ADVOCACY IN FAMILY PROCEEDINGS
A PRACTICAL GUIDE

ADVOCACY IN FAMILY PROCEEDINGS: A PRACTICAL GUIDE

David Bedingfield
BA, Florida State University
JD, Emory University School of Law

Published by
Jordan Publishing Limited
21 St Thomas Street
Bristol BS1 6JS

British Library Cataloguing-in-Publication Data

A catalogue record for this book is available from the British Library.

ISBN 0 85308 873 X

Typeset by Etica Press Ltd, Malvern
Printed and bound in Great Britain by Antony Rowe Ltd, Chippenham, Wilts

PREFACE

I began practising law in London in December 1991, two months after the Children Act 1989 came into effect. Since that date, I have been pestering solicitors, barristers (and, sometimes, judges) with questions about advocacy techniques in family proceedings in this jurisdiction. Not surprising, really, given my pracitce in Atlanta, Georgia, from 1983–1990, had been wholly concerned with other areas of laws altogether. I therefore thought nothing of detaining colleagues, opponents – and strangers on the street for that matter – with questions about advocacy techniques in family proceedings. I have often, in the pages that follow, quoted the advice I was given without attributing the quotation. I do that because on most occasions those barristers and judges did not know they were being invited to help with this text. To all these advocates and judges who have answered my questions over the years, I give you my thanks. Any mistakes that follow, sadly, remain my own responsibility.

The law is stated as at 20 January 2005.

David Bedingfield

DEDICATION

For Deborah Postgate, William Bedingfield, and Nicholas Bedingfield.

For the brothers: Walter Hilbert Bedingfield, Jr; William Eli Bedingfield; and Sidney Edward Bedingfield.

And for Martha Bedingfield of Vidalia, GA.

LIST OF ABBREVIATIONS

AA 1976	Adoption Act 1976
AEA 1971	Attachment of Earnings Act 1971
AJA 1999	Access to Justice Act 1999
ALTE	Apparent Life Threatening Event
AR 1984	Adoption Rules 1984
CA 1989	Children Act 1989
CACA 1985	Child Abduction and Custody Act 1985
C(AHE)O 1992	Children (Admissibility of Hearsay Evidence) Order 1992
C(AP)(A)O 1991	Children (Allocation of Proceedings) Appeals Order 1991
C(AP)O 1991	Children (Allocation of Proceedings) Order 1991
CCA 1981	Contempt of Court Act 1981
CCA 1984	County Courts Act 1984
CCR	County Court Rules 1981
CETV	Cash Equivalent Transfer Value
CJCSA 2000	Criminal Justice and Court Services Act 2000
CLSA 1990	Courts and Legal Services Act 1990
CPR 1998	Civil Procedure Rules 1998
CPR 1998, Sch 1, RSC	Rules taken from the Rules of the Supreme Court 1965 and set out (as amended) in Schedule 1 to CPR
CPR 1998, Sch 2, CCR	Rules taken from the County Court Rules 1981 and set out (as amended) in Schedule 2 to CPR
CSA 1991/1995	Child Support Act 1991/1995
C(SA)R 1991	Children (Secure Accommodation) Regulations 1991
C(SA)(No 2)R 1991	Children (Secure Accommodation) (No 2) Regulations 1991
FLA 1986/1996	Family Law Act 1986/1996
FPC(CA 1989)R 1991	Family Proceedings Courts (Children Act 1989) Rules 1991
FPC(CSA 1991)R 1993	Family Proceedings Courts (Child Support Act 1991) Rules 1993
FPR 1991	Family Proceedings Rules 1991
GALRO(P)R 1991	Guardians Ad Litem and Reporting Officers (Panels) Regulations 1991

MCA 1973	Matrimonial Causes Act 1973
MCA 1980	Magistrates' Courts Act 1980
MCR 1981	Magistrates' Courts Rules 1981
MFPA 1984	Matrimonial and Family Proceedings Act 1984
PD	Practice Direction, Registrar's Direction, Secretary's Circular etc
PD [number]	Practice Direction which supplements Part [number] of CPR 1998
RSC	Rules of the Supreme Court 1965
SCA 1981	Supreme Court Act 1981
SCFO 1999	Supreme Court Fees Order 1999

CONTENTS

TABLE OF STATUTES

References are to paragraph number.

Paragraph references printed in **bold** type indicate where the Act is set out in part or in full.

TABLE OF STATUTORY INSTRUMENTS, GUIDANCE ETC

References are to paragraph number.

Those paragraph numbers in **bold** type indicate where a Statutory Instrument or Guidance is set out in part or in full.

TABLE OF CONVENTIONS

References are to paragraph number.

TABLE OF PRACTICE DIRECTIONS AND PRACTICE NOTES

References are to paragraph number.

Those paragraph numbers in **bold** type indicate where a Practice Direction or Note is set out in part or in full.

For Practice Directions pertaining to the Civil Procedure Rules 1998, see Table of Statutory Instruments, Guidance etc.

TABLE OF CASES

References are to paragraph number.

Paragraph references printed in **bold** type indicate where the case is set out in part.

D

L

M

R

INTRODUCTION

I seek in this book to discuss and explore the craft, and art, of advocacy as it is practised in England and Wales, in particular as it is practised in courts applying principles of law now commonly referred to as 'family law'. Those proceedings share certain characteristics:

- there are no juries;
- rules of evidence allow greater freedom for presentation of cases;
- judges, particularly in cases involving children, often embark on inquisitorial fact-finding expeditions; and, perhaps most importantly,
- the factual background of family break-up often produces extraordinarily emotional witnesses and parties.

In part because of the subject matter of the dispute, advocates in family proceedings owe certain duties, to the court and to clients, that differ slightly from the duties of other advocates.

That being said, any differences between family proceedings and other cases do not mean the basic rules of good advocacy are not applicable in family courts. In preparation for this book I sought the views of many judges and successful barristers, seeking to understand what they found to be effective advocacy techniques in family proceedings. Many disagreements existed, I discovered, but all agreed on this point: there are certain basic rules of advocacy that apply in all legal proceedings. Call them common sense rules, if you like:

- Know your audience. If the fact-finder is the judge, who has tried cases like this for 30 years, your approach will be different than if the fact-finder is a jury.
- Know your theory of your case. All effective advocacy springs from this rule. Everything said in court should be according to your theory of your client's case. Your theory is of course based on the relevant law you contend should be applied. If the facts are found to be as your client contends, in other words, why should the court use its power to give to your client what he or she desires?
- Know that courtesy never lost a case. You can be the most relentless, thorough and rugged cross examiner in the history of the Bar without once appearing to be discourteous, rude or boorish, either to the witness, your opponents, and, most importantly, the judge. Disagreements are what lawsuits are all about. Understanding how to tackle these disagreements is the root of effective advocacy. The best advocates identify and offer solutions to the disagreements without ever becoming disagreeable.

I seek in Chapter 1 to set out in more detail what might be called rules of general application. There are surprisingly few texts devoted to the principles of

advocacy and the various theories of persuasion underlying those principles, and I seek briefly to offer a survey of these in Chapter 1. I also set out what I hope might be considered the consensus view of those judges I interviewed with regard to certain basic rules of presenting cases. In Chapter 2, the basics of the trial are examined: the opening; the examination in chief; cross examination of lay witnesses and experts; the closing submissions.

In the following chapters I attempt to apply those rules to the different types of family proceedings. Private law proceedings involving children are examined in Chapter 3. I include within this chapter those applications regarding alleged acts of domestic violence where relief is sought under Part IV of the Family Law Act 1996. Public law Children Act cases, including applications under s 31 of the Children Act 1989, as well as adoptions under the Adoption Act 1976 (and, tentatively, the Adoption Act 2002), are examined in Chapter 4. I also include within Chapter 4 a brief examination of cases involving abducted children. Ancillary relief applications are considered in Chapter 5. And finally appeals of all cases are discussed in Chapter 6. In the Appendices are those Practice Directions that are relevant to presentation of cases in family proceedings.

Chapter 1

GENERAL PRINCIPLES OF PERSUASION

1.1 WHO, WHAT AND WHY

Any advocate appearing before any tribunal must always answer three essential questions: (1) Who are you appearing for? (2) What does that litigant want? (3) Why should this court grant the relief requested? One immediately sees the questions are easy on one level, damnably complicated on another.

The first question, regarding identity, is not answered simply by saying, 'I appear for the applicant/mother.' Almost invariably, the advocate in family proceedings begins his or her advocacy by choosing how to identify the client. What information about the client's history is relevant to these proceedings, and relevant to the remaining two essential questions to be answered? Your client is the applicant/mother, and she seeks contact with her children, but she is also 20-years-old, unmarried, the victim of an abusive partner, she smokes crack cocaine, she was abused as a child, she has mental health problems, she has seen both children removed from her care by social services, she has been to a detoxification clinic, she seeks to stop consuming crack cocaine, she has a new home, she wishes to resume her relationship with her children. That client's advocate, in his or her skeleton opening, must seek to set out in brief narrative form a biography of this mother, tell the court what this mother now seeks, and convince the court that if it applies the appropriate legal test the court must grant the relief requested.

The second and third essential questions involve both fact and law. What dispute gives rise to the litigation? What does your client now seek in an effort to resolve the dispute? Why, legally and factually, should this court give your client what is sought?

To answer those questions, the advocate must have a credible theory of the case. If one common denominator of bad advocates exists, at least according to my informal survey of judges, it is the failure to present at the first available opportunity a proper theory of the case. The theory should be presented in skeleton form at the beginning of the case, and expanded throughout the evidence. It should do no less than settle the dispute: Why should the court grant your client the relief she seeks? Why should the court decide your client is right and the other side is wrong? 'It does not happen often,' said one District Judge,

'but it does happen: you realise one advocate simply does not have a theory of why his client should win.'

1.2   THEORIES OF PERSUASION

Very little research has been done in the United Kingdom regarding the effectiveness of various adversarial techniques. Jurors in this country, of course, cannot be approached for questioning after a trial, under the terms of the Contempt of Court Act 1981, and it is right to say that judges who make decisions in hard cases are not likely to comment later on what aspect of the advocacy seemed most persuasive.

The best research in this area comes from the United States, Australia and New Zealand. In the States, particularly, it is common for jurors to discuss matters after the trial with lawyers, researchers and anyone else who seeks to discuss the matter.[1] A great deal of this research has been brought together by two professors of speech communication in the US, Richard Rieke and Randall Stutman, in a text called *Communication in Legal Advocacy.*[2] The text is indispensable for the novice advocate because it brings together, and tests, a great deal of the conventional wisdom surrounding oral advocacy.

The fundamental assumption regarding the common law system of trial is that the trial itself offers a reliable method of putting an accurate picture of an event in the mind of the judge or jury.[3] The source of this picture will be the evidence of witnesses, along with the interpretations of experts. The medium will be the questioning of witnesses by opposing counsel. Rieke and Stutman note that this fundamental view of the trial contains a number of assumptions:

- a witness present at the scene of an event is able to perceive that event with reasonable accuracy;
- a single event, existing apart from the perceptions of witnesses, can be communicated successfully to a juror or judge who was not present;
- the witness is able to report the perceptions in such a way that personal judgement will not excessively distort the report;
- a witness's memory is sufficient to provide a complete report of the event after a delay of months or years;
- the accuracy of the report is best obtained through direct questioning by an attorney;
- the credibility and accuracy of the witness are best tested by cross-examination while the decision maker observes the witness's demeanour.

---

1   When I appeared before juries in the US almost invariably a juror would telephone me the day after the verdict had been given, seeking to ask questions about the case, and willing, with a little prompting, to tell everything that was discussed in the jury room.
2   University of South Carolina Press, 1995.
3   See Rieke and Stutman, above, p 46.

Even a cursory examination of what actually happens in court shows there are difficulties with each of these assumptions. In the first decade of the twentieth century, the psychologist Hugo Munsterberg demonstrated that a group of witnesses reporting on the same event presented different reports on each occasion. Munsterberg's findings have never seriously been challenged.[4] More importantly, recent research shows that observers can almost never successfully detect deception on the part of witnesses. In fact, at least some research indicates that it is *harder* to detect deception from oral evidence than it is when jurors or judges attempt to detect deception in a written statement.[5] Rieke and Stutman also note that the assumptions that form the foundation of reality presumed in the trial have also come under attack. Felix Cohen argued in 1950 that instead of a single event existing apart from witness perceptions, there are as many 'events' as there are witnesses. Cohen argues it would be better to describe evidence as the basis from which we construct an event.[6]

As a result of these studies, and as a result of changing perceptions in science regarding reconstructing 'reality', it is now generally accepted that the common assumptions set out above regarding trials simply are not true. If this is so, then how do jurors and judges decide cases?

More recent research tends to show that fact-finders make decisions regarding contested issues of fact not simply through inherent human rationality or by being exposed to a reconstruction of reality, although obviously jurors do not seek to act irrationally or ignore the reconstruction of reality on offer. But more importantly, jurors also use rules of narrative learned through a lifetime of exposure to stories. Rieke and Stutman put it like this:

> 'After all, what is a trial? It is two parties, each telling its story and asking society to endorse its version of reality. This is not all that much different from two children who scream and dispute and tell the parent two divergent versions of what happened, each hoping to be accepted. ... In the court room jurors can find a complex set of claims which must be interpreted. According to the story telling perspective, this task would overwhelm jurors if it were not for their reliance on the common organising tool, namely stories. Through the construction of stories, jurors organise and analyse the vast amount of information involved in making legal judgments. Essentially stories are the systematic means of storing, re-arranging, comparing and interpreting the available information about social behaviour. As such, stories translate legal questions into more easily understood forms.'[7]

Research by Bennett and Theldman in 1981 showed that the use of stories or narrative forms helped jurors in three ways:

---

4   See Hugo Munsterberg, *On the Witness Stand* (Clarke Bordman, 1923); see James Marshall, *Law and Psychology in Conflict* (Bobs Merrill, 1966).
5   See Cody O'Hair, 'Non Verbal Communication and Deception: Differences in Deception Due to Gender and Communicator Dominance', Communication Monographs 50: 175 92 (1983).
6   See FS Cohen Field, 'Theory and Judicial Logic' (1950) *Yale Law Journal* 59, 238–272.
7   See Rieke and Stutman, above, p 48.

(1) jurors locate the central action in a story so as to make sense of other actions
     and events;
(2) jurors construct inferences about a relationship of story elements that
     impinge upon the central action;
(3) jurors then test for consistency and completeness the network of
     connections drawn around a central action.

The jurors therefore apply narrative tests to the stories they hear in an effort
to judge them critically.[8] It is my contention that judges are no different. They
seek, when hearing conflicting evidence, to apply the rules learned from the
'super stories' or meta-stories that we tell ourselves, endlessly, as we seek to
explain the unexplainable.[9]

Another text focusing on the use of narratives in courts is by the American
constitutional lawyer Anthony Amsterdam and the psychologist Jerome Bruner,
entitled *Minding the Law: How Courts rely on storytelling and how their
stories change the ways we understand the law, and ourselves.*[10]

Bruner and Amersterdam query whether the law's tendency to depend upon
narrative for the conduct of its discourse may not produce an overemphasis
on the role of 'agency rather than circumstances, fault rather than unindictable
conditions, intent rather than cultural conscription'.[11] The question goes beyond
the obvious potential of narrative conventions to produce distortion in the
interpretive work of the law through their stereotyped plots, stock characters,
and potted situation. More broadly, the authors wonder whether the inherent
drama of narrative tends to over dramatize legal thinking in a manner out of
keeping with law's function as a cooler of conflict.

The authors are very good at explaining the function of narrative, not only in
the law but in our daily lives. They point out studies in, for example, blue collar
families in Baltimore, Maryland, that showed mothers using narratives with
their children once every seven minutes.[12] These stories give comfort, they
forewarn, the reveal, they legitimize, they convince.

---

[8]   See Bennett and Theldman, *Reconstructing Reality in the Court Room* (Rutgers University
      Press, 1981); see also Fisher, *Human Communication as Narration* (University of South Carolina
      Press, 1987).
[9]   Perhaps the best account of this predicament is Jean-Paul Sartre's novel *La Nausée* (1938,
      Gallimard; English edn 1964, New Directions Publishing). Sartre suggests we are all 'willing
      dupes of our compulsion to narrate, concealing the openness of our possibilities behind the
      specious closures of our stories ... as if there could be anything such as a true story when events
      happen in one direction and we narrate them in reverse.' We constantly, Sartre says, transmute
      our lives into biographies or obituaries, rather than living them first hand.
[10] Harvard University Press (2002).
[11] Bruner and Amsterdam, above, p 112.
[12] Bruner and Amsterdam, above, p 114.

As to why we use narratives, the authors point out that several theories exist. The need for narrative could be inherent either in the nature of the human mind, in the nature of language, or in those supposed programs alleged to run our nervous systems. Another theory argues that narratives and genres of narrative serve to model characteristic plights of culture-sharing human groups. On this view, cultures convert their plights and aspirations into narrative forms that represent both the culture's ordinary legitimacies and possible threats to them.[13] Narratives function not simply to make experience communicable, according to this theory, but also to give a certain practical predictability to the plights of communal life and a certain direction to the efforts needed to resolve them. The authors point out that narratives that engender potentially disturbing conflicts of construction get incorporated in an idealized form into a *corpus juris*, with the objective of minimizing disruption. 'Notions like legitimacy, violation, good faith effort, redress, and so on are prescribed in a form fitted for determination by legal rules and procedures rather than being left to spontaneous, face-to-face working out.'[14]

The authors believe legal narrative conforms to this view of narrative. In litigation, the applicant's lawyer is required to tell a story in which there has been trouble in the world that has affected the applicant adversely and is attributable to the acts of the respondent. The respondent must counter with a story in which it is claimed that nothing wrong happened to the applicant, or that the applicant's conception of wrong does not fit the law's definition. The respondent may say that if there has been a legally cognizable wrong, then it is not the respondent's fault. As the authors note, these are the obligatory plots of the law's adversarial process.

An inevitable consequence of this adversarial storytelling is that it tends to focus the attention of storytellers and hearers alike upon certain considerations rather than others, and to put a premium on type casting the elements of every tale to fit the stock model of the relevant considerations. In family cases, especially, advocates must seek to be aware of this trap. Often times the 'right' answer is not a verdict for one side or the other.

The best illustration of the point is an old story often told by the late US Supreme Court Justice Hugo Black, recounted by Bruner and Amsterdam. A jury in rural Alabama had before them a very poor farmer charged with stealing a mule. The jury's first verdict was: 'Not guilty, provided he returns the mule.' The judge refused to accept the verdict. The jury then came back with a verdict that read: 'Not guilty, but he has to return the mule.' Again, the judge said no. The jury then came back with a third verdict: 'Not guilty, let him keep the damn mule.'

[13] Turner, 'Dramas, Fields and Metaphors: Symbolic Action in Human Society' (1974) Cornell Univ Press.
[14] Bruner and Amsterdam, p 117.

Advocates in family cases must always remember: the adversarial process often offers narratives that do not, in the end, help the client achieve his goal, whether that goal is reuniting the client with an estranged child, or seeking to make a clean break in a contentious divorce matter. Sometimes it is not enough for the parents, for example, to prove the social worker was incompetent and untruthful, or for the husband to prove the wife was deceitful. Neither may actually further the client's case. The advocate must always keep in mind precisely what his client seeks, and understand that always thinking (and acting) in an adversarial manner may not help the client achieve that goal.

That being said, narrative coherence, or narrative fidelity, is a concept that is fundamentally important for an advocate to understand. How does a story 'hang together'? Where is the weak part of a client's narrative regarding the events that are the subject of the lawsuit? In an ancillary relief application, the husband pleads poverty, yet took three trips to Mexico in 1999; in a case regarding claims that a husband has beaten his wife, the husband claims that the bruises around the wife's neck were caused by the wife falling as she walked across the room. Fact-finders constantly test evidence they hear and see by applying it to the stories the fact-finders already know. The fact-finder constantly tests the evidence by asking whether the evidence maintains fidelity to the narrative that both parties accept forms part of the case. The advocate who understands this also constantly tests his own case to make certain he or she understands and appreciates the difficult part of a client's case. The effective advocate will therefore seek not only to present a legal theory of the case, with an understanding of what facts are necessary to show that his client should prevail, but also a narrative theory of the case, showing precisely how his or her client's narrative is more consistent, more 'true' than the opponent's, with the narrative's conclusion being the judgment rendered by the fact-finder.

One of the few texts written by an English judge regarding the judge as a fact-finder is an essay written in 1985 by the Senior Law Lord of England and Wales, Lord Bingham of Cornhill (Bingham LJ, as he then was), entitled 'The Judge as Juror: The Judicial Determination of Factual Issues.'[15] Lord Justice Bingham argues that for a judge, the resolution of factual issues is frequently more difficult and more exacting than the deciding of pure points of law:

> 'In deciding the facts, the Judge knows that no authority, no historical enquiry (save on expert issues) no process of ratiocination will help him. He is dependent, for better or worse, on his own unaided judgement. And he is uneasily aware that his evaluation of the reliability and credibility of oral evidence may very well prove final. So it is, I hope, worth considering what his factual task involves, and how he sets about it.'[16]

---

15   First published in *Current Legal Problems*, Volume 38 (1985), p 1-27; also published in a collection of essays by the same author, entitled *The Business of Judging: Selected Essays and Speeches* (Oxford University Press, 2002).

16   See *The Business of Judging*, above, p 4.

Lord Justice Bingham states that there are three features of the judge's role which do not apply in any other fact-finding investigation:

(1) The judge is always presented with conflicting versions of the events in question.
(2) His determination necessarily takes place subject to the formality and restraints attendant upon proceedings in court.
(3) The judge's determination has a direct practical effect upon people's lives in terms of their pockets, activities or reputations.

There is also, as Bingham LJ notes, one further distinction: the common law judge is not concerned with establishing the truth of what did or did not happen on a given occasion, but merely with deciding, as between adversaries, whether or not the party upon whom the burden of proof lies has discharged it to the required degree of probability.[17] But, as Bingham LJ also notes, in cases where a true fact dispute exists, both parties will have sought to produce a great deal of evidence about that disputed fact. While the burden of proof always exists, according to Bingham LJ few substantial cases turn upon it, and the judge making his factual findings in actuality is usually expressing his considered judgement as to what in truth occurred.

Bingham LJ states that his first step in resolving issues of fact is to establish the common ground between the parties. The pleadings should have identified this, but in some cases – in particular, in family cases – the pleadings do not. Narrowing the issues by determining precisely what disputes exist between the parties is always the first job of the advocate and, according to Bingham LJ, it is also the first job of the fact-finder.

Bingham LJ agrees with the modern view that a judge is unlikely to discover whether a witness is lying simply by observing the witness's demeanour and conduct while giving evidence. Bingham LJ quotes the great English jurist from the 1950s, Lord Devlin:

> 'The great virtue of the English trial is usually said to be the opportunity it gives to the Judge to tell from the demeanour of the witness whether or not he is telling the truth. I think that this is overrated. It is the tableau that constitutes the big advantage, the text with illustrations, rather than the demeanour of a particular witness.'[18]

So how does Bingham LJ discern whether a witness is lying? He points to five primary methods:

(1) The consistency of the witness's evidence with what is agreed, or clearly shown by other evidence, to have occurred.
(2) The internal consistency of the witness's evidence.

---

[17] See *The Business of Judging*, above, p 4.
[18] See Lord Devlin, *The Judge* (Oxford University Press, 1957), p 63.

(3) The consistency with what the witness has said or deposed on other occasions.
(4) The credit of the witness in relation to matter not germane to the litigation.
(5) The demeanour of the witness.

Note that the demeanour of the witness is the least important of the factors that are listed.

It is apparent that what Bingham LJ, and other judges, actually rely on is narrative fidelity. Bingham LJ puts it like this:

> 'If too much attention has over the years been paid to the demeanour of the witness in guiding the trial judge to the truth, too little has perhaps been paid to probability. I do not use that word in any mathematical or philosophical sense, but simply as indicating in a general way that one thing may be regarded as more likely to have happened than another, with the result that the Judge will reject the evidence in favour of the less likely. I think most judges give weight to this factor in reaching their factual conclusions.'[19]

Bingham LJ believes that in practice judges attach enormous importance to the sheer likelihood or unlikelihood of an event having happened as a witness testifies. For example, a witness who everyone agrees has been a meticulous diarist testifies that an event that he claims now to have been important was not an event that he had noted in his diary. It is likely in the absence of some convincing explanation that the court will infer that the event did not occur at all.

Bingham LJ also notes that witnesses very often intend to tell the truth, but in fact are precluded from doing so through no fault of their own. Recent works by psychologists show that when witnesses to an event are later exposed to misinformation about the same event, it often gives rise to an inaccurate recollection by the witness as to what actually occurred. Witnesses in one study who were asked to watch a film of an automobile accident were asked: 'How fast was the white sports car going when it passed the barn while travelling along the country road?' In fact, no barn had existed. Most of the subjects were likely to later 'recall' having seen the non-existent barn.[20] The testing also revealed that once memory is altered in this way, it is difficult to retrieve the original memory.

A loss of recollection is another primary source of unreliability. Most substantive hearings occur some months or even years after the events occurred. Bingham LJ believes recollection fades in a selective and not in a uniform way: in other words, the circumstantial detail falls away or becomes blurred, while recollection of the crucial and striking features of the event usually survives.

---

[19]   See 'The Judge as Juror', above, p 13.
[20]   See 'Misfortunes of Memory', paper submitted by Elizabeth Loftus to the Royal Society in January 1983, cited in 'The Judge as Juror', above, p 16.

Another source of unreliability for witnesses is what Bingham LJ terms 'wishful thinking.' The point of view of the witness always has to be kept in mind, and advocates must of course address this issue when considering how evidence from each witness fits into the narrative as a whole.

Bingham LJ notes that consideration of expert witnesses is wholly different than lay witnesses. It is of course often the worst and least experienced expert who offers the most confident and comprehensive explanation, while the more learned and careful expert is willing to acknowledge an inability to provide a perfect solution to the problems that are raised. Experienced judges prefer the latter expert. There are other methods of testing an expert's reliability, and those methods are set out in some detail in the section on cross-examining an expert.

Another text that is invaluable to the novice advocate is *The Verdict of the Court: Passing Judgment in Law and Psychology* by Professor Jenny McEwan of the University of Exeter.[21] McEwan also brings together much of the research regarding the behaviour of jurors and judges. For McEwan, the most important question is: How do people think? Finders of fact are required to identify the thought processes of another. For example, the question to be answered by the jury might include determining what that witness had been thinking on a past occasion while causing harm to someone else. The fact-finder seeks to assess the mental capacity of the witness, and assess the honesty, the veracity, of the witness. McEwan notes that at times, the legal rules are themselves coloured by the lawyers' assumptions as to how fact-finders themselves think.

McEwan contends that psychological research assists the legal world, if often only by demonstrating to lawyers that many of our assumptions are wrong. She examines the use of heuristics, or reasoning mechanisms commonly employed by people who find themselves required to interpret the behaviour of others. Heuristics serve valuable social functions: they prevent a paralysis of decision-making, which of course would occur if every possible result of every decision is analysed.[22] The 'representative heuristic' is the basis of argument by analogy.[23] The estimation of how probable it is that an event should be classified in a certain category is based on how typical the event is of that category, regardless of how common it is in fact. People therefore assess cause and effect by estimating the likelihood that event X caused effect Y by recalling how often X causes Y. But they ignore the base rate: how often X does NOT cause Y. The 'representativeness heuristic' thus accounts for the inability of

---

[21] (Hart Publishing, 2003)

[22] See McEwan, above, p 16.

[23] See, generally, Kahnman and Tversky, 'Subjective Probability: a Judgment of Representativeness' (1972) 3 Cognitive Psychology 430; Tversky and Kahnman, 'Judgment under Uncertainty: Heuristics and Biases' (1974) 185 Science 1124.

most people to assess probability accurately. McEwan notes that over-prediction of dangerousness in offenders, despite the very low base rate of violent behaviour either in the population at large or in a particular individual, is another example of the effect of the representativeness heuristic.[24]

McEwan argues that the use of stories by fact-finders to fill in the gaps left by the evidence is perhaps best exemplified in family cases, where judges seek to decide what is in the best interests of a child. The judge, as McEwan notes, is seeking to allocate happiness. It has long been noted that this enterprise forces judges into 'predictive, person-specific relational determinations that their legal training ill equips them to provide,'[25] leaving a vacuum that is in many cases filled by idealistic images of family life. These representational heuristic images then have a great impact on the judgment that is rendered. The famous (or infamous) summing up by the trial judge (Caulfield J) in the libel case in 1987 involving Jeffrey Archer and the Daily Star and Archer's payment of £2,000 to a prostitute is a perfect case in point. Caulfield J asked the jury to note whether Lord Archer's wife, who gave evidence, was not 'fragrant, elegant and radiant?' Surely Mr. Archer therefore did not need the services of a prostitute, the reasoning went. The false heuristic proposed by the judge here needs no further explication.

McEwan's chapter on finders of fact is particularly helpful for the novice advocate. She notes the over reliance by lawyers in cross-examination on proving that a witness has either made inconsistent statements in the past, or that his story-in-chief contains an internal inconsistency. Psychologists have long known that consistency may have little relevance to reliability, particularly in the case of children.[26] Children are much less likely than adults to be able to describe a traumatic event in the correct chronological order. Children often include fantasy in a true account.[27] McEwan notes that even Bingham LJ, who obviously has read the literature regarding the over-reliance on consistency as an indicator of truth telling, states in his text, without dismay, that witnesses before him are routinely expected to answer questions designed to reveal tiny inconsistencies in the witness's statement.

McEwan notes that cross-examination plays upon the suggestibility of the witness. (Good lawyers know this after only a few efforts at cross-examination.) Loftus and Palmer's study in 1974 showed that witnesses are

---

[24]   McEwan, above, p 17.
[25]   See Collier, 'The Analysis of Family Dynamics in Child Custody Cases,' in Davies, Lloyd-Bostock, MacMurran and Wilson (eds) *Psychology Law and Criminal Justice* (de Gruyter, 1996); Lloyd-Bostock (ed) *Psychology in Legal Contexts: Applications and Limitations* (Macmillan Press, 1981); McEwan, above, p 20.
[26]   See A Vrij, *Detecting Lies and Deceit* (Wiley, 2000); McEwan, above, p 95.
[27]   See Pynoos and Nader, 'Children who Witness the Sexual Assaults of their Mothers' (1988) 27 *Journal of the American Academy of Child and Adolescent Psychiatry* 567; Pynoos and Nader, 'Children's Memory and Proximity to Violence' (1989) 28 *Journal of the American Academy of Child and Adolescent Psychiatry* 236.

influenced by the language used by the questioner: if asked, 'About how fast were the cars going when they smashed into each other?' the reply consistently gave a higher estimated speed than if a witness was asked 'About how fast were the cars going when they collided with each?'[28]

This research is vitally important for advocates. All advocates should be obsessed with the topic of how people think, how they decide. The content of the narratives that the fact-finder uses is, in the end, down to the advocate's ability to foresee the use of that narrative, to understand the reasons for it, and either to counter it with compelling evidence (if that is the client's goal), or to re-enforce the narrative by framing each question, and each witness's evidence, in a manner intended to offer that re-enforcement.

1.3 ANALYSING AND ASSESSING THE EVIDENCE

The key function of the advocate is to help the client present to the court a version of events based on admissible, credible evidence that compels the court to grant the relief the client seeks. That requires the advocate to have a thorough understanding not only of the 'facts' surrounding the dispute, but an understanding as well of the difficulty of providing content to the term 'facts' in the first instance.

The late Professor Irving Younger was the pre-eminent teacher of trial tactics and techniques in the US. Professor Younger, who died in 1988, had also during his illustrious career served as a trial judge in New York City. After retiring from the bench he taught trial techniques for 10 years, based primarily on his experiences of watching other advocates make a mess of cases. Fortunately, several videotapes of his lectures are still in existence, and law students in the States have for the last 30 years sat enthralled in front of fairly ancient videotapes of Professor Younger discussing how (or more often, how not) to present, or defend, cases in court.

Professor Younger's view of what he called the taxonomy of trial facts is helpful to any advocate seeking to understand the vital importance of fact-finding in the trial process.

In Professor Younger's taxonomy of trial facts, there are eight essential types of facts:

(1) facts perceived through the senses of sight, hearing, touch, taste and smell, or in other words the raw data of the outside world;

(2) facts perceived through the senses with the aid of a device in ordinary use such as binoculars, or eyeglasses, or a hearing aid;

---

[28] See McEwan, above, p 96; Loftus and Palmer, 'The Malleability of Eyewitness Accounts', in Lloyd-Bostock and Clifford (eds) *Evaluating Witness Evidence* (Wiley, 1983).

(3) facts perceived through the senses with the aid of a device not in ordinary use, and requiring special skill and expertise to employ;
(4) facts where no one is able to present any version in court, for example, where both drivers in a collision die, or there are no survivors found in an airline crash, or, as often happens in Children Act cases, social workers who saw or heard an incident and who made entries on social services files can no longer be located;
(5) facts current technology or learning is incapable of finding as true or false;
(6) facts no technology or learning, as currently understood, could ever be expected to prove;
(7) intangible facts, such as the 'fact' of a person's intent when doing an act;
(8) facts that require the decisions of definition, for example, whether the mother could be found as a matter of 'fact' to have caused significant harm to her child, or whether certain behaviour constitutes a treatable mental illness.[29]

The taxonomy is helpful, I contend, because it allows advocates to understand how facts must be proved in court. A fact of the first type might be proved by any witness who saw, heard, smelled, touched, tasted (though it must be said presenting witnesses of taste is a rare task for a lawyer). Facts of the second type might be presented by lay or non-expert witnesses as well, with the understanding that some information regarding the use of the device will be required. Facts of the third type would require expert evidence. Facts of the fourth require use of circumstantial evidence, and/or legal theories such as *res ipsa loquitur,* or the abolition of the hearsay rule. Categories five and six are useful for understanding the reasoning of experts, in particular psychiatrists, who base their conclusions on certain theories that other experts in the field might question. The seventh and eighth categories of fact include the judge's decisions on the 'ultimate issue' of the case, but also include the conclusions of any medical experts or accounting experts regarding the factual background of the case. The fact-finder in family cases will always allow evidence in those two categories, where a Crown Court judge might restrict evidence of this type.

Another useful way of looking at the eighth category of definitional facts is to divide facts into primary facts, capable of being proved by lay witnesses through the senses; and secondary facts, capable only of being proved by experts who might offer opinions regarding definitions, or conclusions, that might be reached regarding primary facts.

---

[29] See Younger, *The Advocate's Deskbook: The Essentials of Trying a Case* (Prentice Hall Law and Business, 1988). Professor Younger further divides the eighth type of fact into three categories: (1) facts defined through ordinary use of language, such as a finding by a tribunal of 'reasonable' care; (2) facts defined through specialised vocabulary of a science, other than law, such as a decision whether a person's behaviour might be classified as a mental illness; (3) facts defined through the specialised vocabulary of the law, such as a decision whether acts constitute murder or manslaughter.

1.3.1 The chronology

Several methods might be used for organising the facts, but in all cases (not just family disputes, but each and every case that appears in any court or tribunal) a chronological time line has to be created. A trial is a story of a dispute, with the judgment to be the conclusion of that dispute. Every 'fact' that is mentioned, from the beginning through to the conclusion, must be relevant to the dispute that brings the litigants to court. Creating a chronology that sets out each and every relevant fact, and sets out with particularity which facts are in dispute (and how that dispute might be settled to the client's advantage), should be one of the first tasks of any advocate. The advocate seeks to understand the nature of each fact on that time line, and decide how to prove (or disprove) the opponent's allegations regarding that supposed fact. Eventually, an edited version of this chronology will be submitted to the finder of fact. (As discussed below, a respondent's chronology would only be presented if the applicant's is woefully deficient, or, better yet, if the applicant's chronology fails to set out a relevant fact that is helpful to the respondent. Being able to show the court that the other side's advocate is willing to fudge with regard to either the truth of a fact, or its relevance, is always good for your client.)

Other methods of analysing and presenting evidence to the court are examined in a collection of essays by lawyers and psychologists entitled *Analysing Witness Testimony: A Guide for Legal Practitioners and other Professionals*.[30] John Shepherd and Ian Mortimer are consultant psychologists. In their contribution Shepherd and Mortimer examine methods of assessing witness statements. Shepherd and Mortimer note that any written statement provides a 'complex interweaving of *episodic* and *identity detail*.' Episodic detail creates for the reader a representation of events. Identity detail is a representation of persons. A lawyer is often presented with a collection of statements, perhaps arranged chronologically, perhaps not. These statements provide, purportedly, the examination-in-chief of that witness. The statements will obviously tell the advocate what the witness is alleged to have experienced. But the good advocate, as Shepherd and Mortimer remind us, will carefully examine the statements and chronology to see what is NOT there.

These basic anomalies in evidential text are usefully identified by Shepherd and Mortimer as follows.

(1) Deficiencies in detail

These deficiencies include deficient descriptions of individuals, leaving an item of information un-stated, stated vaguely or ambiguously; or a statement that

---

30   Heaton-Armstrong, Shepherd and Wolchover, eds, (Blackstone Press, 1999).

fails to identify key individuals, such as a statement in the passive voice that fails to identify the actor. They would include conversational deficits, for example where a witness describes an event where someone enters a room and commits certain acts, but no speech is reported. A deficiency in detail can include sequential and logical discontinuity, where for example there is an obvious missing step in a narrative sequence, resulting in an outcome without a complete triggering cause or reason. Deficiencies in detail can include empty accounts, where no detail is given of the event. Shepherd and Mortimer point out that at times a lack of emotion or response by the witness might prove significant and finally witnesses often refer to other witnesses. The fact no statement is filed might well be a deficiency in detail that has significance for the advocate.

(2)   Anomalous contrast

Witness statements in family proceedings are almost invariably drafted by someone other than the witness. It is therefore important for the advocate to analyse this statement for incongruous use of language, or words and phrases one would not naturally expect this particular witness to use. There may very well be a great amount of detail in a particular description by a witness, giving rise to concerns that the witness was provided with the detail by others. Shepherd and Mortimer use the example of a witness saying it was 'an 8-inch knife with a serrated blade, tapering to a point.' Obviously, it would be unlikely that a lay witness would know the precise details of the measurement and the type of blade, and therefore it would be important for the advocate to note this particular anomaly in the witness statement.

(3)   Invalid descriptions

Those who become expert at reconstructing incidents from interviewing witnesses often have to fall back on the old maxim: what could not have happened did not happen. Therefore if any description within the text simply runs counter to physical reality, obviously the event is unlikely to have occurred. It does not mean, necessarily, that the witness is lying. It means the witness, more likely, has convinced himself of the truth, no matter how unlikely his version of the truth might be.

(4)   Incongruous variation and contradiction

Advocates should seek to identify two types of inconsistency:

- internal inconsistency, where a statement contains two details that do not agree;
- external inconsistency, or detail within a statement failing to agree with accounts others have given. Witnesses may also give evolving descriptions of matters, that is where in an early statement a witness is unable to identify

with specificity a matter of clothing, whereas in a later statement the witness shows an ability to remember perfectly what colour the sweater was and what model or type it was. Shepherd and Mortimer also note the problem of 'migrating of detail,' where a particular witness gives a version of events containing a specific detail, and that detail appears in another witness's account, even though that second witness was unlikely to have seen the same event in the same way.

Shepherd and Mortimer give several examples of how advocates might seek to analyse the details provided when several witnesses seek to describe the same events. One particularly useful method is what the authors call a THEMA grid, or a Thematic Emergence of Anomaly. The grid is particularly useful where, for example, a child witness has given two or three lengthy interviews to police. It would also be useful in situations where there are numerous allegations of domestic violence over a lengthy period of time, where several witnesses might be called to give versions of events.

The grid, when completed, will reveal in table form each account of the incident. For example, in the case of a child victim of abuse who has given two interviews, there may very well be three or four separate accounts of the particular abusive act in question. By setting out each particular account in table form, the advocate is able to grasp quickly the differences, if any, in the accounts.

A grid might also be used where several witnesses give accounts of several different events. A table would be used for each discreet event that is being described. The top of the table, running horizontally, would have cell labels such as Witness 1, Witness 2, and Witness 3. Along the left hand side of the table, running vertically, would be cell labels such as Event of 12-20-01.

By setting out briefly what each witness would be saying about the different events, the advocate would be able to see quickly where the witness accounts differ.

1.4   SKELETON ARGUMENTS

After creating a chronology and then analysing and assessing where in the factual evidence anomalies and difficulties exist, both in her own case and her opponent's, the advocate must then produce a skeleton argument for the court. The skeleton argument by the end of the second paragraph, and first paragraph if possible, should tell the court why your client must prevail.

In the chapters that follow I seek to discuss specific arguments in specific family law disputes. In this section I attempt to set out certain general principles that judges have identified in all effective skeleton arguments.

1.4.1   Identify the issues immediately, and tell the court why your client should win

The United States Supreme Court Justice Felix Frankfurter, writing in a case decided in 1943, put it like this:

> 'In law the right answer usually depends on putting the right question.'[31]

The effective skeleton argument will seek to frame the issues in a way that is most helpful to the advocate's client. Those issues should be framed on the first page of the skeleton.

Use short, simple declarative sentences throughout the skeleton. This is vitally important when framing the issues. Do not burden the judge with lengthy issues of statements that begin with the word 'whether.' Most district judges, in particular, agree that it is far better to break the issue up into short, simple sentences. Given the number of cases district judges are expected to master, how could it be any other way?

A most useful text with regard to creating good skeletons comes from the US, entitled *The Winning Brief: 100 Tips for Persuasive Briefing in Trial and Appellate Courts*, by Brian A Garner. The text is not, despite its title, aimed solely at American lawyers. A 'brief' in US legal parlance refers to the written arguments presented to court by counsel. Judges in the US place much greater emphasis on written arguments than those in the UK, primarily because of the volume of litigation in American courts. As the number of litigants increases in the UK, it is more likely that here, too, written submissions will begin to increase in importance. And, as Garner correctly notes: 'In law, the quality of writing matters.'

* Every skeleton should make its primary point within 90 seconds.
* The framing of the issue must be fair, but also must only have one answer.
* Each issue should be a syllogism, even if part of the syllogism is unstated and assumed.
* The advocate must never write a sentence he could not easily speak.
* In appellate arguments, advocates must always state the standard of review. And, finally:
* Advocates must always, *always* tell the court immediately what it is the court is being asked to do. (Remember: Who are you? What do you want? Why should the court give it to you?)

In my research, District Judges were particularly scathing with regard to those skeleton arguments that do not immediately tell the court what the party seeks. All courts have limited powers. Courts (save for the High Court, in certain circumstances) have only those powers that are given them by statute. The

---

[31]   See *Estate of Rogers v Commissioner*, 320 US 410, at 413, Frankfurter J.

point of all litigation is to ask the court to use, or not to use, those powers granted to the court by the relevant statute. Therefore in every skeleton argument, within 90 seconds of the judge beginning to read the document, the judge should be told not only what order the party wants but also why the court should make the order requested.

Garner is also particularly good with regard to combating legalese. In his view the words 'pursuant to' should be declared illegal. Similarly, the word 'clearly' would also be barred. There are others: 'with respect to', 'as to', 'in order to', 'in connection with' and, perhaps most obviously, 'obviously'.

Good writers also understand the difference between active voice and passive voice, and strive to write in the active voice if possible. There are three reasons, as Garner notes:

- Passive voice adds unnecessary words.
- Passive voice often fails to say squarely who has done what.
- Passive voice subverts the normal word order for an English sentence, and makes it harder for readers to process the information.

Passive voice, of course, is normally comprised of a 'be' verb plus a past participle, usually a verb ending in 'ed'. Often, however, the 'be' verb will not be stated but is implied in the context of the sentence. Garner gives the following example:

> 'Recently I heard it suggested by a client that National Insurance should cover all legal fees.'

That sentence actually contains the implied verb 'being' after the word 'it' and therefore is in the passive voice. To translate to active voice you would write:

> 'Recently I heard a client suggest that National Insurance should cover all legal fees.'[32]

Garner has one other writing tip specifically aimed at legalese. Lawyers are forever burying verbs. A buried verb, or course, is not a verb at all, but is a noun created by a verb. For example the word 'allegation' buries the verb allege. The word 'enforcement' buries the verb enforce. As Garner puts it, given the choice between a noun and a verb, always choose the verb. Given the choice between a word ending in 'ion,' and a word ending in 'ing', choose the latter. By doing so you eliminate prepositional phrases, you avoid 'to be' verbs, and your writing becomes more concrete about people performing actions.[33]

---

[32] See Garner, above, p 158.
[33] See Garner, above, p 151.

Garner also, and it seems to me quite rightly, argues that if given a choice between a passive choice verb and a buried verb, the writer should always choose the passive voice. An example is this:

> 'The Children Act provides rules governing the placement of children in care.'

A better structure of that sentence would be:

> 'The Children Act provides rules governing where and with whom children in care are to be placed.'

Garner's final piece of advice to lawyers is this: remember the importance of ethos. He cites the American lawyer Lloyd Paul Stryker's seminal text on advocacy, *The Art of Advocacy*:

> 'The success or failure of an advocate comes down at last to this: what manner of man is it who is speaking? This is what Emerson meant when he wrote:
>
> > "What you are speaks so loudly I cannot hear what you say."
>
> An advocate might obey every rule that Aristotle and Cicero have laid down, but if he is not sincere in what he says, he will not achieve persuasion.'[34]

The barrister and writer Keith Evans, who has also practised extensively in America and who has written often and well about advocacy techniques, puts it like this: 'be likeable'. As Evans notes, however, that does not mean 'act likeable'. Fact-finders tend to see through that, and it comes through in one's writing as clearly as it does in court. Being likeable, on the other hand, involves never distorting facts for your client's advantage, never engaging in irrelevant attacks on witnesses or parties, or for that matter, opposing counsel; never distorting the applicable legal principles that apply; and always, *always* understanding that reasonable people can disagree.

Advocates must know that skeleton arguments are in fact arguments. While a detailed analysis of the skills of argumentation and rhetoric are beyond the scope of this text, the best advocates know that a basic understanding of those skills is vitally important. A very good introductory text is by the philosopher Chaim Perleman, entitled *The Realm of Rhetoric*.[35] Perleman here sets out what it is people actually do when they argue about values. He reconfirms the ancients' contention that when one's initial premises or assumptions are disputable, the best possible argument can only follow 'a method by which we shall be able to reason from generally accepted opinions about any problem ... and shall ourselves, when sustaining an argument, avoid saying anything self-contradictory'.[36] What Perleman concentrates on is 'How do claims of reasonableness arise in prose that is not formally logical? What does

---

[34]   See Garner, above, p 389; Stryker, *The Art of Advocacy* (New York, 1954), at p 147.
[35]   University of Notre Dame Press, 1982.
[36]   From Aristotle *Topics* in Perleman, above, p 2.

"reasonable" mean for someone who speaks of "reasonable men" or "reasonable doubt".

Perleman shows how argumentation ordinarily proceeds informally, not according to the forms and rules of formal deduction and induction. And, vitally, *arguments are always addressed to audiences for the purposes of inducing or increasing those audiences' adherence to the thesis presented.* To achieve any degree of success with audiences, arguments have to proceed from premises that are acceptable to those audiences. Ambiguity is never entirely avoidable in arguments because the language which must be used is inevitably equivocal in some degree and because the terms that are available are often open to more than one interpretation. Understand that, then seek to minimise it in your arguments, and to point it out to your opponents.

Perleman also helpfully categorises the primary types of argument techniques:

(1) quasi-logical arguments that claim to be rational because they resemble the patterns of formal reasoning;
(2) arguments that are based on claims concerning the structure of reality (for example that phenomena succeed one another, that causes always produce effects);
(3) arguments based on examples, illustrations, and models, all of which imply and allegedly represent the operation of overriding rules or law or principles;
(4) clarifications of one idea by associating it with another, as in analogy or metaphor;
(5) processes by which some features of an idea are detached or disassociated from it so that the primary idea can be seen as without objectionable or incompatible features;
(6) amplification or abridgment of ideas or values;
(7) imposing special order an ideas or arguments.

Professor Alistair Bonnett, who teaches at the University of Newcastle, has put together a useful introductory guide to arguing, aimed not primarily at lawyers but at students.[37] The guide is helpful for lawyers, however, in particular those lawyers who seek to gain a better understanding of the basic structure of an argument.

Professor Bonnett's text is especially useful with regard to criticising opponent's skeleton arguments, and he offers five broad categories for arguments of refutation.

(1) Circularity

The example most often used is this:

---

[37] Bonnett *How to Argue* (Pearson Education, 2001).

'The existence of a personal god is proved by the Bible; and the authority of the Bible must, of course, be accepted because it was inspired by god.'

Here the first claim is proved by reference to a second claim that depends on the acceptance of the first claim. Lawyers all too often do this, though rarely in such an obvious fashion as in this example. As Bonnett points out, when criticising a circular argument it is best to place clear limits on the scope and aim of the argument. For example, counsel for father contends that contact between father and his son is in the best interest of the son. Mother contends no contact should occur because the son has told her that the father has shouted at the child and threatened. Mother argues; in a circular fashion, as follows:

*   Matter 1: The fact of the child's bad relationship with his father is proved by the child's statements to the mother that show the relationship is bad;
*   Matter 2: The child should be believed because the mother 'knows' the child has a bad relationship with his father.

(2)   Simplistic

As Bonnett notes, all advocates simplify in order to be understood. The problems arrive when the process is taken too far. Important complicating factors may be missed, and all too often advocates who contend that the final cause of a phenomenon can be located in one particular thing are guilty of undue simplification. It is not enough, of course, simply to say that the opponent's argument is simplistic. Specific details must be given. Where is the over simplification? What has your opponent missed? Why is that omission relevant to the decision the judge must make?

(3)   Reductionist and determinist

Particularly in children's cases, advocates are tempted to reduce a complex area of processes to a simple cause and effect. A determinist is someone who believes that for everything that occurs there are conditions such that if those conditions are present, nothing else could have occurred. Bonnet notes that in this sense determinism suggests that everything is pre-determined; that whatever happens was bound to happen. This encourages circular argument. A reductionist structures his or her argument in such a way as to mistakenly and simplistically suggest that one particular thing is the cause or root of many other things. In either case, arguments such as this leave themselves open to appropriate criticism.

(4)   Bias

Those with a bias have a specific and prior prejudice in favour, or against, certain interpretations of events. The charge of bias against the opposing party is obviously easy to make, and usually pointless. Of course a party is biased. Why else have we convened the court? The important point is to show how

and where the bias manifests itself. This is also vital in family public law cases where a great many lay witnesses may very well have a bias for or against a parent or a local authority.

(5) Ad hominem

Ad hominem means 'to the man', and ordinarily is used when one seeks to criticise the notion that it is possible to refute an argument by reference to the personal qualities of the person who makes it. As Bonnet points out, however, *ad hominem* attacks can be used in a subtle and effective way:

* *Ad hominem* arguments might test an individual's commitment to a position by identifying possibilities within it that they may not have thought of and may find unacceptable.
* *Ad hominem* arguments might identify contradictions within someone's stated position or between their stated positions and their actions: in other words, the opponent has been hypocritical.

These different methods of attack are also useful in cross-examination, as noted below.

1.5 THE ADVOCATE AND THE CLIENT

Careful readers will note that we are some way into a text on advocacy in family proceedings and no mention has been made of any different approaches to advocacy available only to lawyers working in divorce or children matters. This is not unintentional. Advocates appearing in family cases owe the same duties to their clients as do advocates in other cases, save with these vital exceptions: advocates appearing in cases involving children owe a duty to disclose to the court and, in most circumstances, to the opposing parties, any evidence relevant to the outcome of the case, in particular where the evidence is relevant to the best interests of the child; and advocates appearing in matters under the Matrimonial Causes Act 1973 cannot knowingly allow a client to hide assets or income from the other party. Advocates should make this clear to clients on initial meeting: any information relevant to the best interests of the child, as regarding financial assets in MCA 1973 matters, even if given to the advocate by the client in confidence, will be passed on to the court.

That being said, it is not the advocate's duty to determine what is in the best interests of the child, and then seek to achieve that through the court. The advocate's job instead is to determine what the *client* believes is in the best interests of the child, and then seek to achieve that. This is vitally important for advocates to understand in public law Children Act cases. The advocate is not there to give the client advice about childcare, or about the psychological development of children, or about what the advocate believes would be best

for the child involved in the case. The advocate is a specialist in one area only: the law. But that speciality means the advocate by necessity will know the effect of certain evidence on the judge hearing the case. The advocate must therefore advise the client accordingly.

An example is this: The client has just admitted in conference to beating the child repeatedly, but wishes to argue that each beating was justified. The advocate must advise the client of the likely reaction of the judge to that evidence. The advocate will also tell the client that the client cannot now disavow the beatings, having accepted that they occurred.[38] The advocate will seek to advise the client that if he wishes to argue that each beating was justified the advocate will certainly seek to do so, but the likely result of the argument will be that the child is taken into care.

At this point, a client may ask the lawyer: 'Well, what do I say?' The advocate is not there to tell the client what to say. But the advocate is there to advise the client how lawfully to achieve the result the client seeks to achieve.

The advocate in this example would firmly tell the client that it is for the client to decide what to say and do. But it is hoped the advocate would not simply pronounce this from a soapbox, peer down at the lowly lay client and await instructions. The good advocate would first seek to gain some personal rapport with the client. The advocate cannot simply swan into a first conference, often outside court before a court appearance, and seek to tell the client he should change the behaviour of a lifetime. But the advocate must, in the end, seek to advise the client in family proceedings on matters that are uniquely private and emotional. Therefore that advocate must, it is contended, accept that the circumstances faced by the client (the litigation that might result in, for example, not just the loss of money, but the loss of a home, or a child) will be likely to cause the client to seek personal advice about the conduct of that client's life. The advocate in the above example would seek to advise the violent father that the local authority is offering an anger management course, or a parenting course, that might address the client's parenting problems. If that is not possible, the client would be directed to an NHS-supplied course, which might be accessed through the client's GP. Again, this cannot be presented as advice by a life-style counsellor, concerned about the client's well-being. Instead, it can be presented as an effort by a lawyer to be able to present to the court the best possible (and true) picture of a client. The court will want to understand whether the client has sought to address these difficult problems. Why not tell the client that? He needs to understand that unless he can convince the court that he is serious about attempting a change of behaviour, he may never see his child again.

---

[38]   If the client sought to change his story in a manner that shows he wishes to give false evidence to the court, the advocate would be forced to withdraw from the case. The court would be told only that the advocate was 'professionally embarrassed'. No details would be given.

If the violent client in the above example is opposed to treatment or therapy of any kind, the advocate must seek to understand why. But at some point the advocate must accept that it is the client who will decide. The advocate cannot step over the bounds of his brief and begin to advise the client regarding his personality and his life style. As one can easily see from the example, this is often a fine line, and even experienced advocates have ruefully told me many times they still get this wrong. (They usually do this just after I have made the same admission.) For the younger advocate, the better course is to err on the side of being an advocate for your client's case. Once your client has determined his instructions and given them to the advocate, the advocate is duty bound to present those instructions to the court. If the client seeks to change his story in such a manner that the advocate no longer believes the client is seeking to present truthful evidence to the court, the advocate is duty-bound to seek to resign from the case because of professional embarrassment.

1.6   PREPARING A CLIENT FOR THE WITNESS BOX

All advocates must understand the difference between preparing a client to give evidence, and coaching that client. Barristers appearing in any court must understand Part N of the Bar Code of Conduct. A guidance document is attached to the Code, setting out a checklist of matters it is appropriate to cover when preparing a witness to give evidence:

(1) tell the client he should speak slowly, clearly, and as succinctly as possible;
(2) tell the witness not to guess or speculate;
(3) the witness should ask for the question to be re-phrased if he or she does not understand, or wishes for the question to be made clearer;
(4) explain to the client the process of the hearing, setting out the roles of judge, barrister, solicitors, etc.
(5) set out the way the bundles will be used;
(6) explain why it is that the witness will not be allowed to speak to others during breaks taken during his or her oral evidence;
(7) explain to the witness the primary techniques used in cross-examination; in particular, explain the point of leading questions, demonstrate how they are used, and explain that the witness is not obliged to agree;
(8) test the recollection of the witness about relevant facts, and discuss with the witness the issues that may arise in cross-examination; but note: no mock-cross examinations are permitted.

It goes without saying, perhaps, but I will say it anyway: advocates cannot tell the witness what to say. If for no other reason than self-preservation, no advocate should ever think of urging a witness to say anything other than what that witness believes to be the truth. The self-preservation element is this: if a witness or client is willing to perjure themselves on the advice or urging of a

barrister, that witness is also willing to tell everyone, including the Bar Council, that the reason the case was lost was because the barrister told him to say the wrong thing. No case is worth a career.

Penny Cooper, the director of CPD and Witness Preparation for the Inns of Court School of Law, recommends that advocates prepare witnesses by having them cross-examined by another barrister on another set of facts.[39] While I am certain that would help, I am equally certain that only the wealthiest clients would be willing to pay for such an exercise.

Part N of the Code of Conduct also provides, at 6.1.4, that it is the responsibility of a barrister to ensure that those facing unfamiliar court procedures are put as much at ease as possible. That means instructing your client in what to wear. ('Wear what you would wear to your great grandmother's funeral, and pretend your great grandmother was the Queen of England,' is what a friend of mine in Atlanta used to tell his clients. Others may believe this slightly overstates the case. In any event, the point is that the client should be seen to respect the court.) You should discuss with your client the basics of courtroom etiquette, if you think it necessary. No eating in the courtroom; no chewing gum allowed; no cans of Diet Coke being popped open at inopportune moments during cross-examination.

But you should go beyond this: you must also explain to the witness the basics of giving evidence:

- KISS, or keep it simple, stupid. No lengthy sentences. Make your client speak to you in conference in sentences of 10 words or less. Stop him when he goes over.
- Never talk at the same time as a judge.
- Address the judge appropriately: Madam or Sir for District Judges; Your Honour for Circuit Judges; My Lady or My Lord for High Court Judges. (And when in doubt, promote.)
- Never answer a question with just a 'Yes' or a 'No' if you feel the question requires more than that.
- But never argue with the opposing counsel.

Obviously there is a fine line between the last two points, and counsel should talk to the client about this. Many times, the witness need answer only 'No, that is not right,' to an assertion by an advocate on cross-examination. That witness's counsel will argue the proposition later, at an appropriate time.

---

[39]   See Cooper, 'Witness Preparation – A Stitch in Time Saves Nine' *Counsel Magazine*, July 2003.

1.7 THE DISTRESSED CLIENT

Advocates must understand that the parties engaged in contentious litigation surrounding the break-up of families will almost inevitably present as distressed and emotional. Developing a proper relationship with a distressed client presents difficult problems for the beginner advocate. It may well be the most important skill a young lawyer must develop. Without an ability to develop the trust of a client, an advocate will soon find himself without a client.

The first impression the client receives upon meeting the advocate is crucial. It very likely will be that this first interview is outside court at a preliminary hearing. The location and the precise circumstances, however, are not as important as this: the advocate must show unfeigned interest in the client's legal and personal difficulties. This is crucial, and no advocate I know would seek to disagree. This interest cannot seem false or put on solely for effect. One successful barrister put it like this: 'Of course I am interested in this client's legal problem. My professional life depends upon solving that problem in a way that is seen to be helpful to my client'. In other words, unless you develop the skills to attract and keep clients, all the courtroom skills in the world will not enable you to become a successful advocate.

Jenny Chapman is a law professor in Canada who teaches lawyers on both sides of the Atlantic skills not ordinarily obtained in law schools. In her text on legal skills entitled 'Interviewing and Counselling'[40] she points out that psychologists have discovered that it takes approximately 90 seconds to form a first impression of someone, and that 55 per cent of that view will be based on appearance. Advocates need to think about the effect of their appearance on both clients and judges, and most who do so conclude that 'sober' and 'authoritative' are the impressions successful advocates would seek to impart. If that means black is the new black, then so be it. Wear a dark suit: appear comfortable in it. You seek to project authority, in part so as to reassure your client. For whatever reason, that is more difficult to do when you wear a pink waistcoat and green shoes.

Chapman points out that effective communication requires empathy. This does not mean the same thing as sympathising, which suggests agreement or accord. To empathise means to put yourself in someone else's shoes. As Chapman points out, objectivity and empathy are not mutually exclusive.[41]

It is my submission that on most occasions the best advocates are also the best interviewers and counsellors. Part of the reason is that the good advocate is able to develop a rapport with both the judge and the client. There is a measure of persuasive ability attached to both relationships. Many times the advocate

[40]   Cavendish Publishing Ltd (2nd edn, London, 2000).
[41]   See Chapman, above, 19.

will simply have to advise his client that the course of action sought by the client is not in that client's best interest. In order to be able to do that with any effectiveness, the advocate first has to develop some reasonable personal relationship with the client.

Chapman in her text sets out a check list of what ordinarily happens during the bad interview. In my experience, it is an accurate list. In the bad interview the interviewer was:

- not listening;
- unprepared and disorganised;
- nervous and unsure;
- rude or patronising;
- showed no interest and seemed bored;
- interrogated the client by using closed or leading questions;
- had little or no eye contact;
- made assumptions;
- did not explain clearly and sometimes used jargon;
- was impatient or rushed;
- showed prejudice, for example by asking sexist or racist questions.[42]

The advocate must allow the client to tell the story from his or her own perspective. Again, we live by telling stores. It is almost invariably the case that the advocate's perspective on the 'facts' as set out on papers will change once that advocate has met the client. The allegations and counter-allegations must be read by the advocate with an open mind, and the advocate must seek to gain an understanding – from the client's point of view – of the case that has been set out on paper.

As noted above, there are many occasions when the advocate must offer counsel and advice to his client regarding difficult and emotional questions. Chapman sets out her three principles underlying client-centred counselling:

- interest and empathy on the part of the counsellor;
- a non-judgmental attitude;
- an objective, non-directive attitude.[43]

The advocate must understand that the decision-making process has to be seen by the client to be a collaborative one. The lawyer is not saying to the client: 'If I were you I would do this or that'. Instead, the lawyer seeks to set out with clarity and with particularity the likely consequences of various approaches, and seeks to give advice with regard to the legal problems the client faces.

---

42   See Chapman, above, p 23.
43   Chapman, above, p 60.

The advocate must be able to recognise and understand how to treat the client who becomes overly distressed and emotional. Linda Singer, a psychotherapist and educator, speaks often to the Bar and others regarding counselling skills. Singer notes that psychological distress arises when a person is confronted with a situation in which they perceive that the demands placed on them exceed or threaten to exceed their capacity to cope. There is a consequent loss of problem-solving abilities and a lack of self-awareness. The effect of this sort of stress on those who give evidence is well known to advocates. These witnesses are anxious, irritable, they have poor concentration and are often confused, and they suffer a decrease in their ability to make decisions. Importantly, they begin to misunderstand what is being said.

When your client is clearly exhibiting the symptoms of someone not coping with stress, Singer advises the lawyer first and foremost to seek to restore what she calls 'calm, communication and control'. She advises the lawyer to listen first to what the client is saying, and to acknowledge the client's distress. She advises them to seek to at that point to calm down the client by making certain the client understands you maintain authority, that you are in control of the situation in court (as far as possible), and that there should be no embarrassment because of the distress. Most important for Singer, as it is for Chapman, is that the lawyer must be seen to empathise with the client. This is, again, crucial.[44]

Where the client is unable to give instructions, however, advocates need to be aware of when it is appropriate to seek adjournment. If the client's distress becomes something more serious, and the advocate believes the client cannot either understand the proceedings, or give instructions regarding the evidence to be adduced, the advocate would seek medical evidence regarding the client's mental health. If a psychiatrist states, after examination, that the client is not able to handle his or her affairs, and is not able to give instructions or aid in the client's defence, then a guardian will need to be appointed to appear for that client. Medical evidence is required before this occurs. The next friend or guardian must be represented by a solicitor if the matter appears in the High Court.

The guardian will seek to give to the court the client's views regarding the matter, but will also make certain the court understands that the client is under a disability, and that the views of the client are not necessarily considered by the guardian of the client to be that client's best interest.

The test is not the same as the test for mental impairment in s 1(2) of the mental Health Act 1983. A court may exercise jurisdiction over an adult who is judged as lacking capacity, even though that adult is not mentally impaired. See *A London Borough v BS and S (an adult by her litigation friend The*

---

[44]   Linda Singer spoke at a Seminar of Family Law Advocates, 9 May 2003.

Official Solicitor)[45]. In that case the High Court's inherent jurisdiction was invoked to determine whether a local authority might place an adult who lacks capacity in different, more suitable accommodation, against the wishes of that adult. See also *An NHS Trust v C*, for the test of incapacity as set out by Mr Justice Sumner.

The Official Solicitor should ordinarily be invited to act for an adult who has been assed by a psychiatrist to lack the capacity to aid in the prosecution or defence of any legal claim.

45   [2003] EWHC 1909 [2005] 1 All ER 387.

Chapter 2

THE ADVOCATE'S CRAFT

2.1 PREPARING AND PRESENTING THE OPENING

The length and complexity of any case will govern how an advocate approaches opening submissions. For the normal one-day case in front of a District Judge in ancillary relief proceedings, the opening submissions should be no more than 10 to 15 minutes. This submission should, in a non-contentious way, answer the essential questions:

- Who are the parties (and their advocates)?
- What do the parties seek (or oppose)?
- What (in summary form) are the primary contentions each party makes with regard to the essential issues in the case (in other words, why is each party saying 'I win, he loses'?)?

In a more complicated case, for example a case lasting more than five days and involving several expert witnesses, the opening submissions would need to expand. The judge hearing lengthy and complicated matters will be helped by the applicant's counsel breaking up the contested issues into written schedules. For example, in a case involving a two-year-old child diagnosed with three separate injuries, where the child has been cared for by two sets of carers, the advocate for the applicant might seek to expand the opening submissions by producing short schedules setting out each witness's contentions regarding the disputed issue. There should also be a time line produced, if possible, showing the time when the child was in the care of each carer.

Advocates presenting complex financial cases must always seek to break down complex information into more easily understood schedules. Excerpts from accountant's reports might be used to show the conflicting views that will have to be decided by the court. For example there may be a difference of opinion regarding the valuation of an ongoing business concern. Rather than force the judge to dig out that information within three ring binders of annual reports, a better method would be to use written schedules setting out the appropriate information, with citations to the trial bundle. District Judge Glenn Brasse, who sits in the Principal Registry and often hears large financial disputes, cites this as a first rule for advocates: never force the judge to dive into the trial bundle. Everything at issue should be set out in schedules, with relevant documents attached.

An extremely good text on opening speeches is one that is now some 126 years old. Richard Harris KC first published his *Hints on Advocacy* in 1879, and it quickly became the pupil advocate's Bible. By 1926, the book had gone through 27 editions. Harris's work is certainly of its time, and the reader today must seek to ignore a great number of derogatory, sexist, references to 'girl novelists' and 'female sensitivities'. But Harris also sets out some strikingly good advice with regard to all aspects of advocacy. His comments are mainly aimed at the advocate conducting jury trials, but much of what he says is relevant to cases decided by a judge as well.

Harris first seeks to answer the question of style. In his view, a temperate style is always more effective than a noisy one:

> 'I have never known a verdict obtained by noise: foam has no weight, fury of language no force. I do not intend for a moment to suggest that a conversational style is powerful; and on the contrary, you might as well attempt to fire a bed of growing rushes with a piece of tinder as rouse a jury with a feeble speech. Bad speaking is infinitely worse than silence. Let the facts speak at all events. But a roaring style never persuades; it only astounds if it does not stun.'[1]

Harris believes the advocate must also apply logic to his own case. (In modern terms, he must seek to make certain his own case adheres to narrative fidelity.) The advocate must know that the fact-finder will more readily grasp arguments that are put logically than those which are presented with distortions of premise and sequence.

Harris notes that a good advocate avoids in opening what Harris calls 'fine talking'. This sort of speech, as Harris notes, 'is as unnatural as the spangled dress of the acrobat, and is utterly unfitted for the ordinary business of a workaday life.'[2] Above all things, Harris argues that affectation should be avoided: 'every listener detests it, and cannot help feeling some degree of contempt for the person who indulges in it.'

Harris believed that at the Bar, except in rare cases, the higher gifts of oratory are out of place. As he puts it, in a way that lets us know he's writing in 1879: 'The Empire is not at stake in every trial.'

His basic guide to opening a case has never been improved:

> 'What is really required is a simple well-told narrative of facts in opening your case to the jury. The fewer words the better and the less argument the more likely is your statement to be believed. It must seem a strange story to the jury if it requires arguing upon before the other side has had a syllable to say in contradiction.'[3]

---

[1]   See Harris, *Hints on Advocacy* (Stevens & Sons Limited, 16th edn, 1926), p 4.
[2]   See Harris, above, p 8.
[3]   See Harris, above, pp 8–9.

In other words, *never* seek to argue your case in opening statement. You simply want to set out, with very little fuss, the narrative that your client contends will be proved by the evidence. You should note where disputes exist in the evidence, and you should not seek to minimise the disputes that exist.

Harris also notes that advocates who appear flippant and unserious also appear not to believe in their own case. Harris states that this is a 'fatal blunder of style':

> 'There is nothing which a jury so much detests in the person addressing them as an air of jaunty frivolity. One need hardly say it is quite a distinguishable quality from humour, for which it is often intended. Humour, when it can be introduced with propriety, is one of the most insinuating of qualities; is almost always acceptable, and is one of the most fascinating as well as successful of an advocate's gifts. But you must have the genuine article and not the spurious imitation, between which there is as much difference as between a hardy laugh and the grin of a dog that runs about through the city.'[4]

It perhaps goes without saying that judges are an even less appreciative audience for would-be comics than jurors.

Harris points out one other, seemingly obvious, but often ignored, piece of advice: tell the tale only once. As Harris puts it, redundancy is not a grace, but a deformity; it should be cut off altogether.

The most important parts of an opening speech, according to Harris, are arrangement and order. In the most complicated entangled circumstances there should be no confusion:

> 'It is the business of the advocate and the art of advocacy to separate them, and to show their relations to one another, their bearings upon each other, and their influence upon the main action. Irrelevant matter therefore should be carefully excluded – by no means so easy a task as at first sight appears, and only to be accomplished by diligent study and thoughtful practice.'[5]

The only way to pare away the irrelevancy is to seek to determine with absolute certainty the precise issues of the case. What evidence is relevant to each issue?

Harris is particularly scathing toward barristers who seek to be actors, in particular, by seeking to show or express by facial expressions: for example the barrister's disbelief at certain evidence, or the barrister's anger or contempt that has been aroused because of witnesses allegedly not telling the truth. Harris is surely right when he says *never* should a barrister express any emotion by a look. He puts it like this:

> 'It is only by thoughtful labour and study that the sculpture can explain expression upon the marble which faintly represents the emotions. It is quite clear everyone

---

4 See Harris, above, p 10.
5 See Harris, above, p 14.

is not artist enough to put the right muscles in motion to produce a corresponding effect upon his own features whenever he desires it. Attempts of this kind, therefore, are not only ludicrous but foolish. I have seen an advocate, in trying to look angry, cause a tear all around the court, and set the jury on the grin. He was attempting a piece of acting, and not being an actor, he failed.'[6]

Harris believes moderation is power. He believes it equally necessary to moderate the tone of voice as well as the style of the speaker. One should never exaggerate the facts in opening. In fact, it may be better, as Harris notes, to do precisely the opposite: the evidence will then obviously live up to the opening, and not create the impression in the judge's mind that the case has gone completely downhill since the advocate's opening statement.

Openings, according to Harris, should be slow, sure and short. In the 126 years since that advice was given, no better advice has been given to young advocates seeking to open their first case.

2.2   PRESENTING EVIDENCE-IN-CHIEF

2.2.1   Preliminary considerations about evidence

The Family Proceedings Rules now provide that written statements of all who intend to give evidence shall be exchanged between and among all parties.[7] It was hoped these statements could, in certain cases, stand as the evidence-in-chief, thereby cutting hearing times, reducing complexity and saving money.[8] The reforms cannot be said to have been entirely successful. All judges in all family cases now routinely accept lengthy examination-in-chief, even where there are complete statements available for the court.

That being said, the advocate cannot ignore the existence of the written statements. The advocate must seek to gauge the judge's knowledge of the written statement, and seek to expand on the written statement rather than simply have the witness repeat what the judge has already read.

The advocate conducting examination-in-chief therefore seeks to have the witness tell an intelligible story, and at the same time seeks to integrate that story with the written documents that have been provided. Most judges will tell the advocates early on (or simply indicate obliquely) whether the judge has had an opportunity to read carefully all the statements. In lengthy, complex public law applications, where the number of witnesses and the amount of the

---

6   See Harris, above, p 20.
7   See Family Proceedings Rules 1991, SI 1991/1247, r 4.17(1); Family Proceedings Court (Children Act 1989) Rules 1991, SI 1991/1395, r 17(1).
8   See *Practice Direction of 31 January 1995 (Case Management)* [1995] 1 WLR 332, [1995] 1 FLR 456.

documentation would simply make it impossible for the judge to remember every aspect of each witness's statement, evidence-in-chief is crucially important.

Advocates must know and understand the rules regarding provision of statements in family proceedings:

(1) In proceedings regarding children, statements are filed as directed by the court, or, failing direction, 'before the hearing or appointment'.[9]
(2) No statement may be filed at all in proceedings under the Children Act 1989 (CA 1989) unless the court has made a prior direction, save for cases begun *ex parte*, or in cases where justice requires the statements to be filed and served without direction.[10]
(3) In proceedings for financial relief for and on behalf of children (CA 1989, s 17, Sch 1), a prescribed statement is filed with the application.

Statements must comply with the President's Practice Direction of 31 January 1995, which provides as follows:

> '[The statement] must be sufficiently detailed, but without prolixity; it must be confined to material matters of fact, not (except in the case of the evidence of professional witnesses) of opinion; and if hearsay evidence is to be adduced, the source of the information must be declared or good reason given for not doing so.'[11]

All evidence before any tribunal can be placed in one of four categories: real evidence, demonstrative evidence, documentary evidence or testimonial evidence. All advocates planning to present a case-in-chief must know the difference in those types of evidence, and know the particular objections to each type.

2.2.2 Legal privilege in family proceedings

Advocates must know and understand the rules surrounding privilege, in particular, the rules now governing whether information gained in proceedings regarding children might nevertheless be kept from other parties and the courts.

There are three types of evidence where legal privilege may apply:

(1) reports received from expert witnesses;
(2) communications from third parties (not parties to the case) where no question of leave of the court arises;
(3) communications direct to and from the client.[12]

---

[9] See Family Proceedings Rules 1991, r 4.17.
[10] See Burrows et al (eds), *Evidence in Family Proceedings* (Family Law, 2nd edn, 1999), p 32, where the author notes that such an exception simply has to be read into the current rules.
[11] *Practice Direction* [1995] 1 WLR 332, [1995] 1 FLR 456.
[12] See Burrows et al, above, p 129. The rule is different in the USA, where the lawyer's communication to the client is never privileged. It is why witnesses are routinely asked in American trials: 'Did your lawyer tell you to say that?' To which the well-prepared witness will always reply: 'No. My lawyer told me to tell the truth.'

It has now been held that in cases under the CA 1989, there exists no legal privilege for parties to withhold from other parties and the court reports that are received by experts. See *Re L (Police Investigation: Privilege)*.[13] It is likely that this would apply as well to communications received from third parties. In other words, there is a duty to disclose evidence received by the advocate from third parties, if that evidence is relevant to the welfare of the child.

Advocates acting in financial family proceedings must understand that privilege does not apply to any information gained regarding the client's financial circumstances. By statute, there is a duty of full disclosure imposed on the parties (and their lawyers) regarding all information about the financial condition of the parties. Facts regarding financial information are therefore neither privileged nor confidential.

In the UK, there has been recognised to be an absolute privilege surrounding communications passing between lawyer and client.[14] This means that the client cannot be compelled to give evidence about communications passing between lawyer and client, and a lawyer cannot be compelled to give evidence about those communications. The rule exists to protect the client, not the lawyer. The privilege may therefore be waived by the client. The legal adviser owes a duty to the client not to reveal any communications made by the client to the lawyer for the purposes of legal advice, and commits professional misconduct if he breaches this duty.

That being said, the rule is not rigid, in particular in cases involving children or when a child is a client. The *Guide to Professional Conduct of Solicitors* provides 'truly exceptional circumstances' justify breach of the duty of confidentiality, such as in circumstances where children are at risk of 'serious harm' or where a crime (such as child abduction) may be committed.

The noted family lawyer and advocate David Burrows argues in his book *Evidence in Family Proceedings*[15] that the absolute privilege for lawyers not to reveal client communications should be especially applicable to lawyers advising mature children. The argument here is that otherwise the child would be likely to know that at some point the lawyer will tell those in authority precisely what the child is about to say, depriving the child of an outlet safe from those who otherwise have absolute control of the child's life.

The contrary view, and apparently the view favoured by the judiciary, is put forward by Thorpe J (as he then was) in the case of *Essex County Council v R*.[16]

---

13   [1995] 1 FLR 552.
14   See *R v Derby Magistrates' Court, ex parte B* [1996] AC 487; [1996] 1 FLR 513.
15   Burrows et al (eds), *Evidence in Family Proceedings* (Family Law, 2nd edn, 1999).
16   [1993] 2 FLR 826.

'For my part, I would wish to see case law go yet further and to make it plain that the legal representatives in possession of such material relevant to determination but contrary to the interests of their client, not only are unable to resist disclosure by reliance on legal professional privilege, but have a positive duty to disclose to the parties and to the court ...'

The law at present is not settled. Wall J, in the case of *Re DH (A Minor) (Child Abuse)*,[17] states in dicta that he, too, would seek to have an absolute duty of disclosure imposed on representatives of children who receive information relevant to the proceedings.

My own view, typical of those who practise in this area, is that there can be no hard and fast rule against disclosure, but that there should be no duty to disclose. A child on most occasions should feel confident that the lawyer will not disclose, and there should be no absolute duty to disclose imposed on the lawyer. But there will come a time when the lawyer simply feels compelled to act against the wishes (but perhaps, it is hoped, not the best interests) of his client, in particular when that client is not really emotionally mature enough to see the consequences of his or her actions. When a 14-year-old girl states on the phone to her lawyer that she is about to run away with a known pimp and drug dealer, should the lawyer feel bound by some legal rule from seeking to help that child in some way? Of course not.

The High Court in its wardship jurisdiction does have the power to order a solicitor to reveal client confidences. See *Re B (Abduction: Disclosure)*.[18] In both *Re B*, and *Re L (Police Investigations: Privilege)* there were discussions about the supposed difference in the 'inquisitorial' method of case conduct and the 'adversarial' method. In the experience of most advocates in family proceedings, the difference, if any exists, only arises when considering whether to produce to the other party evidence that in other proceedings would be privileged. It does not mean the advocate should determine beforehand what is 'the truth,' and then offer evidence only supporting that version of events. The experienced advocate understands that he or she is hired to present the client's version of events. Unless the barrister gains specific knowledge that her client is lying, the barrister is duty bound to present that version of events in the most compelling manner possible. To that extent, family proceedings remain adversarial.

2.2.3 Presenting evidence to the tribunal

Real evidence is the thing itself, and not someone's reconstruction or recollection. It might be a bloody shirt; it might be a forged business document; it might be a passport stamped by Customs. All three would be considered

---

[17] [1994] 1 FLR 679, FD.
[18] [1995] 1 FLR 774.

real evidence, and the proponent of each would need to satisfy the court that in fact this is the real item. There are three methods available to prove and introduce an item of real evidence:

- Unique objects.
- Objects made unique.
- Proving a chain of custody.

Advocates in family proceedings almost always use the second and third methods. For example, the wife who has taken the original letter from the husband's business records will have marked the object with an X and the date, and thereby made the object unique. Or the wife may have kept the document in a drawer under lock and key, where no one else has access to that drawer prior to the wife giving the document to solicitors for copying and serving on the opposing party.

Demonstrative evidence seeks to represent an object or a location that is relevant to the issue to be decided by the court. For example, a map is demonstrative evidence. A model or a photograph will also be demonstrative evidence. All courts require certain foundations to be supplied for any demonstrative evidence, in particular where the adverse party objects to the evidence being produced. The proponent must prove the item accurately demonstrates or represents what it purports to demonstrate or represent. Almost invariably, counsel would be able to agree whether, for example, a photograph is a photograph of the relevant area with the relevant items in place. If the photograph is somehow not representative, it would be likely to be a matter for cross-examination and submissions rather than for a preliminary ruling by the judge that the document is inadmissible.

The third type of evidence is documentary evidence, or evidence contained in a document routinely kept by a business or other organisation, where that business or organisation ordinarily relies on the accuracy of information contained in that document. Bank records, accounting statements, letters confirming details of contracts to suppliers – all are examples of documentary evidence. The advocate in ancillary relief proceedings often finds himself or herself buried under an avalanche of financial documents. The advocate must always remember that the judge hearing the case is being asked to master the same number of documents as the advocate in much less time than the advocate has had. The best advocates therefore never ask the judge to read irrelevant documents or documents that have not been agreed and authenticated.

The final type of evidence is oral evidence by witnesses.

All evidence given in court by a witness must first pass two tests:

(1) Is the witness competent to give the evidence?
(2) Is the evidence relevant?

Competence to give evidence refers to the ability of the witness to perceive what occurred, remember it, and communicate it.[19] If the witness is not capable of performing one of those tasks, the witness is not competent to give evidence. It might be that the witness is too young, or the witness is unable to remember anything at all about the incident, or the witness is simply unable for some reason to communicate what he or she remembers.

Memory, of course, is always a ripe area for cross-examination, as discussed below. It is a matter of degree whether a faulty memory simply affects the credibility of the witness, or makes the witness incompetent to testify.

The question of relevance is simple to state, and damnably hard to apply. The test is this: does the evidence have a tendency to prove what the proponent of the evidence is seeking to prove?

2.2.4   The foundation of evidence

Keith Evans, who has practiced in both jurisdictions, has pointed out the fundamental distinction between evidence-in-chief in the US and evidence-in-chief in the UK: the requirement in the States is that a 'foundation' must be laid for all evidence sought to be adduced in chief. The foundation is only this: the advocate must first have the witness establish how the witness is able to know what he or she seeks to give evidence about. In the US, this is a rule relating to competence, that is, whether the witness should be allowed to give evidence to a jury. In the UK, where in family proceedings judges would be hearing the evidence without juries, laying a foundation is less important legally, but it remains important functionally.

Professor Evans helpfully notes that the advocate should ask himself or herself constantly 'how did the witness perceive what she perceived?' The how/what, examination also gives a better rhythm to evidence-in-chief. Most judges take down the most important evidence in long hand. It is difficult to follow a substantive answer – that is one that takes up more than three or four handwritten lines – with another substantive question. Far better to alternate the questions so that witnesses deal first with the how, and then answer the what.

The advocate seeking to conduct examination-in-chief must have a thorough understanding, and the ability to apply that understanding in practice, of two essential concepts:

(1) The difference between a leading question and a non-leading question.
(2) The difference between examination of lay witnesses and examination of expert witnesses.

---

19   See Younger, *The Advocate's Deskbook: The Essentials of Trying a Case* (Prentice Hall Law and Business, 1988), pp 154–155.

Each of these will be considered separately.

(1) Leading questions

It has been a rule in English legal proceedings since man's memory runneth not to the contrary that advocates conducting examination-in-chief cannot use leading questions. The best definition of a leading question is this: the question puts the answer in the witness's mouth. Almost invariably, the leading question can be answered Yes or No. That means the lawyer's question is the substance of the evidence. That is not what trials are for. The judge must hear the witness tell what happened, not the lawyer. Judges know that solicitors prepare their clients' statements. Judges know the statements often contain the sort of precision with regard to dates and events that the witness would be unlikely, in certain cases, to reproduce orally. As one District Judge said to me, that is the primary reason why judges seek to hear from witnesses-in-chief, rather than simply use the statement as evidence-in-chief and then allow for cross-examination. Judges gain a better understanding of a witness when the witness seeks to tell what happened in his or her own words.

Advocates soon learn, however, that not only is the line between a leading question and a non-leading question sometimes difficult to draw, there are exceptions where the court routinely expects the advocate to use leading questions in examination-in-chief. Professor Younger puts it like this: perhaps 30 per cent of all possible questions are leading; 30 per cent are plainly non-leading. In the middle would be about 40 per cent of all questions that would either be leading or non-leading in the sense that reasonable people might disagree. Much depends on the context, whether the judge believes the lawyer is interfering too much, and whether the judge seeks to have the witness give evidence unaided on a particular topic.

Experts agree there are no more than six exceptions to the rule that no leading questions might be used for examination-in-chief.[20] I know of no others. They are as follows:

1 **Preliminary matters.** This might include the witness's name and professional address, the age of the witness (if important), and any other preliminary facts that put the evidence of the witness in context. For example, judges routinely allow advocates to question a witness like this:

> Q: 'You are John Smith?'
>
> A: 'Yes.'
>
> Q: 'And you reside at 45 Park Lane, London, W11?'
>
> A: 'Yes.'

---

[20]   See Younger, above, pp 188–198.

The advocate might then begin his or her examination. 'Could you tell the court your place of employment?' (If that is relevant.)

2   **Uncontested matters.** Advocates will know which matters are not contested in all family proceedings because either witness statements or position statements will have been filed and served. For example, in a case under the Family Law Act 1996, Part IV, where the wife seeks protective injunctions against the husband, it might be the husband's position that he was not at home on the day the wife alleges the injury occurred. His position might be he was nowhere near the home, and no incident at all occurred. Therefore the advocate should not lead with regard to the fact of the incident occurring on a certain date, nor should the advocate direct the complainant's attention to a particular date. In those circumstances, the advocate should, after the preliminaries, approach the matter like this:

> Q: 'Can you describe the relationship you and your husband had during the last few weeks he lived in the home.'
>
> A: 'There were several incidents where we argued, and on several occasions he became violent. He hit me twice.'
>
> Q: ' You say he hit you twice. When did that occur?'
>
> A: 'The first time was on 16 May, and I remember that day because it was my daughter's birthday.' [Or some other manner of noting the date that counsel and the lay client have discussed in conference.]

Counsel will need to have a careful conference with the client with regard to the client's understanding of when, where and how each incident occurred. That will, in some cases, not be possible. In the above example, it might be that the wife's evidence is that she simply cannot put a date on the next occasion, save by reference to other evidence: a medical examination document; or a statement by a friend or neighbour. In that case the advocate would ask, after the witness has stated what happened when the incident occurred, 'What did you do after that?' or 'What happened next?' The witness will then answer 'I went to the hospital' or 'I went to my neighbour's home.' In any event, at this point the advocate will be in position to pinpoint the date, either with medical records, or the neighbour's evidence.

   On the other hand the husband's position might be that he accepted an argument occurred and accepted that there was pushing and shoving, but does not accept the extent of the violence alleged by the wife. If he does acknowledge that an incident occurred on that date, the advocate might simply lead the witness directly to that date and ask the witness to tell the court what happened.

3   **Introducing an area of inquiry.** It is a leading question to say to a witness: 'I direct your attention to 10 January 2001, at the corner of Acre Lane and

Coldharbour Lane. Did an incident occur on that occasion?' Judges routinely allow this sort of introductory question, in part because they are judges who have heard hundreds of these cases in the past and wish to proceed directly to the material and relevant evidence. As noted above, however, in some cases the date or the location is absolutely crucial to a witness's evidence. In those situations, the advocate should not ordinarily use the 'I direct your attention to ...' sort of question. If the witness is a party to the proceedings, he or she will already have read the statements, and very likely will have no difficulty being prompted by the advocate (in a non-leading way) to give the appropriate evidence.

The difficulty arises primarily from non-party witnesses. An example would be a witness to a violent incident between husband and wife, where the date of the incident is crucial to the husband's claim that no incident in fact occurred. In that situation the advocate should be wary of directing the witness's attention to a certain date. Instead, the advocate could approach the matter by asking the witness (who will have provided a written statement in any event) a few foundation questions regarding the date. For example, the witness might be an employee who witnessed the incident between husband and wife while he was making a delivery for his company. In those circumstances documents from the company might be produced to allow the witness to state with particularity which date within them or on which date he saw the alleged incident. If no documents exist, other methods might be used: the witness might remember that it was a Tuesday, or the witness might remember it was the second week in January, or the witness could remember that it was late in the afternoon. Any of these partial identifications of the date might be used, in conjunction with other evidence, to allow the advocate to show in final submissions that the witness is describing an incident that occurred on the date alleged by the applicant.

4 **Inconsequential or irrelevant matters.** Evidence that is clearly irrelevant to the issue to be decided by the judge is often led simply to give a narrative flow to the evidence. For example, if there were incidents occurring on Monday and Wednesday that are relevant to the issue to be decided, and the witnesses finished describing what happened on Monday, the applicant might simply say this:

> Q: 'On Tuesday you and your husband did not see each other, is that right?'
>
> A: 'Yes that's right.'
>
> Q: 'What happened on Wednesday?'

5 **Refreshing recollection.** Other than when rising to cross-examine a hostile expert, nothing strikes more terror in the heart of a novice advocate than receiving from a witness the answer: 'I don't remember'. The advocate

is seeking not to lead the witness to the appropriate answer, and has used every appropriate method of having the witness give the relevant evidence, but has failed. In certain circumstances, it may be that the witness is simply frightened and has become overwhelmed by the prospect of speaking in a courtroom. In those circumstances, courts routinely allow a few leading questions to orient the witness in time. It is always appropriate for the advocate seeking to lead in those circumstances to ask permission from the court. It would not be appropriate to lead the witness throughout his evidence, but it is sometimes acceptable to give the nervous or frightened witness some help in order to allow that witness to complete his/her evidence.

6   **The hostile or adverse witness.** This witness may be a relation of the adverse party; she may be a fellow employee; she might be a former or current lover of the adverse party. Professor Younger usefully breaks down the hostile witness into four specific types:

(1)   the boorish witness;
(2)   the reluctant witness;
(3)   the predisposed witness;
(4)   the adverse party.

In all of these circumstances, courts routinely allow for leading questions to be used.

The boorish witness is simply that witness who seeks to misbehave in the witness box. As ever in law, it is a matter of degree, and a matter of discretion to be used by the advocates and the tribunal. It does occur, however, and the advocate must be ready to deal with the witness who simply wishes to misbehave.

The reluctant witness might be reluctant simply because he or she is nervous or worried about giving evidence. It may also be that the witness is simply not able, for reasons of intellect, to give extended oral evidence unaided by leading questions. Again, this is a matter of degree, and a matter for the discretion of the advocates and the tribunal.

The predisposed witness is that witness who for one reason or another would be likely to support one side or the other. For example, where relatives of one party are giving evidence, courts often allow advocates to lead the witness. Experts expressing an opinion hostile to your client fall into this category.

It is rare in English family proceedings for parties to call the adverse party as part of the case-in-chief, but it is not impermissible. For example, in a public law case under the CA 1989, s 31, a court has the power to allow the local authority to call, as part of the local authority's case-in-chief, the mother or father to give evidence. In a case where the mother and father state they do not seek to give oral evidence, it would not be an abuse of the court's discretion to allow the local authority to cross-examine those

adverse parties. That being said, if the court wished to hear the evidence, it would be likely to indicate that fact to the parents' representatives, who would then be very likely to call their clients and have them give evidence-in-chief in the normal way, prior to cross-examination.

(2)   The expert

In almost all seriously contested family cases, the evidence of experts will be crucial. Accountants will give opinions with regard to the value of a family business; physicians will give evidence with regard to whether a child's injury was caused accidentally or intentionally; child psychiatrists will give evidence with regard to the long-term effect on a child of a change in residence for that child. The rendering of an opinion is of course the fundamental distinction between the evidence of an expert and the evidence of a lay witness.

In the appropriate case, it is a reversible error for a trial judge to prohibit a party from calling expert evidence. A court must give specific, detailed reasons when disagreeing with expert evidence. See, generally, *In Re B (Child)*.[21]

The Children Act's Advisory Committee, set up by the President of the Family Division after enactment of the CA 1989, has periodically issued Best Practice Guidance with regard to all aspects of the Children Act. Section 5 of the 1997 Best Practice Guidance deals with experts. The Section sets out the historic distinction between the role of the expert and the role of the judge. The expert forms an assessment and expresses an opinion within the area of his expertise. This may include an opinion on the issues in the case. It is for the judge to make the decision on that final issue, and no judge is bound to follow the opinion of the experts. That being said, appellate courts are increasingly requiring trial judges to justify any deviation from experts' opinion by a reasoned analysis, and the standard of review for any attempted 'reasoned analysis' is by any view quite high.

The instruction of experts should be one of the first questions considered by those having conduct of a family case. The Best Practice Guidance pointed this out in 1997, and Mr Justice Wall in 2000 made explicit the consequences for advocates and legal representatives who fail to make certain that the evidence of experts is properly prepared.[22] In particular, each expert must be kept up to date with all evidence produced, and advised as to what the other experts are saying. The experts should meet prior to giving evidence and a memorandum of agreement and disagreement should be prepared and served on all parties.

---

[21]   Sub nom *Re B (Split Hearing: Jurisdiction)* [2000] 1 WLR 790, [2000] 1 FLR 334.
[22]   See case of *Re G, S and M (Wasted Costs)* [2000] 1 FLR 52, FD, where Mr Justice Wall made cost orders against legal representatives of the local authority. See also *R (Care: Disclosure - Nature of Proceedings)* [2002] 1 FLR 755; *Re CH (A Minor)* (2000) Times, 6 June.

The question of the type of expert evidence that might be considered useful in each individual case will be considered in the succeeding chapters. There are certain aspects of the advocate's role in presenting expert evidence, however, that are applicable in all cases.

Both the Civil Procedure Rules and the Family Proceedings Rules now provide that leave of the court is required before instructing experts. It is no longer the case that experts might be instructed by each party to counter expert evidence received from the other side. In general, the hope is that one expert might be instructed to present an assessment of the issues to the court. This places an even greater burden on legal representatives to seek to determine the best expert to instruct as quickly as possible. The issue will likely be decided on either the first or second directions appointment before the judge. The party that places before the judge the details of an appropriate expert, with an agreement that the expert will have a report done within an appropriate period of time, is likely to convince the judge to allow that expert to perform the assessment.

Advocates seeking leave to instruct experts have a positive duty to place before the court the following:

- the category of expert evidence that is sought to be adduced;
- the name of the expert;
- the expert's availability for reporting, meeting with other experts and attendance in court;
- the relevance of the expert evidence to the issues in the case;
- whether evidence can properly be obtained by both parties jointly instructing one expert; and
- whether expert evidence may properly be adduced by one party only, that is, usually by the guardian.[23]

Courts have also been directed to make specific orders for leave to disclose papers to an expert that set out the expert's area of expertise, the issues to be addressed, the identity of the expert and the date by which the letter of instruction is to be sent, the date for filing of the expert's report, the date for an expert's meeting, and the date the expert will be likely to have to give oral evidence, if required.[24]

Courts are now adamant that all experts who report in a case must conduct a meeting (whether in person or by telephone) prior to the substantive hearing in the case. The meeting should usually be chaired by representatives for the guardian, and the expert should produce at the meeting a schedule of agreed opinion and a schedule of disagreements.

---

[23]   See Best Practice Guidance June 1997, para 64.
[24]   See Best Practice Guidance, above, para 66.

There are now good model letters of instruction to experts produced by, among others, the publishers of this text.[25] All letters of instruction should:

- define the context in which the opinion is sought;
- set out specific questions for the expert to address;
- identify all relevant issues of fact to enable each expert to give an opinion on each set of competing issues;
- specify any examination to be permitted;
- list the documents to be sent to the expert;
- require as a condition of appointment that the expert hold discussions with other experts appointed in the same field of expertise, and require that the experts produce a statement of agreement and disagreement on the issues by a specific date.[26]

It goes without saying that the letter of instruction should be disclosed to all parties prior to communication to the expert. If possible, the letter should be agreed by all parties. It is almost never in anyone's best interest to seek to exclude information that one party wishes to include in the letter of instruction. That being said, the letter of instruction should not be hopelessly unwieldy.

It is the instructing solicitor's duty to ensure that an expert who has to give oral evidence is kept up to date with relevant developments in the case. The advocate calling an expert has a duty to ensure that the witness has seen all fresh relevant material prior to giving oral evidence. That advocate must make certain the expert is aware of any new developments that have occurred since the making of the expert's report.

2.3 CONDUCTING CROSS-EXAMINATION

Within the drama of a common law trial, nothing approaches the intensity – or the importance – of cross-examination of a hostile witness.

It is easy to see why: the cross-examination is an opportunity for the fact-finder to examine both cases simultaneously. The advocate seeking to cross-examine the opposing expert, for example, is putting to that expert a contrary theory; the advocate cross-examining the hostile or the adverse party is putting to that party adverse evidence that would suggest the witness is lying. The drama is an inescapable result of the decision to determine disputes in fact and law in one sitting, before one judge.

It is therefore not surprising that acres of rain forest have been sacrificed over the last 100 years in order to produce a mountain of textbooks regarding the art of cross-examination.

---

[25] See Model Instructions for Experts (Family Law, 1999).
[26] See Best Practice Guidance, above, para 69.

The student quickly learns, however, that most of these texts are in fact more memoir than textbook. It becomes difficult to extract general rules from any particular cross-examination, save to note that cross-examinations (like many of the best things in life) withstand classification.

There are three texts, however, that helpfully seek to focus on the general rather than the particular. The first is by the English barrister John Munkman, first published in 1957, and re-issued by Butterworths in 1991.[27] The second is an American text by the law professor and trial lawyer Paul Bergman, entitled *Trial Advocacy*.[28] Bergman is particularly good on rules of general application regarding planning cross-examination, and seeking to understand the purpose of cross-examination. Munkman focuses more on an advocate's style of cross-examination. Both texts are indispensable.

The final text is by Irving Younger,[29] which again focuses on American jury trials, but has several useful general rules for any advocate seeking to convince a fact-finder that a witness should not be believed.

2.3.1 The purpose of cross-examination

The primary role of the advocate is to present credible, admissible evidence to a fact-finder that convinces that fact-finder to find in favour of the advocate's client. Every advocate seeking to cross-examine an opposing witness needs to keep this fundamental rule foremost in mind: 'What evidence can I produce from this hostile witness that will help my client?' No rule is as important as this one. And for that reason, every question on cross-examination should do one of two things:

(1) produce an answer that the advocate can use in final submissions in favour of his client;
(2) state to the finder of fact the theory of the advocate's case, even though the answer that is produced is hostile to the client's case.

Each and every question must relate to the advocate's theory of why her client should prevail. Nothing infuriates trial judges more than pointless cross-examination, and nothing is more likely to make that trial judge understand all too clearly that the advocate has no case to offer.

Bergman is especially good on the purpose of cross-examination. If the advocate understands that each question is directed to final submissions, the two most common and amateurish errors might be avoided. The first error is to conduct the cross-examination by simply asking each question that has been

---

[27] See Munkman, *The Technique of Advocacy* (Butterworths, 1991).
[28] See Bergman, *Trial Advocacy* (West Publishing Company, 1979).
[29] Younger, *The Trial Lawyer's Deskbook* (Prentice Hall, 1988).

asked on direct examination, with the difference being that in cross-examination a sneering 'you expect us to believe that' tone of voice is adopted.[30]

If the advocate asked himself prior to asking the question whether the response could be used in his own final submission, he would not simply ask the witness to repeat what has been stated in examination-in-chief.

In the second most obvious amateurish error the examiner probes minute details of the witness's perception. This might be called the 'ant next to the cannon' cross-examination, where the witness is asked countless questions about the insect that crawled around next to the cannon that was used as the murder weapon. The usual basis of this sort of questions is that you seek to test the witness's ability to perceive what happened. In fact, what it proves is that the advocate has no case, and is attempting to produce at least an hour's worth of cross-examination to hide that fact.

The first question the advocate must ask, before rising to cross-examine, is this: 'Do I cross-examine at all?' If the witness has said nothing that harms your client's case, the answer is no. If the witness has stated facts that do harm your client, but your client accepts the truth of what is stated, and argues that for other, perhaps legal, reasons those facts are not determinative of the outcome of the case, the answer is also No. In all other situations, the answer is that the advocate must cross-examine the witness.

But the purpose of each cross-examination depends on the facts that have been adduced by evidence-in-chief. The advocate must determine:

- Which of the facts testified to by the witness are relevant to the outcome of the case?
- What purpose is achieved by cross-examination into that factual area?

With regard to the purposes of cross-examination, advocates must know that there are in fact fairly limited methods available for impeachment of a witness. Five are crucially important:

(1) bias, for personal or family reasons;
(2) financial (or other) interest in the case;
(3) conviction of a serious crime;
(4) inability to perceive what happened;
(5) faulty memory.

Bergman argues (and I think quite rightly) that in fact most cross-examination of witnesses focuses on credibility factors.[31] Those credibility factors are as follows:

---

30   See Bergman, above, p 143.

31   Bingham LJ in his essay on judicial fact finding, in *The Business of Judging: Selected Essays and Speeches* (Oxford University Press, 2002) agrees with Bergman's analysis of the credibility

(1) Credibility of the evidence:
    (a) Is the evidence consistent with common experience?
    (b) Is the evidence consistent with itself?
    (c) Is the evidence consistent with established facts?[32]
(2) Credibility of the witness:
    (a) Is the witness biased or neutral?
    (b) Does the witness have special expertise?
    (c) What is the witness's demeanour?
    (d) What is the witness's background?
    (e) Where does the witness fit in the overall narrative being offered to the court by the opposing party?

As discussed with more particularity below, research has shown that jurors focus more intently on credibility of the evidence rather than credibility of the witness. This should be kept in mind by any advocate preparing cross-examination. The story, not the witness, is the key.

Advocates must remember that each question in cross-examination must relate to the theory of the case. In other words, it does no good to show on cross-examination that the witness is lying if you intend to rely on some aspect of the evidence in support of your case. There is no need to conduct an attack on the witness's interest in the outcome if you intend to argue that the whole of the witness's testimony is irrelevant in any event. Each question on cross-examination shows the fact-finder that the advocate believes the area of enquiry is important. If in fact the area of enquiry is not important, the fact-finder becomes confused, and the advocate loses credibility.

Prior to rising to cross-examine, the advocate will know what it is he seeks to achieve in the cross-examination. But the advocate also must know precisely how to have the witness produce that evidence. There is one way, and one way only, to conduct a proper cross-examination: by leading each witness where the advocate seeks to go.

Irving Younger put it like this:

> 'I promise I will come back from the dead to haunt any advocate who ever asks a non-leading question on cross-examination until that attorney has tried at least 25 cases.'[33]

Bergman, however, cautions that advocates should not overestimate the power of leading questions. A witness is not likely to agree to something he feels is

---

of witnesses. But see the discussion by McEwan, regarding recent psychological research showing that 'consistency' is not always an indicator of reliability; McEwan *The Verdict of the Court* (Hart Press, 2003). See discussion in Chapter 1.

[32] As noted in Chapter 1, however, it is easy to become over enamoured with detecting inconsistency in witness statements. The most effective use of inconsistency is when it is used to prove that the witness is generally not capable of remembering anything at all with particularity.

[33] See Younger, above, p 257.

not true simply because the matter is put to him in the form of a leading question. That is not the point, in the great majority of cross-examinations. The point of putting the question in a leading manner is to make the fact-finder aware of your client's version of the events. Your version must be confidently and assertively put to the witness in the form of a leading question. Many times, the witness will agree to your characterisation of the event, while seeking to maintain that the evidence given in chief is the way the event occurred. Sometimes there is a subtle difference.

Bergman quite rightly notes that no two cases present the same problems in cross-examination, but that certain general rules do exist. He presents what he calls a cross-examination model:

(1) Highest safety questions:
    (a) prior statements of witness are available, either a prior statement in this case or other extrinsic evidence;
    (b) a more believable witness statement or witness evidence is available.
(2) Medium safety questions:
    (a) facts are inconsistent with common experience;
    (b) an assumption by a witness that a third party will refute;
    (c) your client's story is directly opposed to this witness's version of events.
(3) The lowest safety questions:
    (a) fishing, the last resort.

Advocates might usefully use the model when planning cross-examination, making a determination as to which witness must be cross-examined, and determining the point of each cross-examination question.

2.3.2   The technique of cross-examination

John Munkman was an English barrister who practised in the late fifties, until retiring in 1961. At that time, he wrote a fairly brief text on trial techniques, which achieved modest success. Butterworths in 1991 reissued the book, with revisions by the author. It is in my view a terrifically helpful text for the novice advocate.[34]

Munkman is especially good about the limitations of cross-examination. For Munkman, cross-examination can have only four purposes:

(1) to destroy material parts of the evidence-in-chief;
(2) to weaken the evidence, where it cannot be destroyed;
(3) to elicit new evidence helpful to the party cross-examining; and
(4) to undermine the witness by impeaching his credit or showing that he cannot be trusted to speak the truth.

---

[34]   See Munkman, *The Technique of Advocacy* (Butterworths, 1991).

Munkman notes that the actual destruction of a witness's evidence is rare, and usually requires the advocate to have available to him some damning piece of evidence that he can spring on the witness. Outside of television courtrooms, this rarely occurs.

Munkman notes that cross-examination is often overrated. Even a cross-examination that brings out weaknesses may not be decisive. Where, however, a witness has given evidence on a material fact that is disputed by your client, you must seek to cross-examine the witness with regard to that disputed fact, so long as that fact is material to the outcome of the case.

Munkman believes cross-examination is founded on three main techniques:

(1) confrontation;
(2) probing;
(3) insinuation.

Confrontation consists of confronting the witness with a great mass of damaging facts which he cannot deny and which are inconsistent with his evidence.

Probing consists of the barrister seeking to go into the details of the story in order to discover flaws.

Insinuation is the advocate's effort to build up a different version of the evidence-in-chief by bringing out new facts and possibilities, so that while helping to establish a positive case in one's own favour, it also weakens the evidence-in-chief by revealing flaws or inconsistencies. It may consist of nothing more than quietly leading the witness on, little by little. The beginner often uses this method when he or she says to the witness, 'I suggest to you ...' or 'I put to you ...' Sometimes the phrase is necessary; most times, however, there are better ways of putting the questions.

Munkman is especially helpful with regard to probing into the foundations of a witness's statement. Every statement of fact always contains assumptions. The effective cross-examiner seeks to probe those assumptions, in cases where other, reasonable, assumptions might be made. In particular, the assumptions made by experts must be tested. Many times, those assumptions are set out in the written reports. When they are not spelled out, the cross-examiner has no choice but to probe for those assumptions, and, in the appropriate case, to query whether those assumptions render the experts' opinion unreliable.

Insinuation, on the other hand, is related more to an advocate questioning a witness with little hope that probing the underlying assumptions that have been made will achieve much. Instead, insinuation is used as a method that allows the advocate to state his case.

Munkman points out two types of insinuation: general insinuation, which is used with an impartial witness; or firm insinuation, which is used if the witness is

hostile. In both forms barristers or advocates must apply a gradual approach, step-by-step, toward the important question. That question may well elicit a denial, but its intent is to impress upon the fact-finder the likelihood that the witness is mistaken.

This gradual style is characteristic of the technique. Munkman points out one famous advocate, Sir Patrick Hastings, who began all his cross-examinations in the same way. At the outset he put quite plainly the essential points he intended to establish. These might be denied, but at all events the jury and judge saw what was in issue. This was followed up by firm insinuation of detailed facts tending to prove (according to Sir Patrick) the points sought to be proved.[35] By conducting cross-examination in such a manner Sir Patrick always controlled the direction of the examination, always placed his client's case in the forefront of the minds of the fact-finders, and always placed on trial the theory of the case being advanced by his opponents. That, in a nutshell, is what cross-examination is all about.

2.3.3   The manner of cross-examination

As John Mortimer's Horace Rumpole has stated (too many times to count), cross-examination does not mean the advocate 'examines crossly'. Almost invariably, cross-examination should be conducted in a gentle, yet firm manner. The control of the evidence is gained through the formation of the leading questions, not by the attitude of the cross-examiner. Each question should be phrased confidently and firmly. Each question should indicate that only a Yes and No answer really should be expected. You must always be courteous to the witness, in particular, when the witness has just made a statement that skewers your client's case. And, it goes without saying, the advocate should never display emotion, particularly when the witness has given an answer that is harmful to the advocate's client's case.

Argumentative questions force the witness to respond to your argument, rather than to your case. There is a distinction. Argument is based on convincing a third party of the correctness of your position. This involves an interpretation of facts that have been adduced in evidence. A client's 'case', on the other hand, is made up of the facts that have been linked together to form a coherent narrative. When questioning the opposing expert, the distinction blurs a bit, but only slightly. The advocate gently but firmly puts her client's case to the expert, which sometimes requires a contrary interpretation of facts to be placed before that expert. But this contrary interpretation is put to the witness in a manner that is not argumentative.

---

[35]   See Munkman, above, p 86.

Irving Younger, in his lectures on trial techniques, produced 10 commandments of cross-examination. It is interesting to note how often Younger and Munkman converge:

(1) *Be brief.* There are two reasons. First, cross-examination in many, many cases does more harm than good. The second is more important: almost invariably, cross-examination of any individual witness will only have one or two purposes. It is almost always a mistake simply to wander into irrelevant evidence in order to show, for example, that the witness has trouble remembering irrelevant details. Each question in cross-examination should relate to a closing submission. If this rule is followed religiously, most cross-examinations will be brief.

(2) *Use plain words.* Younger ruefully notes that in more than 500 car accident cases he presided over as a judge in New York City, not once did he hear a lawyer use the word car. The questions are always put like this: 'What did you do then with respect to the operation and control of your motor vehicle?' Why not say 'car'?

(3) *Use only leading questions.* The purpose is obvious. You seek to lead the witness in a direction you wish him to go, and if the witness refuses to go there, you, at the very least, wish to put a plausible case before the fact-finder.

(4) *Be prepared.* In other words, always intend never to ask a question to which you do not already know the answer. The sad fact will be, however, that there will be many, many occasions when you rise to cross-examine and you are not certain – no matter the hours of preparation – precisely what the witness will say. In these situations, the advocate must determine precisely why the witness is being questioned. Nine times out of ten, the advocate in that situation should gently probe the underlying factual assumptions made by the witness, firmly put to the witness the opposing view of any disputes regarding relevant facts known to exist between the witness and the advocate's client, and then sit down. If you do not know what the witness is likely to say, you are usually far better off keeping the witness quiet.

(5) *Listen.* Witnesses do say things that are not in their statements. It is the rare cross-examiner who is not thinking of her next question while the witness is speaking. Somehow, the advocate must do exactly that, while also listening to the witness's answer. There are times when a witness simply accepts a statement put to him or her on cross-examination. When that happens, the good advocate stops. The bad advocate, who has not been listening, ploughs on.

(6) *Do not quarrel.* An advocate should never, ever argue or quarrel with a witness. That is not the way cross-examination is conducted. The advocate should be seen to be the reasonable party at all times, seeking to place before the court the reasonable case of his client. When voices are raised,

and emotions interfere with reason, one hopes it is the witness, not the advocate, who is guilty. Younger cites in support the story of the Russian prosecutor at the Nuremberg trials. Day after day, the Russian would hand a document to a witness and say, 'I hand you a document. Does it bear your signature? Did you read it before signing it? Do you now confess yourself to be a fascist beast?' Each time we hear the 'fascist beast' ring to any question we seek to put, the advocate must suppress it.

(7) *Avoid repetition.* Never allow the witness to repeat on cross-examination what was said in evidence-in-chief. Effective impeachment of a witness almost always involves questions that have little to do with the direct examination.

(8) *Do not allow the lay witness to explain an irrational response.* It is very often true that a lay witness gives an answer that is irrational or inconsistent with something that has been said previously. There is no need at this point to say to the witness: 'Please explain how your evidence differs from what was said by X'. The time to do that is in your final speech, when you explain the contradiction in a way that is favourable to your client's case.

(9) *Learn when to stop, and if you are ever ahead, stop there.* It is right to say that the classic 'one question too many' stories are almost all apocryphal. Particularly in the family jurisdiction, where judges would wish to hear complete stories, it is unlikely that the wily cross-examiner can limit the evidence in such a manner. Nevertheless, the advice is useful. Again, the time to stop is when you have made your points for submissions. Once those points are made, sit down. Do not attempt to make a good thing better by piling on the questioning, especially with that gleeful sneering tone often adopted by the novice advocate who thinks he might have scored a point with the previous question.

(10) *Save for closing submissions.* This is another way of saying do not argue your case to the witnesses. You have limited purposes on each cross-examination. On some of these witnesses, for example an expert witness in a public law case, you will in effect be putting your theory of your case to the witness. In almost all other instances, the barrister or the advocate would not be seeking to put his case as a closing submission to any one witness. Remember the purpose of cross-examination: to destroy the evidence; to limit the evidence; to elicit new evidence; and to undermine the witness by impeaching his credibility. The purpose is not to argue the case with the witness.

2.3.4   Question structure and control of the witness

Advocates conducting cross-examination quickly learn that precisely formed questions are the only method available for controlling a hostile witness. Studies

have shown that the 'grammar' of questions by experienced practitioners is in fact very similar from case to case.[36] Certain rules do exist:

(1) *Never use rhetorical questions.* They simply invite the witness to give contrary opinions that contradict the question, and invite argument. The advocate seeks to control the witness, not argue with him.

(2) *Use closed-ended questions* that in the ordinary case are answerable only with 'yes' or 'no'.

(3) *When losing control, be aware of 'loopback' questions.* A loopback question repeats part or all of the answer elicited from a previous question in a new question. The function is to produce a repetition of specific points in order to ingrain those points in the memory of the fact-finder. A loopback question enables the advocate to refer to a question which the witness answered favourably and to continue the questioning from that point. By not refuting the earlier answer or questioning its re-statement, the witness is now forced to work from its premises.[37]

(4) *Be aware of the words you choose.* Consider these examples: teenager/youth; strike/bludgeon; house/residence; outfit/uniform; throw/hurl; bullet/projectile. Research has shown that a particular word, once introduced, will prompt others to adopt the term and its related meanings.[38]

(5) *Be aware of question structure.* There are two dimensions: content and form. The content of the questions will have to come from the context of the case, and the purpose each examiner has for cross-examining any single witness. Form, however, can be looked at in general. Questions vary structurally. Rieke and Stutman, in *Communication in Legal Advocacy*, point out four features of structural variation:

(a) Negative/affirmative construction. Look to see if the negative morpheme 'n't' exists in the main clause. If it is there, re-phrase the question: 'Did you not walk into the house?' 'Did you not look where you were going?' These questions are hard to understand and more difficult to recall than questions stated in the affirmative. They also require longer periods to process than do affirmative sentences. A better way to do it is this: 'You walked into the house, correct?' 'You looked to see what was in front of you, correct?' Always seek to put questions in the affirmative.

(b) Active/passive construction. Always use active voice, for the same reasons you use active voice when you write. It is easier to understand,

---

[36] See Bleiberg and Churchill, 'Notes on Confrontation in Conversation' *Journal of Psycho-social Linguistic Research*, 4, 273–278.

[37] See Rieke and Stutman, *Communication in Legal Advocacy*, (University of South Carolina Press, 1995), p 174. See also JL Kestler, *Questioning techniques and tactics* (McGraw-Hill, 1982).

[38] See Danet, '"Baby" or "Fetus" Language and the construction of reality in a manslaughter trial' *Semiotica* 32, 187–219; Rieke and Stutman, above, p 119.

and uses fewer words: 'Did the boy throw the rock?' is better than 'Was the rock thrown by the boy?'.

(c) Tag questions. This is a device used to turn a non-leading question into a leading question. Generally, it does so by attaching an expected answer to the question. Example: 'Q: The primary value of the business was its employees' expertise, was it not?' The tag (the negative 'was it not') follows the open-ended clause (the affirmative 'the primary value of the business was its employees' expertise'), and turns the question into a leading question. Tag questions are more difficult to understand, but research shows the listeners retain these questions and answers. Research also shows that the witness is more likely to agree with strongly worded, affirmative questions, than weakly worded, open-ended questions.[39]

(d) Leading questions. Why leading questions? To control the witness. The keys to control are well known: (1) do not let the respondent talk; (2) when the respondent must talk, limit her options; (3) design the options to leave the respondent unable to provide narrative responses.[40] In one study, Rieke and Stutman assessed jurors in 15 civil trials in the US in an effort to gain an understanding of the effect on jurors of the questioning used by advocates. Their research shows that when lawyers fail to allow witnesses in examination-in-chief to give open-ended narratives, there results a decrease in the authoritativeness of the witness and the believability of the testimony. It stands to reason: a decrease in storytelling and in increase in control by counsel results in a less believable reality as interpreted by the fact-finder. The results were the same when assessing jurors' reactions to cross-examination. The less narrative allowed, the less believable the testimony. The more control enforced by the advocate, the less believable the witness will be.[41]

Rieke and Stutman's study also revealed jurors do not ordinarily focus on the character of the witness to determine credibility. In other words, juror discussions do not centre on whether a witness is trustworthy or likely to be believed because he is of good character, but instead centre on the probability of the oral evidence fitting in with the other evidence the jurors have heard. It is a question of creating stories that fit. Historically, lawyers are perceived as 'destroying the witnesses' credibility'. A better way of putting it is that the effective lawyer has destroyed the probability of the witnesses' evidence.

---

[39] See Elizabeth Loftus, 'Eyewitness Testimony: the influence of wording of a question' *Bulletin of the Psychonomic Society* 5, 86–88.

[40] This, of course, is key. *You* control the narrative, not the witness.

[41] Rieke and Stutman, above, p 122.

The research tells us no more than what good advocates have said since Richard Harris KC said it in 1879: put open-ended questions to witnesses in examination-in-chief, and let the witnesses tell the story fully and completely; put closed, leading questions to witnesses in cross-examination, and never let them tell the story they wish to tell.

2.3.5   The expert in court

Presenting the evidence of the expert in court, or cross-examining expert, requires the advocate to seek to know as much about the expert's area of expertise *within the narrow confines of the issues in the lawsuit* as the expert. In other words, the advocate must seek to be an expert in, for example, child psychiatry, at least insofar as that area of expertise relates to the narrow issues in any particular case.

Of course this quest to become an expert will fail, and it is the bad advocate who does not understand that an expert with 20 years of experience in his or her area will understand a great deal more about his subject matter than a barrister who seeks to immerse himself for six weeks. Nevertheless, the advocate must learn enough of the subject area to speak the language. Once the language is learned, the advocate must seek to reduce any jargon to plain speaking. Advocates practising family law are fortunate that the fact-finder will for the most part be familiar with the relevant language, whether it is the language of valuation or taxation of financial instruments, or the likely onset of florid symptoms of paranoid schizophrenia.

Experts in family cases almost invariably are offering opinions with regard to probability. There is a probability that this man will not seek to abuse this child; there is a probability that the mother's mental health will remain stable. The good expert will set out in his or her report a prognosis that reveals the proponent of the opinion is not certain, but is seeking to speak in probabilities. It is not right to say that experts' opinions must reach a certain degree of certainty before the fact-finder accepts the opinion as 'more likely than not.' In the close case, the advocate seeks to put to the opposing expert the reasonable conclusions as a question of degree. Where experts exude certainty regarding what unarguably are close cases, the less likely it is that the judge will be equally as certain. This therefore may be a fertile field for cross-examination, and final submissions.

Bergman usefully points out that expert witnesses are treated differently from ordinary witnesses in two respects:

(1) the expert, through the use of hypothetical questions, may testify despite the lack of first-hand knowledge of facts (in other words, an expert is allowed to be a non-percipient witness); and

(2) an expert may give an opinion about conclusions drawn from her knowledge of the case, or from the hypothetical question put to her.

In all other respects, an expert witness will be treated as any other witness.

Advocates must also note that experts are only expert within the area of expertise they profess to have, and might only answer questions that are directly relevant to the issues in the lawsuit. It is wrong in law if a court allows an expert witness to give opinions about questions outside that expert's area of expertise.

Experts all too often refuse to be controlled by the advocate, but instead seek to present a lengthy lecture to the judge about the conclusion the judge should reach. It is the responsibility of the advocate presenting the expert's evidence-in-chief to prevent this from occurring. The advocate must consult with the expert, if only briefly on the day of the hearing, with regard to the order of evidence. The advocate must let the expert know the order in which the various subject matters in the expert's report will be developed in oral evidence. The advocate must also during this meeting discuss with the expert the likely cross-examination. Given that the expert will have met with all other experts in the case, the likely areas of cross-examination will already have been developed. That being said, it is the rare case where every aspect of cross-examination is set out in the various experts' reports.

Advocates should always keep in mind three essential questions when preparing cross-examination of an expert:

(1) How did the expert conduct his assessment? The advocate must always seek to understand the methods used by the expert in order to reach the opinion that was reached.
(2) What did the expert assess? The advocate must seek to understand the factual matrix used by the expert, and seek to pin down the expert on what factual assumptions were made.
(3) Why is the assessment wrong?

The third question, of course, must be answered by the advocate, and put to the expert as a leading question: 'Your conclusion is wrong, Dr X, because you assumed as true allegations that we contend this court will find to be false. You accept, do you not, that if this court finds in our client's favour [on the disputed fact] your conclusions are wrong.' Or: 'Your conclusion is wrong because you failed to take into account the fact the market for businesses of the type owned by my client has collapsed.'

The advocate must seek to question his own expert with regard to the opinions that that expert proposes. The advocate must understand the foundation of each opinion. Again, the three questions posed above must be answered: (1) How did the expert conduct the assessment? (2) What did the expert assess? (3) Why does the expert profess the opinion she professes?

Experts in family cases now have provided to them all the statements, reports and records that have been produced in the case. It is therefore likely that the expert will have taken into account all the various arguments and contentions put forward by both sides. This makes the use of hypothetical questions in court less necessary than perhaps they were in another era. Nevertheless the hypothetical question is often useful in order to narrow the issues each expert must face. A hypothetical question must track with specificity the facts that will be adduced in evidence at the hearing. The general form of a hypothetical is as follows:

Q: 'Professor, I want you to assume the following facts are correct:
   (a) that child A was brought to the emergency ward at 10.51am on 9 June;
   (b) that at that time child A was seen to have [set out injuries the child received];
   (c) that the child had been seen previously by a physician on 6 June, with no abnormalities noted in the relevant limb;
   (d) the child's mother and father have stated they had care of the child for 24 hours previous to the child being presented at the emergency ward and that they accept that prior to that time the child was not complaining of any injury;
   (e) the parents state the injuries occurred as follows: [...]
   On the basis of your examinations of the child, and all the evidence as I have stated in this hypothetical question, are you able to reach a conclusion whether the child's injuries were non-accidental in nature? What is that conclusion?'
Q: 'Could you explain the reasons for your conclusion?'

In a more complex case, any hypothetical question should be part of a schedule that is presented to the other parties and to the judge. It is all too easy to have a complex hypothetical question lose any persuasive power because it is difficult to follow without a written aid. Set down on paper, these types of questions can be powerfully persuasive to the fact-finder.

An expert is subject to cross-examination on the same terms as a lay witness. In other words, if for some reason the expert is biased, or has an interest in the case (whether financial or otherwise), or where the expert has been convicted of a serious crime or had his professional licence suspended or revoked, those areas are open for cross-examination.

There are occasions, particularly in public law cases involving removal of children from families, where the advocate is forced to cross-examine an expert without any expert opinion favouring the advocate's case. In those circumstances, it is nevertheless the advocate's duty to provide to the court a reasonable theory of the case. A fact-finder is more likely to be convinced by a theory that accepts, at least in part, the conclusions and opinions of the expert. For example a child has been removed from the care of the mother because

of uncontroverted evidence showing that two previous children in her care had been physically and emotionally abused. The mother's case is that circumstances in her life have changed and that the child at issue would not be at risk of harm if placed in her care. The experts do not accept this.

The advocate for the mother would seek to probe each expert's opinion. With regard to the changes the mother has instituted, each one would need to be set out by the advocate, with the advocate proposing that each change shows that this mother now has the capacity to care for this child. It will almost invariably be better to attack the expert's interpretation of facts rather than the expert's underlying theory regarding his opinion and conclusion.

Munkman usefully sets out the four primary goals for any advocate attempting to cross-examine the expert:

(1) by the technique of probing, to elucidate precisely the facts and inferences on which the conclusion rests, pointing out any weaknesses that might exist;
(2) to suggest that if the facts are not quite as the expert has been led to believe, the conclusion would be different;
(3) to challenge the validity of inferences made by the expert from facts, an approach Munkman quite rightly notes is the most dangerous and least likely to succeed unless the advocate has contrary expert opinion on his side;
(4) to attack the expert's qualifications or experience.[42] This also is unlikely to achieve much, especially in an age where the expert will have been appointed by the court. That being said, Professor Younger relates his experience watching, as a trial judge, a particularly avuncular, brainy accountancy expert, give opinions in case after case, repelling every advocate's effort at cross-examination, until one day a lawyer asked if the expert had ever been convicted of a crime.[43] The answer? Yes. The crime? Income tax evasion, 20 years ago.

No further questions, Your Honour.

2.3.6   Defending cross-examination

The advocate whose client is being cross-examined should rise only rarely to stop the opponent's questioning the witness. It is likely that the objection only highlights the evidence, and it is now exceedingly rare for a court to rule that a proposed question on cross-examination should not be allowed because of some evidentiary rule.

But there are occasions when, reluctantly, the advocate must rise to interpose an objection. The first example is when the opposing advocate seeks to pose

---

42   See Munkman, above, p 119.
43   The advocate would of course have to have a good faith belief that in fact the expert had been convicted of a crime before such a question would be appropriate.

more than one question at a time. Very often the advocate will ask a question and either interrupt the answer or ask another question before the witness has even begun to answer the first question. If the judge has not intervened, or the witness appears confused, and perhaps even evasive, the witness's counsel must object that the witness has not been given a chance to complete the answer.

Likewise, opposing counsel must rise and (politely) complain to the court when witnesses are asked a question in too rapid a manner. There are often times when the witness begins to respond equally as rapidly. Careless answers are sometimes the result.

The advocate whose witness is being questioned must also make certain the opposing advocate does not misquote the witness. Summarising prior evidence is always an invitation to summarise in an incomplete or misleading way. Summaries sometimes subtly change the thrust of the evidence. Bergman presents the following example:

> 'Q: Alright, you got a pretty good look at the incident, and then ...
>
> Counsel: Your Honour that statement is incorrect. The witness's evidence is that he had stared at the incident for ten minutes at a distance of one foot. Counsel has misquoted the witness.'

There are times when it is right for the advocate whose witness is being cross-examined to point out to the fact-finder those instances where opposing counsel has crossed the line of proper cross-examination. No advocate has the right to badger a witness by, for example, posing argumentative questions: 'So you expect us to believe you, an admitted perjurer?'

Whenever you rise, remember the cardinal rule of advocacy at the Bar: you never address your opponent. You only address the judge. You might politely ask the court's permission to have a word with opposing counsel, if the matter is likely to be non-contentious and you would wish the matter agreed by counsel without the court's intervention. (Better, of course, to have met with counsel before the case begins to work out where any disputes about evidence will arise.)

Several organisations have been established to provide support for experts. These organisations also provide information to solicitors or advocates who seek to instruct experts in subject matters that are often in dispute in family litigation.

The Academy of Experts was founded in 1987. It offers a free, online, searchable directory of more than 1800 experts. References are supplied by solicitors. Experts also provide sample reports and evidence of their expertise along with a full CV.

The Expert Witness Institute began in 1996. EWI's has a quality control process that requires each expert to provide three satisfactory references from barristers

or solicitors or others who have used their services as an expert witness.

The Society of Expert Witnesses was also begun in 1996. It does not attempt to vet those who join. The society has more than 1000 members, and again, provides a free on line service.

The Expert Witness Directory was set up by the publishers Thomson Sweet and Maxwell. All experts on the web site have provided two professional references from solicitors who have instructed the expert within the last two years.

The web sites for those organisations, and others providing information regarding possible experts in family proceedings, are set out below:

(a) The Academy of Experts—www.academy-experts.org
(b) The Expert Witness Institute—www.ewi.org.uk
(c) The UK Register of Expert Witnesses—www.jspubs.com
(d) The Society of Expert Witnesses—www.sew.org.uk
(e) The Royal Insitute of Chartered Surveyors—www.rics.org.uk
(f) The Council for the Registration of Forensic Practitioners—www.crfp.org.uk
(g) The Sudden Infant Death Report (By the Royal College of Paediatrics and Child Health)—www.repath.org/index.asp?Page1D=493.

2.4 RE-EXAMINATION

Your client has just been skewered by the opposing advocate. He (and the judge) now look to you. 'Any re-examination?' the judge asks, eyebrows raised, as if to query why you and your client are wasting his time.

What do you do? Cough nervously and go over the examination-in-chief?

No. Your client has just had a portion (or all) of his case ripped to shreds. Your job is to seek during re-examination to emphasise the strong points of the case, ask non-leading questions that allow the client to respond fully to any cross-examination questions the client failed to explain, and then to sit down. It is not acceptable to lead your witness through your argument. It is not acceptable to cross-examine your witness merely because he has failed to perform precisely as you expected.

Instead, re-examination should be short and sure. There are usually only three or four points that would require re-examination by the advocate. Make your points, and thank the witness, turn to the judge and state that you have no further questions. Some advocates at this point will ask the judge if he has questions. I had always been taught that this is not proper, that the judge will ask questions when and if he wishes, without a need for prompting, but this is a rule that appears to be observed only in the breach.

Munkman, as ever, is very good on the purpose of re-examination: to explain or qualify admissions made by the witness when cross-examined. Munkman's view is that re-examination should simply be:

> '... the insinuation of facts or possibilities which give a different turn to the answers in cross-examination, but as the advocate is examining his own witness, a roundabout approach is unnecessary. The real difficulty of re-examination is twofold. The first difficulty is to think of helpful points – which reduces itself to quick thinking and a detailed knowledge of the case. The second difficulty is to frame simple and straightforward questions without leading, for, in view of the complications introduced in cross-examination, there is a tendency for questions in re-exam to be introduced by lengthy preambles and to be appallingly long-winded.'[44]

Munkman's last point is especially important when re-examining your own expert. Advocates must be prepared for re-examination with a few well-framed, short questions that put the points to the experts without having a long-winded preamble about the points made by other experts.

Munkman points out that because almost invariably it is the technique of insinuation which introduces something new in cross-examination, the object of re-examination is to counteract an insinuation with one of your own. Evidence-in-chief raises a certain probability or inference – for instance, the local authority social worker saw the mother and father, who were supposed to be separated, together on the same train. In cross-examination on behalf of the mother, the witness admits she did not hear the mother and father speak to each other because they were on the other side of the train car. The witness also accepts that the mother's back was turned to the witness, and that she never saw the mother's face or her reactions. The witness accepts that she did not talk to the mother and father, and that the father left the train after a few minutes. The witness accepts that she does not know whether mother and father are seeing each other, save for what she observed on the train. On re-examination, the advocate for the local authority might ask: 'Did it appear the mother and father were talking to each other, even if you could not hear what they were saying?' Yes. 'Could you describe the father's demeanour?' He was smiling, affectionate, he leaned over and was whispering to his wife. 'Could you describe the parting?' He kissed her on the cheek, and left the train.

Munkman also notes that often the re-examiner seeks to exclude a possibility suggested by cross-examination. This often happens in cross-examination of experts, where it will be suggested, perhaps, by one expert that a conclusion should be ruled out, while another says there remains a possibility that the conclusion is the correct one. Your expert must, on re-examination, be given an opportunity to shut the door on the other case, explaining fully and completely (it is hoped) why the conclusion should or should not be ruled out.

---

[44]   See Munkman, above, p 122.

Advocates will know that no new areas if enquiry may be introduced in re-examination. But if there are fresh points elicited, or new evidence brought out, in cross-examination, then it is permissible to allow the witness in re-examination to give a full explanation of the new evidence.

One other point: what do you do on that rare occasion when your client sailed through cross-examination without a single difficulty. Easy - 'No questions, your honour'. Never, never seek to turn up the score when you are ahead. One bad answer in re-examination can render wholly useless all the client's effort in cross-examination.

2.5   CLOSING SUBMISSIONS

Closing submissions bring to the fore one of the primary rules for any advocate: know your audience. Closing speeches, in legal lore, are usually portrayed as emotional appeals to the fact-finder's conscience, a chance for the advocate to trot out his collection of snappy similes and trenchant metaphors to change the minds of jurors who otherwise would have voted to hang an innocent defendant.

These same fictional closing submissions are also inevitably thrown together at the last minute, after all the evidence is before the jury. The advocate sees a connection others have missed, makes that connection in closing argument, and, music rising to a crescendo, his client walks.

Only a couple of difficulties with this scenario:

(1) research shows most jurors believe the evidence is far more important in determining the outcome than anything that might be said during closing submissions, and one can be sure judges are at least equally as unlikely as jurors to find submissions more persuasive than evidence; and,

(2) good advocates know that closing submissions are completed long before the case is opened and evidence is called. Indeed, the evidence that *is* called should always be related to what one or the other advocate is seeking to say in final submissions.

And let us face it, a gut-wrenching, tearful rant about the injustices life and the respondent have meted out to your client is not likely to persuade a tired District Judge on a Thursday afternoon at 4.30, particularly when that judge has heard three cases already that week, each with its own particular emotional difficulties.

It is also true that many advocates and judges, when pressed, accept that in most cases the fact-finders have made up their minds long before closing speeches. As one District Judge put it to me, 'What I'm looking for in final speeches is for the successful advocate to help write the judgment. From the

advocate who will likely not prevail, I'm looking for answers to questions. If those answers are not available, well, that is where I begin my judgment.' Judges are looking for a road map that sets out why one side must prevail.

That being said, research regarding conduct of juries indicates that in fact closing statements can be particularly persuasive in the appropriate case.[45] Jurors in one study ranked closing statements second only to the evidence of witnesses as the factor that most affected their deliberations.[46]

One leading advocate set out her two rules for any closing submission:

(1) do create a narrative that tells a convincing story, interweaving witness evidence with written documentation that proves the advocates' case;
(2) do *not* simply recite each witness's evidence. No single act of an advocate is more likely to induce sleep than to drone on through a recitation of each witness's oral evidence, with the advocate pausing every now and again to look up from his or her notebook to state that his client disagrees, or agrees, with the evidence that has been presented.

The most effective closing submissions are short, to the point, and never lose sight of the inescapable fact that judges seek a plausible narrative. The job of the advocate in final submissions is to provide that narrative, pointing out how the factual evidence supports the narrative that is being presented.

Practitioners and judges agree there are certain unbreakable rules with regard to closing submissions:

- *The advocate should be prepared to give her closing speech before any evidence is called.* This is saying no more than the advocate should have a proper theory of the case, and a proper narrative that will be supported by the evidence, prior to the evidence being called. Obviously in most cases the closing speech will have to change slightly, based on the evidence actually adduced, but the broad, general outlines of the closing speech should be completed well before the case is opened by counsel for the applicant.
- *Limit the number of arguments presented in closing submissions.* Research has shown that jurors, at least, can handle no more than six or seven arguments from either side with regard to why each side should prevail. After that, the difference between the various arguments blurs in the jurors' minds.[47] It is safe to say that a tired District Judge late in the day, after hearing several witnesses give oral evidence, is unlikely to be willing to listen to numerous alternative theories as to why one client or the

[45] See Tarter-Gilgendorf, 'Impact of Opening and Closing Statements' *Trial*, 79–80 (1986).
[46] See Matlon, Davis, Catchings, Derr and Waldron, cited in Rieke and Stutman, above, p 202.
[47] See Calder, Inkso and Yandell, 'The Relation of Cognitive and Memorial Processes to Persuasion in a Simulated Jury Trial' (1974) *Journal of Applied Social Psychology*, 4:62–93.

other should prevail. In the great majority of cases, even the most ingenious legal wizard is unlikely to come up with more than two or three alternative reasons why his or her client should prevail. It is almost always best to choose the best two reasons for prevailing, and go forward with those.

- *Avoid repetition.* It is right, of course, that Aristotle advised speakers to repeat themselves in order to more firmly embed a point in the listener's mind. And it is right as well that one research study after another indicates that at least for lay jurors, repetition works. Rieke and Stutman cite one mock jury study which showed that jurors retained an argument much better when they heard the argument three times as opposed to when they heard it once.[48] That being said, nothing was repeated more often by judges I interviewed than this: lawyers repeat themselves too much. Advocates do need to make certain the judge understands the point and sometimes repetition in final submissions is necessary, but advocates must remember that it is likely that this judge has heard this particular argument, or a variation thereof, on numerous previous occasions.

- *The advocate should always address the opponent's argument.* A one-sided argument raises only those arguments supporting the advocate's position. A two-sided argument also raises, and attempts to refute, the contentions of the opponent. Studies during World War II by the United States War Department revealed sophisticated audiences found two-sided arguments far more effective. Two-sided arguments enhance the credibility of the speaker, and make it easier for the listener to reject subsequent attempts by the opponent to argue an opposing position. The advocate who presents only one side of an issue appears either biased or ignorant. Research has indicated that two-sided arguments are most effective when the supportive arguments appear first, followed by the repetition of the opponent's argument.[49]

- *Avoid rhetorical questions.* Advocates know that a rhetorical question is a question which assumes its own answer. The answer is considered obvious, and requires no response. The question is intended to prompt the audience to respond in a certain way. Used sparingly in front of a jury, a rhetorical question can be effective. It focuses attention on the speaker's argument and stops the flow of the narrative by forcing the juror to generate an answer to the question. Judges, on the other hand, are less likely to be persuaded and more likely to be annoyed by being forced to consider the answer to what the advocate hopes is an obvious question. Far better for the advocate simply to make his argument, without any rhetorical flourishes.

---

[48] See Wiltson & Miller, Repetition, 'Order of Presentation and Timing of Arguments and Measures as to Determinates of Opinion change' (1968) *Journal of Personality and Social Psychology* 9:185; see Rieke and Stutman, above, p 205.

[49] See Jackson and Allen, 'Meta-Analysis of the Effectiveness of one sided and two sided argumentation', cited in Rieke and Stutman, above, p 208.

- *The effective argument will define the issues.* Draw appropriate inferences from the evidence, show the court why the law supports the advocate's theory of the case and set out for the judge the proposed order.
- *Never state your personal belief.* It is the client's case that the advocate puts, not his own. The correct form on submission is: 'I contend on behalf of my client that …', or 'my client contends …'. The good advocate never says 'I contend that …', or, even worse, 'I believe …'. Judges are not interested in the advocate's opinion. Judges are interested, however, in the advocate's contentions made on behalf of the lay client.

The matters available for final submissions include the following, and nothing else:

- Any issue in the case.
- Any evidence in the case.
- All reasonable inferences from the evidence.
- Any argument that is fair.
- Any matters of common knowledge that support the advocate's case.[50]

Those five areas would allow an advocate who chose to do so the opportunity to speak for days regarding even the simplest of disputes. The good advocate knows that judges do not want to hear every argument that is available; they want to hear what your client wants and the best reason why he should win. A good final speech provides answers to those questions.

Irving Younger's 12 commandments for closing speeches deserve repetition:

(1) Be prepared and rehearsed.
(2) Anticipate the arguments from your opponent.
(3) Never forget the equities in a case, and make certain the judge understands the effect of a decision contrary to your client's interests.
(4) Avoid flowery language and rhetoric.
(5) Never speak to your opponent during closing submission.
(6) Always discuss issues, evidence and credibility.
(7) Always include the order or remedy you seek.
(8) Appear to be fair, in particular, when summarising the opponent's argument.
(9) Do not overuse notes. The ideal summation is organised, but sounds spontaneous.
(10) Be explicit, not implicit. Say it plainly.
(11) Be tactful.
(12) Respect the judge's intelligence.

There may come a time in an advocate's career when a judge says or does something that reveals to the advocate that any respect for that judge's intelligence is misplaced. This is the occasion when observation of rule No 12

[50] See Younger, *The Advocate's Desk Book*, above, p 333.

is most important. Never let anyone in the room, including your own client, know that you believe the judge has made a brutal, stupid error. Judges are human; it is why there exists a Court of Appeal. Expressing your disgust, to anyone, about a ruling by a trial court judge does not make it more likely that you will succeed on appeal. So why do it? Far better simply to tell your client that reasonable people will disagree, that you believe the judge made a good-faith error, and that you believe the client should appeal. Clients also are likely to think that the advocate who blames the judge for a bad ruling is looking for an easy way to escape blaming himself. After all, why could not the advocate explain the law and facts to the judge in a way that prevented the error from occurring?

Chapter 3

PRIVATE LAW APPLICATIONS REGARDING CHILDREN

3.1 FINDING THE 'BEST INTERESTS OF THE CHILD'

No other concept in the legal lexicon is as amorphous, vague and uncertain as 'the best interests of the subject child', unless, that is, it is the corollary concept that the best interest of the child should be the 'paramount consideration' when courts determine matters concerning the care and upbringing of children. Advocates soon discover that the 'welfare checklist' at s 1(3) of the Children Act 1989 (CA 1989) provides the right questions; the answers, however, are circumscribed only by the imaginations of the advocates seeking to convince a judge of the rightness of their clients' cause.

The leading judicial pronouncement remains Lord MacDermott's speech in *J v C*:

> '[The principle that a child's best interest is paramount] means more than that the child's welfare is to be treated as the top item in a list of items relevant to the matter in questions. [The words] connote a process whereby, when all the relevant facts, relationships, claims and wishes of parents, risks, choices and other circumstances are taken into account and weighed the course to be followed will be that which is most in the interests of the child's welfare as that term is now understood. ... [It is] the paramount consideration because it rules upon or determines the course to be followed.'[1]

The narrative in private law Children Act applications therefore always centres on the best interest of the subject child.[2] The essential question for the advocate before trial is to determine first and foremost what the advocate's client

---

[1]   [1970] AC at 710–711.

[2]   Advocates will of course know that the welfare principle applies whenever the court is making decisions regarding the care and upbringing of the child. Other statutes require different considerations. The Adoption Act 1976 requires courts to regard the welfare of the child as the 'first consideration'. The Adoption Act 2002 will, when brought in force, require judges to apply the paramountcy principle. The Child Support Act 1991 requires the Secretary of State and child support officers 'to have regard' to the welfare of a child brought before them. There are also slightly different considerations for the court when considering whether to permit local authorities to place children in their care outside the UK. See CA 1989, Sch 2, para 19. The best interests of the child is also not the paramount consideration when considering whether to make a child subject to a secure accommodation order. See CA 1989, s 25. The best interests of the child principle is not paramount when considering whether to grant an unmarried father parental responsibility, or to grant a guardianship order, or to make an emergency protection order.

contends is in the best interest of that child. *It is not the role of the advocate to advise the lay client on what the advocate believes to be in the best interest of that child.*

The advocate is not a child psychiatrist or psychologist; the advocate is not the parent of the child. The advocate should be an expert in two things:

(1) how to argue a case before a court;
(2) how to predict what a judge will be likely to do if given a particular set of facts.

That being said, the advocate in any proceeding, whether under the CA 1989 or any other legislation, must seek to gain a significant understanding of whatever is the subject matter of the dispute. If the parties are two shipping companies, arguing about delivery of wheat to a particular city, the advocate will have to know the language of the industry. What is the common and accepted use of key terms and phrases in correspondence between shipping agents? What is commonly understood by employees of shipping firms regarding loading and shipping requirements? All advocates know that gaining an understanding of how people in the industry act and react is vital to understanding the dispute, and vital to presenting a client's side of any dispute. This means that advocates in Children Act cases must know the research regarding the current views of the medical profession about what is in the best interests of children, as well as how judges hearing cases under the Act will use (or not use) that research in coming to conclusions regarding any individual child. But that knowledge does not make the advocate a childcare expert.

Advocates must make certain their clients understand that the advocate does not pretend to be an expert on childcare, or on what is in the best interests of any individual child. What the advocate is an expert in, however, is in predicting what a judge hearing cases under the CA 1989 will be likely to do with a set of facts. The advocate must know the effect of certain arguments on judges, and must be able to advise the client of what the judge is likely to do in the usual case. That means advising the client of what you believe the judge will say is in the child's best interest. A proper explanation of why the judge believes this or that course is in the best interests of the child will require the advocate to seek to explain to his lay client the evidence of, for example, a child psychiatrist who contends the child has not bonded properly with her mother; or an adult psychiatrist, who believes the father's conviction for assaulting the mother does not necessarily mean the father should have no contact with his son.

Advocates must also understand that if the clients could have agreed, lawyers would not have become involved in the first place. Once advocates have been retained, and the matter reaches final hearing, the participants must understand that this is simply a matter where reasonable people might disagree. An advocate must then zealously represent his client's interest, without regard to

that advocate's private view as to what is actually in the best interests of the child.

But that does not mean advocates should not always be ready to negotiate. Indeed, advocates should encourage negotiation at every stage of the litigation. Peter Jackson QC, who has been handling cases involving children for more than 20 years, puts it like this: ' People in my experience are usually more comfortable with an outcome over which they have some control. They feel – quite rightly – that they have saved time and money, and spared everyone unnecessary conflict.'

Jackson points out that negotiating outside the courtroom is often harder work than conducting the hearing. The barrister must fully understand his or her client's instructions, and must always understand that 'no prejudice' or *Calderbank* discussions have no place in Children Act negotiations. 'In a case under the Children Act 1989, everything you say in the corridor you must expect to be repeated in the courtroom,' Jackson says.

Jackson points out one other crucial fact: the advocate must establish a working relationship with the other side's advocate. Never forget that you will be operating within a very small division. People talk. If you are unnecessarily aggressive (or unusually compliant, for that matter), other advocates will soon know. Put your client's case, seek to agree where possible, note the areas of disagreement and see if discussion is possible on those areas. Even reasonable people will disagree on certain points. The job of the advocate is to seek, as far as possible, to reserve the courtroom for only those points where reasonable people might disagree. All other matters have been settled (in this perfect if unapproachable world) by reasonable people outside the courthouse.

3.1.1 Narratives under the Children Act 1989

In close cases involving children, almost invariably the narrative each party seeks to put forward must emphasise some factors and minimise others. For example, the child's mother seeks to remove the child from the jurisdiction in order to live with her new partner in France. She seeks to emphasise in her narrative the importance of the child living in a happy home where the mother and her partner are working together in harmony to provide a good and safe home for the child. The father who opposes the move emphasises the loss to the child of his relationship with his birth father. He seeks to show the court the importance of the attachment a child has with the father, and the likelihood of damage if that attachment is severed or impaired.

In almost all cases brought under s 8 of the CA 1989, the judge, engaged in the difficult task of predicting the future, is reduced to weighing the pros and cons of any proposed change in the child's life. Judges in CA 1989 cases are profoundly affected, it is contended, by the status quo. If an advocate for the

mother in a residence order dispute can show that the mother was the person who normally provided primary child care during the marriage, the mother is overwhelmingly likely to have a residence order made in her favour when the parents divorce.

Advocates must therefore seek to know and understand the likely effect on children of separation from their birth parents, of removal from their known home and school, of violent change and upheaval in a child's formative years. Advocates must know and understand the literature regarding the effect on children of witnessing domestic violence, and must know and understand how to show the court that a child's actions fit the pattern of those children who have witnessed domestic violence. Advocates should understand in particular attachment theory. A good introduction is Bowlby, *Attachment and Loss*[3] and Erikson, *Identity, Youth and Crisis*.[4] Pagani, Boulerice, Tremblay and Vitaro's research found evidence to support the assertion that the impact of parental separation is worst if it occurs before the child is six years of age.[5] Attachments run along a continuum between secure and unattached. A child with secure attachment, in the classic test of attachment that is often used, will show signs of missing the mother when she leaves the room, and seeks to cling to her upon her return. Infants with insecure/ambivalent attachment will often react differently, showing little anxiety about the presence of strangers and often offering indiscriminate displays of affection.[6] The attachment process is not only seen to be an emotional change in infants; it can also be seen to bring on physiological changes in the child's brain.[7] Advocates will know, however, that it is a mistake to think there is a simple reductive test for attachment relationships. Dr Jonathan Green, a Senior Lecturer in Child and Adolescent Psychiatry at the University of Manchester, notes in a paper presented to a conference of judges and Family Bar members that assessments of attachment need to be embedded in a range of other relevant assessments, including parenting.[8] 'Courts should not consider the presentation or origin of parenting behaviour as an undifferentiated whole' Dr Green argues. In Dr Green's view, attachment assessments should seek to distinguish four factors:

- parental attachment status;
- parental personality structure;

---

[3]   Basic Books, 1969.

[4]   Faber and Faber, 1968.

[5]   See (1973) 38 Journal of Child Psychology and Psychiatry 769.

[6]   This is not the only test for attachment. Dr Claire Sturge, in a conversation with the author, warned about the simplistic approach of many barristers to attachment. 'It is more complicated than simply saying "The child misses mother, therefore there is a secure attachment"', warns Dr Sturge.

[7]   See, generally, Professor Maurice Place, 'Attachment and Identity – Their significance in decisions about contact and placement' [2003] Fam Law 260.

[8]   Green, 'Concepts of Child Attachment' in Thorpe (ed), *Hearing the Children* (Family Law, 2004).

- parental current mood state;
- current social circumstances.

Each of these factors, Dr Green argues, may impact on parenting. The reason for seeking a more differentiated assessment is particularly apparent in the face of a parent suffering from clinical depression. That parent's ability to parent may be adequate, when she is well. Advocates must make certain experts do not make the mistake of simply concluding 'the child has an insecure attachment.'

Advocates must also know and understand the research by Dr Sturge and Dr Glaser, the psychiatrists instructed by the Official Solicitor to provide reports to the court in the cases of *Re L, et al (Contact: Domestic Violence)*.[9] Four points are crucial:

(1) advocates must seek to prove (or disprove) the extent of the violence;
(2) advocates must show the effect of the violence upon the primary carer;
(3) advocates must show the effect of the violence on the child;
(4) advocates must focus on the ability of the offender to recognise his behaviour and attempt to change it.[10]

3.1.2 The checklist

Courts ordinarily use the 'welfare checklist' at s 1(3) of the CA 1989 as a rough guide in giving judgments in private law cases, and advocates often use the list as a guide for closing submissions. This is indeed helpful for the court, but advocates must take care to understand what is actually assumed by the court to be in the best interests of the child, and seek to address those assumptions. (I do not mean legal assumptions, but instead simply those basic notions that we all take into any decision-making process.) Remember Lord MacDermott's speech in *J v C*, when he discussed the best interests of the child '*as it is now understood*'. What Lord MacDermott meant, I contend, is that society's understanding of what is in the best interests of children necessarily evolves. Thorpe LJ, in an interview with the author, noted that these 'assumptions' judges make usually only have a shelf-life of one generation.[11] Advocates must always be aware of these likely judicial assumptions.

The checklist was not intended by the Law Commission that provided the framework for the CA 1989 to be in any way a mandatory box-ticking exercise. The Law Commission believed a checklist could provide a clear statement 'of

---

9   [2000] 2 FLR 334, CA.
10 See Butler-Sloss, 'Contact and Domestic Violence' [2001] Fam Law 355. See also [2000] Fam Law 615, for Sturge's and Glaser's report.
11 See discussion in Chapter 6.

what society considers the most important factors in the welfare of children.'[12]
Advocates will know that other vital factors are missing: the assumption that
siblings should be brought up together, for example; or the assumption that
certain factors are usually more important than others in determining the
welfare of a child.

That being said, the checklist must always be the first source for advocates
looking for a successful theory of the case.

(1)   The ascertainable wishes and feelings of the child concerned (considered in the light of his age and understanding)

Paragraph (a) of the checklist gives to all children a right to express their views
in contested proceedings.[13] There is no test of *Gillick*[14] competence before a
child's views should be recorded and considered. But the child's age and
understanding will be the key to the narrative: if considered old enough, and
mature enough, the child's views will often be decisive. See *Re M (Contact:
Welfare Test)*,[15] where children of seven and eight said they did not wish to
resume contact with their mother.[16] The court determined that ordering contact
against the children's wishes would not be in the children's best interest. As
has been noted by commentators, 'the fervence and persistence of the child's
views may also be influential'.[17] The contrary argument, of course, is that by
placing too great a weight on the child's wishes, the court is delegating the
decision to the child. This places a great burden on the child, who often wishes
to please the parent with primary care of the child, particularly when that parent
now hates the absent parent. There is no set procedure regarding the court's
gaining knowledge of the child's views. The CAFCASS reporter will ordinarily
address the issue. Judges and lay justices may interview children in private in
court, but it is discouraged. The court, and CAFCASS officers, cannot offer
the children confidentiality.[18] Anything the child says that is relevant to the
outcome of the case must be reported to the court.

---

[12]   Law Com. No 172, para 3.19; see the helpful discussion in Cretney, Masson, Bailey-Harris, *Principles of Family Law* (Sweet and Maxwell, 7th edn, 2003), pp 651–655.

[13]   That right is also protected by the United Nations Convention on the Rights of the Child. The European Convention on the Exercise of Children's Rights (1997) has also now been ratified by the UK. This grants children the right to receive information, to be consulted, to express their views and to be represented in family proceedings. The right is limited to those considered to have sufficient understanding. See, generally, Jane Fortin, *Children's Rights* (Sweet and Maxwell, 1998), ch 8.

[14]   See discussion below of child litigants and the case of *Gillick v West Norfolk and Wisbech Area Health Authority and the DHSS* [1986] 1 AC 112, [1986] 1 FLR 224, HL.

[15]   [1995] 1 FLR 274, CA.

[16]   But see *Re C (A Minor) (Care: Child: Wishes)* [1993] 1 FLR 832, where it was held that a girl of 13 who wished to live with her father, was 'too young to carry the burden of decisions about her future.' See also *Re S (Contact: Children's views)* [2002] 1 FLR 1156, where it was noted that the wishes of mature 14- and 16-year-old children must be respected.

[17]   See Cretney, Masson and Bailey-Harris, above, p 654; also see *Re T (Abduction: Child's Objections to Return)* [2000] 2 FLR 192, where an 11-year-old child's letters were particularly compelling for the court, who directed the child not be returned to her mother.

[18]   See *B v B (Minors) (Interviews and Listing Arrangements)* [1994] 2 FLR 489; *Re D (Adoption Reports: Confidentiality)* [1995] 2 FLR 687, HL. The European Court of Human Rights has

Advocates must always remember that children are not simply miniature adults; nor, as the noted clinical psychologist Dr Jan Aldridge notes, are they 'inferior or lesser adults'.[19] Dr Aldridge points out that professionals must remember that children do not process language precisely, the way adults tend to do. Dr Aldridge notes that adult speech structures often pose difficulties for children. Questions for children should be simply phrased, active-voiced sentences with few modifying words. Tag questions ('He went into the house, didn't he?') should be avoided. Professionals must make certain as well that the child understood the words chosen by that profession. All too often children pretend to understand when clearly they do not. And most urgently, advocates and professionals must understand that a child' view of time is often distorted. Placing events in time is a difficult task for the young child. Therefore, an account of an incident that actually occurred may be discounted because the time frame assigned by the child to the incident is clearly not right. Dr Aldridge argues that courts, despite the research show that even young children have the ability to understand and remember events, often discount the evidence of children because of what are arguably irrelevant inconsistencies.

(2) His physical, emotional and educational needs

As commentators have often noted, courts in the past often used judicial assumptions about what was 'good' for a child when giving content to the 'best interests' standard.[20] For example, in *May v May*,[21] the court noted that it was beyond discussion that firm discipline was always in the best interests of a child. Today judges, and advocates, must instead seek to rely on the voluminous research available regarding the needs of developing children. Department of Health Guidance published in 1995, showing children suffer long- term problems when the parenting style is generally low on warmth and high on criticism, has become common knowledge in family courts, and advocates will be expected to know the basics of that research. There is also now almost a judicial assumption that a child needs to maintain a relationship with each parent. (The rub, of course, is whether that means a child should split time with each parent, in those cases where it is possible. Research in the area conflicts: some psychologists and child psychiatrists say a child needs a stable base; others contend the child benefits from seeing both parents, and benefits from reducing parental conflicts.) If the conflict is between a child's natural parents and a child's foster carers, the court will begin with a 'strong supposition' in favour of the natural parents.[22]

---

held that the failure of the court to determine the views of a five-year-old child regarding contact with her father violated the child's rights under Article 8 of the ECHR. See *Sahin v Germany* [2002] 1 FLR 119.

19 See Aldridge, 'Making Sense of What Children Say: Contributions from Developmental Psychology' in Thorpe (ed), *Hearing the Children* (Family Law, 2004).
20 See Cretney, Masson, Bailey-Harris, above, p 656.
21 [1986] 1 FLR 325.
22 *Re M (Child: upbringing)* [1996] 2 FLR 441.

(3)   The likely effect on him of any change in his circumstances

This is a key factor. Indeed, courts admit as much. See, for example, *Re B (Residence Order: Status Quo),*[23] where a decision to transfer a child to the mother after three years with her father was reversed on appeal. Obviously courts will have to weigh this factor in the balance when an absent parent seeks a re-introduction to contact after an extended absence. Sturge and Glaser have noted that this re-introduction needs 'careful planning' to minimise the impact on the child. The research in this area is not conclusive.[24] Advocates for the absent parent should always note that the CA 1989, at s 1(2), provides that delay is likely to prejudice the welfare of the child. Delay may amount to a breach of rights protected under the European Convention and the Human Rights Act 1998. See *H v UK.*[25] It is obvious that parents who have care of the child, and who seek to argue that the status quo should not be disturbed, have motive to delay the proceedings.

Courts have retreated from using gender-based categories in child-care decisions.[26] Therefore there is no longer a legal presumption that the mother is the better primary carer.[27] That being said, courts will also look to the actual history of any individual case: was the mother in fact the primary carer? If that is so, the court will be likely to allow her to continue to provide primary care for the child. Advocates involved in a fact-finding dispute about who provided the care of the child often find themselves arguing against judges who have a traditional view of the roles of mothers and fathers, and who refuse to believe that some families are organised differently.

(4)   His age, sex, background and any characteristic of his which the court considers relevant

The 'characteristics of his which the court considers relevant' could of course include every aspect of that child's life. But courts have again limited consideration primarily to the following: education; religion;[28] medical care (for example, whether to have a circumcision);[29] and race.[30] Advocates in cases where those facts are important must seek to present his or her client's views

---

[23]   [1998] 1 FLR 268, CA.
[24]   See Masson, 'Contact between parents and children in the long-term care of others: the unresolved dispute' (1990) 3 Int. J of Law and Fam 97.
[25]   (1987) 10 EHRR 95. See discussing the European Convention at 3.7 below.
[26]   But see *Re S (Children)* [2002] EWCA Civ where it was held that the difference in men and women should not be ignored.
[27]   See *Re W (A Minor) (Residence Order)* [1992] 2 FLR 332, CA. There is a rebuttable presumption, however, that an infant is better placed with the mother. See *Re W (Residence Order)* [1992] 2 FLR 332; see also *Brixey v Linos* [1996] 2 FLR 1999.
[28]   See *Re P (Section 91(14) Guidelines) (Residence and Religious Heritage)* [1999] 2 FLR 573.
[29]   See *Re J (Specific Issue Orders: Child's Religious Upbringing and Circumcision)* [1999] 2 FLR 678; *Re T and M* [1995] 1 ELR.
[30]   See *Re M* (Section 94 Appeals) [1995] 1 FLR 546.

to the court regarding those issues, and seek to convince the court that the client's view regarding how those issues might best be handled should prevail.

(5) Any harm which he has suffered or is at risk of suffering

Children who have witnessed domestic violence are now universally considered to have suffered emotional harm. This harm must be considered by courts when determining whether those children should resume contact with the violent partner. See *Re L, et al (Contact: Domestic Violence)*.[31]

Again, courts will have to weigh the damage suffered by the child from not knowing or seeing his father, with the damage the child might receive from resuming contact too quickly with someone who has committed these sorts of acts in front of the child.

Research also shows, not surprisingly, that children who are physically abused by a parent are at greater risk of suffering behavioural and emotional problems later in life than children who are not abused.[32]

(6) How capable each of his parents, and any other person in relation to whom the court considers the question to be relevant, is of meeting his needs

This will be a key area of enquiry for advocates in cross-applications for residence, and will prove a damnably difficult area in which to adduce positive evidence. Each party is likely to say the other parent is a poor parent. Each is likely to say that the other parent's discipline is improper, that he (or she) is uncaring and neglectful, and unkind. But courts will usually not believe the self-interested commentary of one party, unless there is corroborative proof from an expert, or from an independent third party. Courts in private law proceedings usually do not have provided for them full-blown assessments of parenting skills by independent experts. Therefore courts often shy away from making findings under this paragraph based on nothing more than unsubstantiated allegations by the absent parent. It is true, however, that courts will assess the impact of the absent parent's behaviour on the primary carer's ability to provide care for the child. Where the absent parent has been violent, and the primary carer suffers from fear of that absent parent, a court will be reluctant to order direct contact between a child and the absent parent.[33] The enquiry here should focus on the practitioner, as well as the status quo: who is available to provide physical care for the child? Who did so in the past?

---

[31]   [2000] 2 FLR 334, CA.
[32]   See Department of Health publications *Caring for children away from home* (1998); *Child protection messages from research* (1995); and *Patterns and outcomes in child placement* (1991). See also Gibbons *Development after physical abuse in early childhood* (HMSO, 1995).
[33]   See *Re L (Contact Domestic Violence)* [2000] 2 FLR 334, CA.

3.2 THE ORDERS AVAILABLE UNDER THE CHILDREN ACT 1989

A competent lawyer is expected to take specific instructions from his or her client regarding the lawful goals of that client, and to advise the client on the prospects of achieving those goals through an order of the court. For example, a lawyer advising a client regarding a contract dispute involving 350,000 apples that client sought to purchase seeks to give advice regarding several matters: Is the contract specifically enforceable, so that the apples might be delivered to the client's supermarket? Is there a damages clause that sets out the damages to be received by our client upon non-delivery? Is our client damaged at all, because he has found a better alternate supplier of apples? The client will tell the lawyer what that client seeks. The lawyer will tell the client whether, on the facts as alleged, a court will give the client what he requires.

In a case involving the care of children, however, lawyers will often find it difficult to translate clients' wishes into orders under the CA 1989. A father who works 10 hours a day, six days a week will inform his lawyer that he wishes to have his child continue to live with him, and in any event, the father wants to make certain that the child attends a certain neighbourhood school. A mother seeks to have her ex-husband prevented from attending the couple's seven-year-old son's school Christmas play. A father seeks to prevent his ex-wife from allowing the couple's 13-year-old daughter to stay over with school friends during school summer holidays.

The inescapable fact is that many 'exercises of parental responsibility' will be made by the parent who has physical care of the child. These decisions will not be subject to review by the absent parent, and will not be likely to form the basis of litigation, despite the fact that the CA 1989 theoretically gives the court jurisdiction to hear every dispute regarding any aspect of a parent's exercise of parental responsibility.

The fact that the father is a terrific father who loves his children and wishes only the best for them will not matter much if the father is not able to provide physical care for the child when that child requires it. If the father's work requires him to be out of the home six days a week, the amount of love and affection the father feels for the child will really not carry much weight. (The same applies for the mother, of course, if she has work that requires her to be absent from home, but it remains more likely, for whatever reason, that the father is the one engaged in work outside the home that requires the father to be physically absent from the home. It is also more likely, but not inevitable, that the mother provided the majority of primary care for the child when the child was less than three. Advocates must of course be acutely aware of those cases where the facts do not fit what judges are likely to believe to be the usual narrative, that is, the father works outside the home, the mother works inside the home.)

Once a decision has been made about physical care of the child, the basic decisions regarding provision of that care will have to be made by the parent that is physically present. What does the child eat for breakfast? When does the child go to bed at night? What television programmes are made available to the child? Courts are extremely reluctant to get involved in disputes regarding basic decisions about childhood care and safety, unless those parental decisions place the child at risk of harm, requiring either a change of residence or local authority involvement.[34] But courts view a change in residence as a major upheaval in the child's life, and will not order a change unless clear evidence is shown that the child's best interests require it. In practice, that is a high standard to meet.

Advocates appearing before any tribunal seek to secure an order that will advance that advocate's client's interests. The assumption is that the order will either compensate the injured party, place the parties back in the position they were before the litigation began, or dictate the legal relationship between the parties in the future. In family law, in particular CA 1989 litigation, the first two goals are impossible. No order under the CA 1989, s 8 will compensate anyone for the damage of a broken relationship; no order will place the parties in status quo ante. And while it is correct in theory to state that an order under s 8 will govern the parties' relationships in the future, it is also correct to state that no order will give an absent parent a legally enforceable right regarding how the primary care taker seeks to parent his or her children, unless the absent parent can demonstrate some level of harm to the child that rises to the level of requiring a change in the child's residence.

One of the most difficult jobs of an advocate in proceedings under the CA 1989 is to explain to the client the true nature of the orders available under the Children Act. Lay clients deal with legal concepts in the language of rights. 'This court has made an order and I therefore have a right', is a common refrain heard by lawyers appearing on behalf of, for example, absent fathers seeking to have contact with their children. It is also a complaint made by absent parents who seek to continue to make basic parental decisions regarding their children, even though their ex-spouses refuse to communicate with them. For this reason, advocates need to have a concrete, logical explanation available for litigants who are caught up in proceedings under the CA 1989. 'What can I achieve?' the client will ask. The advocate must have an answer that realistically addresses the difficulties posed by enforcement of any order that is made.

---

34 The problem is not discussed often by the High Court or Court of Appeal, primarily because lawyers are sensitive to the difficulty and do not press cases where parents are seeking to control basic decisions of the primary carer of the child. In the case of *Re C (A Minor) (Leave to Seek Section 8 Orders)* [1994] FLR 26, Johnson J faced an application by a 14-year-old girl who sought a specific issue order so that she could go on holiday to Bulgaria with friends. Leave was refused. Johnson J noted that making an order would formalise arrangements which would be better resolved by discussion within the family; granting leave might indicate a willingness to side with the child who disagrees with a parent's decision.

The difficulty of enforcing contact orders under s 8 of the CA 1989 is now common knowledge. A good analysis of the research, as well as the cases, in this area has been presented by the barrister, Mark Piercy, who notes the 'depressing familiarity' of intractable contact disputes to those who work in this area.[35] Clients must understand that a court at present has but four available remedies:

(a) imprison the defaulting parent, or impose a sentence of imprisonment, but suspend the sentence upon the defaulting parent's complying with the order;
(b) fine the defaulting parent;
(c) transfer residence to the other parent;
(d) abandon direct contact and seek to work outside the court system to re-institute contact. As has been noted by the President, this is the solution of last resort, and really only serves to bring the law into disrepute. See *Re O (Contact: Withdrawal of Application)* [2003] EWHC 303, [2004] 1 FLR 1258.[36]

It may be that Parliament seeks to add a remedy or two to that list, such as allowing courts to make an order directing that the defaulting parent spend time performing community service work as punishment.

From an advocacy standpoint, the significance is this: you must be able to explain to your client the precise parameters of the orders available under the CA 1989. This includes, necessarily, explaining carefully how each order might be enforced, and the likely prospect of success on that application.

Lord Justice Wall, in a paper delivered in October 2004, to the Children Law Conference, did not seek to sound optimistic:

> 'The message is that if, in the forensic process, we get to enforcement, we have failed. The order we have made is not working ... [I]f we do get to that stage, it is to my mind manifestly unsatisfactory that the only two methods of enforcement currently open to the courts are, first, a fine, and, secondly, prison. It would be difficult to identify two cruder or unsuitable mechanisms.'[37]

The advocate must also be aware of the case law regarding the implacably hostile parent. The mother's hostility is a factor which is capable, according to the circumstances of each particular case, of supplying a cogent reason for refusing contact, especially where the mother's attitude puts the child at serious risk of major emotional harm if compelled to accept contact against her will.

---

[35] See Piercy, 'Intractable Conact Disputes' (2004) Fam Law 815.
[36] See also *Re D (Intractable Contact Dispute)* [2004] EWHC 727, [2004] 1 FLR 1266, where Munby J sought to expose what he believed to be the inadequacies of the court process, and see *Re V (Contact Implacable Hostility)* [2004] EWHC 1215, [2004] 2 FLR 851, where Bracewell J weighed in with a few well-aimed barbs of her own. It is not as if this problem has been ignored by the judiciary.
[37] Wall LJ, 'Enforcement of Contact Orders' (2005) Fam Law 26.

See *Re D (A Minor) (Contact: Mother's Hostility)*.[38] That being said, the court will be reluctant to allow a hostile parent to prevent contact, where the child's welfare otherwise requires contact. See *Re P (A Minor) (Contact)*;[39] *Re W (A Minor) (Contact)*.[40] The European Court of Human Rights has awarded a Finnish father damages against the Finnish government for failing to ensure that he had contact with his child. The applicant had sought contact for eight years, and had been frustrated by the actions of the child's grandparents, with whom he had been living. See *Hokkanen v Finland*.[41] Courts have been reminded that the courts should only refuse contact if satisfied there was a serious risk of harm. See *Re D (Contact: Reasons for Refusal)*.[42] Where there are no rational grounds for resisting contact, the court will order contact unless to do so will create a serious risk of emotional harm for the child. Where the hostility was based upon grounds which were themselves strong enough to justify refusal, the hostility itself should be seen to be largely irrelevant. But where the hostility was based upon rational but not decisive grounds, the hostility could be an important factor, occasionally determinative, provided that what was being measured was the effect on the child. See *Re P (Contact: Discretion)*.[43]

Almost invariably, contact applications where there have been serious incidents of domestic violence cause difficulties for the court. The matter will often be set down for a fact-finding hearing regarding any disputed allegations. The court will then have regard to the factors set out by Butler-Sloss P in the case of *Re L, et al (Contact: Domestic Violence)* [2000] 2 FLR 404, CA. The allegations must first be proved. There is no prima facie barrier if violence in fact is proved, but it is relevant. In assessing the impact of past violence, the ability of the violent party to recognise past conduct, to be aware of the need to change and to make a genuine effort to do so, will be considered.

3.2.1 Parental responsibility

The basics: married fathers and all mothers, whether unmarried or not, acquire automatic parental responsibility for a child. An unmarried father acquires parental responsibility on registration of the birth under the Births and Deaths Registration Act 1953.[44] The effect of this is that an unmarried father obtains parental responsibility only if the mother consents. If she refuses to consent to

---

38 [1993] 2 FLR 1.
39 [1994] 1 FLR 374.
40 [1994] 2 FLR 441.
41 [1996] 1 FLR 289.
42 [1997] 2 FLR 48.
43 [1998] 2 FLR 696.
44 See Adoption and Children Act 2002, s 111, which came into force on 1 December 2003 and amended CA 1989, s 4, so that the father who was not married to the mother at the time of the child's birth has parental responsibility if his name is placed on the birth certificate at registration.

the unmarried father gaining parental responsibility, the only alternative is an application for a court order under s 4 of the CA 1989.

But what does one acquire when an order for parental responsibility is made? Courts have been reluctant to address this dilemma in the language of rights and duties. Courts have stated instead that parental responsibility orders confer on the committed father the status of parenthood for which nature has already ordained he must bear responsibility.[45]

When courts hear a father's application for parental responsibility, the court will seek to assess the father's motive for applying, as well as his commitment to the child. Courts presume that a father invested with responsibilities is capable of exercising rights, performing duties and wielding powers in relation to the child. Where a father is unable to exercise such responsibility his application will be refused.[46] Therefore the court is noting that the term parental responsibility does confer some 'rights'.

But what does it mean for an absent father (or mother for that matter) to 'exercise rights, perform duties, and wield powers in relation to the child'? The fact is that a relationship between a mother, father and child does not fit into the framework of legal rights and duties. When mother and father are living under the same roof, it would be unthinkable for a court to be asked to intervene if the mother felt the father ignored her opinions on where their child should attend secondary school. Is the fact that mother and father are now separated reason to have the courts involved because the mother now ignores the father's opinion about secondary schools?

Section 3(1) of the CA 1989 defines parental responsibility as 'all the rights, duties, powers, responsibilities and authority which by law a parent of a child has in relation to the child and his property'. In other words, do not look just to the CA 1989 for a definition of those powers. Section 3(2) expands the definition to include 'the rights, powers and duties which a guardian of the child's estate ... would have had in relation to the child and his property'. Section 3(4) seeks to separate the term parental responsibility from any obligations that a parent may owe in relation to the child, including a statutory duty to maintain the child. The term parental responsibility is also defined *not* to include any effect on any rights which come in the event of the child's death, he or any other person may have in relation to the child's property.

One can easily see that the definition of parental responsibility only makes sense for parents who have physical care and custody of the child. What rights, duties, powers and responsibilities and authority does the law grant to the non-resident

---

45   See *Re S (Parental Responsibility)* [1995] 2 FLR 648, CA; *Re S (Parental Responsibility: Jurisdiction)* [1998] 2 FLR 921.
46   See *M v M (Parental Responsibility)* [1999] 2 FLR 737.

parent? The short answer is, the right to consult with the primary carer about certain decisions, the right to litigate about certain other decisions. But other than that, not much. Parental responsibility orders do not allow the non-resident parent to overrule the reasonable decisions of the parent with whom the child primarily resides. There are limits to this, however, as set out below.

The court will normally apply a three-part test when unmarried fathers apply for a parental responsibility order and the court will assess:

(1) the father's degree of commitment to the child;
(2) the degree of attachment between father and child;
(3) the reasons why the father is applying for parental responsibility.

The test was originally set out by Balcombe LJ in 1991, in the case of *Re H (Illegitimate Children: Father: Parental Rights) (No 2)*.[47] That test was confirmed by the Court of Appeal, per Ward LJ, in the case of *Re J-S (Contact: Parental Responsibility)*.[48]

3.2.2 Section 8 orders

There are four section 8 orders:

(1) *A residence order.* This is an order settling the arrangements to be made as to the person with whom the child is to live.
(2) *A contact order.* This is an order requiring the person with whom the child lives to allow the child to visit or stay with the person named in the order, or for that person and the child otherwise to have contact with each other.
(3) *A specific issue order.* This is an order giving directions for the purpose of determining a specific question which has arisen, or which may arise, in connection with any aspect of parental responsibility for a child.
(4) *A prohibited steps order.* This is an order setting out a step which cannot be taken by a parent in meeting his parental responsibility for a child without permission of the court.

Residence orders deal only with where the child is to reside. Contact orders are designed only to order the resident parent to produce a child for visits with the non-resident parent. Prohibited steps orders and specific issue orders, however, essentially turn *every* decision regarding the exercise of parental responsibility for a child into an issue that can be litigated. This, of course, is nonsensical, and courts have not allowed non-resident parents to litigate every non-essential decision regarding a child. Certain decisions, however, will be subject to either the approval of the non-resident parent, or subject to the approval of the court:

---

[47] [1991] 1 FLR 214.
[48] [2003] 1 FLR 399.

(1) The decision to move from the general location in which the child and the family resided. In exceptional circumstances, the CA 1989 might be used to restrict a parent from moving the child within the United Kingdom.[49] In the case of *Re S (A Child) (Residence Order: Condition) (No 2)*,[50] the court imposed a condition or a residence order to prevent the mother from removing her nine-year-old Down's Syndrome child to Cornwall. The court held that jurisdiction existed under the CA 1989, s 11(7) to impose any condition that secures the welfare of the child.[51] The greater the restriction on the freedom of the parent subject to the condition, the more exceptional the case has to be to justify it.

Permanant removal from the jurisdiction of the UK, however, will require permission from the non-resident parent, or permission from the court. Section 13 of the CA 1989 specifically grants the power of approval to non-resident parents before a child might be removed from the jurisdiction of the UK. That being said, however, courts have been keen to make certain that the effect upon the applicant parent and the new family of the child of a refusal to leave is carefully assessed. It might be said to be a decisive factor in cases where a parent seeks to remove a child in order to live with a new partner and family.[52] A parent with parental responsibility can veto a child's receipt of a passport.

(2) Major medical decisions regarding the child, including questions regarding abortion or sterilisation, are questions that will be decided by a court, unless both parents agree. Courts have been instructed that these questions are best litigated under the inherent jurisdiction of the court, though s 8 is

---

[49]   See *Re H (Children) (Residence Order: Condition)* [2001] EWCA Civ 1338, [2001] 2 FLR 1277.

[50]   [2002] EWCA Civ 1795, [2003] 1 FCR 138.

[51]   While it is possible for the court to attach conditions to residence orders under s 11(7) of the Act, this does not give the court the power to determine with whom the mother might reside. The court's power to exclude someone from the mother's home could be exercised only under the appropriate statutes, after proof of violence or other acts harmful to the mother or child. In *Re D (Residence: Imposition of Conditions)* [1996] 2 FLR 281, the Court of Appeal granted appeal of an order where the trial court had attached conditions to a residence order made in the mother's favour, prohibiting her from bringing the children into contact with a former co-habitee of the mother's, and prohibiting the mother from allowing the man to live with them. The court held the issue before the trial court would only be this: should the children live with the mother and her co-habitee or with the father? The case was remitted for rehearing.

     Courts are also wary of using s 11(7) of the Act to impose a condition of residence on the primary carer. See *Re E (Residence: Imposition of Conditions)* [1997] 2 FLR 638. But given the appropriate circumstances, in particular, where it is seen that the child's physical or emotional well-being is better served by living in a certain area, the court retains jurisdiction under s 11(7) to impose conditions of residence: *Re H (Children) (Residence Order: Condition)* [2001] EWCA Civ 1338, [2001] 2 FLR 1277.

[52]   The test set out in *Payne v Payne* [2001] EWCA Civ 166, [2001] 1 FLR 1052, seems to have been modified slightly by Thorpe LJ in *Re B (Removal from Jurisdiction); Re S (Removal from Jurisdiction)* [2003] EWCA Civ 1149, [2003] 2 FLR 1043. The Court of Appeal in the latter combined case emphasised that when a mother cared for the children within a new family, the impact of refusal on the new family and the stepfather must be carefully evaluated. It was acknowledged in those cases that *Payne v Payne* did not of itself sufficiently alert the judge to the weight to be given to the relationship between the mother and her new partner and its natural consequences.

obviously an alternative route. The inherent jurisdiction is discussed in more detail below.

(3) Changing the child's name will also be the subject of litigation, unless the parents agree. Again, s 13 of the Act provides a statutory right for the non-resident parent (or at least the one with parental responsibility) to prohibit the child's primary care taker from changing the child's surname. The Court of Appeal has held that it may be appropriate in certain cases for a child to use the surnames of both his mother and father.[53] The President of the Family Division, in the case of *Re W, Re A and Re B (Change of Name)*,[54] sought to lay down guidelines for courts hearing cases regarding the change of a child's surname. The summary given by Butler-Sloss LJ (as she then was) regarding the powers of each parent to change the child's name is helpful:

'A. If the parents are married, they both have the power and duty to register their child's name.

B. If they are not married the mother has the sole duty and power to do so.

C. After registration of the child's names, the grant of a residence order obliges any person wishing to change the surname to obtain leave of the Court or written consent of all those who have parental responsibility.

D. In the absence of a residence order, the person wishing to change the surname from the registered name ought to obtain the relevant written consent or the leave of the Court by making an application for a specific issue order.

E. On any application, the welfare of the child is paramount and the Judge must have regard to the Section 13 criteria.

F. Among the factors to which the Court should have regard is the registered surname of the child and the reasons for the registration, for instance, recognition of the biological link with the child's father. Registration is also a relevant and an important consideration but it is not in itself decisive. The weight to be given to it by the Court will depend upon the other relevant factors or valid countervailing reasons which may tip the balance the other way.

G. The relevant considerations should include factors which may arise in the future as well as the present situation.

---

[53] See *Re R (Surname: Using Both Parents)* [2001] EWCA Civ 1344, [2001] 2 FLR 1358. In that case the child was to move to Spain with his mother and the parents were urged to follow the Spanish practice of using both parents' surnames in order to ease the child's adjustment to a life in that culture.

[54] [1999] 2 FLR 930.

H. Reasons given for changing or seeking to change a child's name based on the fact that the child's name is or not the same as the parent making the application do not generally carry much weight.

I. The reasons for an earlier unilateral decision to change a child's name may be relevant.

J. Any change of circumstances of the child since the original registration may be relevant.

K. In the case of a child whose parents were married to each other, the fact of the marriage is important and I would suggest there would have to be strong reasons to change the name from the father's surname if it was so registered.

L. Where the child's parents were not married, the mother has control over registration. Consequently, on an application to change the surname of the child, the degree of commitment of the father to the child, the quality of contact, if it occurs, between father and child, the existence or absence of parental responsibility are all relevant factors to take into account.'[55]

Courts are much more reluctant to hear cases regarding forenames of the child. The Court of Appeal's judgment in the case of *Re H (Child's Name: First Name)*[56] in one sense showed the difficulties courts face when trying to determine questions regarding what some believe to be non-essential matters regarding childcare. In *Re H* the father and the mother had each registered the child with different forenames. The father's registration was first in time. The child lived with the mother, and had contact with the father. The court held that the mother should be permitted to use the forename she had chosen for the child both at home and when dealing with external authorities. Again, the court was concerned with the fact that the mother was the primary carer of the child, and therefore had to be given primary responsibility for basic decisions regarding that child's care.

(4) A change in the child's religion. In *Re J (Specific Issue Orders: Child's religious upbringing and circumcision)*,[57] the court was faced with an application by a Muslim father, who sought to force the mother of his child to agree to a circumcision of the child according to Muslim law and ritual. The mother refused. The court upheld her refusal, noting that she was a non-practising Christian, that she was the primary carer of the child, and that there would be some risk of harm to the child if the procedure went forward. But the court also noted the importance of the child's religious

---

[55]　[1999] 2 FLR 930 at 933F.
[56]　[2002] EWCA Civ 190, [2002] 1 FLR 973, CA.
[57]　[1999] 2 FLR 678, [2001] 1 FLR 571, CA.

upbringing, and noted that the father has the right, at the least, to consult regarding any changes in religion. See also *Re R (A Minor) (Residence Order: Religion).*[58] The European Convention on Human Rights, Art 9, also provides that freedom of religion is protected, but courts will always use the best interest of the child standard when there are disputes about religions. See *Re J*, above.

(5) A significant change in the child's education. See *Re A (Specific Issue Order: Parental Dispute).*[59] A court's consideration of a child's education will always be an example of why the term 'right' can never be seen in a vacuum, but always must be viewed in the context of the factual dispute in which the question arises. There are countless factual possibilities: a seven-year-old, for example, fails to attend school because the mother neglected him. That child has a right to attend school; the mother has a duty to make certain he attends, or at least provide him with an education at home that complies with state-mandated norms. The state has a duty to provide reasonably adequate education for the child. So far so easy. But if a 12-year-old fails to attend because he is being bullied, or because he develops a behavioural problem, or because he just does not like his school, the matrix of rights and duties becomes infinitely more complicated. Will the state have a duty to provide alternative education? Will the mother have a duty to work with the state to make certain the child is educated properly? Will the child's residence be changed if the father, if absent, offers a better alternative educational plan for the child? Does the child himself have a duty to attend school? How is that duty to be enforced? Even a brief consideration of these questions reveals the almost-infinite complexity of child-care decisions by courts when considering the child's educational needs. The welfare checklist also provides that courts should pay particular care to a child's education. For these reasons, courts will sometimes hear disputes regarding which school a child should attend, and will make a specific issue order. But more often, a court will allow the parent with primary care of the child to decide, noting that it would be difficult to weigh one school over another in family proceedings; *Re S (Specific Issue Order: Religion: Circumcision).*[60]

3.2.3 The Children and Family Court Advisory and Support Service

All advocates appearing in cases involving children must have detailed knowledge of the Children and Family Court Advisory and Support Service (CAFCASS). The Labour Government introduced CAFCASS to an unwitting public in 2000, with the Criminal Justice and Court Services Act 2000. The

[58]   [1993] 2 FLR 163, CA.
[59]   [2001] 1 FLR 121, CA.
[60]   [2004] EWHC 1282, [2005] 1 FLR 236.

new service attempts to rationalise the reporting service to the court. Before the Act, courts were given information about children by three separate agencies: the Guardian ad Litem and Reporting Officer Service, the Family Court Welfare Service and the children's branch of the Official Solicitor's Office. The new Act sought to have one new unified service. The Lord Chancellor was given responsibility under the Act for administering the new service.

The Act gives to CAFCASS four central functions:

(1) to safeguard and promote the welfare of children;
(2) to give advice to any court about applications made to it and any such proceedings;
(3) to make provision for children to be represented in such proceedings; and
(4) to provide information, advice and other support for children and their families.

Advocates must know the difference between reports directed by the court to be provided by CAFCASS reporting officers, and reports to be provided by local authority social services officers. The CA 1989, s 7, provides that the court considering any question with respect to the child under the Act may ask a local authority to arrange for a report on that child. Section 37 of the CA 1989 provides that where in any family proceedings a question arises with respect to the welfare of a child, *and it appears to the court that it may be appropriate for a care or supervision order to be made with respect to that child*, the court may direct local authority social services to undertake an investigation of the child's circumstances. Courts therefore can only order local authority social workers to produce section 37 reports, as they are known, if that court believes a care or supervision order 'may be appropriate' for that child. The section empowers the court of its own motion to direct a local authority to look into the circumstances of the child. The court may make an interim order pending the results of the investigation.[61] Section 37 also gives a time limit of eight weeks to report, unless the court otherwise directs. As from 1 November 2003, all cases in which a section 37 direction is made must be conducted in accordance with the new Protocol for judicial case management in public law Children Act cases.

Courts have been directed to spell out carefully the reasons for making the section 37 order, and a transcript or note of the judgment should be made available to the local authority at the earliest opportunity.[62] The court in its order should also state how and by whom the order will be communicated to the local authority.

---

61 See CA 1989, s 38(1).
62 See *Re M (Intractable Contact Dispute: Interim Care Order)* [2003] EWHC 1024 (Fam), [2003] 2 FLR 636.

Directions made under s 37 are vitally important for a court to consider, not least because it also empowers the court to appoint a guardian for the child.[63] The court can only appoint a guardian if the court makes or 'considers whether to make' an interim care order.[64]

The difference between section 7 referrals to local authorities and section 37 referrals are really a matter of degree. Section 7(1) referrals are for those cases where the court desires a welfare investigation and report, but would not be likely to seek to remove the child from the care of one parent. For example, the court may be concerned that the child had been excessively bullied at school, and suffer harm, but the harm came not necessarily because of the care given the child by the parent.

It is possible to use section 37 in intractable contact disputes. It empowers the court to remove children who were being denied all contact with the non-resident parent and who are suffering significant harm because of the resident parent's faults and distorted belief system about the non-resident parent.[65] In *Re M* (above), Wall J noted that the procedure is not a panacea; it must only be used when the circumstances truly justify. Wall J also noted that it will not always be appropriate to appoint a children's guardian when proceedings have become specified. In the case of *In Re C E (Section 37 Directions)*,[66] Wall J noted that a guardian should not be appointed automatically at the time a section 37 direction is made. Wall J also noted that a guardian should be appointed at once if the court decides to make an interim care order under section 38(1)(b) at the same time as making a section 37 direction. Otherwise, there must be a prospect that a public law order may be appropriate before a section 37 order can be made in the first place. Courts are careful not to allow advocates to use section 37 to argue that a guardian should be appointed in private law proceedings.

Wall J discussed the purpose of a section 7 referral in *Re A and B (Minors) No 2*.[67] Wall J described the section 7 report as the principal weapon in the court's armoury in ensuring coordination of private law proceedings with statutory local authority child abuse investigations. Wall J believed section 7 referrals would be the first step in a case where there were parallel private law proceedings and local authority investigations. In that case, courts would use section 7 to direct the local authority to provide detail of the nature, progress and outcome of the investigation. The local authority must make the social

---

63 See CA 1989, s 41(6)(b).
64 Ibid.
65 See *Re M (Intractable Contact Dispute: Interim Care Order)* [2003] EWHC 1024 (Fam), [2003] 2 FLR 636.
66 [1995] 1 FLR 26.
67 [1995] 1 FLR 351.

worker who writes the section 7 report available to give evidence and to be cross-examined at the substantive hearing.[68]

Welfare reports and any recommendations that the CAFCASS reporter makes must be taken into account by the court that directed preparation of the report.[69] A court must give reasons for failing to follow the recommendations of the CAFCASS reporter.[70] The reporter, on the other hand, must also undertake an adequate investigation. Seeing the children in the welfare office is not normally seen to be adequate. A home visit is required.[71]

It is a matter for the court's discretion whether to adjourn a case to make certain that the welfare officer or CAFCASS reporter is available to give oral evidence. It is almost always an abuse of discretion, however, for the court to disagree with the recommendations of the CAFCASS reporting officer or welfare officer without giving to the reporter an opportunity to explain his or her views in court, and to deal with the judge's differing recommendations.[72]

Advocates cross-examining CAFCASS reporters or local authority social workers must remember that these reporters and welfare officers are expert witnesses. These witnesses perceived almost nothing first hand, and received their narrative background of the case from written documents. The advocate should therefore always examine the quality of the written documentation given to the social worker or CAFCASS reporter. If it is poor, then the perception of the expert witness is affected.

3.3   THE CHILD AS LITIGANT

One of the great virtues of the CA 1989 is that it provides that children involved in care proceedings not only are the subject of the proceedings, they are parties to them as well. The legislation seeks not only to give a voice to the child, but it seeks to change the notion that children do not exist as legal entities. In private law applications under the Act, however, the child is ordinarily not a party, or a witness. Instead, the child's views will be given to the court by (ordinarily) a CAFCASS reporting officer, who will visit the child once, or at most twice, in order to gain an understanding of those views.

---

68   See *W v Wakefield City Council* [1995] 1 FLR 170.
69   *Re P (Custody of Children: Split Custody Order)* [1991] 1 FLR 337.
70   *Re J (Children) (Residence: Expert Evidence)* [2001] 2 FCR 44; *Re C B (Access: Attendance of Court Welfare Officer)* [1995] 1 FLR 622, CA. Also see *Re V (Residency Review)* [1995] 2 FLR 1010.
71   *Re P (A Minor) (Inadequate Welfare Report)* [1996] 2 FCR 285.
72   *Re C B (Access: Attendance of Court Welfare Officer)* [1995] 1 FLR 622; *Re C (Section 8 Order: Court Welfare Officer)* [1995] 1 FLR 617, where the Court of Appeal said that *Re C B* is not a hard and fast rule of law.

The common law, of course, provides that children (those under the lawful age of majority, now, after 1969, defined as 18 years of age) must be treated as 'being under a disability'. This disability means a person may not:

(1) bring or make a claim in any proceedings;
(2) acknowledge service, defend, make a counterclaim or intervene in any proceedings; or
(3) appear in any proceedings under a judgment or order, notice of which has been served upon him.

The only way to appear in any of those proceedings set out above would be through an appointed representative. This has traditionally been known as a 'next friend' for the person bringing the proceedings or a 'guardian ad litem' for the person defending or responding to the proceedings. The Civil Procedure Rules 1998 now provide that the term 'litigation friend' is to be used for both categories.

The Family Proceedings Rules 1991 (FPR 1991) now govern family proceedings, but nowhere in those Rules is the term 'family proceedings' fully defined. Rule 1.2(1) provides that family proceedings has the meaning assigned to it by s 32 of the Matrimonial and Family Proceedings Act 1984. Section 32 of the 1984 Act provides that 'family business' means business of any description which in the High Court is for the time being assigned to the Family Division and to no other division under s 61 of (and Sch 12 to) the Supreme Court Act 1981. Family proceedings also means 'proceedings which are family business,' according to the gnomic provisions of s 32.

In any event, it is well settled that proceedings brought under any Act regarding the upbringing and welfare of children may be denoted as family proceedings. This means that, at the least, proceedings brought under the Matrimonial Causes Act 1973, the Matrimonial and Family Proceedings Act 1984, the Family Law Act 1986, the CA 1989 and the Child Support Act 1991 are family proceedings. Proceedings under the Adoption Act 1976, however, are covered by the Adoption Rules 1984.

The CA 1989 presumes that certain applications within family proceedings might be brought by the child, so long as that child has sufficient understanding to enable him to give instructions to a solicitor. An example is an application by a child in care to increase contact with another child in care.[73] Ordinarily, the child will be represented by a litigation friend.

Part IX of the FPR 1991 will apply to all cases involving children, save for children who are the subject of applications in 'specified proceedings' within the meaning of the CA 1989, s 41(6). Specified proceedings, under s 41(6), are defined as applications for a care order or a supervision order, or discharge

---

[73] See CA 1989, s 34.

of a care order or a supervision order, or an application for a residence order for a child currently in care. Specified proceedings also refer to applications for contact between a child who is the subject of a care order and any other person.

If the application is a specified proceeding under s 41(6), the child is automatically a party, and automatically a guardian is appointed to appear on behalf of the child. The guardian's duties are set out under r 4.11(a) of the FPR 1991. The guardian shall appoint a solicitor to represent the child unless a solicitor has already been appointed, and give advice to the child as is appropriate having regard to the child's understanding. Section 41(2)(b) of the CA 1989 provides that the children's guardian is under a duty to safeguard the interests of the child in the manner prescribed by the Rules of Court. Rule 4.12 of the FPR 1991 provides that the solicitor appointed for the child shall be instructed by the child's guardian. If the child's solicitor or guardian determines that the child wishes to give instructions which conflict with those of the children's guardian, the solicitor and the guardian must first seek to determine whether the child is able to give such instructions on his own behalf, having regard to the child's age and understanding. If the guardian and solicitor determine that the child is able to do so, then the child will be able to instruct the solicitor directly with regard to the course of the litigation. The guardian will remain involved in the litigation, but will seek separate legal representation.[74]

It is also possible for certain minors to sue without a litigation friend. Rule 9.1A of the FPR 1991 provides that a minor shall be entitled to apply for the leave of court for an order under the CA 1989 without a litigation friend where he has obtained the leave of court for that purpose, or where a solicitor considers that the minor is able to give instructions in relation to the proceedings, having regard to the minor's understanding. Courts have been directed to grant leave, or remove the litigation friend, if it considers that the minor concerned has sufficient understanding to participate as a party in the proceedings without a litigation friend.[75] The court, rather than the solicitor, always has the ultimate right to decide whether a child who comes before it as a party without a next friend or without a litigation friend has the necessary ability, having regard to his understanding, to instruct a solicitor.[76] The test used by a court on applications to dispense with a guardian is a one-stage test. The essence of it

---

[74] Advocates who appear on behalf of (or who cross-examine) guardians must make certain the guardian has not exceeded the bounds of her expertise. An example is the case of *B v B (Child Abuse: Contact)* [1994] 2 FLR 713. Wall J in that case found the guardian to have gone beyond the proper bounds of her role in two respects. First, the guardian had adopted a judicial role in effectively finding that a child in the case had been subject to sexual abuse. Second, the guardian sought to assess material which, in the judge's view, she did not have the expertise to assess. Guardians must only report their factual observations and assessment within the guardian's professional expertise as a social worker. Expert advice must be sought on the interpretation of controversial material, especially relating to allegations of sexual abuse.

[75] FPR 1991, r 9.2(6).

[76] See *Re CT (A Minor) (Wardship: Representation)* [1993] 2 FLR 278.

is that the court has to consider whether the minor has 'sufficient understanding to participate as a party in the proceedings concerned'.[77]

Guidance on the application of the test regarding a child's ability to give instructions on his own behalf has been given by Thorpe J in the case of *Re H (A Minor) (Care Proceedings: Child's Wishes).*[78] Thorpe J stated in that case that a child of 15 would not *necessarily* have sufficient understanding to instruct. Thorpe J did reject the argument that emotional disturbance could not, on its own, negate the ability to instruct. In cases involving an able, intelligent but emotionally disturbed child, Thorpe J believed that the court should apply rr 4.11 and 4.12 realistically to ensure that the court heard not only the professional view of the child's guardian, but also the wishes and feelings of the child himself.

In the case of *Re C (Residence: Child's Application for Leave),*[79] a 14-year-old child sought leave under the CA 1989, s 10 to make a section 8 application that she be permitted to live with her mother. The girl was found to have sufficient understanding to make the proposed application. In *Re N (Contact: Minor Seeking Leave to Defend the Removal of the Guardian),*[80] Coleridge J held that the essential question was not whether the child was capable of articulating instructions, but whether the child was of sufficient understanding to be able to cope with all the ramifications of the proceedings and to give considered instructions of sufficient objectivity. In considering this question, the court would have regard to the nature of the proceedings, the length of time the proceedings had been before the court, the likely future conduct of proceedings and future applications that would need to be made. Where the court terminates the appointment of a solicitor or children's guardian, the rule now requires the court to give reasons for doing so and requires that none of the reasons be taken by the court or by the proper officer.[81]

Rule 9.5 of the FPR 1991 also provides a route for children into family proceedings. This rule provides that if in any family proceedings it appears to the court that it is in the best interests of any child to be made a party to the proceedings, the court may appoint a CAFCASS officer, or, if he consents, the Official Solicitor, or, if he consents, some other proper person, to be the litigation friend of the child with authority to take part in the proceedings on the child's behalf. Where a guardian is appointed under this rule, and that guardian is an officer of the CAFCASS service, rr 4.11 and 4.11A shall apply to that guardian as they apply to a children's guardian appointed under the CA 1989, s 41. This means that the duties required of this guardian will be the same

77 See *Re N (Contact: Minor Seeking Leave to Defend and Removal of Guardian)* [2003] 1 FLR 652.
78 [1993] 1 FLR 440.
79 [1995] 1 FLR 927.
80 [2003] 1 FLR 652.
81 FPR 1991, r 4.12(5).

as required of a guardian in care order applications. It is still relatively rare for a court to allow a child to intervene or to be made a party in private law Children Act applications.

Advocates seeking to make children parties in private law proceedings must be aware of the President's Practice Direction *Representation of Children in Family Proceedings Pursuant to Rule 9.5 of the Family Proceedings Rules 1991*,[82] as well as the accompanying *CAFCASS Practice Note*.[83] Advocates must remember that children are not entitled as of right to participate as parties in private law litigation. The President's Direction provides that 'making a child a party to the proceedings is a step that will be taken only in cases which involve an issue of significant difficulty and consequently will occur in only a minority of cases.' The President notes that consideration should be given to whether an alternative route might be preferable, such as asking an officer of the CAFCASS to carry out further work or by making a referral to social services, or by obtaining an expert's report.[84]

The President notes as well that the decision whether to make the child a party is exclusively the judge's, made in light of the facts and circumstances of the case. The President then sets out 10 examples of cases where the judge would likely be justified in making the child a party:

(a) where a CAFCASS officer has notified the court that in his or her opinion the child should be made a party;
(b) where the child has a standpoint or interests which are inconsistent with or incapable of being represented by any of the adult parties;
(c) where there is an intractable dispute over residence or contact, including where all contact has ceased, or where there is irrational but implacable hostility to contact or where the child may be suffering harm associated with the contact dispute;
(d) where the views and wishes of the child cannot be adequately met by a report to the court;
(e) where an older child is opposing a proposed course of action;
(f) where there are complex medical or mental health issues to be determine or there are other unusually complex issues that necessitate separate representation of the child;
(g) where there are international complications outside child abduction, in particular where it may be necessary for there to be discussions with overseas authorities or a foreign court;

---

82   [2004] 1 FLR 1188.
83   [2004] 1 FLR 1190.
84   See also *A v A (Contact) (Representation of Children's Interests)* [2001] 1 FLR 715, where the President noted that the Human Rights Act 1998 would likely lead to increased use of guardians in private law proceedings.

(h) where there are serious allegations of physical, sexual or other abuse in relation to the child, or there are allegations of domestic violence not capable of being resolved with the help of a CAFCASS officer;
(i) where the proceedings concern more than one child and the welfare of the children is in conflict or one child is in particularly disadvantaged position;
(j) where there is a contested issue about blood testing.

The President points out that separate representation almost inevitably means a delay in the case. When a child is made a party and a guardian is to be appointed, consideration should first be given to appointing an officer of CAFCASS as guardian; before appointing an officer, the court will cause preliminary enquiries to be made of CAFCASS. If CAFCASS is unable to provide a guardian without delay, the court will look to r 9.5(1), which makes further provision for the appointment of the guardian.

If the matter is in County Court, the Circuit Judge must consider transferring to the High Court.

If a court has decided to appoint an officer of CAFCASS to be guardian, the order should simply state that '[the child] is made party to the proceedings and pursuant to FPR 1991 r 9.5 an officer of CAFCASS be appointed as his/her guardian.' The decision about which particular officer of CAFCASS to allocate as guardian is a matter for CAFCASS.

CAFCASS is to make a decision within five working days of receiving the papers in the case whether the matter should be allocated to a member of the service locally, or to CAFCASS Legal (that part of the service which has taken over responsibilities previously exercised by the children's branch of the Official Solicitor's Office). In most High Court cases, CAFCASS Legal will act as guardian. It is the responsibility of the local CAFCASS service manager and CAFCASS Legal to liaise whenever necessary to ensure that the most appropriate CAFCASS officer is appointed as guardian.[85] If the CAFCASS officer to be appointed as guardian is based at CAFCASS Legal, there will normally be no need for a solicitor for the child also to be appointed because the litigation will normally be conducted in-house pursuant to s 15 of the Criminal Justice and Court Services Act 2000.

The Practice Note sets out certain categories of cases that should be referred to CAFCASS Legal:

(1) cases in which the children's divisions of the Official Solicitor or CAFCASS Legal previously acted for the child;
(2) exceptionally complex international cases where legal or other substantial enquiries abroad will be necessary or where there is a dispute as to which country's courts should have jurisdiction over the child's affairs;

---

[85] See *CAFCASS Practice Note* [2004] 1 FLR 1190.

(3) exceptionally complex adoption cases, for example, a suspected illegal adoption;

(4) all medical treatment cases where the child is old enough to have views which need to be taken into account, or where there are particularly difficult ethical issues such as the withdrawal of treatment, unless the issue arises in existing proceedings already being handled locally when the preferred arrangement will usually be for the matter to continue to be dealt with locally but with additional advice provided by CAFCASS Legal;

(5) any freestanding human rights applications pursuant to s 7(1) of the HRA 1998 in which it is thought it may be possible and appropriate for any part to be played by CAFCASS or its officers;

(6) any additional categories of case for referral to CAFCASS Legal that may from time to time be added to the list.[86]

Lawyers involved in emergency proceedings before any court should know that CAFCASS Legal take it in turn to carry a mobile telephone through which the department might be contacted any day of the year by the High Court out-of-hours duty judge. This is helpful in particular in cases involving medical emergencies.

3.4　THE INHERENT JURISDICTION OF THE HIGH COURT AND WARDSHIP

Advocates appearing in any application regarding children must always bear in mind the powers available only to a judge of the High Court. Understanding the inherent jurisdiction of the High Court, and wardship jurisdiction, on first glance requires the advocate to dig 'deep in the murky history of feudal times'.[87] In actuality, however, the inherent jurisdiction exercises an entirely modern function: the jurisdiction enables a judge of the High Court to craft orders to fit the particular circumstances of any case, notwithstanding a lack of statutory powers available for the judge, and notwithstanding that the case might present novel legal or factual issues.

The inherent jurisdiction of the High Court is derived from the Crown. The Sovereign has an obligation to protect those who owe allegiance to the Crown. In one sense, protection of the weakest members of society is entirely symbolic: it demonstrates the power of the Sovereign, as well as the beneficence. Where there is cruelty and injustice, the Crown must become involved. Otherwise, the Sovereign forfeits its powers.[88]

---

[86]   See *CAFCASS Practice Note* [2004] 1 FLR 1190 at 1192.
[87]   See Ward LJ in *Re Z (A Minor) (Freedom of Publication)* [1996] 1 FLR 191, at 196–197.
[88]   See generally *Re P (GE) (An Infant)* [1965] Ch 568, [1964] 3 All ER 977, CA.

Ward LJ, in the case of *Re Z (A Minor) (Freedom of Publications)*[89] explained the origin of the High Court's wardship jurisdiction like this:

> 'The origins of wardship lie buried deep in the murky history of feudal times. It was an incident of tenure, by which, upon a tenant's death, the Lord became guardian of the surviving infant's land and body. Although the entitlement to the profits of the land carried with it the reciprocal duty of maintaining and educating the ward according to his station, a cynical historian may well take the view that this valuable source of revenue to the Crown which, in about 1540, was transferred from officials of the Royal Household to the Court of Wards and Liveries, was more concerned to protect the rights of the guardian than those of the ward. When that entitlement in the Court were abolished in 1660, wardship did not wither away. *Cary (Lord Falkland) v Bertie* [1696] 2 VERN 333, at 342, saw the jurisdiction transferred to the Court of Chancery.'

Wardship jurisdiction is merely one part of the High Court's inherent jurisdiction. As courts have noted, in one sense all British children might be described as wards of court because they are subject to the parental jurisdiction now entrusted to the High Court.[90] When minors are made wards of the court, the court exercises its inherent jurisdiction on behalf of that minor.[91] The then Master of the Rolls, Lord Donaldson, put it like this:

> 'Since there seems to be some doubt about the matter, it should be made clear that the High Court's inherent jurisdiction in relation to children – the *parens patriae* jurisdiction – is equally exercisable whether the child is or is not a ward of Court. Indeed, the only additional effect of a child being a ward of Court stems from its status as such and not from the inherent jurisdiction, e.g. a ward of Court cannot marry or leave the jurisdiction without the consent of the Court and no important or major steps on a ward's life can be taken without that consent.'[92]

Advocates who practised at the Family Bar prior to 1991 and the implementation of the CA 1989, remember wardship as one of the more important, and often used, routes for a child into care. Prior to October 1991, a child could be made subject to a local authority care order in no less than 17 different ways. It was generally believed by most practitioners that the wardship route into care was often abused.[93]

The CA 1989 changed this. After the implementation of the Act, the only method available to place a child in the care of a local authority is under ss 31 and 38 of the CA 1989. The proper use of the wardship jurisdiction after the CA 1989's implementation is set out by Waite LJ in *Re T (A Minor) (Child: Representation)*:[94]

[89]   [1996] 1 FLR 191.
[90]   See *Richards v Richards* [1984] AC 174, [1983] 2 All ER 807, HL, per Lord Scarman.
[91]   See Administration of Justice Act 1970, s 1(2), Sch 1, which delegated to the Family Division of the High Court the *parens patriae* jurisdiction.
[92]   See *Re W (A Minor) (Medical Treatment)* [1992] 4 All ER 627 at 631, [1993] 1 FLR 1, CA.
[93]   See Masson and Morton, 'The Use of Wardship by Local Authorities' [1982] 52 MLR 762.
[94]   [1993] 4 All ER 518.

'The Court's undoubted discretion to allow wardship proceedings to go forward in a suitable case is subject to their clear duty, and loyalty to the scheme and purpose of the Children Act legislation, to permit recourse to wardship only when it becomes apparent to the Judge in any particular case that the question which the Court is determining in regard to the minor's upbringing or property cannot be resolved under the statutory procedures in Part 2 of the Children Act in a way which secures the best interests of the child; or where the minor person in a state of jeopardy from which he can only be protected by giving him the status of a ward of Court; or where the Court's functions need to be secured from the effects, potentially injurious to the child, of external influences (intrusive publicity for example) and it is decided that conferring on the child the status of a ward will prove a more effective deterrent than the ordinary sanctions of contempt of Court which already protect all family proceedings.'

Section 100 of the CA 1989 prohibits the High Court from utilising the inherent jurisdiction to make public law orders that the local authority might otherwise obtain through the provisions in Parts 3 and 4 of the Act. These orders are discussed in Chapter 4. The High Court can no longer place wards of the court into the care of a local authority.

The CA 1989 does give to the High Court, however, a residual power: the local authority might apply for leave for the court to use its inherent jurisdiction, where the result to be achieved might not be achieved through any other statutory order.

Local authorities now seek to use the inherent jurisdiction in the following situations:

(1) To stop undesirable publicity for a child in care.[95]
(2) For declarations regarding significant medical treatment, such as abortions.[96]
(3) For a declaration that the child might be sterilised.[97]
(4) Where the child faces an operation where the life of the child is at risk, or where the child's interests seem contrary to continuing the life of that child.[98]

Private parties might also use the wardship jurisdiction for the four categories as noted above. In addition, a private party whose child has been abducted, and it is believed the child is being hidden by the party who has taken that child, might also apply to the High Court for the child to be made a ward. The child becomes a ward of the court immediately upon an application by any 'interested person'. The court might then direct that government agencies, including

---

95   See *Re M and N (Minors) (Wardship: Publication of Information)* [1989] 3 WLR 1136.
96   See *Re B (Wardship) (Abortion)* [1991] 2 FLR 426.
97   See *Re B (A Minor) (Wardship: Sterilisation)* [1988] AC 199.
98   See *Re B (A Minor) (Wardship: Medical Treatment)* [1990] 3 All ER 930. See discussion in *Encyclopaedia of Social Services and Child Care Law* (Sweet & Maxwell), p B1-30.

agencies dealing with income support payments or child benefit payments, to disclose the address of the alleged abductor to the court and to the applicant. The court might also direct that all port authorities be alerted to the identity of the child and the abductor. The court also might direct Tipstaff, which is a law enforcement arm under the direction of the High Court, to assist the applicant in searching for the child. Tipstaff officers might carry out basic surveillance of an address, or carry out more detailed searches for the child and the abductor.

The inherent jurisdiction is most often used, however, in order for physicians or hospitals to seek a declaration regarding the continued medical care of those with irreversible medical conditions. An example of this is *Re C (A Baby),*[99] where the President of the Family Division faced an application by parents to allow discontinuation of feeding to a child aged three months. The baby had been born eight weeks prematurely. Two weeks later the baby developed meningitis. The baby was brain damaged and required both artificial ventilation and tube feeding. The child was blind, deaf and suffered pain and distress. Doctors gave evidence that there was no prospect of improvement. Both doctors and parents agreed that it was in the child's best interests that the artificial ventilation be stopped. The court granted the relief sought.

The High Court has now issued a Practice Note governing applications to terminate medical treatment for those in what has been called a 'persistent vegetative state'.[100] The guidance provides that PVS diagnosis may not reasonably be made until the patient has been in a continuing vegetative state following a head injury for more than 12 months, or following other causes of brain damage for more than six months. Before those dates, rehabilitative measures such as coma arousal programmes should be begun. Courts should properly refuse to hear applications to terminate artificial feeding and hydration until the condition is judged to be permanent. Clinical and other observations of a patient over a period of time would probably need to be commissioned.

Applications to the court should be by originating summons issued in the Family Division of the High Court. Applications to the court in relation to minors should be made within wardship proceedings and applicants should seek leave of the court for the termination of feeding and hydration, rather than a declaration. The relief to be sought is also set out in the Practice Direction.

---

[99]   [1996] 2 FLR 43, FD.

[100]   See *Practice Note (Declaratory Proceedings) (Medical and Welfare Decisions for Adults Who Lack Capacity)* [2001] 2 FLR 158. See also *Practice Direction (Family Division: Declaratory Proceedings Concerning Incapacitated Adults' Medical and Welfare Decisions)* [2002] 1 FLR 177; *Practice Note: Official Solicitor: Appointment* [2001] 2 FLR 155; *Re B (Consent to Treatment: Capacity)* [2002] EWCA 429, FD, [2001] 1 FLR 1090. See also *NHS Trust A v H* [2001] 2 FLR 501.

3.5   CHILD ABDUCTION

A parent whose child has been abducted by that child's other parent seeks from the law certainty and speed. Sadly, the law often offers neither. Lawyers conducting litigation under the Child Abduction and Custody Act 1985 and the Hague Convention must understand this, and must always seek to prepare their clients for this.

It may well be that because of the speed with which applications are issued under the Child Abduction and Custody Act 1985 that the client has not had an opportunity to have explained to him or her the background of the Hague Convention. Advocates must seek to do this as quickly as possible in the initial conference, in particular those advocates whose clients are accused of abducting a child from a settled residence. The object of the Hague Convention is to process the expeditious return of any child under the age of 16 who has been 'wrongfully removed or retained in another contracting state'. The child is returned, if the Act operates appropriately, to the country of the child's habitual residence. The parent who has taken the child from the child's settled residence to a jurisdiction that has signed up to the Convention must understand that the court will ordinarily order a prompt return of the child. That does not mean the court in the original jurisdiction will refuse to hear the abductor's case; indeed, the point of the Convention is not to decide who wins a dispute regarding the residence of a child. Instead, it is to decide which court will answer the question.

A secondary purpose of the Hague Convention is to ensure that rights of custody under the law of one contracting state are effectively respected in other contracting states. It is therefore vitally important that the client understands immediately that the first application will not determine where and with whom the child will live; instead, the application of the Hague Convention is merely to return the child to the court that has personal jurisdiction over the child.

Applicants under the Hague Convention in the High Court will seek to use the court's interim powers.[101] A court might use the inherent jurisdiction of the High Court in order to take all appropriate steps to ascertain the whereabouts of the child and to ensure the child's return. The court might exercise its jurisdiction even before the child arrives within England and Wales.[102] The court may make a collection and/or location order, ordering the defendant to deliver the child to the plaintiff. The court may order any person who has relevant

---

[101]   See the Child Abduction and Custody Act 1985, s 5. Of course, the first question to be answered is whether the child is now in a country that recognises the Hague Convention. The second consideration is practical: can the respondent be served?

[102]   See *A v A (Abduction: Jurisdiction)* [1995] 1 FLR 341.

information about the child to disclose that information.[103] This includes the solicitor representing the abductor. The solicitor may be ordered to disclose all documents in his or her possession relating to the abductor's whereabouts. It has been held, however, that an order may be made forbidding the solicitor to disclose any information to the abductor, but the solicitor cannot be ordered to lie to the client or to mislead him.[104] The court may also issue injunctions, order a CAFCASS officer to prepare a report, and might order that the plaintiff be permitted to place an advertisement or seek to have the matter publicised in a newspaper.[105]

Advocates conducting child abduction litigation must explain to the lay client, in simple, plain language, the meaning of the following terms:

(1) *Custody and access rights.* A right of custody is the right to determine the child's place of residence. A right of access includes the right to take a child for a limited period of time to a place other than the child's habitual residence.[106] Where an issue is raised regarding whether the foreign law gives the applicant custody rights or not, the court will determine the issue on expert evidence. Where the court is faced with conflicting expert evidence, it is for the applicant to prove his rights under the relevant forum law.

(2) *Wrongful removal or retention.* Removal is wrongful when it is breach of someone else's custody rights, or someone else's rights of access.[107] Removal can be wrongful where it is in breach of an express court order.[108] A unilateral decision by one parent not to return a child to the country of the child's habitual residence may constitute wrongful retention.[109] Retention has been held to include not only physical restraint, but also orders obtained in court on the initiative of the abducting parent.[110] A removal which is not in breach of domestic law may nevertheless be wrongful for the purposes of the Convention.[111]

(3) *Habitual residence.* Habitual residence is not defined in the Act or the Convention. Two features must be proved to establish habitual residence: (a) a person was present in a place or country voluntarily and (b) for a settled purpose with a settled intention to remain.[112] In the case of *C v S*

---

[103]   FPR 1991, r 6.16.
[104]   See *Re H (Abduction: Whereabouts Order to Solicitors)* [2000] 1 FLR 766. See also *Re B (Abduction: Disclosure)* [1995] 1 FLR 774.
[105]   See *Re D (A Minor) (Child Abduction)* [1989] 1 FLR 97.
[106]   See Hague Convention, Art 5.
[107]   See *C v S (A Minor) (Abduction)* [1990] 2 FLR 442, HL.
[108]   See *Re C (A Minor) (Abduction)* [1989] 1 FLR 403.
[109]   See *Re S (Minors) (Abduction: Wrongful Retention)* [1994] Fam 70, [1994] 1 FLR 82.
[110]   See *Re B (Minors) (Abduction) (No 2)* [1993] 1 FLR 993.
[111]   See *Re F (Child Abduction: Risk if Returned)* [1995] 2 FLR 31. See Practice Note of 14 October 1997.
[112]   See *Re H (Abduction: Habitual Residence: Consent)* [2000] 2 FLR 294.

(A Minor) (Abduction),[113] Lord Brandon said this in his speech regarding the issue of habitual residence:

> 'The question whether a person is or is not habitually resident in a specified country is a question of fact to be decided by reference to all the circumstances of any particular case ... There is a significant difference between a person ceasing to be habitually resident in country A, and his subsequently becoming habitually resident in country B. A person may cease to be habitually resident in country A in a single day if he or she leaves it with a settled intention not to return ... Such a person cannot, however, become habitually resident in country B in a single day. An appreciable period of time and a settled intention will be necessary to enable him to become so. During that appreciable period of time the person will have ceased to be habitually resident in country A but not yet have become habitually resident in country B.'

When the parents separate the child's habitual residence will follow that of its principal carer. In the case of a married couple, it is not possible for one parent unilaterally to terminate the habitual residence of the child by removing the child from one jurisdiction to another, if that removal is wrongful or in breach of the other parent's rights.[114] The habitual residence of a newborn child will be that of the parent who has parental responsibility for and primary responsibility for care of the child. The fact that the child was born abroad does not inevitably mean the child is habitually resident in the country where the child was born. Once the evidence produced satisfies the court of the applicant's residence, the burden shifts on to the defendant to show that he is not so resident. The issue of whether the child has acquired a new habitual residence after removal by one party will depend upon the facts of each case. The longer the child lives in the new jurisdiction without challenge, the more likely it is that the child will be said to acquire the habitual residence of those who continue to care for him without opposition.[115]

Article 12 of the Convention provides that where a child has been wrongfully removed or retained, and at the date of the commencement of the proceedings a period of less than one year has elapsed from the date of the wrongful removal or retention, the authority concerned shall order the return of the child forthwith. This means that where more than 12 months have elapsed, the court has jurisdiction to hear the application, but the court will consider any delay in the making of the application and consider whether this means the child has now become settled in his or her new jurisdiction or new residence.

---

113 [1990] 2 FLR 442.
114 See *B v H (Habitual Residence: Wardship)* [2002] 1 FLR 388.
115 See *Re G (Abduction: Rights of Custody)* [2002] 2 FLR 703.

Three primary defences are available where parents allege a wrongful removal:

- Consent or acquiescence.
- There would be a grave risk of harm to the child if returned.
- The child objects to being returned and has attained an age and degree of maturity which is appropriate to take account of the child's views.

These defences are set out in Article 13 of the Convention. Consent must be clear, compelling and unequivocal. It is normally required to be in writing or evidenced in documentary form. It cannot be passive. It must be positive consent to the removal of the child.[116] The burden of proof rests on the person who seeks to prove consent. The means of proof will vary according to the circumstances of each case. A court may hear oral evidence from the parties. It is possible for consent to be inferred from conduct.[117]

The defence regarding grave risk of harm to the child if returned has been given a narrow reading. There must be a weighty risk of substantial harm. Wood J, in the case of *Re D (A Minor) (Child Abduction)*,[118] stated that 'Article 13(b) is likely to apply in the most extreme cases, where evidence of the exposure to physical or psychological harm or otherwise place the child in an intolerable situation'. It must be a risk to a particular child, not a general risk of harm.[119] The burden of proof on the defendant to establish this exception is a very heavy one.[120] Where the abductor alleges fear of violence from the applicant as a basis to establish grave risk of psychological harm to the children, the court will look to whether courts in the requesting country are able to provide protective orders for the abducting party.[121]

It is also a question of fact and degree in cases involving a child's objection to return. It is a matter for discretion for the court to decide, if the evidence presented appears insufficient at first hearing to make a finding one way or the other, whether to order a further investigation into the matter.[122] The court must also seek to determine whether the child is actually giving his or her genuine views or whether the child has been influenced by the abductor or someone in contact with the child.[123]

The court will apply a two-stage test when considering the application of the Article 13 defences:

---

[116] See *Re W (Abduction: Procedure)* [1995] 1 FLR 878.
[117] See *Re M (Abduction: Consent: Acquiescence)* [1999] 1 FLR 171; *Re H (Abduction: Acquiescence)* [1997] 1 FLR 872.
[118] [1989] 1 FLR 97.
[119] See *Re S (Abduction: Custody Rights)* [2002] 2 FLR 815.
[120] See *Re E (A Minor) (Abduction)* [1989] 1 FLR 135.
[121] See *TB v JB (Abduction: Grave Risk of Harm)* [2001] 2 FLR 515.
[122] See *P v P (Minors) (Child Abduction)* [1992] 1 FLR 155.
[123] See *B v K (Child Abduction)* [1993] Fam Law 17, where children aged nine and seven years were held to have attained an age and degree of maturity which was appropriate to take account of their views.

(1) Has a prima facie case been made out under the Article?
(2) Should there be an order to return the children?

The Article 13 threshold is strictly applied. It is only in exceptional circumstances that the court will consider not returning the children.[124]

3.6   FAMILY HOMES AND DOMESTIC VIOLENCE

Advocates struggling with the meaning of 'cohabitants', 'relevant child' and 'associated persons'[125] should always keep in mind that the Family Law Act 1996 (FLA 1996) in fact simplified and streamlined the law in this area. Prior to the effective date of the 1996 Act, advocates struggled with three separate statutes, as well as the inherent jurisdiction of the High Court, any of which might be invoked in order to exclude a violent partner from the family home.

3.6.1   The basics of Part IV of the Family Law Act 1996

(1) A 'relevant child' is:
   (a)   any child who is living with or might reasonably be expected to live with either party to the proceedings;
   (b)   any child in relation to whom an order under the Adoption Act 1976 or the Children Act 1989 is in question in the proceedings; and
   (c)   any other child whose interests the court considers relevant.
(2) 'Cohabitants' are a man and a woman who, though not married to each other, or living together as husband and wife.
(3) A person is 'associated' with another person if:
   (a)   they are or have been married to each other;
   (b)   they are cohabitants or former cohabitants;
   (c)   they live or have lived in the same household, otherwise than merely by reason of one of them being the other's employee, tenant, lodger or boarder;
   (d)   they are relatives;
   (e)   they have agreed to marry one another (whether or not that agreement has been terminated);
   (f)   in relation to any child, they are both parents or have parental responsibility for the child;
   (g)   they are parties to the same family proceedings.

The basic purpose of the FLA 1996 is to regulate the occupation of the family home in the short term, where one party 'associated with' another has been violent, either to the other party or to a relevant child. Three primary orders are available:

---

[124]   See the commentary in *Emergency Remedies in the Family Courts* (Family Law). See also the commentary in the Red Book, 2004.
[125]   See FLA1996, s 62.

(1) A non-molestation injunction, prohibiting the alleged perpetrator of the violence from committing any acts of violence, or otherwise molesting the applicant.
(2) An occupation order, regularising the occupation of the family home, and if necessary excluding the respondent from certain areas of the family home.
(3) An exclusion order, requiring the perpetrator of the violence to vacate the family home.

All of the orders are designed to be temporary in nature. The FLA 1996 is not intended to determine ownership rights of the family home.[126] Advocates appearing for applicants must first determine whether the applicant fits under one of the provisions of the statute. The applicant must be:

(1) entitled to occupy a dwelling-house by virtue of an interest in a lease or contract; or
(2) have matrimonial rights in relation to a dwelling-house, either by being a current spouse of someone who has rights to that home, or a former spouse of someone contending they have a right to occupy that home; or
(3) be a cohabitant or former cohabitant with someone who has an existing right to occupy the dwelling house; or
(4) be a spouse or former spouse of someone where neither party has a right currently to occupy the former matrimonial home, yet is occupying the home (or claiming to have a right to occupy the home) through a bare licence. (These situations are rare, but exist. For example, two squatters might claim a right to occupy, even though no legal right to occupy will exist.)

Occupation orders may be made under any of five different sections, and each of the sections is a self-contained code.[127] The correct section depends upon the status of each of the parties. The most common application is by a wife or female partner of a violent man under s 33, where the applicant has an estate or interest in or matrimonial home rights in the dwelling-house. Section 33(6) sets out the test for the court. The court will assess the following:

(a) The housing needs and resources of each of the parties and any relevant child.
(b) The financial resources of the parties.
(c) Likely effect of any order or any decision by the court on the health, safety and well-being of the parties and of any relevant child.
(d) The conduct of the parties in relation to each other and otherwise.

---

[126] FLA 1996, s 36 orders, applying to cohabitants and former cohabitants, may only last for six months. See s 36(10). The order may be extended once, for a further six months. There is no time limit on s 33 orders, but courts will usually hear within a short period of time ancillary relief applications that will result in orders that terminate any occupation orders that have been made prior to the application.
[127] See FLA 1996, ss 33, 35-38.

If it appears to the court that the applicant or any relevant child is likely to suffer significant harm attributable to the conduct of the respondent if an order under s 33 containing one or more of the provisions mentioned in s 33(3) is not made, the court shall make the order unless it appears to the court that:

(a) the respondent or any relevant child is likely to suffer significant harm if the order is made; and

(b) the harm likely to be suffered by the respondent or child in that event is as great as, or greater than, the harm attributable to conduct of the respondent which is likely to be suffered by the applicant or a child if the order is made.

This test – now known as the 'balance of harm' test – has caused courts some difficulties. It has now been held that courts must consider s 33(7) the balance of harm test, before looking at the factors under s 33(6).[128]

Advocates for either party must address the balance of harm test as an item of urgency when discussing the matter with the client. In cases where there are serious acts of violence, the court will have no difficulty in finding the balance of harm test in favour of the applicant.

Courts are now directed to set these matters down as quickly as possible for a fact-finding hearing. What this means, in practice, is that the cases are listed within several days or weeks, but in a time slot not sufficient to allow extensive evidence. Therefore documentation is the key. If there is a Police report, or a hospital report, these must be produced on behalf of the applicant in order to convince the court of the seriousness of the alleged acts. One District Judge who hears many of these applications at the Principal Registry said to me that only with documentation, or with independent evidence by some reasonably unbiased third party, could he justify making an order excluding the respondent from the family home. Many times, there simply is not sufficient time for the district judge to make a decision regarding which party is exaggerating or lying regarding any incident. What happens then is that a district judge will be likely to make an occupation order, regulating the occupation of the home. A certain room will be likely to be set aside for the applicant. Enforcement of these orders, however, is problematic. Again, unbiased third party confirmation is required in most cases before a court will act.

Advocates must also explain to respondents that if the court makes a relevant order, and if it appears to the court that the respondent has used or threatened violence against the applicant or a relevant child, the court is obliged to attach a power of arrest to one or more provisions of the order, unless the court is satisfied in all the circumstances of the case the applicant or the child will be adequately protected without such a power of arrest.[129]

---

128   See *Chalmers v Johns* [1999] 1 FLR 392.
129   See FLA 1996, s 47.

In practice, courts routinely attach powers of arrest where violence is proved.[130] Advocates must explain carefully to the respondent the result of a breach of an order where there is a power of arrest. The respondent will be arrested upon notice to the police of the alleged breach. The respondent will be held overnight at a police station and delivered the next court day to the court where the order was made. The constable need not have an arrest warrant to arrest the respondent, as long as there was reasonable cause for suspecting the respondent to be in breach of the order. Where a person arrested under a power of arrest cannot be brought to a court, he may be brought before the relevant judicial authority at any convenient place.[131]

Children under 16 may not apply for an occupation order or a non-molestation order save with the leave of the court. The court may grant leave only if it is satisfied that the child has sufficient understanding to make the proposed application for the occupation or non-molestation order.[132]

Many cases are settled at the door of the court with the acceptance by the applicant of undertakings given to the court by the respondent, usually in the form of undertakings not to use or threaten violence, and/or undertaking not to enter or attempt to enter the former matrimonial home, or a part of that home. The virtue of undertakings is that it avoids a fact-finding exercise by the judge. No admissions are made when a party gives an undertaking.[133] The point of doing so is to avoid litigation where possible, in the situation, for example, where the husband has already left the family home. Explaining this to the clients, both applicants and respondents, is difficult. It seems counter-intuitive to an innocent party to give an undertaking not to do something that the party claims he has never done in any event. Nevertheless, on many occasions it is in the respondent's best interests not to fight an application under the FLA 1996, unless the respondent seeks to remain in the home, or unless the respondent is able to show that the applicant is lying or exaggerating. Clients must understand that the occupation orders are temporary. All property disputes will eventually be resolved under the Matrimonial Causes Act 1973 in the usual way, once the ancillary relief application has been made.

3.7 THE HUMAN RIGHTS ACT 1998 AND THE EUROPEAN CONVENTION FOR THE PROTECTION OF HUMAN RIGHTS

There was some debate, when the Human Rights Act 1998 (HRA 1998) came into effect, whether application of the European Convention in family

---

130 See *Chechi v Bashier* [1999] 2 FLR 489.
131 See President's Direction of 17 December 1997. The court also has the power to remand the respondent under Schedule, either on bail or in custody.
132 FLA 1996, s 43.
133 FLA 1996, s 46.

proceedings would really change judicial behaviour in this area. After all, the CA 1989 was compliant with the European Convention. There was no doubt that the 'best interests of the child' principle complied with the European Convention. It was felt that those who claimed that the incorporation of the European Convention into domestic law would radically change our approach to family proceedings would quickly be shown to be mistaken.

In fact, however, the application of the European Convention to family proceedings *has* radically changed the behaviour of lawyers and judges, even though the actual changes in the law brought about by application of the HRA 1998 have been minimal. But every lawyer and every judge must consider - in each and every case - the implications of Convention rights[134]. In other words, the narrative of the case must always be recast in terms of the European Convention. This serves, I submit, to work subtle changes on the lawyers' perception of the essential narrative of each case. Perhaps this was best summed up by Brooke LJ in the case of *Mubarak v Mubarak*[135], where the court sought to apply the European Convention to the Debtors Act 1869:

> 'The [European Convention] is doing work of considerable value in shining light into some of the dustier corners of our law. The experience of this case shows, at any rate to my satisfaction, that corners do not get much dustier than those inhabited by section 5 of the Debtors Act 1869 and the prescribed procedures of that Act.'

For family lawyers, Article 8 obviously is the most important source of law contained in the Convention. Article 8 provides as follows:

(1) Everyone has a right to respect for his private and family life, his home and his correspondence.
(2) There shall be no interference by a public authority with the exercise of this right except such as in accordance with the law and is necessary in a democratic society in the interest of national security, public safety or the economic well-being of the country, for the prevention of disorder or crime, for the protection of health or morals, or for the protection of the rights and freedom of others.

---

[134] Indeed, the HRA 1998, at s 3, provides that all primary and subordinate legislation must be read and given effect in a way compatible with Convention rights. Therefore, every court or tribunal determining any question which has arisen in connection with a Convention right must take into account judgments, decisions, declarations or advisory opinions of the European Court of Human Rights, any opinion of the European Commission of Human Rights, any decisions of the Committee of Ministers taken under Article 46 of the Convention. In retrospect, how could it ever have been argued that the HRA 1998 would not change how we look at family law cases?

[135] [2001] 1 FLR 698, CA. In that case, Brooke LJ was referring to the new CPR Practice Directions regarding committals, which provided that the burden of proof was that the allegations be proved beyond reasonable doubt. The applicant in committal proceedings argued in *Mubarak* that this burden did not apply to judgment summonses. Brooke LJ emphasised that in order to comply with Article 6, it would be necessary to read into the Direction a requirement that this burden also applies to an application for a judgment summons.

A father who has wrongly been denied any contact with his child has rights protected by s 8 of the CA 1989. To recast the narrative in Article 8 terms, the father has a right to a family life. The government, by failing to provide an adequate remedy for the father who is being wrongfully refused contact with his child, has breached the father's rights under Article 8 for a family life.[136] The interference by the public authority with the exercise of the father's rights would not be in accordance with the law, would not be necessary in a democratic society in the interests of public safety or for the prevention of disorder or a crime, and would not be necessary for the protection of the rights and freedom of others.

In most cases, the recasting of the narrative does not result in a change of judicial behaviour. But in each and every case that exercise must be undertaken. There are cases where the source of law will prove vitally important.[137]

Perhaps the most important application of the Convention in family proceedings came in the public law case of *Re C and B (Children) (Care Order: Future Harm)* [2001] 1 FLR 611. In that case, the Court of Appeal, per Hale LJ, reframed the questions before it and, by doing so, created new law. The court, in seeking to frame the question in a way that takes account of the rights claimed under the Convention, held that the actions of public authorities must be 'proportionate'. By that rule, the action taken by a local authority to protect a child has to be proportionate to the nature and gravity of that feared harm. The principle that also arises from that case is that under the Convention the local authority must work to support, and eventually to reunite, the family unless the risk is so high that the child's welfare requires permanent removal. This case is discussed more extensively at Chapter 4, section 4.4.2. The important point for present purposes is this: the reframing of the issues into Human Rights Act terms radically changed not only the outcome of the case, but no doubt the future landscape as well.

Advocates must be prepared to raise all questions concerning breaches of the European Convention within any family proceedings, whether under the CA 1989, the Matrimonial Causes Act 1973, or any other Act. Section 7(1)(b) of

---

[136] Note that it is not claimed that the mother breached the father's Article 6 rights. The Convention is aimed solely at government actions, or those who actively conspire with government actors. Section 6 of the HRA 1998 provides that 'It is unlawful for a public authority to act in a way which is incompatible with a Convention right.' But a court is itself a 'public authority' and therefore cannot act in a way that violates rights protected by the Convention: HRA 1998, s 6(3)(a).

[137] See HRA 1998, s 8(2), (3). No award of damages is to be made unless, taking account of all the circumstances of the case, the court is satisfied that the award is necessary to afford satisfaction to the person in whose favour it is made. The court will look to see if any other relief has been granted by any other court. Damages can only be awarded by a court with jurisdiction to do so. Theoretically, however, the inherent jurisdiction of the High Court to be used to support a claim for damages. In the ordinary case, a claim for damages would have to be made in civil free-standing proceedings or within judicial review proceedings. See Supreme Court Act 1981, s 31 and CPR 1998, Part 54.

the HRA 1998 provides that complaints regarding Convention rights might be brought in any court or tribunal in which proceedings are brought by or at the instigation of a public authority, or constitute an appeal against the decision of a court or tribunal. It is possible, under s 7(1)(a) of the 1998 Act, to file a separate claim regarding the violation of a right protected by the Convention. Where the claim under s 7(1)(a) relates to a judicial act, the claim must be by way of judicial review or by way of appeal.[138] A claim under s 8(1)(a) in relation to a judicial act must be brought in the High Court. Otherwise, a claim in relation to an act of a public authority may be brought in any court.[139]

A free-standing claim should be made under CPR 1998, Part 8.

Article 8 claims involve a two-stage process:

(1) Does the applicant have a family life that has suffered an interference?
(2) Is the interference with family life justified?

To answer the second question, the court will ask:

(a) whether the interference was in accordance with law;
(b) whether the interference was in pursuit of a legitimate aim; and
(c) whether the interference was necessary in a democratic society.

The Convention does not define family life. At present, it is accepted that the term encompasses at least the following:

(1) relationships between all children and their parents, regardless of their marital status or their living arrangements;[140]
(2) relationships between siblings;[141]
(3) alternative relationships, for example that between a female to a male transsexual, his partner and the child born in to that relationship by artificial insemination by donor;[142]
(4) relationships between extended family members such as between grandparents and their grandchildren, or nieces and nephews and uncles and aunts;[143]
(5) relationships between adoptive parents and children;
(6) relationships between parents and children born into second relationships, or children born as a result of an adulterous affair.[144]

---

[138]   See HRA 1998, s 9.
[139]   See CPR 1998, r 7.11; see discussion in *The Family Court Practice* (Family Law, 2004).
[140]   *Johnson v Ireland* (1986) 9 EHRR 203; *Boughanemi v France* (1996) 25 EHRR 228.
[141]   *Olsson v Sweden (No 1)* (1988) 11 EHRR 259.
[142]   *X, Y and Z v UK* (1997) 24 EHRR 143.
[143]   *Boyle v UK* (1993) 19 EHRR 181.
[144]   *Jolie and Lebrun v Belgium* (14 December 1986, unreported).

The European Court has not held, however, that same sex couples and their children enjoy a family life. Adoption will extinguish family life. Taking a child into care will not. Divorce will not end family life under the Article. An absent parent therefore has an Article 8 right to have reasonable contact with his or her child.

Advocates must be aware of European jurisprudence regarding family law issues. In *Yousef v The Netherlands* [2003] 1 FLR 210, the European Court of Human Rights held that when the Article 8 rights of parents and those of a child are at stake, the child's interests are the paramount consideration, so that if any balancing of the interests is necessary, the child's interests must prevail.[145] The European Court has also held that the phrase 'in accordance with law' refers not only to domestic law, but also to a more general notion of the rule of law as a protection against arbitrary interference by the state.[146] It would therefore arguably be a breach of Article 8 for a court to give social workers unfettered discretion to remove a child from the family home.

The President's Practice Direction of 24 July 2000 sets out the procedure to be followed when raising an issue under the HRA 1998. Where the proceedings were care proceedings or public family proceedings which have come to an end, the appropriate remedy may well be a free-standing application under s 7(1)(a) of the HRA 1998. Where the proceedings are ongoing, however, the complaint should normally be dealt with within the context of the proceedings and by the court dealing with those proceedings.[147] Only in an exceptional case would it be appropriate to treat human rights arguments as raising a discrete issue to be heard in the High Court. If the case requires transfer to the High Court, the whole case must be transferred.[148]

Article 6 of the Convention provides that everyone is entitled to a fair and public hearing within a reasonable time by an independent and impartial tribunal established by law. The concept of a 'fair' hearing means that each side should have roughly 'equality of arms'. Each side must have an opportunity to present his or her case under conditions that do not unduly penalise either party.[149] Both parties must have access to all evidence.[150] The European Court of Human Rights has held that the current system in this jurisdiction of hearing

---

145 See also *L v UK* [2000] 2 FLR 322; *K and T v Finland* [2000] 2 FLR 118; *P, C and S v UK* [2002] 2 FLR 631 (ECHR). See also *Venema v The Netherlands* [2003] 1 FLR 551, where the European Court held that a decision by a Child Welfare Board to remove a child from the care of a mother suspected of harming the child, without first putting to the mother the concerns of the doctors, breached the mother's and child's Article 8 rights.

146 See *Olsson v Sweden (No 1)* (1988) 11 EHRR 259.

147 See *Re L (Care Proceedings: Human Rights Claims)* [2003] EWHC 665, [2003] Fam Law 466; *Re L (Care: Assessment; Fair Trial)* [2002] EWHC 1379, [2002] EWHC 1379, [2002] 2 FLR 730.

148 See *Re L* (above).

149 See *Dombo Bebeer BC v The Netherlands* (1994) 18 EHRR 213.

150 *Saunders v UK* (1996) 23 EHRR 313.

cases involving children in private did not violate Article 6. The court in that case also held that the prohibition against the disclosure of documents from the case did not run foul of Article 6.

In the case of *L v Finland* [2000] 2 FLR 118, the court held there was a violation of Article 6 because no oral hearing had been held prior to the decision to take a child into care.

3.8   CASE LAW UNDER THE CHILDREN ACT 1989

The following cases show courts struggling with the difficulties of monitoring and limiting the discretion of trial judges in a jurisdiction where discretion is supposedly encouraged. It is difficult at times to draw general conclusions from the reported cases. Advocates must learn to recognise these disputes. Where the cases are otherwise unreported, they may be found on the online service Lawtel. Unreported cases are not useful as citations in court, but, again, the cases help the beginning advocate gain an understand of the conflicting narratives that courts frequently face.

That being said, the following cases give the beginning advocate a good background to the essential principles of the CA 1989. And more importantly, the cases reveal the conflicting narratives judges must face in every contested hearing. These narratives, in turn, reveal the fault lines in the CA 1989 or, more precisely, show how certain disputes in family relations arise repeatedly. Advocates must learn to recognise these disputes where the cases are otherwise unreported; they may be found on the online service LAWTEL. Unreported cases are not useful as citations but, again, the cases help the advocates gain an understanding of the narratives that a court will face.

Re S (Specific Issue Order: Religion: Circumcision)

Fam Div [2004] EWHC 1282 (Fam) (Baron J)

A parent must gain the consent of the other parent, or the court, before subjecting a child to circumcision.

Re B (A Child)

CA (22 April 2004, unreported) (Thorpe LJ, Buxton LJ)

An order under the CA 1989, s 91(14) was not to be made by the court of its own motion without giving a proper opportunity to the affected party, particularly where that party was a litigant in person.

Re H (A Child)

CA [2002] EWCA Civ 190 (Thorpe LJ, Buxton LJ)

An order restricting a mother from using her preferred forenames for her son rather than those officially registered by the father in external dealings within the community of the primary home was set aside.

Re A (Children) (Specific Issue Order: Parental Dispute)

CA (1 September 2000, unreported) (Simon Brown LJ, Robert Walker LJ)

On the facts of this case, the judge did not err in making an order that children of a French father and an English mother living in England were to attend a French-speaking school in England, though there was no general principle that such a course should be followed in other cases.

Re U (A Minor) (Specific Issue Orders: Muslim Upbringing and Circumcision), sub nom Re U (A Minor), sub nom Re J (Child's Religious Upbringing and Circumcision)

CA [2000] 1 FLR 571, (2000) 52 BMLR 82 (Dame Elizabeth Butler-Sloss (President), Schiemann LJ, Thorpe LJ)

Notwithstanding the provisions of the CA 1989, s 2(7), where more than one person (or a local authority with a care order under s 33(6) of the Act) shared parental responsibility, no one holder could have a male child circumcised against the wishes of the other(s) without an order of the court. In deciding whether to make that order the court would consider each case upon its own facts.

Camden London Borough Council (Applicant) v (1) A (2) B (3) C (by her Guardian ad Litem) (Respondents), sub nom Re C (A Child)

Fam Div [2000] 2 WLR 270, (1999) 50 BMLR 283 (Wilson J)

In deciding whether to order that a baby be subjected to a blood test with a view to determining whether she had been infected with HIV, a court invited to override the wishes of the parents had to move extremely cautiously, but where the case for testing was overwhelming, the court would make such an order. The law could not, however, prevent a mother from breastfeeding her baby despite the fact that there was a risk of infection to the baby therefrom.

W (A Child): A (A Child): B (Children)

CA [2000] 2 WLR 258: [2000] 1 WLR 634: [1999] 2 FLR 930 (Butler-Sloss LJ, Auld LJ, Manetell LJ)

Three appeals concerned the circumstances in which a child registered at birth in one surname might have that name changed by deed poll by one parent against the wishes of the other parent, in the light of the House of Lords' decision in *Dawson v Wearmouth* [1999] 2 WLR 960. Approach of the appellate courts in cases under the CA 1989. Leave to appeal to the House of Lords refused.

Dawson v Wearmouth, sub nom Re W (A Minor)

HL [1999] 2 WLR 960, [1999] 2 All ER 353, [1999] 1 FLR 1167 (Lord Slynn of Hadley, Lord Mackay, Lord Jauncey, Lord Clyde, Lord Hobhouse)

In order to justify an order requiring a change of name, considerations relative to the child's welfare had to be advanced for that purpose. A court should not make an order for the change of name unless there was some evidence that this would lead to an improvement from the point of view of the welfare of the child. The change of the child's name was not an infringement of the father's rights under Article 8 European Convention on Human Rights.

Re G (Children)

CA (25 January 2005, unreported) (Thorpe LJ) (available on LAWTEL)

A judge has erred in his assessment of the emotional impact that a refusal would have on a primary carer applying for permission to permanently remove children from the jurisdiction.

B v B

CA [2004] EWCA Civ 681 (Arden LJ, Wall LJ)

Court orders that were on the face regular, but were in fact made without jurisdiction, remained in force until they were discharged. The English court had jurisdiction to make orders under the CA 1989 in relation to a child who had resided with her mother and father in Scotland before her parents separated and she and her mother came to live in England.

Re R (A Child)

CA (13 October 2003, unreported) (Thorpe LJ, Jonathan Parker LJ, Dyson LJ) (available on LAWTEL)

The judge had not been wrong to grant a residence order in favour of the natural parent, where the exceptional hallmark of the case was the expert evidence to the lack of the child's attachment to the foster parents.

In the matter of G (A Child), sub nom PG v LMR, sub nom In re G (A Child) (Contempt: Committal)

CA (2003) (Dame Elizabeth Butler-Sloss (President), Mummery LJ, May LJ)

A father who had placed details of the case between himself and his child's mother on the website 'Families Need Fathers' had been wrongly committed for contempt of court due to procedural flaws in the committal hearing.

Re D (Stay of Children Act Proceedings)

Fam Div [2003] 2 FLR 1159 (Bracewell J)

The choice between international jurisdictions was not an issue that was directly related to the upbringing of a child; therefore, although the issue was important, it fell outside the ambit of the CA 1989, s 1(1)(a).

H (Children)

CA [2001] 2 FLR 1277 (Thorpe LJ, Astill J)

Where the father sought leave to remove his children to Northern Ireland, the Court of Appeal would not interfere with a judge's findings to refuse such leave where it was quite apparent that the children needed the help and support of both parents, which could only be achieved if they remained in England.

Re L (A Child): Re V (A Child): Re M (A Child): Re H (Children)

CA [2001] 2 WLR 339, [2000] 4 All ER 609, [2000] 2 FLR 334 (Dame Elizabeth Butler-Sloss (President), Thorpe LJ, Waller LJ)

In cases where contact was refused against a background of domestic violence, there was no presumption that on proof of domestic violence the offending parent had to surmount a prima facie barrier of no contact. As a matter of principle, domestic violence of itself did not constitute a bar to contact.

Re C (Child) sub nom Re C (Leace to Remove from the Jurisdiction)

CA [2000] 2 FLR 457 (Morritt LJ, Thorpe LJ, Chadwick LJ)

The Court of Appeal should not substitute its own decision where a judge at first instance had the advantage of seeing and hearing the witnesses. The judge's decision whether to grant a mother leave to remove a child form the jurisdiction had been difficult and finely balanced and it is important to respect his judgment.

Re G (Abduction: Wrongful Removal)

CA [2000] 1 FLR 78 (Swinton Thomas LJ, Mummery LJ)

An order demanding that a child be returned from South Africa was upheld. Where the law provided for the challenge of an order made ex parte there was no breach of Article 6 of the European Convention on Human Rights.

W v T sub nom Re W (Minor) (Contact Application: Procedure)

Fam Div [2000] 1 FLR 263 (Wilson J)

There was a wealth of authority to the effect that the granting of leave to apply for contact under the CA 1989 was a substantial judicial decision. Accordingly the magistrates had fallen into error in despatching the application for leave without arranging a hearing to which both parties were invited to attend.

Re Z (Abduction: Non-Convention Country)

Fam Div [1999] 1 FLR 1270 (Charles J)

In an application for the return of a child to a country which was not a signatory to the Hague Convention there was a presumption that, in the absence of good reasons to the contrary, generally the welfare of a child was promoted by his return to the country where he was habitually resident.

Re S (Removal from Jurisdiction)

Fam Div [1999] 1 FLR 850 (Richard Anelay QC)

A father's contact with his son, who the mother was removing from the jurisdiction to live in Chile, could be adequately safeguarded by the authentication of the English contact order by the Chilean Supreme Court.

Re D (Abduction: Acquiescence)

Fam Div [1999] 1 FLR 36 (Cazalet J)

Habitual residence was a matter of fact to be determined by reference to all the circumstances and relevant authorities.

E v E (Child Abduction: Intolerable Situation)

Fam Div [1998] 2 FLR 980 (Hughes J)

The wishes and needs of the mother were not the test in deciding to return children under the Hague Convention. Instead the test was whether the children would be placed in an intolerable situation if returned.

Re K (Application to Remove from Jurisdiction)

Fam Div [1998] 2 FLR 1006 (Charles J)

In an application to remove a child from the jurisdiction an assessment of what was in the best interests of the children was not determined by reference as to who had been the best primary carer but was governed by considering who the children had been living with and their relationship with the custodial and the non-custodial parent. Consideration was also given to where the children had been living and the competing advantages and disadvantages of the countries.

Re W (Minors) (Child Abduction: Unmarried Father): Re B (A Minor) (Child Abduction: Unmarried Father)

Fam Div [1998] 3 WLR 1372, [1998] 2 FLR 146 (Hale J)

Two cases in which applications under the Hague Convention on the Civil Aspects of International Child Abduction 1980 were made by unmarried fathers with differing results. A child could not be removed from the jurisdiction whilst a parental responsibility order was pending.

Re P (A Minor) (Abduction), sub nom P v P (Abduction: Acquiesce)

CA [1998] 2 FLR 835 (Hirst LJ, Ward LJ, Chadwick LJ)

Where parties are conducting without prejudice negotiations to reach an agreement following the abduction of a child, the wronged parent cannot be

held to have acquiesced to the removal of the child if those negotiations do not result in an agreement.

M v M (Abduction: England and Scotland)

CA [1997] 2 FLR 264 (Butler-Sloss LJ, Millett LJ, Aldous LJ)

Child abduction of children by wife from Scotland and successful appeal in England as to forum conveniens being Scotland for matrimonial proceedings by the husband.

Re G (A Minor) (Revocation of a Freeing for Adoption Order)

HL [1997] 2 WLR 747, [1997] 2 All ER 534, [1997] 2 FLR 202 (Lord Browne-Wilkinson, Lord Lloyd, Lord Nicholls, Lord Steyn, Lord Hoffmann)

The revocation of a freeing for adoption order under the Adoption Act 1976, s 20 does not necessarily involve sole parental responsibility for the child being wholly restored to the former parent. That responsibility may be shared with the local authority.

C v W (Contact: Leave to Apply)

Fam Div [1999] 1 FLR 916 (Hale J)

An order under the CA 1989, s 91(14) was entirely suitable where a father had shown complete disregard for the requirements of the court and for his son when seeking contact and residence. The court was entitled to ask for a demonstration of care for the child rather than the father's own convenience and interests.

Re D (Prohibited Steps Order)

CA (1996) 2 FLR 273 (Neill LJ, Ward LJ)

A prohibited steps order cannot be used to prevent a father of children staying overnight at the matrimonial home following contact with the children. This was not a permissible order under the CA 1989, s 11(7).

Re C S (Expert Witnesses)

Fam Div (1996) 2 FLR 115 (Bracewell J)

Guidance on proper procedure for instructing expert witnesses and preparing for hearing in child cases.

Re H (Minors: Prohibited Steps Order)

CA [1995] 1 WLR 667, [1995] 4 All ER 110 (Butler-Sloss LJ, Sir Ralph Gibson)

Making a prohibited steps order against a non-party.

Re W (A Minor) (Welfare Reports: Appeals)

CA (1995) Times, 25 January

Judge's request for a welfare report in the course of prohibited steps proceedings not appealable.

Chapter 4

CHILD PROTECTION LITIGATION

4.1 INTRODUCTION

Litigation is necessarily concerned with the past: a corporation's employee decides to drop a supplier and break a contract; a careless driver runs a red light; a desperate man robs a bank. Juries and judges seek to determine precisely what occurred in the past, and once this fact-finding exercise is completed, the law assigns certain reactions: compensation is paid to the non-breaching supplier; damages are paid to the injured pedestrian; a desperate man is sent to jail.

Public law litigation involving children, however, is different. The past is important, obviously, but the primary role of the judge is to predict the future. The judge must seek to discover what will be in the best interests of a child throughout the child's minority. Historically, judges have sought to do this by applying the moral norms of upper middle class, male barristers. More recently, however, in particular after the 1960s and the onset of public funding of child protection litigation, judges increasingly have placed before them evidence from 'experts': psychiatrists, psychologists, paediatricians, and social workers. These experts are explicitly instructed to seek to predict the future. Judges therefore now base their own predictions of the future welfare of a child not on 'common sense' or simply the received wisdom of an elderly lawyer, but instead on the expert medical evidence that has been presented during the trial.

The increasing reliance by courts on expert evidence in all areas of law has been commented on extensively and it is not the intention here to rehearse the arguments about the proliferation of experts, nor to join the debate about the efficacy of restricting experts in the manner contemplated by the civil procedure reforms of 1998. What advocates practising in this area must know and understand, however, is that in public law child protection litigation, the experts almost always drive the narrative. That is, the experts, unless challenged, will set the framework for the story the court must tell. Advocates appearing for clients who do not accept the expert opinion on offer in a case must seek to prevent the expert from controlling the narrative.

In Chapter 1 of this text, it was noted that advocates seeking to cross-examine experts must concentrate on three questions:

(1) How did the expert conduct the assessment?

(2) What did the expert assess?

(3) Why did the assessment reach a conclusion that was reached?

In order to take back control of the narrative from an expert, an advocate must seek to show how an expert has made an error on one of the three fundamental questions posed above. For example, with regard to question (1), the advocate would query the method used by the expert, pointing out a flaw in the method that would result in an erroneous conclusion. With regard to question (2), the advocate would seek to show that the expert based his or her opinion on erroneous factual assumptions. The expert would be seen not to have assessed the actual facts in this case, but to have made assumptions that were in fact not proved to be true.

Question (3) poses different problems for the advocate. Almost invariably, an attack on the conclusion reached by an expert will fail unless there are appropriate attacks on questions (1) and (2). The only exception to this is where there is contrary evidence available supporting the advocate's case.

I seek in this chapter to set out briefly the legal context for public law applications under Part IV of the Children Act 1989 (CA 1989), briefly describe the five types of cases commonly seen in public law cases in England and Wales, and explore the types of evidence that will likely be confronting the advocate in each of those cases.

4.2   CHILD PROTECTION UNDER THE CHILDREN ACT 1989

All advocates seek to use legal language precisely. Lawyers are often criticised for speaking only in legal jargon, but lawyers often do so because they wish to speak in words that are clearly understood by the judge and the opposing party. Advocates in child protection litigation quickly learn that several phrases bear particular attention. The first, of course, is 'significant harm'.

The CA 1989, at s 47, provides that a local authority must make enquiries about any child in that local authority's area whom the authority has reasonable cause to suspect may be suffering significant harm. If the local authority brings the matter to court, the court must then determine if there are reasonable grounds for believing the child is suffering or likely to suffer significant harm as a result of care given the child by his parents before it makes an interim care order.[1]

---

1   The 'threshold criteria' definition is needlessly complex and lawyerly: is the child suffering, or likely to suffer, significant harm from the care given the child by the parents, that care not being what it would be reasonable to expect a parent to give to that child, or the child is suffering significant harm and the child is beyond parental control.

And at the substantive hearing of the case, the court cannot make a care order or a supervision order unless it finds the child is suffering or likely to suffer significant harm from the care given the child by her parents.

It would make matters easier for advocates and judges if the phrase that is at the very centre of all public law children litigation were capable of precise definition. But of course that is impossible. The harm depends on the context of each situation, and advocates must understand that the phrase 'significant harm' has to be redefined in each and every case.

Section 31 of the CA 1989 defines harm as 'ill treatment or the impairment of health or development'. Harm must be 'significant' in the sense that it is 'full of meaning or import; highly expressive or suggestive'. There are two slightly different meanings that might be given to the term significant. The first is simply that the word is meant to mean 'more serious' harm than what might ordinarily be expected. The emphasis is on degree, on measuring the amount of harm. The second meaning, however, is more appropriate: this is that harm is significant in that it is *suggestive* of harm that is more than what might ordinarily be expected. It is harm that is full of meaning or import and suggests that there is a need for restriction of the parents' rights.[2]

Each local authority is by statute obligated to maintain a Child Protection Register. There are four categories on the register:

(1) Neglect
The term is defined in *Working Together Under the Children Act 1989* as persistent or severe neglect of a child or the failure to protect the child from exposure to any kind of danger, including cold or starvation or extreme failure to carry out important aspects of care, resulting in the significant impairment of the child's health or development, including non-organic failure to thrive.

(2) Physical injury
The term is defined as actual or likely physical injury to a child. The term includes both failure to prevent physical injury, as well as deliberate acts by a parent to injure the child.

(3) Sexual abuse
The term is defined as actual or likely sexual exploitation of a child or adolescent.

---

2   See discussion of this in White, Carr & Lowe, *The Children Act in Practice* (Butterworths, 2nd edn, 1995), pp 183–190.

(4) Emotional abuse

This category in one sense is recognised as a catchall category. It involves all abuse or involves some emotional ill treatment.[3] The category is defined as actual or likely severe adverse effect on the emotional and behavioural development of a child caused by persistent or severe emotional ill treatment or rejection.

Advocates or parents must note that parents do have certain rights during the investigation process, both under Article 6 and Article 8 of the European Convention on Human Rights, and under relevant guidelines issued by the Secretary of State and made applicable to local authorities by s 7 of the Local Authority Social Services Act 1970. These rights are not confined to the purely judicial part of Children Act proceedings where local authorities seek public law orders. Unfairness in any stage of the litigation process might also involve breaches of the parents' rights to a fair trial under Article 6. If this proposition had not been clear to all, Mr Justice Munby has now removed all doubt in his judgment in the case of *Re L (Care Assessment: Fair Trial)*.[4]

In *Re L*, the parents had been excluded from certain meetings held by the local authority where the family had been discussed. Mr Justice Munby held that this meant that the decision-making process, seen as a whole, had not involved the mother sufficiently to provide her with the required protection of her interests. She had been wrongly excluded from meetings, and crucially, had been wrongly excluded from the decisive meeting which she had specifically asked to attend. She had therefore had no opportunity to answer criticisms of her which had been put to the psychiatrist at the decisive meeting. The mother had been kept in the dark by the local authority's failure to disclose a series of documents and communications. The mother had been marginalised by the lack of direct contact with the local authority key worker.[5] Social workers will also have copies of health visitors' reports and copies of any correspondence between the social workers and health visitors and GPs. Again, where criticisms of the parents have been levelled in these communications, the parents should be given a copy and should be given a right to reply.

The local authority in most but certainly not all cases brought under Part IV of the CA 1989 will have investigated the family for a considerable period of time prior to initiating proceedings. Even a short investigation will generate reams of documents, and advocates in public litigation for and against local authorities

---

3   Experts have often complained that local authorities seek findings in sexual abuse cases that are impossible to make, and fail to seek findings of emotional abuse that might also be present in a sex abuse case. Findings of emotional abuse are also easier for the judge to make. See Brophy, et al, *Child Psychiatry and Child Protection Litigation* (Gaskell Academic Series, Royal College of Psychiatrists, 2001), p 85.

4   [2002] EWCA 1379 (Fam), [2002] 2 FLR 730 (FD).

5   Mr Justice Munby also sought to set out what he termed the 'decision-making matrix' in cases involving potential future neglect of a child. This discussion is mandatory reading for advocates appearing in neglect cases. See *Re L (Care Assessment: Fair Trial)* [2003] EWCA 1379, [2002] 2 FLR 764.

need to understand precisely how these documents are generated, the purpose for which they are retained, and whether the documents are discoverable by parties to public law child protection litigation.

One of the first documents in any social services file on a child and family will be a running chronology of local authority involvement with the family.[6] The chronology will almost always consist of handwritten entries by a number of different social workers and the entries should be all inclusive, that is the information revealed will be both the good and the bad regarding the family under observation. Social services files will also contain copies of professionals' meetings, including meetings between and among social workers, health visitors, members of the medical profession who have had contact with the family, mental health services (if they are involved) and police, if there are ongoing criminal investigations. While it is possible for the local authority to exclude parents from these professionals' meetings, the parent must be given a copy of any minutes generated by the meeting. The parent must be given an opportunity to respond to any factual allegations that are made during the meeting. Any response made by the parents should be presented to all the experts involved.

Of course the advocate for the parent will seek to convince the court that the local authority has treated that parent unfairly, but the advocate must not lose sight that treating the parent fairly is not, in the end, the goal of the CA 1989, nor is it likely to stop the court from making an order that is seen to protect the child in the appropriate case. It must be remembered that in *Re L*, above, Mr Justice Munby in the end made a care order regarding the child, finding that while the local authority had acted unfairly, the judge's duty was to make a care order if the local authority showed that the grounds existed for one, and the court was convinced that a care order was in the best interest of the child.[7] The advocate for the parent must always keep in mind that the end result sought by the client is the return of the child. All narratives offered by the advocate must necessarily focus more on the parent than on the social worker.

---

[6] High Court Judges have not been reluctant to set out the requirements of social work investigations, and advocates appearing for social services departments must make social workers aware of these requirements *before* the social worker begins his statement. See, generally, *Re E (Care Proceedings: Social Work Practice)* [2000] 2 FLR 254 (Bracewell J); *Re D and K (Care Plan: Twin Track Planning)* [1999] 2 FLR 872 (Bracewell J); *Re R (Child of a Teenage Mother)* [2000] 2 FLR 660 (Bracewell J); *Re R (Care: Disclosure: Nature of Proceedings)* [2002] 1 FLR 755, FD. See also Local Authority Circular of 28 August 1998 (LAC(98)20), which sets out the requirements for social workers who are preparing care plans where adoption is the preferred option. Note the various steps and timetables that must be set out in these care plans.

[7] Mr Justice Munby did keep open in *Re L* the question of whether the parent's Article 6 rights would in the appropriate case trump the child's right to have his best interests be the paramount concern of the court. Munby J opined, however, that the best interests would not necessarily be paramount when considering relief for the parent whose Article 6 rights have been breached because that decision would not be about an aspect of parenting the child. Munby J did note, also, that the child also has Article 6 rights: the right to have the litigation decided without undue delay. All of Munby J's musings, however, are *dicta*.

In the end, the social worker's competence (or lack of it) is not what is being judged.

The social worker's file should also have copies of the minutes of any child protection conferences that have been held. Advocates should note the attendance list, which should be set out at the beginning of each minute. Advocates should note who is *not* on that list: perhaps no school report had been made available; perhaps the health visitor who liked the mother was not there; perhaps the parent had not even been notified of the meeting.

There should also be in the local authority files copies of school reports and copies of reports from any members of the public who might have sought to tell social services what had occurred which placed a child at risk of harm. Very often the names of the accusers will be omitted. These reports must be produced to the parents, even if there is no request to do so. It is vitally important that parents have produced to them all copies of reports regarding adverse comments made about their parenting.

Health visitor reports are almost always vitally important in neglect cases. The health visitor is not, strictly speaking, a social worker. She does not work for the same department as the children's social workers who will be running the Children Act litigation. The health visitor is a National Health Service employee who may not have a great understanding of the principles underlying child protection litigation. But the evidence from the visitor about the condition of the home will often give to the court a more reliable picture of the family's life than a social worker's report, in part because parents do not believe the health visitor is a part of the child protection team. All health visitor reports must be produced to opposing parties, and the local authority must notify the health visitor early in the litigation process that her attendance is likely required at the substantive hearing.

4.2.1   Local authority intervention under the Children Act 1989

Local authorities are of course creatures of statute, and can only act as provided by statute. The CA 1989 provides that local authorities may seek the following public law orders:

(1) a child assessment order;
(2) an emergency protection order;
(3) a supervision order;
(4) a care order.[8]

---

[8]   See CA 1989, ss 31, 43 and 44. A court in any family proceedings also has the power to make a family assistance order, which might mandate that a probation officer or another local authority social worker 'advise, assist and (where appropriate) befriend any person named in the order'. The statute demands that there be exceptional circumstances, and judicial definition for that term has not been given. It has been held that the purpose of the family assistance

Advocates for the parties must as quickly as possible formulate a theory of the case that takes into account the following: first, and most important, any risks the child might suffer harm in the future, and the gravity of the harm that might be suffered; secondly, the likelihood of harm to the child from separation from his parents or carers. The second question will involve considerations of the child's age, his attachment to his carers, his attachment to his siblings, his physical and emotional needs, and the ability of the parents to provide for them in the short term while this litigation proceeds. Underlying all these assessments is the understanding that children are damaged by separation from their psychological parents, even in situations where those parents have caused the children harm. It is a question (as ever in the law) of balancing and contrasting the gravity and likelihood of the harm the child will likely suffer. .

A theory of the case is vitally important early on in the child protection process because the litigation (unlike, say, personal injury litigation, or criminal litigation) is an ongoing, continuous process where theories sometimes are tested on the ground. For example counsel for a 15-year-old mother may propose at the first hearing of the local authority's application for an interim care order that the maternal grandmother will help with care of the child, and therefore the child should remain with mother and grandmother. A court might well make no order and leave the child at home. But when the local authority determines that in fact maternal grandmother is addicted to alcohol and sleeps most of the day, that finding might be presented to the court at a later interim hearing. The mother's theory of the case, in other words, will be tested. It is therefore vitally important that the theory be considered carefully with the lay client before presenting to the court or to the local authority.

4.2.2   The legal framework

Framers of the CA 1989 sought to separate the responsibilities of courts and local authorities. It had been assumed by the framers of the Act, mindful of the supposed evils of wardship jurisdiction where proceedings might last for years, that once a court had determined that a local authority should care for the child the court's oversight for that child should end. That particular framework, however, has now been superseded, in part by the Human Rights Act 1998, but also in part because appellate judges in this country came to understand that this framework provided neither fairness to the parents nor sufficient protection for children in care. The Court of Appeal therefore in a succession of cases sought, in effect, to amend the CA 1989 to comply with the supposed dictates of the European Convention of Human Rights. But the House of Lords refused to allow the most radical judicial amendments to be put into effect. The uncertainty arising from the House of Lords speeches in

---

order is to provide short-term help to a family, to overcome the problems and conflicts associated with their separation or divorce. Help may well be focussed more on the adult rather the child. See *Re DH (A minor) (Child Abuse)* [1994] 1 FLR 679 at 702.

the case of *Re S (Minors) (Care Order: Implementation of Care Plan);
Re W (Minors) (Care Order: Adequacy of Care Plan)*[9] continues, as I write,
to be felt throughout the family court system. The Adoption Act 2002 has now
created new duties for local authorities after the making of care orders. The
Act amends s 26 of the Children Act 1989, and provides a method for
CAFCASS officers and others to bring matters back to court after the making
of final care orders.

The framework for making public orders is as follows:

(1) The local authority must
  (a) prove by a balance of probabilities facts sufficient to convince a trial
      court that the child is suffering significant harm as of the date
      proceedings were initiated or local authority protections were put in
      place; and/or
  (b) show there is a real possibility that the children might suffer significant
      harm in the future; and
  (c) prove this harm was caused (or will be caused) by the care given the
      child by the carers, that care not being what was reasonable to expect
      the parent to give; and/or
  (d) prove facts sufficient to show that the child is beyond parental control
      and would suffer significant harm as a result of being beyond parental
      control.
(2) If the local authority prove the threshold criteria as set out above, the court
    must then consider which public law order, if any, is in the best interest of
    the child. The welfare of the child will be the paramount consideration for
    the court, and the court is directed to consider the welfare checklist set out
    at s 1(3) of the CA 1989.

Advocates for local authorities in particular will be aware of the judgment in
Re R (Care: Disclosure: Nature of Proceedings),[10] where it was held that
those responsible for the preparation of public law cases must have a proper
understanding of the relevant legal principles, the issues in the case and the
procedures of the court. There must be a proper examination of the background
material and the relevant files. There must be a full and proper discussion with
the relevant witnesses, to ensure that, so far as possible, their statements contain
a full and proper account of the relevant matters, which include central matters
seen or heard by that witness, the sources of hearsay being recorded, and the
relevant background to and the circumstances to which the matters set out
took place. The advocates must give full consideration to whether there should
be disclosure of any contemporaneous notes made by witnesses, including those
of the guardian. There must also be a proper consideration of what further
information or materials should be obtained.

9   [2002] UKHL 10, [2002] 1 FLR 815, HL.
10   [2002] 1 FLR 755.

There will often be discussions between counsel for the parents and the local authority prior to the hearing regarding reaching agreement about the conditions necessary for the court to make a public law order. An example is a case where the father is accused of sexually abusing his children. Counsel for the parents states that the father will accept that he caused the children significant harm by emotionally abusing them by, for example, allowing the children to see pornographic videos, or perhaps by not making certain the children did not see the parents' sexual activities; but he denies sexually abusing the children.

Counsel for the local authority will need first to determine whether the facts that are admitted will support the care plan it has drawn up. If the local authority is seeking to remove the children permanently from the care of the father, it is likely that those bare admissions would not permit the court to approve the plan. The local authority would therefore likely have no choice but to go forward with the fact-finding hearing regarding the allegations of sexual abuse, if cogent evidence exists to support the allegation.

The agreement of the parties does not deprive the court of its duty to satisfy itself by evidence that the strict criteria for a care order have been fulfilled. The degree of investigation required, however will vary from case to case. It is a matter for the discretion of the judge as to whether the concessions made by the parents are sufficient to meet the justice of the matter and the best interests of the children. See *Re B (Agreed Findings of Fact);*[11] *Re M (Threshold Criteria: Parental Concession);*[12] *Re W (Children) (Threshold Criteria: Parental Concessions.*[13] In the latter case, the parents' concessions were not accepted. The court held that because the parents accepted no responsibility for the children's sexualised behaviour, there was no firm basis upon which to deal with future applications by the parents for contact with the children. There is no 'issue estoppel' under the Children Act, so the fact the parties present the court with an agreement does not stop the court from directing there be further evidence given. See *Re D (Child: Threshold Criteria).*[14] See also *Oxfordshire County Council v L.*[15]

Courts will now often direct there be split hearings, with the first hearing to be used to make findings of fact regarding disputed allegations of fact. The second hearing, or placement hearing, will be used to make decisions about the children's permanent placement.[16]

Where findings are made on a preliminary issue at a split hearing, there is jurisdiction to hear an appeal if those findings are of crucial importance to the final decision to be made by the trial court. *Re B (Split Hearings:*

[11]   [1998] 2 FLR 968.
[12]   [1999] 1 FLR 728.
[13]   [2001] 1 FCR 139.
[14]   [2001] 1 FLR 274.
[15]   [1998] 1 FLR 70.
[16]   See *Re S (Care Proceedings: Split Hearings)* [1996] 2 FLR 773; para 55 of the Case Management Checklist in the Public Law Protocol.

Jurisdiction.[17] If there is new evidence adduced, a trial judge may change his decision regarding the initial findings.[18]

Judges are directed to express at the preliminary hearing such views as they are able to, in order to assist social workers and experts in making assessments and drafting the care plan. The judge hearing the first part of the case should be requested to direct that the matter be reserved to him or her. The court will do so, but will not make it an absolute requirement. There are often cases where judges, for whatever reason, will not be available to hear the case in five months' time. Therefore, care must be taken that the original judgment is either transcribed at public expense, or a careful note is agreed by the judge.

4.2.3   The threshold criteria

The threshold criteria should be considered by the court as at the time the local authority initiated care proceedings, or when the local authority began to provide continuous protective measures for the child.[19] Evidence that is discovered by the local authority after initiating proceedings nevertheless might be used by the court to find that the child was suffering or likely to suffer significant harm as of the date proceedings began.[20]

The House of Lords in the case of *Re H (Minors) (Sexual Abuse: Standard of Proof)*[21] sought to clarify the standard of proof to be met by the local authority in establishing the threshold criteria. The following points emerge from the speeches of the House of Lords:

(1) the person who makes the allegation must prove it;
(2) the standard of proof is a balance of probability;
(3) the more serious the allegation the more convincing must be the evidence to prove it.[22]

Lord Nicholls of Birkenhead gave the leading speech, holding unequivocally that judicial doubts or suspicions about allegations would not be enough to support findings that the child was suffering or likely to suffer significant harm.

---

[17]   [2000] 1 FLR 334.
[18]   *Re B and H (Children)* Lawtel 29 October 2003.
[19]   See *Re M (A Minor) (Care Order: Threshold Conditions)* [1994] 2 AC 424, [1994] 3 All ER 298, HL. See *Southwark London Borough Council v B* [1998] 2 FLR 1095, which provides that the relevant date is the same whether it is alleged that the child is suffering harm or is likely to suffer harm. Protective measures would include, inter alia, taking the child into accommodation, or having the child made subject to an emergency protection order. It may also include having the family live together in a residential assessment unit.
[20]   See *Re G (Children) (Care Order: Threshold Criteria)* [2001] EWCA Civ 968, [2001] 1 WLR 2100, [2001] 2 FLR 1111.
[21]   [1996] AC 563, [1996] 1 FLR 80.
[22]   See discussion of *Re H* in *Essential Family Practice 2002* (Butterworths), p 2328.

Lord Nicholls also stated, however, that facts, even trivial or minor facts, taken together, may suffice to satisfy the court of the likelihood of future harm:

> 'It is open to a Court to conclude that there is a real possibility that the child will suffer harm in the future although harm in the past has not been established. There will be cases where, although the alleged mistreatment itself is not proved, the evidence does establish a culmination of profoundly worrying features affecting the care of the child in the family. In such cases it would be open to a Court in appropriate circumstances to find that although not satisfied the child is yet suffering significant harm, on the basis of such facts as are proved there is a likelihood that he will do so in the future.'[23]

Lord Nicholls believes that the 'likelihood' threshold is therefore comparatively low. The court must only be satisfied that there is a real possibility that cannot be ignored. Nevertheless, the court must make findings of fact, on the balance of probabilities, sufficient to show why there is a real possibility that cannot be ignored that the child is likely to suffer significant harm in the future.

A court might find that a child has suffered or is likely to suffer significant harm, even though the perpetrator of the harm is not identified with particularity. The House of Lords in *Lancashire County Council v B*,[24] held that the threshold conditions could be satisfied when there was no more than a possibility that the parents, rather than other carers, could have inflicted the injuries which the child had suffered. Courts were instructed, however, that it is relevant at the disposal stage of the hearing to note that the parents had not been shown to be responsible for the child's injuries.[25]

It has been held that where there is insufficient evidence to make a finding identifying the perpetrators of harm, the court should apply the following test: is there a likelihood or a real possibility that one or more of a number of people with access to the child was the perpetrator or a perpetrator of the injuries? See *North Yorkshire County Council v SA*.[26] In uncertain perpetrator cases, the correct approach is for the case to proceed at the welfare or placement stage on the basis that each of the possible perpetrators is treated as such. See *Re O and N; Re B*.[27] The House of Lords held that the judge conducting the welfare hearing should have regard to the facts found at the preliminary hearing when those facts leave open the possibility that a parent or carer was a perpetrator of proved harm. The conclusion must not be excluded from the court's consideration when determining the long-term interests of the child.

Advocates in family proceedings will also note the judgment of the President in the case of *Re T (Children)*.[28] The President noted that the court understood

---

[23]   [1996] 1 FLR 80, per Lord Nicholls at 101c–e.
[24]   [2000] 1 FLR 583, HL.
[25]   See Lord Nicholls at 589g–590b.
[26]   [2003] EWCA Civ 839, [2003] Fam Law 631.
[27]   [2003] UKHL 18, [2003] 1 FLR 1169.
[28]   [2004] EWCA Civ 538.

'that in many applications for care orders counsel are now submitting that the correct approach to the standard of proof is to treat the distinction between criminal and civil [standards of proof] as "largely illusory". In my judgment this approach is mistaken. The standard of proof in Children Act cases is the balance of probabilities, and the approach to these difficult cases was set out by Lord Nicholls in his speech at *Re H.*'[29]

4.2.4　The placement or welfare stage

Once a court determines that the threshold criteria have been met, the court then must determine which (if either) of the two public law orders available should be made, or if the court should make an interim or a final order. The court should take into account the presumption of the CA 1989 that where there is agreement between the parties, the court should make no order, if possible. In determining the future of the child, the court must consider carefully the care plan produced by the local authority. However, the term 'care plan' has acquired quasi-statutory significance.[30] The Department of Health *The Children Act 1989 Guidance and Regulations*, Volumes 3 and 4, do set out matters to be included in the care plan in particular at para 2.62. These matters are also set out in the case of *Manchester City Council v F.*[31]

The Adoption and Children Act 2002, s 124 inserts a new s 31A into the CA 1989. This new clause, once it comes into effect, will give a statutory underpinning to what has become a rule in any event: that is, that local authorities file and serve a care plan in every case in which it seeks a care order. The statutory duty does not apply where the authority is only seeking an interim care order, although it is at present common practice for all local authorities to set out an interim care plan for the child. It is likely that a failure to set out some sort of interim care plan would violate the child's rights under Article 8. The local authority will be required by the new s 31A to keep the care plan under review and to make changes as and when necessary.

Advocates must also be familiar with the Local Authority Circular of 12 August 1999 (LAC(99)29) 'Care plans and care proceedings under the Children Act 1989'. This Circular covers practice and policy matters, and seeks to make consistent the practices of local authorities across the country. The Circular contains a guide to the structure and contents of care plans, and requires local authorities to give reasons as to why a particular placement or course of action has been chosen. Local authorities must consider 'achievable timescales leading up to specific outcomes', a common failure of local authority care plans in practice. Paragraph 17 of the Circular notes that interim care plans for interim hearings do not set out the final views of the local authority, and that the interim care plan must be designated as such. A separate care plan is needed for each

---

[29]　See para 28 of Butler-Sloss P's judgment, *Re T (Children)*, above.
[30]　See, generally, *The Family Court Practice 2004* (Family Law, 2003), pp 546–554.
[31]　[1993] 1 FLR 419.

child subject to the proceedings, even though some of the information for siblings may be similar or identical.

Where the care plan designates a local authority other than the applicant, the care plan must be prepared in cooperation between the two authorities.[32] The court and the advocates must always have available the *Handbook of Best Practice in Children Act Cases*, produced by the Children Act Advisory Committee.

Advocates for parents often seek to argue that even if the court finds that the children have suffered significant harm, nevertheless the court should make a supervision order rather than a care order. The primary difference is that under a supervision order the local authority will not share parental responsibility for the child, and will therefore not be allowed to remove the child from the care of the parents without a further order of the court, unless there is an emergency.

Courts will ordinarily ask itself the questions set out in the case of *Re D (Care or Supervision order)*:[33]

(1) Is the stronger order need to protect the child?
(2) Can the risk be met by a supervision order?
(3) Is there a need for the speed of action that a care order allows the local authority?
(4) Is the parent able to protect the child without the need for the local authority to share parental responsibility?
(5) Can parental cooperation only be obtained through the use of a draconian care order?
(6) Can the child's needs be met by advising, assisting and befriending the child rather than by sharing parental responsibility for the child?
(7) Have the parents improved their ability to care for the child during the proceedings?
(8) Will the duration of a supervision order (12 months, with the authority able to extend it for a further 12 months) be sufficient to protect the child?

The role of the guardian continues for the duration of a supervision order, unless terminated by the court. See *Re MH (Child) (Care Proceedings: Children's Guardian)*.[34]

If the court makes a care order, the guardian's (and the court's) roles will cease. The child will then be in the care of the local authority. Concerns were raised by the House of Lords in the case of *Re S (FC) and others*,[35] that the fact there was little or no judicial oversight of the local authority's

---

[32] See *L v London Borough of Bexley* [1996] 2 FLR 595.
[33] [2000] Fam Law 600.
[34] [2001] 2 FLR 1334.
[35] [2002] UKHL 10.

decision-making process after a care order was made meant the CA 1989 was not compliant with the European Convention, Article 8. The Court of Appeal in that case had in effect amended the Act to allow, in certain cases, for the guardian to remain involved after care orders had been made. The House of Lords allowed the appeal of that decision, but the speeches that were given prompted the government to act. The Adoption Act 2002 provided a power for independent reviewing officers to seek a remedy from the courts in appropriate cases. Regulations were issued in 2004 to extend the functions of CAFCASS to take court proceedings on behalf of a child following a referral from an independent reviewing officer.[36]

Once the threshold criteria have been established, advocates for parents often will seek to argue that the court should not make a final care order, but should make an interim care order in order for the parents to be further assessed by the local authority or by other experts. Jurisdiction for the court to make an interim care order and to order a further assessment is provided by CA 1989, s 38(6), and the guidance provided by the House of Lords in the case of *Re: C (A Minor) (Interim Care Order: Residential Assessment)*.[37] The court in *Re: C*, and Holman J in the case of *Re: M (Residential Assessment Directions)*[38] set the parameters for a section 38(6) order:

(1) the power extends to an assessment of the parents together with the child;
(2) assessment should be interpreted more generally than a reference simply to a medical or psychiatric assessment;
(3) section 38(6) is to be broadly construed;
(4) the assessment must not be contrary to the overall best interests of the child;
(5) it must be necessary to enable a court to reach a decision;
(6) it must not be unreasonable or require the local authority to fund the proposed assessment;
(7) the court must consider whether the assessment is appropriate in light of all the circumstances.

There had been considerable confusion in the Family Division regarding the distinction between assessment and therapy, in particular when work is provided by institutions such as the Cassel Hospital in Oxford, which provides as part of its assessment process quite a bit of therapeutic work. The Court of Appeal in the recent case of *Re: G (Interim Care Order: Residential Assessment)*[39] rejected the distinction drawn between assessment and therapy. That distinction had first been drawn by Holman J in the case of *Re: M (Residential Assessment Directions)*. The Court of Appeal, with Thorpe J

---

36   See new s 26(C) of the Children Act 1989, as amended by the Adoption Act 2002 and SI No 1419.
37   [1997] AC 489, [1997] 1 FLR 1 HL.
38   [1998] 2 FLR 371.
39   [2004] EWCA Civ 24, [2004] 1 FLR 876.

giving the judgment of the court, held that the essential question should always be:

> 'Can what is sought be broadly classified as an assessment to enable a Court to obtain the information necessary for its own decision?'

In reality, a permissible assessment to enable a court to obtain the information necessary for its own decision was likely to contain the provision of a variety of services, supports and treatments, with or without accommodation. Applications under s 38(6) would fail if what was proposed was not required to enable a court to obtain the information necessary for its decision. The application would also fail if the child was only peripherally involved, or if the proposal was for a treatment programme for one or both of the parents that contained no element of assessment for the court. The application may also be refused if the costs are prohibitive.

Advocates in public law cases must be particularly concerned about the application of the Human Rights Act 1998, and Article 8 of the European Convention for the Protection of Human Rights. The advocates must note the President's Practice Direction of 24 July 2000, and must be acutely aware of Munby J's judgment in the case of *Re L (Care Proceedings: Human Rights Claims)*.[40] Munby J held that it is not necessary or desirable to transfer care proceedings under the CA 1989, Part V from the county court to the High Court merely because of a breach of human rights under the European Convention. This rule has been confirmed by the Court of Appeal in the case of *Re V (A Child)*.[41]

Advocates should be particularly concerned where a local authority seeks to remove children permanently based on the allegation of future harm. The Court of Appeal considered these types of cases in the case of *Re: C & B (Care Order: Future Harm)*.[42] In that case care orders were made some three years previously regarding the eldest child of the family and her half sister. The care orders were made on the basis that the eldest child had suffered actual harm to her intellectual emotional development. The care order was made regarding the younger child based on the likelihood of future harm. A year later the mother gave birth to a son. Shortly thereafter, the local authority began investigating that child's welfare. The conclusion reached by the local authority was that the newborn child would suffer similar significant harm as his sisters. Three months later the mother gave birth to another child. Shortly thereafter interim care orders were made regarding both children and both children were removed from mother and placed with foster carers. At the substantive hearing on the

---

[40]   [2003] EWHC 665, Fam, [2003] Fam Law 466. See also *Re L (Care: Assessment: Fair Trial)* [2002] EWHC 1379, [2002] 2 FLR 730.

[41]   [2004] EWCA Civ 54, CA (Tucky LJ, Wall LJ).

[42]   [2001] 1 FLR 611.

matter, the judge found there was a likelihood of each child suffering significant emotional harm in the future. She made final care orders under s 31(2) of the 1989 Act.

On appeal, the parents argued that the mother's history (she had suffered from depression and possibly a manic episode some years previously) did not justify the extreme action of removing both of the children. The Court of Appeal agreed. The court, in allowing the appeal held that when the local authority's case involved only a real possibility of future harm to a child, the action taken by the local authority had to be proportionate to the nature and gravity of that feared harm. The principle had to be that the local authority work to support, and eventually to reunite, the family, unless the risk was so high that the child's welfare required removal.

Advocates must be aware of European jurisprudence in this area.[43] The European Court has often dealt with claims that a country's system of child protection violates Article 8 rights, and the judgments do provide a certain safety net of rights for parents and children. In particular, all significant decisions regarding a state's interference with family life must be subject to judicial review.[44] In *Johansen v Norway*,[45] the European Court noted that in deciding whether the removal of a child from care is compatible with respect for family life a fair balance was to be struck between the interests of the child in remaining in public care and the rights of the parents in being reunited with the child. The result of the balance, however, does not disturb the 'paramountcy' principle. Note, too, that the European Commission (not court) concluded in *Hendriks v The Netherlands*[46] that the conflicting rights of the child will always prevail over those of the parent. The European Court has not gone that far.

The court has held that if the care order is 'temporary' or interim, the implementation of the order must be guided by the ultimate aim of family reunion.[47] The order must be implemented in a manner 'consistent' with family life. Placement of siblings miles apart violates their Article 8 rights.[48] The local authority must provide suitable education.[49] The child has a right under Article 63 not to be mistreated. This means a local authority may be held liable for damages if it fails to remove a child from an abusive family.[50]

---

43   A good text is Swindells, Neaves, Kushner and Skilbeck, *Family Law and the Human Rights Act 1998* (Fam Law, 2000). For an overview of the Convention, see Starmer, *European Rights Law* (Legal Action Group, 1999).
44   See *Olsson v Sweden (No 1)* (1988) 11 EHHR 259; *Boughanemi v France* 25 EHRR 228.
45   (1996) 23 EHRR 33.
46   (1982) 5 EHRR 223.
47   See *K and T v England* (27 April 2000).
48   *Olsson v Sweden (No 1)* (1988) 11 EHRR 259.
49   *Campbell and Cosans v UK* (1982) 4 EHRR 293.
50   See *Z v UK* which arose from the English case of *X v Bedingfordshire CC* [1995] 2 AC 633.

4.2.5 The Protocol

Public law Children Act litigation is a notoriously lengthy and complex process. Indeed, some would wonder how could it not be, given the difficulty of the questions the tribunal will be asked to decide. This lengthy process, however, is also seen to further damage the child who is the focus of the litigation. The CA 1989 enshrines this principle, providing at s 1(2) that delay in Children Act proceedings is ordinarily not in the child's best interests. The crucial difficulty, of course, is finding the right balance between efficiency and fairness, between delay and justice.[51]

Some ten years after the implementation of the Children Act, in 2001, the Lord Chancellor's Department began to seek remedies for the perceived over-long and inefficient litigation process under Part IV of the CA 1989. The Scoping Study published by the Lord Chancellor's Department in March 2002, set out some of the causes of the delay, and inefficient court procedures came top of the list. The Lord Chancellor's Advisory Committee therefore set out to present a Protocol that would govern all Part IV litigations. The Lord Chancellor's Advisory Committee published its conclusions in May 2003. The Lord Chancellor, and the President of the Family Division, adopted the new Protocol by issuing a Practice Direction providing that all applications issued after 1 November 2003, or for proceedings transferred after 1 November 2003 from a family proceedings court to a Care Centre, or from a county court to a Care Centre, or from a Care Centre to the High Court, shall be governed by the new Protocol.

The Protocol for Judicial Case Management contains six steps:

(1) The application

The objective of the application is for the local authority to provide sufficient information to identify the issues and to make early welfare and case management decisions. Historically, the local authority had merely filled out a form C1, with a note stating that evidence would soon be filed. This practice has been stopped by the Protocol. Under the new Protocol, the local authority must file and serve its statement and other supporting documents by day three.

(2) The first hearing in the family proceedings court

Family proceedings courts are directed to hold a hearing on the matter before day six after filing of the application. The objective here is to decide what immediate steps are necessary, including scheduling any contested interim care order hearings. Directions should be given, if possible, for scheduling

---

[51] See, generally, *C v Solihull Metropolitan Borough Council* [1993] 1 FLR 290; *Re W (Welfare Reports)* [1995] 2 FLR 142, CA, for discussions on the delay principle. Any delay in Children Act proceedings must be 'planned and purposeful and in the best interests of the child'.

a case management conference and final hearing, along with filing of evidence, disclosure of other documents, and the preparation by the local authority of a core assessment. The parties are directed to use a standard directions form which is annexed to the Protocol. At this hearing a decision will be made regarding whether the case should be transferred to a Care Centre (county court), or transferred to the High Court.

(3) Allocation hearing and directions

If the matter is transferred to a Care Centre, the Care Centre court is directed to hold an allocation hearing by day 11 after the application. If transferred to the High Court, the High Court is directed to hold this hearing within 15 days of the application. The objective is to provide for judicial continuity through to final hearing. The judge at the allocation hearing will consider a further transfer of the matter (either laterally or vertically), consider whether an interim care order hearing should be held, consider disclosure issues, and consider completion dates of the local authority core assessment.

(4) The case management conference

A case management conference should be held in the case, no matter the level of court, between day 15 and day 60 after the application. Local authorities are directed to provide case management documents and a court bundle five days prior to the hearing. The other parties are to provide their statement of position two days prior to the hearing. There should be an advocates' meeting one day prior to the hearing. At the case management conference the judge will consider a schedule of issues, go through the Case Management Checklist[52] and the judge will also make certain the timetable for evidence, and for production of any expert reports, is agreed by all parties.

(5) The pre-hearing review

Courts are directed to hold a pre-hearing review by week 37 after the filing of the application. There should be an advocates' meeting at least one week prior to the pre-hearing review. The court at the review will go through the pre-hearing checklist, determine the schedule of issues, make certain that all documents and bundles have been produced. Advocates are to note that a pre-hearing review might be dispensed with by agreement if all issues are agreed, and the pre-hearing review is optional in a family proceedings court.

---

[52]   The checklist is provided in the Appendix to this book.

(6) The final hearing

Local authority solicitors must have ready for the court the trial bundles at least two days before the final hearing and all parties must have filed by that time the case management and practice direction documents.

4.3 THE ISSUES AT THE SUBSTANTIVE HEARING

Child protection litigation under the CA 1989 falls principally into five categories:

(1) neglect of the child causing physical harm;
(2) neglect of the child causing emotional harm;
(3) a non-accidental injury suffered by the child and perpetrated by a carer;
(4) sexual abuse of the child;
(5) long-term physical or emotional abuse of the child caused by inappropriate chastisement or by inconsistent or neglectful parenting.

One can easily see that within these five broad categories are an infinite number of factual circumstances. The neglect of the child's physical health might be temporary, caused by a parent's grief over the death of a loved one, or it might be caused by a parent's inability to recover from an illness. It might be caused by the parent's own physical infirmities, or it might be caused by the continued inability of the child's carer to resist the lures of narcotic drugs. The child suffering a non-accidental injury may have been abused many times throughout his childhood, until finally the abuse became public. Or the child might have suffered only one injury from a parent who showed immediate remorse and understanding. Advocates for local authorities and for parents and children quickly understand that the factual situations in family proceedings are as infinite and varied as families themselves.

4.3.1 Social work assessments

Advocates tackling a child protection case must know and understand what social workers seek to do when undertaking a core assessment of the family. The quality of social work assessments varies considerably.[53] Social workers should examine practical issues. Parenting skills, social networks, support for parents – all of this should be assessed by social workers, following the *Framework for the Assessment of Children in Need and their Families*.[54]

Advocates should look to see whether there are assessments of the following:

---

[53]   See in this regard Brophy et al, *Child Psychiatry and Child Protection Litigation* (Gaskell, 2001) p 39, where psychiatrists were asked to comment on the quality of social work assessments they had seen. One psychiatrist said the social work assessment is 'almost valueless. It's badly written about families that don't exist'. Others note that the assessments vary enormously, with some of them being quite helpful.

[54]   Department of Health, 2000.

- the history of a parent's background;
- family history;
- family functioning;
- the parents' current relationship;
- the quality of parenting offered;
- the functioning of the child;
- description/observation of the child;
- the child's wishes and feelings;
- a basic chronology of local authority involvement;
- a plan for local authority action;
- an assessment of the parents' ability to change, including whether the parents accept responsibility for any alleged abuse or neglect.

Primary users of the core assessment will be any experts who later seek to provide opinions about the family. Therefore any mistakes in the original statements by the local authority, or in its core assessments, often are reflected in the reports of experts who appear later in the case.

Advocates should become familiar with the 'decision-making matrix' of social workers, as set out by Munby J in the case of *Re C (Care Assessment: Fair Trial)*.[55]

4.4   THE EXPERTS – GENERAL OVERVIEW

The decision about what type of expert evidence to seek has to be made at an early stage of the litigation. The choice, of course, depends on the type of harm the child has allegedly suffered. In neglect cases, it is often the case that a child psychiatrist will be able to give evidence about the emotional harm the child might have suffered because of neglect. In non-accidental injury cases, and in those cases where the child has suffered physical harm from neglect, a consultant paediatrician will be able to give evidence about the harm the child has suffered. In those cases where sexual abuse has been alleged, medical evidence regarding the child's physical condition will be adduced, as well as evidence from a child psychiatrist regarding the condition of the child.

I seek in the next sections to discuss briefly each of these types of expert evidence.

A text that is invaluable for advocates involved in child protection litigation is a collection of research pieces edited by the consultant psychiatrist Julia Brophy entitled *Child Psychiatry and Child Protection Litigation*.[56] The research was funded by the Department of Health, and supported by the Lord

---

55   [2003] EWCA 1379, [2002] 2 FLR 764.
56   Gaskell, 2001.

Chancellor's Department. The research included interviews of consultant child psychiatrists and others involved in the child protection process regarding their experience in the family courts. Most agreed that one of the major achievements of the CA 1989 has been to increase the dialogue with experts. Most agreed that the pre-trial meetings between experts who disagree had improved presentation of the experts' differing opinions, and served to narrow the issues at trial. Most also agreed that the pre-trial meeting reduced in importance the cross-examination to be faced by the expert at final hearing. Few experts expressed a liking for being cross-examined. Most also agreed that the letters of instruction they had received have improved considerably during the last several years.[57]

Certain consultants believed that at least a few experts have their own agenda in these cases, and often seek to campaign for that agenda. One consultant said it was clear that certain experts think parents or fathers in particular get a bad deal in court, and therefore seek to present evidence favourable, if at all possible, to the father.[58] Certain other experts are known constantly to disagree with paediatric opinion about whether an injury was likely to have been non-accidental. Certain other experts, mindful of the damage children suffer in care, often encourage parents to contest the uncontestable by recommending rehabilitation even in the most hopeless of cases.[59] Advocates should therefore seek to gain an understanding whether experts presenting evidence often give evidence for only one side of the question or another.

One of the interesting conclusions offered by at least some of the consultants who were interviewed was that their own work had not been sufficiently challenged in court. They believe their work was treated with too much respect, and the conclusions were not sufficiently challenged. The consultants believed that the best challenges would be to the methods that were used and the basis of the opinions that were reached.[60] The consultants believe that at least a few judges were also too ready to accept what the experts had said.

Advocates will note the judgment by Butler-Sloss P in the case of *Re LU (A Child); Re LB (A Child, sub nom Re U (A Child) (Serious Injury: Standard of Proof)*,[61] regarding the use of expert evidence by judges in family

---

57   See Brophy et al, above, p 70.
58   See Brophy et al, above, pp 80-81.
59   See Brophy et al, above p 81. Readers might also remember the case of Dr Colin Patterson, who was found guilty of serious professional misconduct by the General Medical Council and struck off the roll of doctors because of his evidence in Children Act cases. Dr Patterson diagnosed the disputed condition known as temporary brittle bone disease in infants, despite being presented with medical evidence that did not support his findings. The General Medical Council decided Dr Patterson had been more concerned with acting as an advocate for his own theory, defining a condition which only a handful of doctors worldwide believed existed, rather than as an impartial expert witness. See *The Times*, 5 March 2004.
60   See Brophy et al, above, p 92.
61   [2004] EWCA Civ 567, [2004] 2 FLR 263.

proceedings. The court in that case sought to apply the lessons of *R v Angela Cannings*,[62] where Angela Cannings' criminal conviction for the murder of her child was overturned on appeal. The Court of Appeal held in *Cannings* that it did not necessarily follow, from the current state of knowledge, that three sudden unexplained infant deaths in the same family led to the inexorable conclusion that the deaths must have resulted from the deliberate infliction of harm. The original trial court jury had relied (it was assumed) on expert evidence presuming to show that even where no physical injury or abuse had been shown, a jury could presume on statistical evidence alone that multiple unexplained deaths had to have been caused by the child's carers.

The issues before Butler-Sloss P in the case of *Re LU* included whether the judgment by the Court of Appeal in *Cannings* changed any rule in family proceedings. The court had no difficulty in holding that nothing in *Cannings* changed the approach to be taken by judges hearing allegations in family proceedings. The court held that the burden and standard of proof as set out in the case of *Re H and R (Minors) (Sexual Abuse: Standard of Proof)*[63] remained the correct approach for trial courts hearing family proceedings.

But the court in *Re LU* did provide the following guidance for trial courts:

(1) The cause of an injury or an episode that cannot be explained scientifically remains equivocal.
(2) Recurrence is not in itself probative.
(3) Particular caution is necessary in any case where the medical experts disagree, one opinion declining to exclude a reasonable possibility of natural causes.
(4) The court must always be on guard against the over-dogmatic expert, the expert whose reputation or *amour propre* is at stake, or the expert who has developed a scientific prejudice.
(5) The judge in care proceedings must never forget that today's medical certainty may be discarded by the next generation of experts or that scientific research will throw light into corners that are at present dark.

Most cases that are brought by local authorities in family proceedings courts involve parental neglect. One study produced in 1996 covering five family proceedings courts found that almost two-thirds of cases did not contain allegations of sexual or physical abuse.[64] More likely than not, what experts will face will be not one issue but several: a parent may abuse drugs while neglecting the child; another child might have severe physical disabilities that impact on the parents' abilities to care for the entire family; there may be an

---

[62]   [2004] EWCA Crim 01.
[63]   [1996] AC 563.
[64]   See Bates and Brophy, *The Appliance of Science? The Use of Experts in Child Court Proceedings: A Court-Based Study*, a research report for the Department of Health (Archer: Centre for Family Law and Policy, 1996).

inappropriate male partner in the family who perpetrates violence on the mother of the children. It has been repeatedly argued, at least by child psychiatrists, that a diagnosis of emotional abuse in cases such as this is a complex exercise. The prognosis is also likely to require skills and clinical training only a child psychiatrist will have.[65]

However complex the problems that face families, however, the basic framework for assessment of parenting rarely varies. The consultant psychotherapist Dr Roger Kennedy provides an overview of the process used by parenting assessors in his article 'Assessment of Parenting'[66]

Dr Kennedy sets out the primary criteria for assessing parental skills as follows:

- Is there adequate provision of physical care?
- Is there consistency of behaviour and function in regard to the child?
- Is there capacity to empathise with the child?
- Is there capacity for trust?
- Is there capacity for change?
- What historical factors are relevant, for example were the parents abused themselves?

Dr Kennedy noted the delicate balance that had to be drawn between giving the parents another chance and affecting the child's ability to make attachments at any given age. A baby's needs were the most urgent, primarily because of statistics showing that adoptions have a better chance of success where the child was adopted as an infant. Children of eight or nine, on the other hand, have probably suffered damage from poor early attachment already, and therefore no 'undue' harm might occur if additional time is given for assessment.

4.5 EVIDENCE REGARDING SEXUAL ABUSE

Since the mid 1970s, and the advent of the technology of videotape, interviews of children by police or child care professionals have routinely been videotaped for later viewing, either by a court or by an investigative agency or local authority. High Court judges first began viewing videotaped evidence in wardship cases in the 1980s and, from the beginning, the High Court and Court of Appeal have criticised the use of improper interviewing techniques by social workers and the police.

---

[65] See DPH Jones, *Working with the Children Act: Task and Responsibilities of the Child and Adolescent Psychiatrist* (HMSO, 1991); Caplin & Thompson, 'Emotional Abuse of Expert Evidence' [1995] Fam Law 628–631. Cited in Brophy et al, above, p 109.

[66] [1996] Fam Law 74 (now published in a text edited by Mr Justice Wall and entitled *Rooted Sorrows: Psychoanalytic Perspectives on Child Protection, Assessment, Therapy and Treatment* (Fam Law, 1997)).

Video interviews that do not follow the guidelines first set out in the *Report of the Inquiry into Child Abuse in Cleveland* in 1987 will be disregarded by judges. The case of *Re A and B (Minors) (No 1) (Investigation of Alleged Abuse)*[68] is instructive. In that case, the father applied for contact with his two children in divorce proceedings. The issue concerned allegations that the father had sexually abused his eldest child. The mother informed social workers that she believed the father had abused A. On examination, nothing abnormal was found. The mother later reported the child had made comments which led her to suspect that abuse had occurred. The child was interviewed by an inexperienced social worker and a policewoman on three occasions. The interviews were recorded on video. Nothing indicated abuse in the first interview, but in a later interview the child made comments suggesting abuse had occurred.

The mother also introduced into evidence a later interview of the child by a child psychotherapist from Great Ormond Street Hospital in London. In that interview the child refused to talk about the father, but simply said that the father's actions 'had hurt'. The psychotherapist gave evidence that the child's reactions were 'not uncommon' in a child who had been sexually abused. Later, three distinguished child psychiatrists criticised aspects of the first three interviews. One pointed out that discussions between the mother and the eldest child must have occurred between the second and the third interviews, and two of the psychiatrists were of the opinion that during the interview with the psychiatric social worker considerable pressure was placed on the child and leading questions were asked.

Wall J made an order allowing contact to occur. He noted that the social worker had uncritically accepted the mother's statement even though the mother had suffered from transient psychotic episodes where fantasy and reality had become confused. The video interviews were rejected because they contained breaches of the guidelines in *The Memorandum of Good Practice*.[67]

Wall J also noted the distinction between interviews of the child intended for therapeutic work with the child, and interviews that are intended for use by police and the courts. During the interview by the psychotherapist, the child made no statement indicating sexual abuse, even after the psychotherapist had made unwarranted references to sexual abuse and sexual boundaries. Wall J noted that even six years after the Cleveland Report, profound differences existed between distinguished psychiatrists on the approach to child sexual abuse. The judge was very concerned that after the guidelines had been in

---

[67]   *The Memorandum of Good Practice on Video Recorded Interviews with Child Witnesses for Criminal Proceedings,* Department of Health (HMSO, 1992).

[68]   [1995] 3 FCR 389, FD (Wall J). Wall J was also highly critical of the lack of coordination between social workers and the police shown in this case. See *Re A and B (Minors) (No 2)* [1995] 1 FLR 351, FD, and Wall J, 'The Courts and Child Protection – The Challenge of Hybrid Cases' a lecture given at All Souls College, Oxford on 1 July 1997 and reported in [1997] CFLQ 345.

operation for several years elementary errors of investigation were still committed by the police and the local authorities.[69]

The Memorandum of Good Practice has been the subject of a great deal of research, culminating in two vitally important Home Office publications:

(1) the Home Office consultation document entitled *Speaking up for Justice*, published in 1999;

(2) a document edited by Graham Davies and Helen Westcott entitled *Interviewing the Child Witnesses under the Memorandum of Good Practice: A research review.*[70]

Video interviews are admissible in evidence in all proceedings regarding the care and upbringing of children. These videotapes are hearsay, in that they are 'statements made out of court offered in court for the truth of the matter asserted therein'.[71] Hearsay evidence is now admissible in all civil actions by virtue of the Civil Evidence Act 1995. Prior to the effective date of that Act, however, hearsay evidence in proceedings regarding children had been made admissible under the CA 1989. Even though the evidence of an out-of-court statement is now admissible, the party against whom the evidence is offered must be given an appropriate opportunity to rebut the evidence. The rule is set out in the case of *Re: G (Minors) (Welfare Report: (Disclosure):*[72]

> 'In a jurisdiction … in which the normal rules governing the admission of a hearsay evidence have been relaxed by statute … the fundamental rule providing that a party should be informed of all the evidence against him should only be relaxed in the most exceptional circumstances amounting to a serious threat to the welfare of the child.'

Where video evidence is to be adduced in care proceedings, specific guidelines exist as to the manner in which it should be presented.[73] Leave of the court is required before any child might be medically or psychiatrically examined or otherwise assessed for the purpose of preparation of expert reports, including videotapes.[74] The child's view must also be taken into account by the judge, depending on the age and maturity of the child involved.[75]

---

[69] See also *Re R (Child Abuse: Video Evidence)* [1995] 1 FLR 451, FD; *Re M (Child Abuse: Video Evidence)* [1995] 2 FLR 571, FD, for the manner of making police video evidence available for use in care proceedings.

[70] Both documents were published by HMSO, in 1999. The research has been applied to create a new memorandum, published by HMSO in 2000.

[71] See, generally, Keen, *The Modern Law of Evidence* (Professional Books Limited, 1985) p 183.

[72] [1993] 2 FLR 293.

[73] See *B v B (Court Bundles: Video Evidence)* [1994] 1 FLR 323; *Practice Note: Case Management* [1995] 1 All ER 586, [1995] 1 FLR 456.

[74] FPR 1991, r 4.18(1); Family Proceedings Courts (Children Act 1989) Rules 1991, r 18(1). Application for leave should be served on all parties unless otherwise directed, FPR 1991, r 4.18(2); Family Proceedings Courts (Children Act 1989) Rules 1991, r 18(2).

[75] In *Re P (Witness Summons)* [1997] 2 FLR 447, CA, the trial court in a care order case involving allegations of sexual abuse refused to allow the alleged abuser to issue a witness summons against the 12-year-old victims. The Court of Appeal refused appeal, holding the court below was within its discretion. See *Morgan v Morgan* [1977] Fam 122.

Judges now routinely allow child and adolescent psychiatrists to see the video interviews of children who are alleging they have been sexually abused, read all the reports and statements, and then render an opinion on whether the child's evidence is credible. There had long been a judicial disquiet about this, which in fact allows the expert to intrude on what has traditionally been seen to be the function of the trial judge.

These psychiatrists do not ordinarily approach the matter in the same way an untrained judge might. Instead, most child psychiatrists have been schooled in one of several assessment techniques. Perhaps the two most popular of these are Statement Validity Analysis (SVA) and Fact Pattern Analysis (FPA), which are often used together.

SVA is a systematic procedure for assessing the credibility of memory reports. It has been used with child witnesses for decades in Germany.[76] SVA consists primarily of a Criteria-Based Content Analysis (CBCA). Some 19 CBCA criteria have been proposed to reflect qualitative and quantitative differences between credible and non-credible reports. A high degree of detail is considered important: it is believed witnesses who are lying find it difficult to embellish false tales with details not actually existing in memory. Research has indicated that deceivers provide less information than non-deceivers.[77] One of the best known studies of CBCA was conducted in 1988. CBCA was applied to 40 child abuse statements. Twenty were confirmed cases of abuse (ie, because of confessions or physical evidence); 20 were 'doubtful'. The CBCA was shown strongly to differentiate the groups. All criteria were more prevalent in the confirmed cases. Some were present in all of the confirmed cases (logical structure, quantity of details). Certain criteria found in most of the confirmed statements were completely absent in the unconfirmed statements (for example, related external associations, attributions of perpetrator's mental state).[78]

In 1996, Porter and Yuille tested the efficacy of 18 proposed verbal clues to deceit taken from several statement analysis techniques.[79] In particular, participants were recruited for a study addressing 'security effectiveness'. The subjects either committed a theft 'to test the effectiveness of a new security guard', or carried out a similar but innocuous task. The participants then provided either a truthful alibi, a partially deceptive account, a completely false alibi, or a truthful confession. Results indicated that only three out of the 18 clues tested

---

[76]   See Undeutsch, 'Statement Reality Analysis' in Trankell (ed), *Reconstructing the Past: The role of psychologists in criminal trials* (Kluwer, The Netherlands, 1982).

[77]   De Tuck and Miller (1985) 'Deception and arousal: Isolating the behavioural correlates of deception' in Human Communication Research, 12, 181.

[78]   Raskin and Esplin (1991) 'Assessment of children's statements of sexual abuse' in Doris (ed), *The Suggestibility of Children's Recollections* (American Psychological Association), pp 153–164.

[79]   Porter and Yuille (1996) 'The language of deceit: an investigation of the verbal clues in the interrogation context' Law and Human Behaviour, 20, 443.

significantly differentiated the truthful and deceptive accounts. All three clues were derived from the SVA technique. These were: amount of detail, coherence, and admissions of lack of memory.

FPA examines statements for: (a) factual consistency/inconsistency; (b) logical patterns/fallacies; (c) factual plausibility/implausibility. This is a less formal and less researched procedure that serves primarily to complement SVA.[80]

SVA consists of the following:

(1) Coherence. A statement is considered coherent if the various parts fit together in a logical, coherent and consistent fashion.
(2) Spontaneous reproduction. A statement is considered to exhibit spontaneous reproduction if it occurs in an unstructured, spontaneous fashion. Rigid structure would result in a low rating.
(3) Sufficiency of detail.
(4) Contextual embedding. This is present if a memory account relates an event anchored in the appropriate context, including space/time interrelations in the person's life.
(5) Descriptions of interactions with other people present during an event.
(6) Reproductive conversation.
(7) Unexpected complications during the incident.
(8) Unusual details that are realistic, but not usual.
(9) Peripheral details.
(10) Accurately reported details that were not understood by the witness.
(11) Related external associations.
(12) Accounts of subjective mental state.
(13) Attribution of perpetrator's mental state.
(14) Spontaneous corrections.
(15) Admitting lack of memory.
(16) Raising doubts about one's own evidence.
(17) Self-deprecation.
(18) Pardoning the perpetrator.
(19) Details characteristic of the event.

Dr Clare Sturge, a child and adolescent psychiatrist who often gives evidence in child abuse cases, states that she uses portions of the SVA and the CBCA, but does not strictly follow them. 'That would imply that there is a scientific basis to these approaches', she says. 'The state of the art has certainly not yet reached that stage.'

---

[80] Houran and Porter (1998) 'Statement Validity Analysis of The Jim Ragsdale Story: Implications for the Roswell Incident' *Journal of Scientific Exploration*, pp 57–71.

Lamb, et al, in 1997 recommended that in addition to the SVA questions above there should also be a Validity Checklist.[81] This would take account of background characteristics, including cognitive factors, suggestibility and affect. It would seek to set out the interview characteristics which relate mainly to the conduct of the interview by the interviewer. The Checklist would include an analysis of motivational factors, including possible motives for the allegation, the context and influence by others on the child. It would include investigative issues, including an analysis of whether the allegations are consistent with what is known of these types of incidents.

The decision-making process used by child and family psychiatrists investigating allegations of sexual abuse has been usefully set out by Dr Kirk Weir in a recent article 'Evaluating Child Sexual Abuse'.[82] Dr Weir tells us that cases fit into one of several broad categories:

- allegations of abuse made by the child or by an adult as a result of conversations with a child, along with observations of the child;
- evidence that the child is unduly preoccupied with sexual matters or displays unusual sexual knowledge;
- circumstances where the risk of child sexual abuse is thought to be high, including those cases where known offenders have access to the child;
- non-specific signs of emotional disturbance;
- medical findings suggestive of sexual abuse.

Dr Weir notes that it is rare where medical evidence will prove the sexual abuse, and, in any event, evidence proving the identity of the sexual abuser is rarer still. The medical evidence will usually concern abnormalities of the child's genitals or anus, and almost invariably the conclusion to be reached by the doctor will simply be that the condition is either consistent or not consistent with sexual activity having taken place.[83]

Dr Weir assesses the evidence of children by using the following criteria:

- spontaneity;
- repetition;
- internal consistency;
- corroboration;
- embedded responses;
- the amount and the quality of detail;
- the consistency of a child's description with his developmental level;

---

[81]   Lamb, et al, *Assessing the Credibility of Children's Allegations of Sexual Abuse: A Survey of Recent Research* (HMSO, 1997).

[82]   [1996] Fam Law 673.

[83]   Dr Weir notes that in only 15 to 30 per cent of cases in which child sexual abuse has occurred is there medical evidence suggestive of abuse. Reasons for this lack of medical evidence include the fact that often the abuse consists of fondling and masturbation or oral sex, often leaving no physical evidence.

- the consistency of the child's emotional state with disclosure;
- 'accommodation syndrome';
- consistency in the face of challenge;
- details characteristic of the offence.[84]

Child psychiatrists also believe that many false allegations have certain characteristics in common. This might be a lack of emotion during disclosure, lack of a sense of threat, a lack of detail and a stereotypical presentation. Dr Weir notes the difficulty of distinguishing a 'stereotypical presentation' from the presentation of a truly abused child who has been forced to tell the story many times. Other circumstances also often produce false allegations:

- professional bias, where an over-concerned professional prematurely commits himself or herself to believing abuse has occurred;
- hostile witnesses, for example where absent parents allege abuse for litigation purposes;
- stereotyping where children are repeatedly given information critical of the so-called abuser;
- post-traumatic stress disorder, where an adult with a history of being sexually abused over-identifies with the child involved and may confuse his own experiences with the child's experiences;
- serious psychiatric disorder, including over-involvement with the child, fantastic and naïve allegations by parents;
- post-traumatic stress disorder in a child or adolescent, including teenagers who suffered previous child sex abuse and may experience 'flash back' phenomena and misinterpret innocent situations as abusive;
- manipulation, especially by parents who make false allegations of abuse in order to achieve certain ends;
- coaching.[85]

Advocates should also understand the concept of 'suggestibility'. That term has been defined as 'the act or process of impressing something (an idea, attitude or desired action) on the mind of another'.[86] Advocates must know that the simple notion that children are infinitely suggestible and can be encouraged to make plausible allegations of abuse against an adult on the basis of a few leading questions has been refuted by the research, in particular by Goodman, et al, in 1991.[87] But there are instances where children, particularly younger children,

---

[84] [1996] Fam Law 673 at 675.
[85] See also Spencer and Flin, *The Evidence of Children: The Law and the Psychology* (Blackstone Press, 1993); Weir and Wheatcroft, 'Allegations of Children's Involvement in Ritual Sexual Abuse: Clinical Experience of 20 Cases' (1994) 19(7) *Journal of Child Abuse and Neglect* 491; Ney (ed), *True and False Allegations of Child Sexual Abuse: Assessment in Care Management* (Branner/Mazel, 1995).
[86] See Fundudis, 'Young Children's memory: How good is it? How much do we know about it?' (1997) *Child Psychology and Psychiatry Review*, 2: 150–158.
[87] Goodman et al, 'Children's testimony for a stressful event: Improving children's reports' (1991) *Journal of Narrative and Life History*, 1:68–79.

are susceptible. Ceci and Bruck in 1993[88] concluded that children in general were prone to incorrect responding under certain circumstances:

(1) an accusatory context, where neutral or ambiguous actions by adults are always interpreted negatively by another authority figure;
(2) repeated suggestive interviewing;
(3) post-event misinformation, in particular where witnesses who observe an event later read a misleading account of it;
(4) memories implanted by others.

Pezdek and Roe[89] found that it is much easier to change a memory than to implant a totally false one. But research by Hyman, et al, in 1995 seems to show that adults repeatedly presented with a mix of real and fictitious events from their own lives will over time claim to remember at least some of the fictitious events.[90]

4.5.1 Sexual abuse – physical examination

Advocates in all cases involving the alleged sexual abuse of children must be familiar with the guidance on paediatric forensic assessment prepared jointly by the Royal College of Paediatrics and Child Health and the Association of Police Surgeons.[91] The health needs of the child are paramount. A comprehensive assessment of the child must also be undertaken prior to any physical examination. Good practice also requires that a permanent record of the findings by photograph (video or still image) should always be made in order to allow a second expert to give a second opinion. The poor quality of this photographic evidence has long been a subject of complaint. Dr Raine Roberts, the clinical director of St Mary's Sexual Assault Referral Centre in Manchester, a physician with more than 30 years of experience handling sexual abuse cases in court, also notes in a paper given to members of the Bar that there has been a considerable problem with regard to the taking of intimate photographs when it cannot be guaranteed that these photos will not be shown in court.[92]

There are only two questions to be asked by the examiner:

(1) Is the finding normal or abnormal?

---

[88] Ceci and Bruck (1993), 'Suggestibility of the child witness: A historical review and synthesis' *Psychological Bulletin*, 113: 403–449, cited in Davies and Westcott, above.

[89] Pezdek, K and Roe, C, 'The suggestibility of children's memory for being touched: Planting, erasing and changing memories' (1997) *Law and Human Behaviour* 21: 95–106, cited in Davies and Westcott, above.

[90] Hyman, Husband, Kellen, Gallas and Cleason, 'Faulty and non-productive questioning techniques: Potential pitfalls of the child interview' a paper presented to the Meeting of the Society for Applied Research in Memory and Recognition on 16 July 1995, cited in Davies and Westcott, above.

[91] Royal College of Paediatrics and Child Health, April 2002.

[92] See Roberts, *Medical Evidence in Child Abuse Cases* (Jordan Publishing Ltd, 2002).

(2) If the finding is abnormal, what has caused it? In other words, what is the reason for the abnormality? Could the finding be caused by a natural act, such as an injury in play?

Dr Roberts notes that in many cases the questions simply cannot be answered. It is now well understood that sexual abuse can occur without leaving signs of injury. Only a full thickness tear of the hymen, the findings of traces of semen in young girls, or the existence of a pregnancy will serve as incontrovertible proof of sexual activity.

Advocates must know and understand the terminology and use it correctly in court:

(1) The vulva – the labia majora and the labia minora, the outer thick lips and inner small folds of skin surrounding the entrance to the vagina, the clitoris and the urethral opening.
(2) The vestibule – the area enclosed within the labia minora and including the bladder opening.
(3) The fossa navicularis – the hollow, depressed area just behind the opening into the vagina. It is part of the vestibule.
(4) The introitus – the hymen and its orifice.
(5) The hymen – a membrane of modified skin attached to the sidewalls of the vagina and partly covering the opening into the vagina. The clock face is used to describe the findings with regard to hymen tear. 12 o'clock is toward the front of the child; 6 o'clock toward the back of the child. As Dr Roberts has pointed out in his lectures to the Bar, the hymen is commonly heart-shaped, with areas of deficiency toward the front of the child which have commonly been mistaken for tears. The hymen is not necessarily symmetrical. There may be a deeper cleft on one side than the other in a crescentic hymen. Deficiencies at the 10–11 o'clock and the 1–2 o'clock positions are often found in normal children. 'Attenuation' of the hymen refers to a narrowing or rubbing away of the hymen which is seen in association with abuse. The attenuated area is usually posterior or posteriolateral. As set out by the Royal College of Physicians in *Physical Signs of Sexual Abuse in Children*: 'Since it is not possible to assess a minor degree of attenuation unless it has resulted in gross asymmetry, significant attenuation implies that at least a portion of the hymen has completely disappeared usually after repeated trauma leaving the hymenal ring irregular and hymenal orifice enlarged.'

4.6 PHYSICAL HARM AND UNCERTAINTY – THE SHAKEN BABY SYNDROME

As long ago as 1860, when the French reformer and physician Tardieu noticed similar symptoms in a number of French children who had been reported by

parents to have died with no obvious cause, numerous medical researchers have suspected that children might be easily injured by being shaken by their carers.[93]

The brain is lined by three membranes: the innermost one, which is not visible to the naked eye, known as the pia; the arachnoid, a thin, usually clear membrane; and the dura, a dual-layered membrane along the inner surface of the skull. The space between the dura and the arachnoid is known as the subdural space. Blood vessels that feed or drain the brain of blood run through this space. Most of these blood vessels are thin-walled veins carrying blood under low pressure from the brain. A number of thick-walled arteries carry blood under pressure to the brain through the same subdural space.

Certain abnormalities cause subdural bleeding: clotting abnormalities, amino acid abnormalities, copper abnormalities and structural abnormalities, particularly aneurysms or arteriovenous malformations which rupture. Most experts agree that in the absence of these abnormalities the only possible source of blood in the subdural space is trauma.

Accidental trauma causing subdural haemorrhaging has been believed to require a significant force. Injuries such as high-speed road accidents or falls from a first-floor window or higher are usually used as the benchmarks for the force needed to cause these injuries. In the absence of that, the remaining traumatic cause of subdural haemorrhaging of infants is a non-accidental shaking or deceleration injury. The combination of subdural haemorrhaging and retinal haemorrhaging is highly suggestive of shaking.

In 1972 American researchers noted that infants with intra-cranial intra-ocular haemorrhages in the absence of signs of external trauma or skull fracture, and with no history of trauma, were likely suffering from 'whiplash shaken infant syndrome'.[94] Shaken baby syndrome was formally recognised by physicians in the UK in the 1970s. Surveys were published showing the possible effects on children of forceful shaking, including infantile subdural haematoma. Several high profile cases in the late 1990s, including the allegation concerning the British nanny Louise Woodward in the US, brought the matter great public attention.

The difficulty is that children who are allegedly victims of shaken baby syndrome vary considerably in their presentation. Some seem to be acute emergency cases. Others are admitted to hospital on several occasions before

---

[93] See Tardieu, '*Etude medico-legal sur les services et mauvais traitments exerces sur des enfants*'. See Cobley, 'Shaking Forces – Shaken Baby Syndrome and the Level of Violence involved' [2003] Fam Law 51.

[94] See Caffey 'On the theory and practice of shaking infants: its potential residual effects of permanent brain damage and mental retardation' (1972) 124 AJDC 161, cited in Cobley, above, p 52. See also Hobbs, Hanks, Wynne (eds), *Child Abuse and Neglect: A Clinician's Handbook* (Churchill Livingstone, 2nd edn, 2002), pp 92–96.

a diagnosis might be made.[95] Therefore determining the timing of the injury is difficult. Many times the physician simply will not be able to make a finding regarding the timing of the injury.

More problematic in family proceedings, however, is that experts are uncertain as to the amount of force that is required. Research published in 2001 regarding 37 infants who had died through inflicted head injuries concluded that in the majority of the cases the brain damage suffered by the infant was due to a lack of oxygen, and not due to the application of direct force to the brain. It had previously been believed that the force had caused the head injuries, which had caused the death.[96] The researchers believed that the lack of oxygen was attributable to an injury in the infant's neck which starved the brain of oxygen. Therefore since the force was directed against the neck, rather than the brain, the force to be applied need not be severe. The authors of the research commented that:

> 'Although mechanisms of shaking must vary, nobody really knows how babies are injured, it may not be necessary to shake an infant very violently to produce stretch injury to its neuroaxis.'

The difficulties in the research were pointed out in the case of *Re A and D (Non-Accidental Injury: Subdural Haematomas).*[97] In that case a five-week-old baby boy was admitted to hospital suffering from convulsions. CT scans revealed two small and symmetrically situated acute subdural haemorrhages. There was another small focus of a fresh haemorrhage. Five days later, an ophthalmologist examined B and discovered bilateral retinal haemorrhages. After discharge from hospital, the child was cared for by his maternal grandparents. At the initial care proceedings, the local authority sought a finding that the parents caused the injuries. The parents denied responsibility, arguing that it could have been caused by a bouncy chair and/or rough play on the part of the child's older siblings. Six consultants gave oral evidence, including one who was a co-author of the research noted above. This particular expert refused to exclude the possibility that the child's injuries had been caused by the bouncy chair. The other experts refused to support those conclusions, although all experts came round to the opinion that the degree of force required to cause subdural haemorrhages need not be as great as previously believed. The court found that the threshold conditions had been satisfied, but the court also made clear that it required a showing that the force used must be out of the normal rough and tumble of family life. The force must be *'unacceptable and inappropriate and obviously so'*. The President of the Family Division, Lady Justice Butler-Sloss, noted the research regarding the degree of force that might be necessary to cause these injuries, but also noted that further research is necessary.

[95] See Cobley, above, p 52.
[96] See Geddes et al, 'Neuro pathology of Inflicted Head Injury in Children' (2001) (1247) Brain 1299. Cited in Cobley, above, p 53.
[97] [2002] 1 FLR 337.

Advocates must be aware of a study by Kemp and others entitled *Apnoea and Brain Swelling in Non-accidental Head Injury*.[98] Researchers found evidence that the victims have a significantly high level of associated injuries. This suggested that the victims usually had suffered from a considerable degree of violence at or around the time they were shaken. The researchers disagree with the suggestion that it may not be necessary to shake a baby very violently to produce stretch injury to its neuroaxis.

Advocates must also note the methods used by paediatricians in determining whether the subdural haematomas exist. Care must be given regarding the timing question, in particular in those cases where several carers are involved.

Retinal haemorrhages are present in between 75 per cent and 90 per cent of shaken babies. However, even on those infants with no haemorrhages, detectable on clinical examination, intracranial and optic sheath abnormalities are demonstrable by other tests.[99] In child abuse cases, it has been shown that the retinal haemorrhages persist much longer and occur in association with brain trauma.[100]

4.7   FACTITIOUS ILLNESS BY PROXY, OR MUNCHAUSEN'S SYNDROME BY PROXY

Perhaps no other form of child abuse identified by experts during the last two decades has caused as much controversy as the condition physicians have labelled factitious illness by proxy, or Munchausen Syndrome by Proxy (MSBP). The term MSBP is used to describe two related types of child abuse:

(1) A parent fabricates an account of an illness in a child, forcing the child to be taken for medical treatment; if the story is sufficiently convincing the child is then exposed to a number of tests and treatments, all of which are needless and therefore are abusive.
(2) The parent directly causes an illness in a child, for example by poisoning the child or suffocating the child.[100A]

---

[98]   See Archives of Disease in Childhood, January 2003.
[99]   See Hobbs, Hands, Wynn (eds), above, p 94.
[100] Ibid.
[100A] The latest pronouncement on factitious illness is by Ryder J in the case of *A County Council v A Mother* [2005] EWHC 31 (Fam). 'The terms Munchausen's syndrome by proxy and Factitious/fabricated (and induced) illness (by proxy) were not a disease, but merely descriptions of a range of behaviours whose context and assessments could provide insight into the degree of risk a child might face.' In that case Ryder J noted that the court was not bound to follow even uncontradicted expert evidence, though of course the court must be cautious before declining to do so. See also *Re B (Minors) (Care Proceedings: Case Conduct), sub nom Re CB and JB (Care Proceedings: guidelines)* [1999] 1 WLR 238, [1998] 2 FLR 211, where Wall J set out guidelines for courts hearing cases where abuse is alleged and denied by the parents. A split hearing should be held, with the first hearing concentrating solely on the factual matrix. Ordinarily, there would be no need for psychiatric or psychological examination of the adults prior to this fact-finding exercise.

Both forms of abuse are labelled MSBP because both have the same end result: that is, medical treatment is given to the child which is unnecessary.

Munchausen Syndrome was first identified in 1951 by a general physician who noted that certain patients fabricated evidence of disease in order to gain medical attention.[101] In 1997, Sir Roy Meadow coined the term Munchausen Syndrome by Proxy because it obviously is related to the adult Munchausen Syndrome identified first by Asher in 1951. It is right, of course, to note here that Sir Roy Meadow's evidence in criminal cases, and in certain children's cases, has now been discredited. In particular, Meadow's use of statistical evidence has been held to be improper. Meadow attempted to show courts that the chances of a child receiving an accidental injury in certain situations (in particular, after another child in the family had died) were astronomical. Courts have now noted that this use of statistical evidence is not appropriate.

But that should not preclude courts from finding that MSBP does in fact exist. There have been numerous studies involving families placed in residential units where hidden cameras were used to record a parent (usually the mother) attempting to suffocate an infant, or attempting to administer drugs to an infant.

Experts now generally agree there are four common features in presentations of MSBP:

(1) the child's illness is either falsified or procured by a parent or carer of the child;
(2) the child's persistent presentation for medical assessment and care usually results in multiple medical procedures;
(3) the perpetrator denies any knowledge of the cause of the child's illness;
(4) acute signs and symptoms of the illness abate when the child is separated from the perpetrator.[102]

Dr Tim David is Professor of Child Health and Paediatrics at the University of Manchester, and a paediatrician who has given evidence in child abuse cases numerous times during the last decade. Dr David, who speaks often at seminars for specialist practitioners, points out that there are a number of fairly well recognised patterns to the presentation by parents who attempt to deceive physicians regarding the illness of their children:

(1) Haematuria (blood in the urine)

The presence of blood in the urine always warrants medical investigation, and these investigations ordinarily are highly invasive. Adding blood to the child's urine therefore will ordinarily force physicians to follow up with these invasive tests. This might include removing a piece of the kidney for examination under the microscope.

[101] See Asher, 'Munchausen Syndrome', The Lancet 1951, cited by Professor Tim David in a speech given to the Family Bar on 28 November 2002 entitled 'Munchausen Syndrome by Proxy: Fictitious Illness Abuse'.

[102] See paper by Professor Tim David of Booth Hall Children's Hospital, presented to the Family Bar on 28 November 2002.

(2) Vomiting

Dr David notes that the mother or father might simply fabricate reports regarding vomiting. Genuine blood in vomit is often black in colour and resembles coffee grounds. This is a result of gastric acid on the red haemoglobin of the blood. Dr David notes that one child of four years has been in hospital for a total of 18 months because doctor's feared there was blood in the child's vomit. (This is called haematemesis.) Later it was discovered the mother had been adding cocoa to the vomited material, making the vomit look much like the coffee grounds appearance of the vomit of a child who has vomited blood.

(3) Diarrhoea

Again, it is easy to fabricate a report of diarrhoea. There have been reported instances of mother's administering laxative drugs to their child. In this case, a trace of laxative will be detectible in the stool and/or urine of the child. Another method identified by physicians as an effort to fabricate diarrhoea is for a parent to add water to stool samples to simulate loose stools.

(4) Epileptic convulsions

Sir Roy Meadow first reported in his article in 1984 in the Lancet[103] that 21 of 32 children he had identified with fictitious epilepsy had suffered fits by partial suffocation by a parent with a pillow. Sixteen other children had false symptoms, including loose stools, blood in the urine and vomiting blood. Again, the evidence regarding epileptic convulsions must be examined carefully by the assessing physician, and it is difficult for a physician to ascribe the cause of these epileptic fits, even in cases where the parent is not suspected of inducing the fit.

(5) Suffocation

Studies in the UK and the USA using covert video surveillance demonstrate without question that the suffocation by a parent of an infant is not a fantasy of social workers and paediatricians. Suffocation is achieved by the parent placing her hand over the child's mouth and nose, or by the parent covering the mouth and nose with a pillow or another object.

Professor David points out that one feature of deliberate suffocation that does not appear to occur in accidental suffocation or in Sudden Infant Death Syndrome is the finding of fresh blood coming from the mouth or nose of the infant. It is believed (at least in some cases) that this blood is a result of direct trauma to the mouth and nose. There is now a special technique which is routinely used when examining the lungs of babies who have died unexpectedly. Suffocation can cause bleeding within the lungs. Recent

[103] See 'Factitious Epilepsy' *Lancet* 1984 2: 25–28.

research shows that it is possible to detect traces of recent bleeding using special staining techniques. Physicians are able to detect whether there has been bleeding within the lungs more than 48 hours before death. Research indicates that deliberate suffocation might be one cause of this bleeding into the lungs. A number of other medical causes would have to be excluded before this theory might be sustained in any individual case.

(6) Drowsiness and falling into a coma
Where a parent has administered sedatives to a child, the correct diagnosis is only made after tests of the urine or blood reveals the presence of the sedative drug that had not been prescribed for the child.

(7) Poisoning
Cases have been reported where children have been poisoned with salt. This leads obviously to raised levels of sodium in the blood and urine.[104]

4.8   SUDDEN INFANT DEATH

Any advocate handling a case where an infant has died suddenly and unexpectedly must seek to understand what is now commonly known as 'Sudden Infant Death Syndrome'. The best introductory text is *Sudden Unexpected Deaths in Infancy* edited by Peter Fleming, Pete Blair, Chris Bacon and Jem Berry.[105]

Doctors refer to the syndrome as Sudden Unexpected Death in Infancy. In about four unexpected deaths out of five, no clear cause can be found. Sudden Infant Death Syndrome comprises the largest category of deaths occurring in England and Wales between the age of one month and one year.[106]

The American pathologist John Beckwith formulated the definition of Sudden Infant Death Syndrome in 1969:

'The sudden death of a baby that is unexpected by history and in whom a thorough necropsy examination failed to demonstrate an adequate cause of death.'

Advocates must understand that Sudden Infant Death Syndrome is not a 'cause' of death. Instead, the category is in one sense simply a catchall: it refers to the fact that no cause is known. In 1972 Sudden Infant Death Syndrome

---

[104]   Roy Meadow, 'Non-accidental Salt Poisoning' Archives of Diseases in Childhood (1993) 68:448-452; Rogers, Tripp and Bentovin et al 'Non-accidental poisoning: an extended syndrome of child abuse', (1976) *British Medical Journal*: 1:793–796.
[105]   HMSO, 2000.
[106]   Professor Tim David, lecture given to the Family Bar, 6 March 2003.

became registrable as a cause of death in England and Wales. There is some controversy about the extent to which the term 'Sudden Infant Death Syndrome' should be abandoned altogether. Professor Michael Green, a retired forensic pathologist, has published an article in the British Medical Journal which advocated a 'think dirty' campaign and argued for increasing the use of the term 'unascertained' as the cause of death.[107]

If an infant dies suddenly and unexpectedly but is found to have one or more suspicious injuries, by common practice the diagnostic label Sudden Infant Death Syndrome cannot be used. Instead, the term 'unascertained' is used when noting the cause of death.

The term often used by physicians in this area is 'Apparent Life Threatening Event' (ALTE). An apparent life threatening event, as defined by the 1986 National Institute of Health and Consensus Panel on Infantile Apnoea, is an event characterised by the combination of apnoea (stopping breathing), colour change, change in muscle tone, choking or gagging.[108]

Physicians will be aware of several studies in cases of ALTE that are wildly contradictory. Some studies seem to indicate that as many as 20 per cent of the children suffering ALTE actually had been suffering from abuse by one parent or another. Other studies show that less than 3 per cent of the patients in that study group had been suffering from parental abuse.[109] In any event, for advocates, and in particular for advocates cross-examining experts in this area, the studies do reveal that infants do suffer apnoea during sleep, and infants do suffer from hypoxia, and these events are not caused by parental neglect or assault.

A number of genetic disorders have been identified as causing sudden death in infancy. Metabolic diseases and heart disorders are both ordinarily inherited conditions. The gene mutation in some studies has been identified in relatives

---

[107]   See Green, 'Time to put Cot Death to Bed?' (1999) *British Medical Journal* 3 19: 697–698. Also see Limerick, 'Not Time to Put Cot Death to Bed' (1999) *British Medical Journal* 3 19: 698–700.

[108]   See Rahilly, 'The Pneumographic and Medical Investigation of Infants Suffering Apparent Life Threatening Episodes' (1991) *Journal of Paediatrics and Child Health*: 27: 349–353; cited by Professor Tim David in his speech to the Family Bar, 6 March 2003.

[109]   See Rahilly 'The pneumographic and medical investigation of infants suffering apparent life threatening episodes' (1991) *Journal of Paediatrics and Child Health* 17: 349-353.; Samuels, Poets, Noyes, Harmtann, Hewertson, Shouthall, 'Diagnosis and management after life threatening events in infants and young children who received cardiopulmonary resuscitation' (1993) *British Medical Journal* 306: 489–492; Pitetti, Maffei, Chang, Hickey, Berger, Clyde, 'Prevalence of retinal hemorrhages and child abuse in children who present with an apparent life-threatening event' (2002) *Pediatrics* 110: 557–562.

or in the preserved tissue of the dead infant.[110] Research regarding a 'cot death gene,' however, would seem to be inconclusive.[111]

4.9 THE ASSESSMENT OF PARENTS SUSPECTED OF ABUSE

Dr Kerry Bluglass is a Consultant Adult Psychiatrist at the Woodbourne Priory Hospital in Birmingham and a Senior Clinical Lecturer in the Department of Psychiatry at the University of Birmingham. He has for more than a decade given evidence with regard to assessing parents' mental state in alleged cases of abuse, and he often speaks at seminars of family lawyers. He notes that it is difficult to discern any malevolent or deliberate intent on the part of any mothers/parents who kill, or almost kill, their children. Of course underlying psychodynamic facts may later emerge, indicating failure of bonding, or transgenerational attachment distortions, or ambivalent attitudes to mothering,[112] according to Dr Bluglass.

Bluglass contends that it is difficult to describe common characteristics of parents who perpetrate this type of abuse. It has been noted that the majority of MSBP perpetrators are mothers, although fathers, grandmothers, nurses, foster care mothers and day care workers have all been reported to be perpetrators of this type of abuse.[113] It has been noted that some parents who have been found to have injured their children intentionally show little emotional attachment to the child when left alone, and seemed more interested in spending time in the hospital with the medical and nursing staff than with their ill child.[114] MSBP mothers seem to welcome tests being performed on a child. They become resentful when they do not get what they want. It is easy to see, however, wholly innocent mothers might also welcome tests being performed on the child, and may also become resentful when a test is not provided.

It has also been noted that between 10 and 25 per cent of MSBP perpetrators suffer from Munchausen Syndrome themselves. In these cases there is likely to be a long and bizarre maternal medical history. Professor David notes that in trying to understand MSBP, it is helpful to see the condition as part of a spectrum of parental behaviour, from one extreme of complete neglect to the

---

[110] Ackerman, Tester, Driscoll, 'Molecular autopsy of sudden unexplained death in the young' (2001) *American Journal of Forensic Medicine and Pathology*; 22:105–111.
[111] Summers, Summers, Drucker, Barson, Hajeer, Hutchinson, 'Association of IL-10 genotype with sudden infant death syndrome' *Human Immunology*, 61: 1270–1273. See criticism of these findings by Professor David, 'Identifying the Subset of Sudden Infant Deaths that are Suspicious', a paper given to the Family Law Bar Association on 6 March 2003.
[112] See Bluglass, 'Characteristics of parents/carers who kill babies', a paper given to the Family Bar in February 2003.
[113] See Professor Tim David, above; Bluglass, *Munchausen Syndrome by Proxy* in Weldon & Van Velson (eds), *A Practical Guide to Forensic Psychotherapy* (Jessica Kingsley, 1997).
[114] See Professor David, above.

other extreme of procuring symptoms. Professor David agrees that the most common diagnostic area, particularly when concrete forensic evidence of procuring or perpetrating the abuse is unavailable, it is for a physician to see if the mother fits some general profile of MSBP perpetrators. Professor David believes this is a serious error: the profile of the mother may help one to understand why she has abused the child, but it cannot be used to indicate whether or not the child has been abused.[115]

Most experts now agree that MSBP should be considered when the following factors have been noted:

- an illness is unexplained, prolonged and so extraordinary that it prompts experienced physicians to note that it seems unprecedented;
- symptoms and signs are inappropriate and incongruous, or present only in the presence of the perpetrator;
- treatment is ineffective or poorly tolerated;
- the parent is not as worried about the child's illness as the nurses and doctors;
- the parent is constantly with the ill child in hospital, and is happily at ease in the ward;
- attacks occur more often at home than in hospital;
- the family has experienced sudden infant or child death;
- the family contains members alleged to have a serious incident of medical disease;
- the parent has had the Munchausen Syndrome diagnosed with regard to that parent.[116]

Many times adult psychiatrists will be asked to assess parents who have alleged to harm the children. It must be kept in mind that the diagnosis or confirmation of MSBP is a paediatric matter, not a psychiatric condition. Dr Bluglass has argued in the past that the existence of a personality disorder in a parent is not an axiomatic pointer to MSBP, or any particular form of child abuse.[117]

An adult psychiatrist in a case involving MSBP will be asked to consider the history of the parent's illness behaviour, and assess the understanding of the parent of the symptoms that the child has exhibited. The psychiatrist will also seek to assess relationships between adults in the family. The psychiatrist will seek to determine whether it is possible to exclude an obvious psychiatric disorder or illness as a cause of the parent's behaviour.

---

[115] See Professor David, above.
[116] See Samuels, Southall, 'Munchausen Syndrome by Proxy' (1992) *British Journal of Hospital Medicine* 47: 759–762.
[117] See Bluglass, *Munchausen Syndrome by Proxy*, above; Weldon & Van Velson *A Practical Guide to Forensic Psychotherapy*, above.

As Dr Bluglass has noted, to look for confirmation in the mental state of the perpetrator before the facts have been established is often unhelpful, reinforcing denial from the parent.[118]

Dr Bluglass notes that none of the features such as a parent's previous history of violence, alcohol or substance abuse, or a personality disorder or even poor relationship with the baby can be diagnostic in themselves. The medical, pathological, and paediatric evidence is *always* more important. That being said, psychiatrists have noted there are certain dynamic factors that need to be kept in mind:

(1) Was there rejection by the mother, after an unplanned and unexpected pregnancy?

(2) Is there an abnormality in the baby, ie a congenital abnormality such as a missing limb or facial dysmorphia?

There are certain methods used repeatedly by parents who kill. The first is upper airway obstruction. Suffocation by the child will look like a hypoxic event, and because the amount of force used is minimal, bruises are not always present.

The second obvious method is by shaking the child. This is discussed in the section on shaking injuries to children (at section 4.6). Advocates will know there is a great deal of controversy and dispute in this area at present regarding the amount of force necessary to cause severe injuries in infants.

The third method is the administering of noxious substances to the child. Mothers have been found to give salt to their child, to give to them laxatives or diuretics, or to give to the children medication such as paracetamol or anti-depressants. Sometimes this comes about because of ignorance, and the intent is not always necessarily to harm the child. The mother may very well be extremely 'disassociated,' according to Dr Bluglass.[119]

Advocates for a parent accused of killing her child must seek to work with the experts to understand whether an appropriate diagnosis of the parent can be made. If the parent is suffering from a psychotic illness, that illness will usually be treatable. The recovery may bring an enormous risk of suicide to the mother and consequently places other children in the home at risk. The mother's grief would need sophisticated professional management and mental health follow up. Experts now agree that with good professional help, a mother who has killed as a result of a psychotic illness can be in a position to care safely for children in the future, with appropriate safeguards. (Whether a court would allow that to occur is another matter altogether.)

---

[118] See Bluglass 'Characteristics of parents who kill babies', above.

[119] See paper given by Dr Bluglass to the Family Bar, February 2003, above.

For a parent not diagnosed as suffering from psychotic illness, but instead assessed to be providing poor quality parenting over a wide range of categories, the situation is quite different. If a parent suffers from a personality disorder, it is ordinarily a long process to address that disorder, if the personality is changeable at all. Parents who suffer from disordered attachment are more problematic. Dr Bluglass notes that there is some evidence that parents can modify their behaviour. Physicians and mental health professionals offering help to parents must emphasise the distinction between treatment and intervention for the individual as opposed to treatment of the individual with no likelihood of rendering that individual safe as a parent. Dr Bluglass notes that any treatment or intervention is very uncertain of success.

4.10   NON-ACCIDENTAL INJURIES – FRACTURES

Advocates appearing for or against a parent accused of causing a child to suffer a fractured or broken limb will need to have a basic understanding of the role of the radiologist. These experts will be asked to define the abnormalities revealed on the x-rays or scans, offer a differential diagnosis, suggest the cause of the injuries, date the injuries, determine if there is likely to be an underlying brittle bone disease, and, most importantly, asked to decide if the injuries are consistent with the explanation offered by the accused.[120]

It has been known since at least the early 1950s that many childhood fractures are clinically undetectable and cause surprisingly little pain. The fractures become evident only after the entire skeleton had been x-rayed.[121] In particular, rib and spine fractures often went undetected. Researchers found it hard to believe that children who were in no obvious pain, and with no history of parental abuse, could have suffered the injuries at the hands of the parents. Indeed, at first it was assumed that the injuries were likely caused in most cases by 'metaphyseal fragility of bone.'[122] In 1961, a paper presented in the Journal of the American Medical Association sought to argue that in many of these cases of discovered fractures the cause was child abuse. The term 'battered child' dates from this article.[123]

Advocates must have at least a basic understanding of the language used by paediatricians and radiologists.

The outer layer of bone is made up of a hard, compact material that forms rings around canals (called haversian canals) inside the bone. Inside each canal

---

120   See Kempe et al, 'The Battered Child Syndrome' (1962) *Journal of American Medical Association* 181: 17–24.
121   See Astley, 'Multiple Metaphyseal Fractures in Small Children' (1979) *British Journal of Radiology* 26: 577–583.
122   See Astley, above.
123   Kempe et al, 'The Battered Child Syndrome' (1961) *Journal of American Medical Association* 181: 17–24.

are blood vessels. The compact bone is covered with an even tougher layer, called the periosteum. The inner part of a bone (the spongy bone) is ordinarily very strong. Bone strength derives from a protein called collagen. The hardness comes from phosphorus and calcium. A broken bone will ordinarily heal itself. Doctors seek to heal simple fractures by placing the broken ends together, allowing the repair cells (osteoblasts) to knit the bone together.

'Compound' or open fractures are those fractures that also cause tissue damage. A compound (open) fracture might require the treating physician to insert a pin to hold the bone in place. A simple (closed) fracture occurs when there is no communication between the site of the fracture and the skin. A greenstick fracture is an incomplete break in the bone. A displaced fracture is when the ends of the bone are not aligned.

Assessors will seek to determine whether the fracture was caused by direct impact, or by indirect violence transmitted along the bone. Assessors will seek to discover whether the fractures were discovered accidentally, and whether there are multiple fractures, in particular where the fractures are of different ages. And most obviously, the assessor will seek to determine whether the fracture is consistent with the history given by the parent or carer.

A joint is the place where two or more bones meet. Hinge joints (elbow and knee) allow movement in one direction only. Swivelling ball and socket joints (hip and shoulders) allow for a circular movement. The saddle joint is at the base of the thumb. The pivot joint allows the forearm to twist.

A basic glossary is set out below:

Diaphysis	Tubular shaft of bone
Ephiphysis	Expanded articular (or joint) end of bone
Osteolysis	Removal or loss of bone resulting in areas of reduced bone density
Osteopaenia	Loss of bone density due to a lack of calcium and mineral content
Perosteum	Membrane covering bones; bleeding beneath the membrane results in new bone formation
Physis	Cartilage growth plate at ends of longer bones
Radiograph	Picture taken with x-rays
Sutures	Joints between the plates of bone which form the skull vault
Wormian bones	Small bones that lie within the suture or joint between the curved plates of bone that form the skull
Osteogenesis Imperfecta, aka brittle bone disease	Underlying cause is a defect of collagen, which forms part of the connective tissue of the bones. Condition is hereditary. Biochemical analysis allows for a precise diagnosis

Rickets

A nutritional disorder caused when the sufferer fails to consume sufficient minerals, particularly vitamin D. It is now more commonly the result of kidney or liver disease rather than diet. Fractures that might be mistaken for non-accidental injury can be found in children suffering from rickets.

Parts of the body:

Cranium	Skull
Mandible	Jawbone
Clavicle	Collar bone
Scapula	Shoulder blade
Ulna	Main forearm bone
Radius	Small forearm bone
Pelvis	Hip bone
Carpels	Wrist bones
Femur	Thigh bone
Patella	Kneecap
Fibula	Small shin bone
Tibia	Main shin bone

4.11   THE MEDICAL HISTORY

Despite the wealth of knowledge paediatricians and radiologists bring to investigations of child abuse, by far the most important aspect of the assessment is the taking of the medical history from the parents. Experts agree the following must be analysed carefully:

(1) What events happened just before the injury occurred? When did the carers first notice the injury? How did the symptoms develop? When did the child last eat? What, and how much, did the child eat?

(2) Who was with the child just before the injury? Who were the carers? Who else was in the home? Could they have heard anything?

(3) Was there a 'precipitating event?' Was there a difficult feeding episode? Was there a problem with nappy changes? Were the parents involved in a dispute at the time?

(4) What is the child's normal nature? Is the child in a difficult developmental stage?

(5) What was the first response of the carer after the injury? Did they seek care promptly?

(6) What is the child's medical history? Was the child's birth difficult? Were there illnesses in the neonatal period? Has the child been immunized against communicable diseases? Has the child received regular physical check ups?

(7) Is the child's developmental level age appropriate or delayed? Can the child

do the things the carers say he can do? (In other words, if a carer says the child climbed into a bath, is that possible?)

(8) Can the child tell you any part of the history?

Assessors (not exclusively paediatricians) will also want to know who lives in the family home. Are they related? What is the family support system? Who cares for the child ordinarily? Is the family suffering from poverty or recent unemployment? Is a family member in prison? Is there a history of domestic abuse, or drug or alcohol use? Are the parents divorced or separated?

More intrusive assessors will also want to inquire into the parents' history: were they abused as children? Was either parent taken into the care system?

Assessors will want to know how the parent normally disciplines the child. Assessors will seek to determine whether the parents understand the nature and severity of the child's injury.

Paediatricians will take careful measurements of the child's height, weight and head circumference. These will be plotted on standard growth charts and compared with the child's height and weight at birth. If the head size shows a rapid increase that might indicate the time of an infant's head injury. Low weight or poor growth are obvious indicators of neglect, or what is called 'non-organic failure to thrive'.

The child's skin should be carefully examined. Were there bruises? Abrasions? Cuts? Lesions? The scalp must be examined for bruises or redness. Advocates must note when any of these examinations are omitted, in particular in those cases where physicians are confident that the child suffered a non-accidental injury. Were the ears, nose and throat examined? Was there bleeding of the gums, or bruising or abrasions inside the lips? Are there retinal or pre-retinal haemorrhages? Was there bleeding into the chambers of the eye?

Doctors ordinarily will wish to know about the other children in the home. Are there siblings with similar symptoms or injuries?

Skull fractures cause special problems for physicians and experts. The diagnosis is usually only made after x-ray examination. Skull fractures are difficult to age because they heal without leaving a callus. The usual timetable of fracture healing is therefore not applicable.

Skull fractures ordinarily occur because of an impact between a solid object and the skull. The parietal bone is large and relatively thin and vulnerable to injury. Frontal fractures, on the other hand, are much more rare. The occipital bone fracture has been noted to occur often in abused children.[124] Advocates will need to understand that physicians will likely not accept that a child has

---

[124] See Professor Tim David, 'Fractures: General Assessment of Suspected Abuse' a paper given to a seminar of the Family Law Bar Association, 5 July 2002.

suffered a fractured skull as a result of falling out of bed. Research in 1977 showed that of 246 children less than five years old observed to fall out of bed from a height of more than 90 centimetres, no life-threatening injuries were reported.[125] Numerous studies have confirmed this. It is unlikely a child has suffered serious life-threatening injuries merely by falling out of a bed, no matter the angle of the fall.

4.12   EMERGENCY PROTECTION ORDERS

The CA 1989, s 44 gives to a local authority certain emergency powers with regard to a child, dependent upon the court making a finding that there is reasonable cause to believe that the child is likely to suffer significant harm if not removed from the home. In those circumstances, the court may make an emergency protection order (EPO). The order may also be made if the court finds that the parents are frustrating the reasonable efforts of the local authority to make enquiries regarding the child.

The advocate for the parents will need to use the EPO hearing for an emergency conference and planning session. What brought about the need for the EPO? What can be done to remedy the situation? What are the alternative care arrangements in the family, should the local authority not seek to return? Where are the factual disagreements between the local authority and the parent? Can the child be returned under a protective order of some type?

Almost invariably, EPOs will lead to further applications for interim care orders. Advocates for the parents and the local authority should seek to go ahead and plan the litigation. Will it need to be transferred? Are there other parties to notify and serve? Are there previous proceedings? Is there a need for disclosure of any of those papers?

Advocates should also seek a measure of agreement, if possible. What are the essential factual issues? Is the local authority seeking to exclude anyone from the family home? Who are the witnesses the local authority seek to rely on with regard to factual disputes? What areas of the case will likely need expert attention? When will a guardian be appointed?

The legal framework surrounding EPOs is set out at ss 44–45 of the CA 1989. The orders are for eight days, and may be renewed once for a further seven days. No appeal may be made against the making of, or the refusal of EPOs, or the extension or the refusal to extend the EPO. Where the court makes an EPO with an exclusion requirement, the court may attach a power of arrest to the requirement. The child or a parent or someone else with parental responsibility may apply to discharge the EPO.

---

[125]   (1977) *Pediatrics* 60: 533–636.

If magistrates act unreasonably with regard to making or refusing to make an EPO, the only remedy is judicial review. See, generally, *Re P (Emergency Protection Order)* [1996] 1 FLR 482; *Essex County Council v F* [1993] 1 FLR 847.

4.13 SECURE ACCOMMODATION ORDERS

Advocates appearing for parents or children at applications for secure accommodation orders often have the Kafka-esque feeling that their presence is not really required by the relevant law, or even acknowledged by the magistrates. It is right to say that the law in this area is subject to the dictum that hard cases make bad law.

Children involved in secure accommodation cases are invariably hard cases. The section of the CA 1989 that allows for secure accommodation is set out in the negative: that is, that the local authority must never place a child in secure accommodation *unless* certain requirements are met: (1) the child has a history of absconding and is likely to abscond from any other description of accommodation; and (2) if the child absconds, the child is likely to suffer significant harm. The Act provides, as an alternative, that the child may be placed in secure accommodation if the child is likely to injure himself or others if he is placed in any other type of accommodation. If the court determines that the relevant criteria have been made out, the court must make the order. The court may make an interim order permitting the child to be kept during the period of the adjournment in secure accommodation. The court's authority is not required for the first 72 hours that a child is placed in secure accommodation. Exceptional circumstances can justify the making of an application where a child is not already in secure accommodation. The lack of suitable accommodation in the area is not an exceptional circumstance.[126]

The court does not have to find both s 25(1)(a) and (b) before making an order; either limb is sufficient.[127] The child's best interest is not the paramount consideration. Instead, the court will look to s 25 of the Act.

The phrase 'likely to abscond' should be interpreted in the same way as 'likely' in s 31 of the CA 1989. That is, it is used in the sense of a real possibility, a possibility that cannot be sensibly ignored having regard to the nature and gravity of the feared harm in the particular case.[128]

Almost invariably, the child will wish to attend. The court has the discretionary power to permit the child to attend, but the Court of Appeal has indicated its displeasure with this course. The child should not be permitted to attend if the

---

[126] See *Re AK (Secure Accommodation Order)* [2000] 1 FLR 317.
[127] *Re D (Secure Accommodation Order)* [1997] 1 FLR 197.
[128] *Re D (Secure Accommodation Order)* [1999] Fam Law 311.

court is satisfied not attending is in the best interests of the child. The fact that the child would need to be physically restrained during the hearing in order to control him would, not surprisingly, be sufficient ground for refusing to allow the child to attend court.[129]

The Court of Appeal has now held that the secure accommodation procedure is compliant with the European Convention. The court in *W Borough Council v DK, DJK, AK*[130] held that detention under s 25 of the Children Act 1989 is lawful so long as the child detained is kept there in connection with that child's education. The education requirement is vital, given that the European Convention, at Article 5, justifies detention only if necessary for the purposes of educational supervision. In the context of the detention of minors, however, educational supervision did not just mean attending classroom education. According to Butler-Sloss P, educational supervision necessarily embraced many aspects of the exercise by the local authority of parental responsibility for the child.

The difficulties of representing children in these applications were spelled out in bold relief in the case of *Re M (Child) (Secure Accommodation Order: Representation)*.[131] In that case, C was placed in secure accommodation. She was 15 years old. She had been a registered drug addict for a year. She had a child, who was also the subject of separate care proceedings. Shortly before this application, C had presented at hospital with severe abdominal pains. She had signed herself out of hospital against medical advice. She clearly was taking cocaine that had been adulterated with ammonia.

C was placed in a secure unit under s 25(1)(a)(i) of the CA 1989, which gives authorities permission to place the child in secure accommodation for 72 hours prior to a court application. Social services sought a secure accommodation order. C was questioned in the unit. The guardian for C attempted to convince her to remain in the secure unit. C refused. C sought to retain separate legal representation. C wanted the solicitors who were appearing for her in the care proceedings to handle the application for a secure accommodation order.

C was brought to court from the secure unit. She met her own solicitor, who had not been served with the application. C's solicitor did not feel that she could adequately represent C. The magistrates first granted the local authority's application to dispense with formal service of the papers. The magistrates then adjourned the matter until the afternoon to give C an opportunity to give instructions to her solicitors.

In the afternoon, the social worker gave evidence. The court then made an interim care order as well as a secure accommodation order. C appealed both

129   See *Re W (Secure Accommodation Order: Attendance at Court)* [1994] 2 FLR 1092.
130   [2001] HRLR 12, [2001] 2 WLR 1141, [2001] 1 FLR 526.
131   [2001] EWCA Civ 458, [2001] 2 FLR 169.

decisions. Johnson J heard the case, and found that C and her solicitor were fairly treated by the magistrates, who had sought to give C time to discuss the papers with her solicitor prior to the hearing that afternoon. Johnson J further held that the magistrates were right to make the order. C appealed to the Court of Appeal. The Court of Appeal dismissed the appeal, holding that the child had been treated fairly, and that the magistrates had complied with the dictates of Article 6 of the Convention. Thorpe LJ noted that appellate courts

> 'had to review with scrupulous care a hearing that gave a frightened and vulnerable teenager only a few hours with her solicitor before embarking on a hearing that resulted in her loss of liberty for six weeks. The social worker's evidence [regarding the child's chaotic life] was a matter of record, and in many important respects was neither contested nor capable of contest. There were no other steps that could have been taken had an extensive adjournment been granted.'

And there, in a nutshell, is the advocate's dilemma: he or she must determine whether any facts might be contested. If so, will an adjournment provide a fair opportunity to do so? Is the client likely to remain in placement during the adjournment?

Again, advocates need to plan ahead for the interim care order and for the care proceedings that will ensue. What is the local authority's plan? Is there a treatment plan available? Where will the child move to when she leaves the secure unit? What are the contact implications? What experts will be required? All of this should be in place when the matter comes back before the court for the first interim care hearing.

4.14 ADOPTION

4.14.1 Overview

The law of adoption is currently in a state of flux, awaiting full implementation of the Adoption and Children Act 2002 (ACA 2002). But students of this area of the law know that adoption has always caused difficulties in English law, ever since the implementation of the first Adoption Act in 1926. A movement for reform of the first Act began almost immediately after its implementation.

One of the difficulties in adoption law is the uneasy alliance with care proceedings. This is not simply that the Adoption Act 1976 (AA 1976) places the child's welfare as a first consideration, while the CA 1989 makes it the paramount consideration. The difficulties instead surround the concept that the parents' approval is required for adoption, unless the court determines that the parents' failure to give their consent is 'unreasonable'. The consent is difficult to explain to lay clients who are about to see their child adopted. How could it be unreasonable to want to keep your child?

The ACA 2002, when fully implemented, will change that narrative. The new Act makes the child's welfare the court's paramount consideration. And the Act allows courts to dispense with the consent of parents by one of two methods: a finding that the parents cannot be found; or a finding that the welfare of the child requires the consent to be dispensed with.[132]

Advocates must know and understand the reasons that underpin our current law of adoption, in particular the widely accepted notion in the psychological literature that children require a permanent psychological parent.[133] Studies performed primarily in the US have indicated that children needed this feeling of permanence above almost all else, and that this role might be adequately filled by foster parents or adoptive parents, so long as the child understood that this was in fact his psychological parent. This view is almost universally accepted, and underpins adoption law.

Because almost all adoptions now are initiated by local authority adoption agencies, contested adoptions usually either precede or occur alongside care proceedings under the CA 1989. Indeed, one of the reasons for the enactment of the ACA 2002 is to streamline the procedures, and to place the child's best interests as the paramount consideration under both Acts.

If a local authority in a care case seeks to place a child for adoption, the authority must follow the Local Authority Circular of 28 August 1998 (LAC(98)20) entitled 'Adoption – Achieving the Right Balance'. Paragraphs 28 to 33 of that document were issued in an amended form in the Chief Inspector's letter of June 1999 (CI(99)5). The Circular requires the local authority to set out the likely steps and timescales required to implement the plan for adoption. Paragraph 29 of the Amended Circular provides that when the choice of placement depends on findings of fact, the care plan must still seek to explain the key steps which would need to be taken before an adoptive placement could be made. The authority must give estimated timescales for each of these steps. Where the facts of the care application are not disputed and the preferred option is adoption, paragraph 30 makes it clear that local authorities must satisfy themselves that sufficient and appropriate assessment has taken place. The authority must rule out rehabilitation or placement with relatives.

Paragraph 31 sets out the steps which should always have been addressed before final hearing: (a) the coordination of information between the teams responsible for the care proceedings and those responsible for family findings; (b) the completion, as far as possible, of the Form E giving details about the child; (c) consideration of the case by the Adoption Panel with a view to making

---

[132]   The welfare checklist at s 1(3) of the CA 1989 will be used to help guide judges in their task. See s 52(1) ACA 2002.
[133]   See Jordan, 'Contested Adoptions and the Role of the State in Family Matters', in Ryburn, ed, *Contested Adoptions: Research, Law, Policy and Practice* (Arena, 1994).

a recommendation on whether adoption is in the child's best interests; (d) the identification by the local authority of the key steps and timetable which would lead to an adoptive placement if the court made a care order; (e) a contingency plan to be used if the preferred option for adoption cannot be achieved; and (f) consideration as to whether a freeing application is appropriate.

Paragraph 33 of the Amended Circular makes it clear that it is not appropriate before the final care hearing for there to have been introductions between the child and the prospective adopters or for the agency to have confirmed the Panel's recommendations.

When the ACA 2002 comes into force there will be a new process implemented in adoption cases. As discussed below, courts will no longer be able to free children for adoption. Instead, the court will be asked to make a placement order, authorising the Local Authority Adoption agency to place a child with prospective adopters.[134]

Courts hearing contested adoption applications under the AA 1976 will apply a two-part test, as follows:

(1) Is adoption in the child's best interests?
(2) If so, the court must determine whether:
    (a) the birth parents have consented to the application;
    (b) if they have not consented, the court must determine whether that consent should be dispensed with on grounds set out in the AA 1976.[135]

In order to determine whether adoption is in the child's best interests, the court will apply s 6 of the AA 1976. That section provides that any court or adoption agency in making any decision relating to the adoption of a child shall have regard to all the circumstances of the case, but give first consideration to the need to safeguard and promote the welfare of the child throughout the child's childhood.[136] So far as practicable, the court and adoption agency must ascertain the wishes and feelings of the child regarding the decision, and give due

---

[134] See ACA 2002, ss 18–29.

[135] In the AA 1976, unmarried fathers are given no rights to withhold consent to an adoption. A father's agreement is required only if he is married to the mother of the child, or if the father has a parental responsibility order or parental responsibility agreement. The unmarried father without parental responsibility need not be a party to the adoption application, *Re C (Adoption: Parties)* [1995] 2 FLR 483; AA 1976, s 72.

[136] Lord Simon set out the difference between the Adoption Act's 'first consideration' and 'paramount consideration' in the case of *Re D (An Infant) (Adoption: Parent's Consent)* [1977] 1 All ER 145. 'In adoption proceedings the welfare of the child is not the paramount consideration (ie outweighing all others); but it is the first consideration (ie outweighing any other) ... The new statutory provisions are explicit that in adoption proceedings it is the welfare of the child throughout childhood that is to be considered, not merely short-term prospects.' Where a court is considering consolidated applications under the CA 1989 and the AA 1976, the welfare of the child subject to the CA 1989 application will be considered paramount to the welfare of the child subject to the AA 1976 application, if there is a conflict of interest between the two. See *Re T and E (Proceedings: Conflicting Interests)* [1995] 1 FLR 581. See also, with regard to

consideration to them, having regard to the child's age and understanding.[137] (The ACA 2002 will require the courts to consider the child's welfare as the paramount consideration, and will consider the welfare of the proposed adopted child throughout his life).

If the court determines adoption is in the child's best interests, the court then is directed to consider the grounds under s 16 of the 1976 Act for determining whether the court should dispense with the consent of the non-consenting parents.

4.14.2   Grounds for adoption under the Adoption Act 1976, s 16

(1)   The birth parents cannot be found or are incapable of giving agreement[138]

The AA 1976 requires notice of the adoption application be served on each person(s) whose agreement is required under the Act if there is a known address where a parent can be found.[139] If the applicant does not know the address of the birth parents, assistance from government agencies must be sought. If that is unavailing, newspaper advertisements are usually the next step. Research has shown that 11 per cent of non-agreeing mothers and 5 per cent of non-agreeing fathers were unable to be found or were incapable of giving agreement.[140] In the case of *Re L (A Minor) (Adoption: Parental Agreement)*,[141] the court refused to accept a certificate from a psychiatrist of the birth mother, stating that the birth mother was incapable of giving consent. The court held that the fact the parent was irrational was insufficient. The court also noted that minority does not per se prevent a person having the capacity to agree.

(2)   The birth parents are withholding their agreement unreasonably[142]

Lord Hailsham, in the case of *Re W (An Infant)*,[143] laid down three guiding principles for contested adoption applications, settling the law in this area for a generation. The case arose because of conflicts between two separate panels

---

'throughout childhood', the case of *Re D (A Minor) (Adoption Order: Validity)* [1991] 2 FLR 66, where the court held that a benefit which might accrue to the child after the age of 18 should not be considered as a relevant factor to a court considering an adoption application. See also *T v T (Minors: Custody Appeal)* [1987] 1 FLR 374. That now changes with the 2002 Act.

137   *Re D (Minors) (Adoption by Step-Parent)* [1981] FLR 102 ('fairly clear reason needed to go against the wishes of a mature child').

138   AA 1976, s 16(2)(a). This section was part of the Adoption of Children Act 1926.

139   *Re B* [1988] 1 QB 12.

140   See Murch, *Review of Adoption Law* (HMSO, 1992).

141   [1987] 1 FLR 400.

142   AA 1976, s 16(2)(b).

143   [1971] AC 682, HL.

of the Court of Appeal.[144] The different panels disagreed whether the test for determining the reasonableness of withholding agreement should include determinations of culpability and blame with regard to the birth parents' behaviour to the child. The Court of Appeal in the case of *Re W* had allowed the birth mother's appeal on the ground that her conduct had not been culpable or blameworthy.[145] A different panel in the Court of Appeal held instead that courts should not focus on the blameworthiness of the birth parents' behaviour, but rather the reasonableness of their refusal in the totality of the circumstances.

Lord Hailsham and the majority of the House of Lords believed that focusing on the parents' blameworthiness would lead the trial court into error. Section 16(2)(b) of the AA 1976 lays down a test of reasonableness, noted Lord Hailsham, and it does not lay down a test of culpability or self-indulgent indifference, or a failure or probable failure of parental duty:

> 'From this it is clear that the test is reasonableness and not anything else. It is not culpability. It is not indifference. It is not the failure to discharge parental duties. It is reasonableness, and reasonableness in the context of the totality of the circumstances. But, although welfare per se is not the test, the fact that a reasonable parent does pay regard to the welfare of his child must enter into a question of reasonableness as a relevant factor. It is relevant in all the cases if and to the extent that a reasonable parent would take it into account. It is decisive in those cases where a reasonable parent must so regard it.'[146]

The time for making the determination of the reasonableness of the birth parents' refusal to agree to adoption is the time of the application. This means that where the child has been placed with prospective adopters for some time, and has developed attachments to the adopters, it makes it more difficult for the birth parents to convince a court that it is still reasonable to refuse to agree to adoption. The Court of Appeal in the case of *Re H (Infants) (Adoption: Parental Consent)*[147] held that even though s 6 of the AA 1976 does not apply to the issue of determining the reasonableness of the birth parents' refusal to agree, nevertheless:

> 'the relative importance of the welfare of the children is increasing rather than diminishing in relation to dispensing with consent. That being so, it ought to be recognised by all concerned with adoption cases that once the formal consent has been given, or once a child has been placed with the adopters, time begins to run against the mother and, as time goes on, it gets progressively more and more difficult for her to show that the withdrawal of her consent is reasonable.'[148]

---

[144] See *Re B (CHO) (An Infant)* [1971] 1 QB 437, [1970] 3 All ER 1008, CA.
[145] [1970] 2 QB 589, [1970] 3 All ER 990, CA.
[146] Judgment of Lord Hailsham of St Marylebone LC [1971] AC 682 at 690.
[147] [1977] 2 All ER 339, [1977] 1 WLR 471.
[148] Judgment of Ormrod LJ. See also *Re D (a Minor) Adoption: Freeing Order)* [1991] 1 FLR 48, CA, where Butler-Sloss LJ noted that the questions in contested freeing order applications are the same as in applications for adoptions, namely 'Is adoption in the best interests of the child?' and 'Is the natural mother unreasonable in withholding her consent?' The court must in local authority applications determine first whether the child's future would best be served

Courts hearing adoption applications will now determine 'reasonableness' in the following manner:

(1) the test is to be applied at the date of the hearing;[149]
(2) all the circumstances of the case must be considered;[150]
(3) the welfare of the child is not the sole or necessarily paramount concern;[151]
(4) the test is objective (would a reasonable parent in the same or similar circumstances agree to adoption?);[152]
(5) the test is reasonableness, and nothing else;[153]
(6) the court must not substitute its own view for that of the reasonable parent;[154]
(7) there is a range of decisions that might be 'reasonable', depending on the circumstances of the case.[155]

(3) The birth parents have persistently failed without reasonable cause to discharge the obligations of a parent[156]

At first glance, it would seem that this provision merely duplicates the provision above with regard to a parent withholding agreement unreasonably. The Court of Appeal has held, however, that past neglect of the child does not by itself show that the parent is now unreasonably withholding consent. For example, a parent may be able to show the court that he or she has changed and would now be able to provide a safe home for the child.[157] Studies have shown that only 9 per cent of cases utilise this section to dispense with parental agreement.[158] This ground was first introduced in 1958, primarily to broaden the grounds available to the court for making an order.[159] Courts now apply a two-part test as follows:

(1) Has there been a persistent failure to discharge the obligations of a parent?
(2) Has the failure been without reasonable cause?[160]

---

by rehabilitation with the birth parents or by placement in a substitute home. Once that decision is made, the court must then decide whether a reasonable parent would object to placement in a substitute home.

149 *Re L (A Minor) Adoption: Statutory Criteria)* [1990] 1 FLR 305.
150 *O'Connor v A and B* [1971] 2 All ER 1230.
151 *Re H; Re W (Adoption: Parental Agreement)* [1983] FLR 614.
152 *Re W* [1971] AC 682, HL.
153 *Re E (Adoption Freeing Order)* [1995] 1 FLR 382.
154 *Re E (A Minor) (Adoption)* [1989] 1 FLR 126.
155 *Re H; Re W,* [1983] FLR 614; *Re W* [1971] AC 682, HL. For full discussion of this issue, see Hershman and McFarlane, *Children Law and Practice* (Family Law, 2004), H (123)–(145).
156 AA 1976, s 16(2)(c).
157 See *Re H; Re W* [1983] FLR 614.
158 Murch, 'Agreement and Freeing', in *Review of Adoption Law* (HMSO, 1997), para 37.
159 See discussion in Cretney and Masson, above, p 928.
160 See *Re D (Minors) (Adoption by Parent)* [1973] Fam 209; *Re M (An Infant)* (1965) 109 SJ 574; *Re P (Infants)* [1962] 1 WLR 1296; *W v Nottinghamshire County Council* [1981] 3 WLR 959.

(4)   Has the birth parent abandoned or neglected the child?[161]

Studies have revealed that this section is ordinarily used only in conjunction with other grounds.[162] The Divisional Court in the case of *Watson v Nikolaisen*[163] has held that where the mother of an illegitimate child had placed the child directly with prospective adopters and signed a form she believed at the time to have ended her parental rights, she still had not 'abandoned' the child within the meaning of the section. Abandonment requires conduct contrary to the criminal law. It has also been held that placing children in the care of the local authority because of inability to care for the child is not 'neglecting' a child under this section.[164]

(5)   Has the birth parent persistently ill-treated the child?[165]

Again, the studies quoted in the *Review of Adoption Law* showed this section was relied on only in conjunction with other grounds. It has been held that the agreement of both parents might be dispensed with even though it is impossible to prove which one of the two actually ill-treated the child.[166]

(6)   Has the birth parent seriously ill-treated the child, making rehabilitation in the parents' household unlikely?[167]

The Houghton Committee in 1974[168] recommended that this section be introduced in the Children Act 1975 and it was duly enacted. Bevan and Perry, in their text in 1978 shortly after the section came into force, argued that there need be no causal link between the ill-treatment and the poor prospects of rehabilitation. Section 6 of the 1975 Act applies to the question of the likelihood of rehabilitation to the birth parents' household.[169] Cretney and Masson argue that because this is true, agreement might be dispensed with where the local authority had failed to provide sufficient assistance to the family.[170]

Dispensing with parental consent will be different when the 2002 Act is implemented. The child's welfare will not be the paramount consideration (see s 1(7) of the ACA 2002). Instead, 'consent may be dispensed with when the child's welfare requires it'. Case law will no doubt be required to give flesh to this requirement.

---

[161]   AA 1976, s 16(2)(d).
[162]   See Murch, *Review of Adoption Law* (HMSO, 1992).
[163]   [1955] 2 QB 286.
[164]   See *Re JM Carroll* [1931] 1 KB 317; *Re P (Infants)* [1962] 1 WLR 1296.
[165]   AA 1976, s 16(2)(e).
[166]   *Re PB (A Minor) (Application to Free for Adoption)* [1985] FLR 394.
[167]   Adoption Act 1976, s 16(2)(f).
[168]   HMSO, 1974.
[169]   See *Re PB (A Minor) Application to Free for Adoption* (1985) FLR 394.
[170]   See Cretney and Masson, p 930.

4.14.3   Freeing orders

As commentators have often noted, adoption law under the AA 1976 is an uneasy combination of two issues: the court must determine whether the child's links with the birth parents must be severed; and the court must then make the determination whether it is in the best interests of the child to create a new legal relationship with prospective adoptive parents. It was felt by those who contributed to the Houghton Report, as well as the framers of the AA 1976, that in certain situations it would be better to separate those issues.

The provision first enacted in 1975 providing for an application for a 'freeing order' was finally implemented in 1984. Most observers agree that the procedure has not been a success, for a variety of reasons.[171] The ACA 2002 will eliminate freeing orders. Within care proceedings, local authorities will be able to apply for placement orders under ACA 2002, s 18, which in effect replace freeing orders.

Freeing orders, the Houghton Committee believed, should be used to provide a speedy process for mothers to give their consent quickly and easily, while in contested cases the court might dispense with the parents' agreement at an early stage of the proceedings.[172]

Research has shown, however, that in the decade of their availability, freeing orders have only been used for about 10 per cent of adoption placements.[173] Most applications are made by local authorities and the majority of those applications concern children in care. Frequent delays in the legal process mean agencies see little use for the freeing application.

For these reasons, the ACA 2002 will mean the end of freeing orders. The 'freeing' system will be replaced by the 'placement' system. The crucial difference is that under the placement system, the birth parents retain parental responsibility with adoption. If parents have consented to the placement, local authority adoption agencies will place the child with prospective adopters under s 19(1) of the ACA 2002. If no consent is forthcoming, the court will be asked to make a placement order under s 31(2) of the ACA 2002. The court will be asked to dispense with parental consent under either of the two routes set out at s 52 of the ACA 2002.

Freeing is not appropriate where foster parents seek to adopt a child who has been living with them.[174] Freeing orders are also not appropriate where there

[171]   See particularly Lowe and Borkowski, *Freeing for Adoption* (HMSO, 1993).
[172]   See Houghton Committee Report, above, para 173; Lowe and Borkowski, above, p 2.
[173]   Lowe and Borkowski, above, p 4.
[174]   *Re H (A Minor) (Freeing Order)* [1993] 2 FLR 325.

is to be a degree of openness or contact between birth parent and adoptive parent.[175] Applications for freeing orders might only be made by adoption agencies.[176] The consent of the parent or guardian is required, unless the applicant seeks to dispense with parental agreement and the child is in its care.[177] The court must determine that the parents have had an opportunity to make a declaration that they do not want to be involved with the adoption.[178] Parents not making this declaration must be told after one year whether the child has been adopted or placed for adoption.[179] Research has shown that approximately one-sixth of parents declare they do not wish to be further involved.[180]

If agreement to the freeing order is being withheld, the court must determine whether the agreement should be dispensed with on the ground set out in the AA 1976. These grounds have been discussed above. Courts have said that because there would be no relationship with prospective adopters which might be broken if the order were not made, it is more difficult for a court to find that the parent is withholding consent unreasonably. Perhaps because of this, some 84 per cent of freeing applications result in orders, compared with the 96 per cent success rate for applications in adoption proceedings.[181]

Courts must also make the determination that the father, if unmarried, has no intention of seeking a parental responsibility order or a residence order. If a court determines the father does or might have such an intention, the court must further make the determination whether the application will be likely to be refused.[182] The effect of the freeing order is that the parents' parental responsibility for a child is terminated. The birth parent would then require leave for any further application to the court concerning the child, save for an application to revoke the freeing order.[183]

Courts might make section 8 contact orders when hearing applications for freeing orders. If the adoption agency then seeks to place a child for adoption and disagrees with the level of contact set by the court during the freeing application, the only remedy is through the inherent powers of the High Court.[184]

[175] *Re H (A Minor) (Freeing Order)* [1993] 2 FLR 325.
[176] AA 1976, s 18(1).
[177] AA 1976, s 18(2)(b).
[178] AA 1976, s 18(6).
[179] AA 1976, s 19. Parents not notified of a subsequent decision to place a child might apply to have that placement quashed, see *R v Derbyshire County Council, ex parte T* [1990] 1 FLR 237, CA.
[180] See Lowe and Borkowski, above, Table 3.45.
[181] See Lowe and Borkowski, p 55. See also *Re E (A. Minor) (Adoption)* [1989] 1 FLR 126, CA.
[182] AA 1976, s 18(7); see *Re H (Minors) (Local Authority: Parental Rights) (No 3)* [1991] Fam 151, CA.
[183] See *Re C (Minors) (Adoption: Residence Order)* [1994] Fam 1, CA.
[184] See *Re C (Contact: Jurisdiction)* [1995] 1 FLR 777, CA.

During the interim between freeing order and adoption order, the adoption agency has parental responsibility for the child.[185] The agency has a duty to hold reviews regarding the child every six months if the child is not placed for adoption.[186] Some commentators have argued that freeing orders create a group of parentless children who drift in care.[187]

Research has shown that as many as half of all adoptions are contested at the final hearing.[188] Contested hearings fall into two categories:

(1) where the adoption agency or local authority seek to remove the child from the prospective adopters; and

(2) where the birth parents are refusing to agree to the adoption.

The status of a child that had been freed for adoption, and then not adopted, had been seen as a lacuna in the law of adoption. The House of Lords in the case of *Re G (Adoption: Freeing Order)*[189] has now solved the dilemma. In that case, a child in care had been freed for adoption, thereby extinguishing both the birth parents' and the local authority's parental responsibility for the child. The adoption placement broke down. Section 20 of the AA 1976 allows the birth parent to apply to the court for revocation of the freeing order if the child has not been adopted within one year of the order.

The difficulty was that the freeing order had of course also extinguished the care order. When the birth parent in *Re G* applied for revocation of the freeing order, parental responsibility would have vested solely in her if the court acceded to the application. For that reason, the county court refused on first instance to grant the mother's application. The Court of Appeal dismissed the appeal, rejecting the mother's evidence that she would agree to a care order being made if the application was allowed.

The House of Lords allowed the mother's appeal. The court held that the proper course for a court to take in these circumstances would be to agree to the freeing order being revoked, conditional upon the local authority seeking and obtaining a care order.

4.14.4   Trans-racial adoptions

Research from the 1980s pointed out the difficulties mixed race or ethnic minority children have in a majority white culture. These children often reject

---

185   AA 1976, s 21.

186   Adoption Agencies Regulations 1983, SI 1983/1964, reg 13. Local authorities are governed by the Review of Children's Cases Regulations 1991, SI 1991/895 and the CA 1989, s 22(1)(b) in that the child will be 'looked after' by the local authority and therefore reviews must be held.

187   Cretney and Masson, above, p 909.

188   See Murch, Lowe, Borkowski, Copner and Griew, *Pathways to Adoption: Research Project* (HMSO, 1993). The researchers note that the statistics are skewed because the data included cases where agreement was not given but the final hearing was not contested.

189   [1997] 2 FLR 202, HL.

their own race and culture, perhaps because they are taught nothing about that background except that it is different, and less favoured, than the majority culture. Many local authorities, responding to this research, have instituted policies of attempting, wherever possible, to place ethnic minority or mixed race children with couples of the same or similar background. The reason is obvious: these children need positive reminders of their own racial identity and positive reinforcement about their cultural background, in order to achieve a healthy understanding of that race and culture within a majority white country. The Court of Appeal has held that it is not an improper exercise of discretion for a judge to accept the desirability of a child of mixed race being brought up by black or mixed race families, even where this would require the child to be removed from a stable home.[190] That being said, it has also been held by the Court of Appeal that the 'principle' that a black child should never be placed with white parents 'puts undue emphasis on the issue of colour to the exclusion of other matters important to the security and welfare of a child, such as security in a long-term relationship'.[191] Where an adoption agency has a number of valid reasons for placing a child of mixed race with prospective adopters other than the short-term foster parents who had cared for him for the first two years of his life, including the fact that the adopted child would have adopted siblings of mixed race in his new family, that agency will not be held to have acted unreasonably so as to justify intervention by judicial review.[192]

The Chief Inspector, Social Services Inspectorate, has produced a circular to local authorities entitled *Issues of Race and Culture in the Family Placement of Children*.[193] The guidelines contained in the document, however, do little more than state that local authorities should be sensitive to the issues of race and culture, but that in the end, the best interests of the child must govern the local authority decision. Where there is a conflict between the policy of an adoption authority to avoid trans-racial placements and the welfare of the child, the adoption by persons of the same racial origin is not to be considered an overriding objective. The welfare of the child must prevail.[194] Adoption agencies have no legal duty to consider the child's racial origin or cultural background. Local authorities or voluntary organisations looking after children, however, do have a duty to consider the child's racial background when making decisions about the care and upbringing of those children.[195]

---

190 *Re P (A Minor) (Adoption)* [1990] 1 FLR 96, CA.
191 *Re N (A Minor: Adoption)* [1990] 1 FLR 58 at 62. The court in that case refused to allow the adoption of a Nigerian child by a white couple, citing the fact that adoption is not recognised in Nigeria and noting that the father, who had a role to play in the child's life, would suffer 'shame and distress' if the order were made. The child was made a ward and custody was awarded to the white foster parents who had sought the adoption.
192 *R v Lancashire County Council, ex p M* [1992] 1 FLR 109, CA.
193 CI(90)2.
194 See, in this regard, *Re JK (Adoption: Transracial placement)* [1991] 2 FLR 340, FD; *Re O (Transracial Adoption: Contact)* [1995] 2 FLR 597, FD.
195 CA 1989, ss 22(5) and 61(3)(c).

The thorny question of trans-racial adoptions will always present difficulties for courts. It is recognised that there is the distinct possibility that trans-racial placements damage the child's racial identity.[196] It is also clear that judges, when faced with trans-racial placements where the prospective adopters are caring, loving people who will provide a safe home for the child, are little concerned about the child's future racial identity problem.[197] The Conservative government indicated that 'common-sense values' should determine what is in the best interests for the child and, as commentators have indicated, it is difficult to see how that might be translated into legislation.[198]

4.14.5 Religious upbringing of the adopted child

Section 7 of the AA 1976 provides that an adoption agency shall have regard, so far as is practicable, to any wishes of the child's parents or guardians as to the religious upbringing of the child. The judge is not justified in refusing an adoption order, however, solely because the religious faith of the applicant differs from that of the natural mother.[199]

Advocates for applicants must always keep this rule in mind where those applicants are proposing to change the child's religion. The general rule is that the younger the child is, the less likely it will be that religion will play a huge role in the court's determination. That being said, it is highly unusual for a local authority to place, for example, a Muslim child with a Jewish couple.

4.14.6 Contact after adoption

The CA 1989 gives to the courts the power in adoption proceedings to make a section 8 order allowing for contact between the child and the birth family.[200] Very often contested adoption applications in the end turn into philosophical disputes about the virtues of open adoption. What is clear is that each case must be considered on its individual facts. The law as written applies in the same way in adoption applications for infants as it does for 15-year-olds. The questions for consideration by the courts, however, depend on the distinct factual circumstances of the child. Where that child has a history of care with the birth family, and the birth family wishes to continue contact, even after adoption, courts must be cognisant of recent research showing that children who were in touch with their parents sometimes nevertheless wanted very much

---

196 See, in this regard, Hayes, 'The Ideological Attack on Trans-Racial Adoption' (1995) *Int J Law and Family* 1.
197 See, in this regard, *Re N (A Minor) (Adoption)* [1990] 1 FLR 58; *Re P (A Minor) (Adoption)* [1990] 1 FLR 96; *R v Lancashire County Council, ex parte M* [1992] 1 FLR 109 CA; *Re O (Transracial Adoption: Contact)* [1995] 2 FLR 597.
198 See Cretney and Masson, above p 901.
199 *Re G (An Infant)* [1962] 2 QB 141, [1962] 2 All ER 173, CA.
200 The 1989 Act does this providing that courts hearing 'family proceedings' might make any section 8 order and designating adoption as a 'family proceeding'.

to be adopted; and sometimes children having no parental contact nevertheless felt a strong sense of natural family identity, making adoption a less viable option.[201]

Studies by Rowe and Lambert in 1973 showed that children who were separated from their birth parents and then drifted in care almost invariably emerged from care more damaged than when they entered. Studies published in the late 1970s and early 1980s showed that children living in a number of temporary foster homes began to develop even more deep anxieties and concerns than they had when they entered the care of the local authority.[202]

In 1991, the Department of Health pulled together a great deal of this research in a publication entitled *Patterns and Outcomes in Child Care*.[203] The reports showed that frequent access to parents seemed to be associated with fewer fostering breakdowns.[204] In particular, Thoburn and Rowe showed in 1988 that when other variables were held constant, fewer placements broke down when family links were maintained.[205]

A study published in 1991 showed that even among a group of children who were being placed in permanent substitute families, the children who had maintained links with birth families suffered less damage from long periods in care than those without contact.[206] The 1991 study showed that half of the children referred for permanent placement had some link with their birth family at the time. These were older children who might normally be able to maintain the links themselves. The research has concluded that the growing trend towards access of family members to children in care needs to be extended. By doing so, children might acquire and retain self-identity which is a crucial component in healthy emotional development.[207]

The editors of *Patterns and Outcomes in Child Care* noted that studies had shown that family links which children wish to maintain were not always preserved. Berridge and Cleaver noted in their research an 'anti-family ideology' in some local authority social services departments where social workers believed that a fresh start would help the abused child. Research shows, however, that while a fresh start might be required, this fresh start must include, in most cases, the entire family unit. State intervention must be exercised

---

[201] See Rowe et al, *Long Term Foster Care* (London: Batsford & Baaf, 1984) and discussion of the permanency movement, above.

[202] See Morris, 'The Permanency Principle in Child Care Social Work' (1984), cited in Hoggett, Pearl, Cookes and Bates, eds, *The Family, Law and Society* (Butterworths, 4th edn, 1996), p 640.

[203] HMSO, 1991.

[204] See Berridge & Cleaver, *Foster Home Breakdown* (Oxford University Press, 1987).

[205] Thoburn & Rowe, 'Research: A Snapshot of Permanent Family Placement' (1988) 12 *Adoption & Fostering* 29, cited in *Patterns and Outcomes in Child Care*, above.

[206] See Wedge & Mantle, *Sibling Groups and Social Work* (Gower, 1991).

[207] See Wedge and Mantle, above.

in a more sophisticated manner than simply eliminating all contact with the birth family.

Studies also showed that relationships between siblings were also a vitally important consideration for social workers. Berridge and Cleaver reported more breakdowns when the child had siblings in care, but was separated from all of them, than when placed with all siblings in care or with some siblings in care.

The most important conclusion drawn by the authors of the report is that the concept of permanence must be broadened to include consideration of continued family contact through open adoption or permanent fostering.[208] Informal barriers to contact are widespread and ordinarily not recognised. Local authorities must examine their stated policies, but also examine the prevailing climate of opinion among social workers about birth parents and maintenance of family contact. It is vital that advocates for birth parents explore with experts the experts' knowledge of this research.

The White Paper, *Adoption: The Future*,[209] provides that 'it may be sensible and humane to encourage an open adoption approach, provided that the prospects for a secure and successful adoption are not jeopardised'. Courts are increasingly aware of the value of some contact being maintained, but are also mindful that where the prospective adopters do not wish the contact to take place, the courts risk undermining the placement. The difficulties were discussed by Simon Brown LJ in *Re E (A Minor) (Care Order: Contact)*,[210] where he stated that 'although the value of contact may be limited by the parents' inadequacy, it may still be of fundamental importance to the long term welfare of the child unless … it can be seen that in a given case it will inevitably disturb the child's care'.

Courts hearing freeing order applications might make contact orders, with the issue of contact to be reviewed when the child is to be adopted.[211] Where an unmarried father applies for contact with his child at the same time as the mother and stepfather apply for an adoption order, the court should hear all applications together in one hearing.[212] A former parent after an adoption has been made would require leave of court to apply for further contact. This of course relieves the adoptive parents of receiving notice of the case unless a court has first

---

208   It must be noted that these findings were not entirely supported by other data reported in the various studies collated. As in all social studies of this type, extreme care must be taken in considering the figures produced. Efforts are made by researchers to keep variables to a minimum, but all child-care professionals know that, in actuality, variables are always present because no two cases are ever alike.

209   (1993) Cm 2288.

210   [1994] 1 FLR 146.

211   See *Re A (A Minor) (Adoption: Contact Order)* [1993] 2 FLR 645. See also *Re C (Contact: Jurisdiction)* [1995] 1 FLR 777, CA.

212   *Re G* [1993] Fam Law 93.

granted leave to the birth parents.[213] In the latter case the court held that where the adopters had agreed to give annual reports and refused to do so, leave should be granted for an application for an order that the reports be provided.

Courts have held that while there is ordinarily a presumption that contact with an absent parent is in the best interests of a child, that presumption does not survive an adoption order. In the case of *Re L (A Minor) (Adoption: Statutory Criteria)*,[214] Balcombe LJ held unequivocally that there is no presumption in the case of all children that access by the natural parent is desirable. Counsel for the birth mother had sought to argue that those who wished to stop contact had the burden of showing contact was not desirable. Balcombe LJ noted that the submission was misconceived.

The question of contact after a care order is made inevitably places the care plan of the local authority at risk.[215] Where a local authority has decided on adoption and a cessation of contact with the mother after a care order, and the mother wishes to remain a part of the child's life after the order, the court must weigh the evidence of the benefit of that contact in the future against the possibility that the child would not gain the sort of permanence the child requires and deserves. An example of the difficulty of the exercise is the case of *Re D and H (Care: Termination of Contact)*.[216] Here a local authority sought care orders for two girls, D and H. The mother had admittedly neglected the children. The plan was to place the children with long-term foster parents, with the mother to have generous contact. Mother agreed to the care order and the care plan. That guardian, however, considered adoption to be the better course. She argued that contact should gradually be reduced, then stopped.

The judge at first instance made the care order, but considered adoption to be the preferred course. He therefore made an order under s 34 of the CA 1989, ordering that contact be gradually reduced and then terminated upon placement with prospective adopters.

The Court of Appeal allowed the mother's appeal and discharged the judge's order. The court held the judge had failed to assess the local authority care plan, and had failed to consider the recent improvements in contact between the mother and the two children.

The court noted that the serious nature of the order demanded that the judge in his judgment deal explicitly with the benefits to the children from unhindered contact. The court also held that the judge's reasoning, with regard to the effect of his making the adoption order, was faulty. The judge at first instance had

---

[213]   See *Re E (Adopted Child: Contact: Leave)* [1995] 1 FLR 57; *Re T (Adopted Children: Contact)* [1995] 2 FLR 792.
[214]   [1990] 1 FLR 305, CA.
[215]   See discussion of this in Chapter 6.
[216]   [1997] 1 FLR 841.

believed the making of the adoption order meant he did not have to consider the authority's long-term foster plan. The Court of Appeal noted that while the judge had the power to make the order he made under s 34(2) or (5), he should have instead made an order authorising the local authority to refuse contact under s 34(4).[217]

4.14.7 The orders available

Advocates for birth parents must have available to them arguments supporting less draconian orders than adoption orders. Adoption ends the child's relationship with the birth family, with lifelong effect. The adopted child has a new legal existence. It confers citizenship (perhaps) and the adopted child will inherit from the adoptive parents, if the adoptive parents die intestate. The ACA 2002 provides for the appointment of a special guardian, who may make all parental decisions for the child; special guardianship does not, however, change the child's legal status, or give the child inheritance rights. Legal security does exist. Birth parents may only apply to negate the special guardianship order with leave of court.

4.14.8 The agreement of the child

The AA 1976 requires that 'due consideration' be given to the child's wishes and feelings, but does not mandate that mature children agree to the adoption.[218] The guardian ad litem is not specifically required to ascertain the child's wishes, though it is certainly considered good practice for guardians to do so.[219] The child must attend the adoption hearing unless excused, making it almost certain that mature children at least have a right to be heard before adoption. Cretney and Masson, as well as other commentators, have noted that these provisions may not be adequate to satisfy obligations under the United Nations Convention on the Rights of the Child, Article 12.[220] The review of adoption law in 1992 proposed that the law in England and Wales with regard to consent of a child aged 12 or more be changed to the rule prevailing in Scotland, under the Adoption (Scotland) Act 1978. That Act provides that the consent of a child aged 12 or more is required before an adoption might be made.

---

[217] See also *Re T (Adopted Children: Contact)* [1995] 2 FLR 792, CA; *Re T (Adoption: Contact)* [1995] 2 FLR 251, CA; *Re E (Adopted Child: Contact: Leave)* [1995] 1 FLR 57, FD.

[218] AA 1976, s 6.

[219] See Adoption Rules 1984, SI 1984/265, rr 6(6)(b) and 18(6)(b). See also *Manual of Practice Guidance for Guardians ad Litem, etc* (HMSO, 1992), p 123; discussion in Cretney and Masson, above p 915.

[220] See also *UK Agenda for Children* (Children Rights Development Unit, 1994), p 45.

4.15 CASE LAW – PUBLIC LAW ORDERS

Again, the cases chosen here are selected not merely because of the principles involved, rather, each case should be read by students as examples of narratives that often occur in public law litigation. How trial courts, and the Court of Appeal, react to those narratives sets out the parameters of the CA 1989, s 31.

A County Council v (1) F (2) M (3) X (A Child Through its Guardian)

Fam Div [2004] EWHC 2720 (Fam) (Hogg J)

Where the father was identified as the perpetrator of injuries to his first child, a care order was made in respect of his second child because the father was considered a risk to small children and the threshold criteria had been satisfied. However, a care order was not made in respect of his eight-year-old stepson as it was not in his best interests.

A Borough Council v (1) Mrs E (2) Mr E (3) C (A Child by his Children's Guardian)

Fam Div [2004] EWHC 2580 (Fam) (Ryder J)

An interim care order was necessary and proportionate to protect the interests of a child, who was believed by his carers to have been born as a result of a miracle birth, where the medical evidence proved that the carers were not his parents.

Re V (A Child)

CA [2004] EWCA Civ 1575 (Thorpe LJ, Wall LJ, Holman J)

The act or omission of a social worker engaged in pre-birth investigations would not normally render subsequent care proceedings unfair as a whole or lead to a breach of rights under the European Convention on Human Rights 1950 Article 6.

Re C-B (A Child)

CA [2004] EWCA Civ 1517 (Thorpe LJ, Wall LJ, Holman J)

The refusal to grant an adjournment where a child's guardian had reversed her opinion had prejudiced the applicant's case for a residence order to the extent that it was a breach of her right to a fair trial under the European Convention on Human Rights 1950 Article 6.

Re H

Fam Div [2004] EWHC 1270 (Fam) (Hedley J)

An allegation of a serious criminal act within family proceedings was still subject to the civil burden and standard of proof, although the more serious the charge the less likely its occurrence, hence the stronger the evidence required to prove it.

S (A Child) v (1) Knowsley Borough Council (2) Julie Raymond Walters (3) Donna Cusick (4) Alan Shaw

Fam Div [2004] EWHC 491 (Fam) (Charles J)

In most cases where a person sought to challenge the role that a local authority had during the currency of a secure accommodation order, judicial review was likely to be the most appropriate recourse because it could naturally be combined with legal rubrics of the Human Rights Act 1998.

Re V (A Child)

CA [2004] EWCA Civ 54, [2004] 1 WLR 1433, [2004] 1 All ER 997, [2004] 1 FLR 944 (Tuckey LJ, Wall LJ)

It was not necessary or desirable to transfer care proceedings under the CA 1989, Part IV from the county court to the High Court merely because a breach of human rights under the European Convention on Human Rights 1950 was alleged.

Mr and Mrs W v (1) Vale of Glamorgan Council (2) AG (3) JG (4) The Child's Guardian

Fam Div [2004] EWHC 116 (Fam) (Hedley J)

In local authority care proceedings, the court's decision to refuse to entertain an application by the grandparents to become a party in those proceedings had been unfair.

Re G (A Child)

CA [2004] EWCA Civ 24 (Thorpe LJ, Latham LJ, Dame Elizabeth Butler-Sloss (President))

The judge had jurisdiction under the CA 1989, s 38(6) to direct the continuation of the assessment of a family as inpatients at a hospital and, as a matter of

discretion, should have concluded that the continuation of the assessment was reasonably required to enable the judge at a final hearing to balance the arguments for and against the parents as primary carers of their child.

Re M (A Child) (Care Order: Freeing Application)

CA [2003] EWCA Civ 1874, [2004] 1 FLR 826 (Ward LJ, Mantell LJ, Carnwath LJ)

As a matter of statutory interpretation and on authority, applications for a care order and for a freeing for adoption order being dealt with at a single hearing had to be individually assessed. The care proceedings should be dealt with first and only if a care order was made should the freeing application be considered.

Re R (A Child)

Fam Div [2003] EWHC 2927 (Fam), [2004] EMLR 8, [2004] 2 FLR 949 (Munby J)

A 17-year-old girl, who had sufficient understanding and maturity, could decide for herself whether her private life could be shared in a media interview.

Re H (A Child) (Care Order: Appropriate Local Authority)

CA [2003] EWCA Civ 1629, [2004] Fam 89, [2004] 2 WLR 419, [2004] 1 FLR 534 (Thorpe LJ, Jonathan Parker LJ, Dyson LJ)

The judge's decision that the appellant county council should be the designated local authority in respect of a care order had been inappropriate. There were circumstances, although not those relied on by the judge, that justified the conclusion that the case was an exceptional one justifying a departure from the test identified in earlier decisions of the Court of Appeal.

Re B (A Child)

CA [2003] EWCA Civ 1842, [2004] 1 FLR 527 (Thorpe LJ, Scott Baker LJ)

The judge's rejection of the mother's evidence to rebut legitimacy, founded on her assertion that the child was that of an unknown man who had raped her, rather than that of her husband, was inevitable.

A Local Authority v C

Fam Div [2003] EWHC 2206 (Fam), [2004] 1 FLR 415 (Hedley J)

The best interests of children involved in care proceedings was achieved by the High Court invoking its wardship jurisdiction in order to fill a lacuna created by the Fostering Services Regulations 2002, SI 2002/57. The result was that the children could be placed with their grandparents despite them having not been approved as foster parents.

Re D (Children)

CA (28 July 2003, unreported) (Thorpe LJ, Sir Swinton Thomas)

The judge had been fully entitled to preclude the continuation of the process of trial without the need to hear further evidence, and make an interim care order in the light of his concerns that the mother might have done something physical if she had had advance notice of the order that he proposed to make.

A Local Authority v (1) W (2) A Police Authority

Fam Div [2003] EWHC 1624 (Fam), [2004] 1 WLR 1494, [2004] 1 All ER 787, [2003] 2 FLR 1023, (2004) LGR 150 (Wall J)

A local authority could disclose the substance of allegations based on sensitive and confidential information received from the police and made against a mother whose children were subject to an interim care order where the case for disclosure was compelling.

Re B (Children), sub nom In Re B (Children: Patient Confidentiality)

CA [2003] EWCA Civ 786, [2003] 2 FLR 813 (Bodey J, Thorpe LJ)

Judge erred in failing to consider the options that were open to him once he had found that the CA 1989, s 31 threshold for making a care order had been crossed. He was not entitled to sanction removal of children unless he was satisfied that it was both necessary and proportionate and that no other form of order achieved the essential end of promoting the welfare of the children.

Re B (A Child)

CA [2003] EWCA Civ 881, [2003] 2 FLR 1035 (Thorpe LJ, Bodey J)

If an application for permission to appeal on the ground of lack of reasons was made to the appellate court and it appeared to the appellate court that the application was well founded, it should consider adjourning the application and remitting the case to the trial judge with an invitation to provide additional reasons for his decision. It was unsatisfactory to use an omission by a judge to deal with a point in a judgment as grounds for an application for appeal if the matter had not been brought to the judge's attention where there was a ready opportunity to do so.

Re A (Children) (Care Proceedings: Asylum Seekers): A Local Authority v (1) M (2) N (3) The Secretary of State for the Home Department

Fam Div [2003] EWHC 1086 (Fam), [2003] 1 FLR 291 (Munby J)

Where a family's claim for asylum and exceptional leave to remain had been rejected, it was an abuse of the court's process for the family to attempt to use care proceedings to frustrate the removal process which was a separate and distinct function of the Home Secretary.

Re M (Intractable Contact Dispute: Interim Care Order)

Fam Div [2003] EWHC 1024, [2003] 2 FLR 636 (Wall J)

Where two children were the subject of an intractable contact dispute, the court made an order under the CA 1989, s 37 directing the local authority to investigate the children's circumstances, and subsequently made a residence order in the father's favour, a supervision order to the local authority and required contact between the children and their mother to be at the discretion of the local authority.

A Metropolitan Borough Council v JJ and S (A Child by his Guardian) sub nom In Re J (A Child) (Care Proceedings: Disclosure)

Fam Div [2003] EWHC 976 (Fam), (2003) 2 FLR 522 (Wall J)

A guardian in care proceedings had a right to examine and take copies of local authority documentation relating to a child under the CA 1989, s 42. The local

authority had been wrong to mislead the court on the issues in the case and to resist the guardian's application in the first place. Public interest immunity did not apply.

Re (1) O (2) N (Children) (Non-accidental Injury): In Re B (A Child) (Non-accidental Injury)

HL [2003] UKHL 18, [2004] 1 AC 523, [2003] 2 WLR 1075, [2003] 2 All ER 305, [2003] 1 FLR 1169 (Lord Nicholls, Lord Hoffmann, Lord Millett, Lord Scott, Lord Walker)

Where the evidence at a preliminary hearing in care proceedings was not sufficient to exclude a parent as the perpetrator of harm to a child it would be wrong to proceed at the disposal hearing on the basis that that parent had been found not to be the perpetrator.

Re L (Care Proceedings: Human Rights Claims)

Fam Div [2003] EWHC 665 (Fam), [2003] 2 FLR 160 (Munby J)

Just as applications for judicial review were to be deprecated where there were pending care proceedings, so were applications under the Human Rights Act 1998, ss 7 and 8. The court gave guidance on the proper forum for such cases, which was almost always the court where the care proceedings were being tried.

Re H (Children)

CA [2003] EWCA Civ 369 (Thorpe LJ, Dame Elizabeth Butler-Sloss (President))

Where an applicant was the only blood relative who was willing and able to advance a case for care of the child, she should have been granted permission to apply for residence under the CA 1989, s 10(9) and to be a party to the care proceedings.

Re (On the Application of (1) R and Ors (2) P and Ors) v Children and Family Court Advisory and Support Service

QBD (Admin) [2003] EWHC 235 Admin, [2003] 1 FLR 953 (Charles J)

CAFCASS was not under an obligation to make one of its officers available immediately for appointment as the children's guardian in specified proceedings when requested to do so by the court.

Re H (A Child)

CA [2002] EWCA Civ 1932 (Thorpe LJ, Lawrence Collins J)

An interim hearing could not be allowed to be a substitute for a full trial of a local authority's concerns about the safety of a child. In the present case the judge had undoubtedly been invited to reach a conclusion on the assessments of the long-term future prospects for the child in question which would be inappropriate at an interim hearing.

B County Council v L and Ors

Fam Div [2002] EWHC 2327 (Fam) (Charles J)

Where an assessment of parenting ability had been terminated early and without good reason, a further assessment was ordered before a full care order could be considered.

A Chief Constable v (1) A County Council (2) AB (A Child) (By his Children's Guardian SM) (3) DH & RW

Fam Div [2002] EWHC 2198 (Fam), [2003] 1 FLR 579 (Wall J)

Medical evidence filed in care proceedings would be disclosed to the police for use in potential criminal investigations into the deaths of two young children.

Re J (A Child) (Leave to Issue Application for Residence Order)

CA [2002] EWCA Civ 1346, [2003] 1 FLR 114 (Ferris J, Thorpe LJ)

In deciding whether to grant leave for an application for a residence order by the child's maternal grandmother, the test to be applied was the statutory criteria set out in the CA 1989, s 10(9) and not whether 'the applicant satisfied the court that he or she had a good arguable case'.

Re H (Morris) (Sexual abuse: standard of proof)

HC [1996] AC 563, [1996] 1 FLR 80

Sets out the appropriate approach by a trial judge to questions of fact, establishes and clarifies the standard of proof in public law Children Act 1989 cases.

Re (1) O (2) N (Children)

CA [2002] 2 FLR 1167 (Ward LJ, Sir Martin Nourse)

The judge had applied the correct standard and burden of proof when deciding issues of fact to determine whether the threshold conditions had been established.

Re K (A Child)

Fam Div [2002] EWHC 1438 (Fam), [2002] 2 FLR 868 (Dame Elizabeth Butler-Sloss (President)

A human rights application was outside the duties of a guardian ad litem.

Re B (Children)

CA [2002] 2 FLR 599 (Thorpe LJ, Rix LJ, Arden LJ)

A judge in care proceedings had erred by preferring the lay evidence of a mother to clear and unambiguous expert evidence and by concluding that the mother had not failed to protect her child from harm.

Re J

Fam Div [2002] EWHC 766 (Fam), [2002] 2 FLR 618 (Charles J)

A Jordanian public authority was not treated as a child's guardian for the purposes of s 16 of the AA 1976 because it could not consent to the child's adoption given that adoption was prohibited under Sharia law.

Waltham Forest London Borough v (1) JR (2) NH (3) C (By her Litigation Friend Christine Smith, sub nom R v Waltham Forest London Borough, ex parte C (By Christine Smith, her Litigation Friend)

QBD (Admin) [2002] EWHC 568 (Admin), [2002] 1 FLR 1119 (Wilson J)

Where a child with a mixed ethnic and cultural background was to be placed for adoption, it would possibly be in the child's best interests to choose an adoptive home where only one strand of the child's heritage was reflected provided that the adopters were sufficiently sensitive to help the child understand and take pride in all elements of the child's identity.

Re M (A Minor) (Care Order) (Threshold Conditions)

[1994] 2 AC 424

Establishes the relevant date for determining the question of whether the child 'is suffering' harm under the CA 1989, s 31. The court is to look to the date when the local authority put 'protective measures' in place for the child: *Southwark London Borough Council v B* [1998] 2 FLR 1095. The relevant date is the same under both limbs of the CA 1989, s 31.

Re S & Ors: Re W and Ors, sub nom Re W & B (Children): W (Child) (Care Plan)

HL [2002] UKHL 10, (2002) LGR 251, [2002] 2 WLR 720, [2002] 2 All ER 192, [2002] 1 FLR 815, [2002] HRLR 26, [2002] UKHRR 652 (Lord Nicholls of Birkenhead, Lord Mackay of Clashfern, Lord Brown-Wilkinson, Lord Mustill, Lord Hutton)

The Court of Appeal had exceeded its role in deciding that the essential milestones of a local authority care plan were to be elevated to starred status. An interim care order was not intended as a means by which the court could continue to exercise a supervisory role over the local authority's care of a child. The CA 1989 was compatible with the European Convention on Human Rights.

Chapter 5

ANCILLARY RELIEF

5.1 INTRODUCTION

Advocates in ancillary relief applications quickly learn that in no other area of the law, save perhaps for the murkier areas of criminal law, will there be encountered clients as emotionally fraught, disputes as contentious, or decisions as difficult for advocates and judges. It is inevitable, of course: intense disagreements are what one would expect from two people who until very recently shared each other's most intimate moments but who now are involved in a complex property dispute, the resolution of which will satisfy neither party. Separating the legal arguments from the emotional arguments sometimes seems impossible; it is also an absolute requirement for all advocates practising at the Family Bar.

5.2 SEEKING A NARRATIVE – THE FRAMEWORK OF THE DISPUTE

Judicial revolutions are said to happen rarely in English jurisprudence. Significant changes in the substantive law, trite theory has it, come from Parliament. But all advocates know that courts often make new law when interpreting the broad mandates handed down by Parliament, particularly in those areas of law where Parliament has granted to courts broad discretion to make each decision fit the facts of each case.

The history of the Matrimonial Causes Act 1973 (MCA 1973) fits this pattern. Parliament in 1973 provided no overarching statutory principle for decisions to be made under the Act, save that children should be a first concern. (Parliament did state in 1984 that courts should, insofar as justice allows, seek to achieve a clean break between the parties, a statutory goal that merely added another bit of uncertainty to an area of law already gaining renown as wholly unpredictable.)

The advocate in any legal dispute always asks: what admissible evidence will convince the tribunal to rule in the advocate's favour? In order to answer that question the advocate must know and understand the legal test that the decision-maker will apply. Commentators have long noted that the virtually untrammelled

discretion given to courts by the MCA 1973 made it difficult if not impossible to answer the most important question the client will ask, which is, what will the judge do on this set of facts? The checklist at s 25, some of which is in fact contradictory, allows the court to justify different results in cases with similar facts.[1]

But when Parliament fails to act, courts must fill in the gaps. Parliament in effect delegated to the Court of Appeal and House of Lords the power to determine the correct approach to decisions under the MCA 1973. These broad rules were fixed in large part by the Court of Appeal, based on the judiciary's view of the principles that should apply. In cases such as *Duxbury v Duxbury*,[2] the Court of Appeal held that trial judges exercising discretion under the MCA 1973, s 25 should focus primarily on the reasonable needs of the non-income producing spouse. The Court of Appeal made the essentially legislative decision that marriage should not be seen as a joint enterprise, where property and assets obtained by either party to the marriage are presumed to be joint assets, to be divided equally. The Court of Appeal instead told trial judges to make certain, after meeting the needs of any minor children, that the reasonable needs of the non-income producing spouse were met. After those 'needs' had been met, the income-producing spouse (usually the husband) was free to take the remaining assets for himself.

The court also defined 'reasonable needs' to mean that the non-income producing spouse should have enough capital and income to provide her with a lifestyle similar to the one she enjoyed. That spouse would not receive the right to leave half of the property acquired during the marriage to her heirs.

This point of view culminated in the case of *Dart v Dart*.[3] It meant that husbands with property in two jurisdictions would almost always choose England and Wales as jurisdiction for their divorce applications. This jurisdiction had come to be seen throughout the Western legal world as one where the assets of the income-producing spouse would find a safe home.

The House of Lords decision in *White v White*[4] was in fact a judicial overturning of the accepted order. In *White*, the House of Lords held that judges making decisions in 'high income' ancillary relief applications, where resources are greater than needs, had been focusing too much on the needs of the non-income producing party (usually the ex-wife), and too little on seeking an overall equitable division of matrimonial assets. In other words, lawyers and judges have been getting the narrative of the dispute wrong. Where previously the narrative had been: 'What does the non-income-earning spouse need to continue

---

1   For an excellent discussion of this, see Mears, '*White v White* yet another "turkey"' [2001] 151
     NLJ 61.
2   [1987] 1 FLR 7.
3   [1996] 2 FLR 286, [1996] Fam Law 607, CA.
4   [2001] 1 AC 596, HL.

living as she has in the past?' the narrative is now: 'Why should the court deviate from an equal division of the assets?'

The reasons for the abrupt reversal of narrative will likely occupy the time and attention of a small legion of legal scholars, and I do not seek to add to the literature here. But it is important for the student of advocacy to understand how the narrative has shifted, and it is instructive to note how a shift in the law causes all advocates in that area of the law to change the terms of the debate. You know there has been a shift in the legal tectonic plates because the disputes are different now. The same assets, the same factual background, but a different case altogether.

White may also increase certainty in the law, allowing legal advisers to predict with more certainty the likely outcome of any contested case, and thereby increasing the likelihood of early settlement. It is far too soon as I write to make predictions about that. But what *White* undeniably does, however, is change the narratives courts will use when they divide assets after the break up of a marriage.

So what narratives are available after *White*? At the least, these: value the assets accumulated by both parties during their relationship, and divide by two; or argue the following:

(1) there are children to be cared for by the non income-producing spouse;
(2) the assets cannot be equitably divided because, for example, the primary asset is a small family business with little capital value;
(3) this was a short marriage;
(4) the resources do not match needs, either because of poverty, or because one party has a particular physical or mental disability that requires a greater share of the assets, or because the party has a far greater earning capactiy than the other;
(5) one spouse or another either brought money and property into the marriage, or brought an exceptional amount of assets into the marriage through exceptional efforts or through inheritance;[5]
(6) one party engaged in gross deception, financial mismanagement, violence, or is hiding assets from the courts;
(7) after a relatively lengthy relationship, one party has far less earning capacity than the other, and it would inequitable to ignore it;
(8) the parties signed an agreement prior to the marriage that reveals the parties' views at that time about what would be a fair distribution;
(9) some combination of (1) to (8).[6]

---

[5] See in this regard Mance LJ in *Cowan v Cowan* [2001] EWCA Civ 679, [2001] 2 FLR 192, where he states that one should first take out material inheritances and material assets, then divide fairly, probably by equality. See also Lord Nicholls of Birkenhead's speech in *White*, discussing property acquired 'external to the marriage'.

[6] For an interesting (and equally valid) summary of the current state of the law, see Hodson, Green and de Souza, 'Lambert Shutting Pandora's Box' [2003] Fam Law 37.

Experienced advocates know that disputes will occur even in cases where you seek to add up and divide by two. The problem is that in large asset cases, each party will seek not only to maximise their share of the assets, but will also give greater value to certain assets than merely market value. For example, the wife wants to remain in the family home, or wants to remain in the neighbourhood where the children have gone to school, or she wants the summer home because the oldest daughter takes riding lessons from there every summer and would fall apart if told she could not. All of this has to be considered by the advocate, who must then set out the various options and argument for his or her client. The client, in the end, must make the choice, but the advocate must set out the likely results of those choices. For example, an all out effort to keep the family home may result in the loss of another asset that was also cherished, and worth more to the client, in monetary terms, than the family home will be, once the children leave home. The advocate must let the client decide, but must give the client sufficient facts to decide intelligently.

The 'stellar contributions' argument would seem to have had a short shelf life. Criticised the moment it was introduced as opening a Pandora's Box and shifting ancillary relief hearings inevitably toward examinations of conduct,[7] the 'contributions' argument sought to provide a reason for giving the large wage earner (usually the husband) a greater share of the assets. Those arguments culminated in the case of *Cowan v Cowan*,[8] where the Court of Appeal held that in fact in certain cases stellar contributions could be considered as a reason for deviating from equality.

Advocates understood that the Court of Appeal had created an enormous area for disagreement and dispute. The Court of Appeal responded one year later in the case of *Lambert v Lambert*.[9] In that case Thorpe LJ made it clear that courts exercising broad discretion under the MCA 1973, s 25 criteria must look to fairness in the division of assets as the overarching principle, and the court should not engage in intricate analysis of each party's proposed reasons for deviating from equality.

In *Lambert*, the husband argued that his special contribution as the sole breadwinner in the family meant that he should be awarded the greater share of the family assets. Connell J agreed, and awarded the wife 37.5 per cent, the husband the remainder. Thorpe LJ and the Court of Appeal allowed the appeal. The court noted that 'once the judge had concluded that H was not a

---

7   See Coleridge J in *G v G (Financial Provision: Equal Division)* [2002] EWHC Civ 1339, [2002] 2 FLR 1143. See also T Glen Brussen, 'Pandora's hostage to fortune' [2003] Fam Law 101.
8   [2001] EWCA Civ 679, [2001] 2 FLR 192.
9   [2002] EWCA Civ 1685, [2003] Fam 103, [2003] 2 WLR 631, [2003] 4 All ER 342, [2003] 1 FL 139.

genius and that W could not have done more' he should not have elevated one contribution above the other, as the two were equally incommensurable.[10]

The Court of Appeal attempted to answer the question of whether 'fairness' meant equal distribution of future income as well as distribution of capital in the case of *McFarlane v McFarlane; Parlour v Parlour*.[11] In those cases, both wives sought a larger share of the husbands' future incomes, arguing that there was no reason for deviating from the yardstick of equality with regard to future income, in particular where present capital is insufficient to produce a fair award. The cases involved husbands who were likely to earn millions in the future. Counsel for the wives contended that the future income should be divided equally. The Court of Appeal panel disagreed, holding that the yardstick of equality should not be applied and that the courts should not don a straightjacket and apply one model in determining the outcome of different cases. Thorpe LJ did note, however, that the objective is fairness, and that discrimination between the sexes must be avoided.

Thorpe LJ pointed out that the facts in both cases were exceptional. Most couples do not argue about millions of pounds of future income. But there are cases where present capital is simply not enough to provide a fair award. Therefore, in those cases it is open to the judge to award a higher share of future income as periodical payments, notwithstanding the normal principle that a clean break should be sought wherever possible.

Unfortunately,[12] the Court of Appeal offered little guidance on what proportion of the payer's income should be paid. Mrs McFarlane had stated that her needs were £128,000 per annum. The district judge had awarded her £250,000 as periodical payments. Bennett J then reduced that to £180,000. The Court of Appeal re-instated the award of £250,000. The Court of Appeal gave no statement of principle, however, telling practitioners how this exercise should be approached.

Certainty in this area of the law would be even harder to achieve, most judges agree, if courts constantly heard arguments about the cause of the breakdown of the marriage. Marriage as an institution is a legal creation. The intimate relationship of a couple is not a legal creation. The breakdown of a relationship, with all its attendant irrationalities and unknowns, does not fit well into a dispute about a purely legal creation. Courts therefore seek as far as possible to avoid drifting into impossible-to-answer questions about conduct that may or may not have caused the relationship to end.

---

[10] Also note the judgment of Coleridge T in *H-J v H-J* [2002] 1 FLR 415, which was specifically approved by Thorpe LJ in *Lambert*.
[11] [2004] 2 All ER 921.
[12] As noted by Lisa Jones in [2004] 154 NLJ 1494.

Parliament dealt with the problem in the time-honoured manner: by passing the problem on to the courts. The MCA 1973 provides that the court may consider the conduct of each of the parties, if that conduct is such that it would in the opinion of the court be inequitable to disregard it.[13] (Surely no better example of Parliamentary delegation of power exists. Conduct should be considered, unless it should not be. Courts must decide.)

Courts have been loath to allow advocates to introduce conduct into the equation for the very good reason that no outward bounds would likely be placed on the evidence one party or the other would consider relevant. Hearings would quickly descend into fruitless efforts to prove that one party or the other actually caused the marriage to break down.

Therefore it is possible to reduce to several broad categories the types of conduct that have been considered by courts to be relevant:

(1) conduct that involves financial mismanagement and a depletion of the family's assets;[14]
(2) conduct that includes deceiving the court during the litigation process;[15]
(3) conduct that involves violence against the other party or children;[16]
(4) conduct that involves gross deception, though simple adultery is usually not enough to qualify.[17-18]

Parties must note that allegations of conduct must be set out on Form E, and district judges at the first directions appointment will determine whether these issues should be litigated, and if so, what evidence is to be adduced.

---

[13]   See MCA 1973, s 25(g).

[14]   See *Le Foe v Le Foe and Woolwich plc* [2001] 2 FLR 970; *Martin v Martin* [1976] Fam 335, [1976] 3 All ER 625; *Moorish v Moorish* [1984] Fam Law 26, CA; *Beach v Beach* [1995] 2 FLR 160. The difficulty in predicting when conduct might be considered in this area is exemplified by the case of *Singer v Sharegin* [1984] FLR 114, CA, where the court held that the husband's error of judgement leading to a term of prison in Russia should not be considered as conduct, even though the prison term cost the business dearly.

[15]   See *T v T (Interception of Documents)* [1994] 2 FLR 1083; *P v P (Financial Relief: Non-disclosure)* [1994] 2 FLR 381; *M v M (Financial Provision: Party Incurring Excessive Costs)* [1995] 3 FCR 321; *H v H (Financial Relief: Conduct)* [1998] 1 FLR 971.

[16]   See *H v H (Financial Provision: Conduct)* [1994] 2 FLR 801; note the Court of Appeal's warning in *Griffiths v Griffiths* [1974] 1 All ER 932, however, that mere proof that one party was 'callous and unkind' will not be sufficient to prove conduct under this section.

[17-18]   See *S-T (Formerly J) v J (Transsexual: Void Marriage)* [1998] Fam 103; *A v A (Financial Provision)* [1998] 2 FLR 180, FD; *Rampal v Rampal (No 2)* [2001] EWCA Civ 989, [2002] Fam 85 (husband's bigamy was conduct to be taken into account in the broad discretionary exercise of the trial judge).

5.3 THE ADVOCATE'S TASK – ANALYSING THE PAPERS

Several questions must be answered by advocates immediately upon receipt of the papers. Those questions will frame the narrative to be presented throughout the case, and will do nothing less than set out the issues in every case:

- How long a marriage is this?
- Are there any minor children?
- Will the children be living with husband or wife?
- Have the parties already separated?
- Is there a question of interim relief, including interim maintenance?
- How will costs be paid?
- What are the capital and income positions of both parties?
- What are the debts of both parties?
- Are there pensions or insurance policies available, or is either party likely to receive in the near future an inheritance?
- Is either party cohabiting with another partner, in a situation where that partner provides income or capital for the couple?

Each one of the above bullet points simply sets out a broad framework of questions that must be answered. For example, if the children are staying with the mother, are there going to be increased childcare costs because mother now has to seek employment? The earning capacity of the parties almost invariably causes dispute, in particular where a husband contends his ex-wife should be able to earn more than she does.

The trend among district judges is to assume that both parties, women as well as men, will likely have to provide income after divorce, in those cases where resources do not meet needs.

Advocates must seek to find a legitimate reason for the court to deviate from the yardstick of equality. The three most obvious examples are the low income case, the short marriage, and the small family business that, if sold, would not produce assets sufficient for both parties to begin new businesses.

5.3.1 The low income case

White v White by its terms applies to those cases where substantial assets are to be divided. But the Court of Appeal have also indicated that even in cases where needs are greater than resources, equality of outcome should be a consideration to be kept in mind by the court.[19] In low income cases, there obviously will be a likelihood that the court will have to look first and primarily at making certain the children or any children of the marriage are housed. The

---

[19]   See *S v S (Financial Provision; Departing from Equality)* [2001] 2 FLR 246.

court will also have to consider the reasonable needs of the caring parent. Therefore in most low income cases there likely will be a deviation from equality. Where, in low income cases, there is only the former matrimonial home as an asset, the temptation will likely be to argue that the court should seek a more equal division of the assets by allowing the caring parent to remain in the home with the children until the children reach majority, then order a sale of the home at a time soon after that date. The other triggers for resale would be death or remarriage of the occupying spouse, or her cohabitation with another partner for more than 12 months.

This order, commonly known as a *Mesher* order and approved by the Court of Appeal in the case of *Mesher v Mesher and Hall*,[20] is of course contrary to one of the stated principles of the MCA 1984, which mandates that the court achieve a clean break between the parties, if possible. District Judge Million, in a talk he gave to the Family Bar in June 2003, indicated that in his opinion district judges would continue to refuse to make orders for later sale of the property. In his opinion, these orders were likely to cause further litigation, as well as work hardship on the spouse who remained at home caring for the children.[21] The orders are unlikely to be made unless it is proved the occupying spouse will be able to re-house herself when the home is sold.

Another possible order allowing the non-occupying spouse to recover his or her investment at a later date is an order that provides for the continued occupation by a spouse of a property until the death or remarriage of the occupying souse, or the court making a further order. The intent here is to focus on the occupying spouse's finances, and if she is later in a position to re-house herself (or she has no need of the house because she has died), the husband should be allowed to recoup a portion of his initial investment.[22] The order should always be considered when there is a possibility a re-marriage will occur.

In the low income case the s 25 criteria should be closely examined:

- income, earning capacity, property and other financial resources;
- financial needs, obligations and responsibilities;
- standard of living;
- age of parties, duration of marriage;
- physical or mental disabilities;
- contributions (including to welfare of family both in past and in foreseeable future);
- the conduct of either spouse when it is inequitable to disregard it;
- loss of one spouse that occurs as a result of the divorce.[23]

---

20   [1980] 1 All ER 126, CA.
21   See *Harvey v Harvey* [1982] Fam 83, 3 FLR 141, CA, where the order was criticised as merely postponing the evil day.
22   See *Martin v Martin* [1978] Fam 12. See also *Clutton v Clutton* [1991] 1 FLR 242, CA, per Ewbank J.
23   In effect, this last category almost invariably refers to pensions.

In any low income case the most important question will be housing, in particular housing for any minor children. In the case of *M v B*,[24] the Court of Appeal held that the paramount consideration in applying the s 25 criteria is to provide housing, if possible, for both parties, but in particular for the spouse who will be caring for any minor children. That being said, as Philip Moor QC has pointed out in seminars he has given in this area of the law over the last several years, advocates run into difficulties when they overemphasise housing, in particular in moderate income cases. The House of Lords in *Piglowski v Piglowski*,[25] held that there is no rule that the spouse's housing needs should be given greater weight than any other of the s 25 criteria.

Advocates in low income cases should always have available to them the latest statistics from the Expenditure & Food Survey (EPS) published by the National Statistics Office. This will show the average weekly expenditure per household during the latest calendar year. During 2001/2002, the weekly expenditure was some £398. The EPS data shows that spending extremes ranged from £127 in the lowest of the ten income groups, to £885 per week in the highest of the ten groups. The average gross income per household was £550 per week.[26] The 2003/2004 Expenditure & Food Survey can be downloaded free at www.statistics.gov.uk.

5.3.2   The short marriage

White v White applied to a lengthy marriage. The question that is likely to be asked by the court, however, is not so much how long the marriage has existed, but how much of the couple's assets were produced during the marriage. Where there is a wide disparity in wealth between the couple prior to the marriage, the court will likely hear arguments regarding the length of the marriage. In other words, an advocate for a woman who brought a considerable fortune into a marriage that lasted for seven years will contend that it is simply unfair to allow the husband to receive half of all of the assets, such as the former matrimonial home, that in effect were purchased with the assets of the woman.

The court's struggle with the definition of fairness and equality is exemplified in the case of *Foster v Foster*.[27] This was an extremely short marriage of some three years' duration. The parties were both aged 33. Both were employed throughout the marriage, the wife earning twice as much as the husband. The parties owned five properties with a total net value of £400,000. The district judge sought to return the parties to the position in which they had been before the marriage, and accordingly the order resulted in a division of the assets of 61 per cent to the wife and 39 per cent to the husband.

---

24   [1998] 1 FLR 53.
25   [1999] 2 FLR 763, HL.
26   While households with the lowest 20 per cent of incomes received only £114 on average per week, those in the top 20 per cent earned £1,314 per week.
27   [2003] EWCA Civ 565, [2003] 2 FLR 299, CA.

The wife appealed, claiming she should receive more because she had paid most of the mortgages on the various properties. The circuit judge agreed and increased her share to 70 per cent. The husband appealed to the Court of Appeal, and that court allowed the husband's appeal, reinstating the order of the district judge. The Court of Appeal first noted that it would be wrong for advocates to focus on the length of the marriage. In cases where a substantial number of properties were purchased during the marriage, it does not matter how long that marriage lasted. The Court of Appeal affirmed the joint enterprise method of looking at marriage. The court noted that 'Where a substantial surplus has been generated by their joint efforts it cannot matter whether they have taken a short or long time to do so'.

5.3.3   The small business

An accepted reason for deviating from equality is the situation where husband and wife (or either alone) operate a small business that does not have sufficient liquid assets to afford either spouse an opportunity for investment in another, similar business. Any advocate seeking to advise a divorcing spouse with regard to the division of a family business must have, at the least, a working knowledge of the law surrounding business organisations and the different tax rules that apply to each type of organisation, and must be able to make sense of a spreadsheet.

A business may be one of three legal entities:

- a limited company;
- a partnership;
- a sole trader.

The legal entity of the business will have been decided upon based on several factors:

- the sophistication of the enterprise;
- the profitability of the enterprise;
- the tax efficiencies that might be realised from incorporation. An incorporated business will have its profits charged at income tax rates up to 40 per cent. A company that does not make profits, after paying directors' salaries of more than £300,000, will have tax charged at the small companies rate of 25 per cent. For sole traders, the higher rate tax of 40 per cent will start to bite on profits in excess of about £28,000, before taking into account personal allowances and reliefs.

David Salter, a solicitor with two decades' experience handling substantial asset divorce matters, has usefully set out a list of the initial questions to be answered by advocates handling cases involving family businesses:[28]

---

28   See 'Interpreting and Using Financial Information', a paper presented by David Salter at the 2003 Family Finance and Property Seminar, June 2003, London.

(1) What is the profit history of the business? Note that s 2.14 of Form E requires copies of the last two years' accounts to be attached. Section 2.14 of Form E also requires a party to estimate the current value of his interest in the business asset as well as any possible capital gains tax payable on a disposal, indicating the basis of his or her valuation.

(2) How should a business be valued? Any expert must consider the stock on hand, the premises of the business, as well as the goodwill of the business.

(3) If there is a partnership, is there a written partnership agreement or deed? Parties should note that the Partnership Act 1890, s 24(1) provides that in the absence of an agreement to the contrary, all partners are entitled to share equally in the capital and the profits of the business. Thus, on dissolution, the accrued profits, including any profit made from selling any fixed assets, are usually to be divided equally. In other words, the partners' capital accounts would not govern the division of the assets. See the case of *Popat v Shonchhatra*.[29]

(4) The advocate should determine whether the Limited Liability Partnership Act 2000 applies to this business. This Act creates a new form of legal corporate entity which seeks to combine the tax status of a partnership with limited liabilities for its members. LLPs are available to two or more persons carrying on any trade or profession, they must be registered at Companies House and there are requirements for the filing of audited accounts. LLPs must file an annual return at Companies House.

(5) Advocates should consider whether in cases involving partnerships between husband and wife, proceedings should be filed initially in the Chancery Division, subject to a later transfer to the Family Division.

(6) In cases of private companies, advocates should be looking for hidden benefits. David Salter points out that in his experience advocates should be on the lookout for the following: car allowances, telephone payments, payment of rent, entertainment allowances, arrears of dividends and service charges payable to a service company.[30] Salter also advises advocates to look into loan accounts, that is money owed to a party by the company which will therefore count as an asset of that party. Advocates should also look at any outstanding debts which seem difficult to explain. If those debts are called in, it might put a different perspective on the company's trading position.

All businesses might be evaluated simply using a dividends/assets/earnings basis of valuation. But in the case of smaller businesses, it might make more sense to value the business's goodwill, that is, the price a willing purchaser would pay to acquire the right to own or control the company's profitability. Advisers should seek to ascertain the sustainable profits before tax. This would involve adding back any proprietors' salaries, bonuses and pension contributions paid,

---

[29] [1997] 1 WLR 1367, CA.
[30] See David Salter, 'Interpreting and Using Financial Information', above.

any dividends and any other non-recurring items of expenditure; and deducting a notional salary for what it would cost to put in a manager to run the business in lieu of the current family management team. Advisers must seek to assess the personal involvement of the proprietor. If the purchaser needs to secure the proprietor's services under a contract for a transitional period, that would have to be included in the assessment.

Small limited liability companies also present a minefield for advocates. Upon determining the existence of the company, and the division of ownership shares in the company, advisors must discover whether there are any shareholder agreements restricting the normal voting rights attached to ordinary shares.

Advocates will know that a lack of liquidity in the assets that are to be divided can be used as a reason for departing from the yardstick of equality.[31] In the case of *Wells v Wells*,[32] the wife had been awarded at first instance the secure assets while the husband was left with illiquid and risk laden assets. Thorpe LJ in allowing the appeal, stated as follows:

> 'Had the marriage survived, the family will undoubtedly have shared adversity as it had shared prosperity ... but the future years look hazardous. In principle it seems to us that the separation of the family does not terminate the sharing of a result of the company's performance ... in [a clean break case], sharing is achieved by fair division of both the copper bottom assets and the illiquid and risk laden assets.'

Many times families use a small business to shelter expenses that in fact are personal or family expenses. Small businesses are often used to send income to nominee accounts, sometimes held in offshore enterprises.

Therefore certain questions have to be addressed immediately by any advisers facing the break up of a small business:

- Has the business been run in a lawful and ethical manner?
- Has one party or the other funnelled profits illegally to another account?
- What are the tax and tax penalty implications regarding any criminal activity?

Jeffrey Nedas FCA, a solicitor with many years' experience in high-end divorce cases, predicts that *White v White* will result in an increased use of accountants to value middle-class business assets.[33] As noted by Coleridge J in *N v N (Financial Provision: Sale of Company)*[34] the court will want to be satisfied that the goose that lays the golden egg has been correctly weighed. Nedas argues that any accountant seeking to carry out an in-depth examination of an individual company will need to research the industrial section of that company in order to understand the company's competitive position. The accountant (and

31   See *Cowan v Cowan* [2001] 2 FLR 192 and *S v S* [2001] 2 FLR 246.
32   [2002] 2 FLR 97.
33   See Nedas, 'Valuation issues after *White* and other cases' [2004] 34 Fam Law 187.
34   [2001] 2 FLR 69.

advocate) needs to be aware of current trends and issues. The accountant will require the same quality *and* quantity of information that would be made available for the financial due diligence process of a corporate transaction or pre-lending review.[35]

5.3.4 Analysing the assets

Even a regime that simply calls for the division of all assets into equal shares will still likely cause disputes in most middle class and wealthier families, if only because of the difficulty in valuing the various financial instruments that most middle class families now possess. What I seek to do here is to go through the basic financial instruments that many, if not most, middle class and wealthier families now own.

(1) Traditional life assurance

The basic life assurance plan has a great number of variations. There are two primary differences, however. The first basic type of insurance is term insurance, which is nothing more than a bet with the insurance company: the owner pays premiums for an agreed period and if the owner dies during that time, the insurance company pays a sum for which the life had been insured. If the owner survives through the term, no money is paid. The second basic type of insurance is whole life insurance, which pays a lump sum when you die at any age.

(2) Endowment insurance

Endowment insurance is a savings vehicle for the owner as well as protection for his or her dependants. The owner pays the premiums and at the end of the term of the insurance, there should be received a lump sum. If the owner dies earlier than the term set out in the policy, dependents will receive a lump sum, just as with whole life insurance. The premium income is placed by the insurance company into life funds, where it is invested. This is an area of uncertainty: the return the insurance company will earn on its investments is never guaranteed. In the case of a with-profits policy, the policyholder is entitled to a share of the profits from the growth of the fund, provided that in fact the fund does grow.

Advocates must keep in mind two essential points regarding life assurance:

(1) First, returns on investment (particularly equity investments) may turn out to be considerably lower than they had been in the 1990s. Certainly it is correct that during the short term the with-profits element for policyholders looks much less attractive than in the past 10 years.

---

[35] See Nedas, above.

(2) Many investors who enter into a life assurance contract find themselves unable to maintain payments. If money is taken out early, the surrender value is usually very low compared to what has been paid in. Salesman's commissions usually come out of the early payments. If the insurance company documents are supplied, advocates will see just how much front end loading the policy provides. Advocates need to note the surrender value of any endowment assurance policy.

Advocates also need to understand how endowment policies are valued. There are several types of value that advocates need to keep in mind:

(1) Surrender value

The surrender value is what the policy is worth if encashed immediately. The surrender value of a with-profits policy nearing maturity will still show a significant under value, because it will likely exclude the terminal bonus.

(2) Fund value

The fund value represents the insurer's estimate of the current value of the policy if it is not encashed. The fund value will be higher than the surrender value because the initial administrative charges may be disregarded. This valuation in fact will only be achieved if the policy is kept until maturity.

(3) Sale value

The sale value is the value of a policy if sold by the original policyholder to a third party for consideration other than the policy's surrender value. These policies are known as Traded Endowment Policies, Traded Insurance Policies, or Second-hand Endowment Policies.

(4) Paid-up value

The paid up value is the value of the policy if the premiums are discontinued, but the policy is allowed to remain in force until the maturity date.

(5) Maturity value

The maturity value is the value of the policy on the maturity date, that is at the conclusion of the policy term or at the death of the owner of the policy during the term. The maturity value will include any accrued bonuses as well as the terminal bonus. Advocates should know that if a policy is nearing maturity, it is much more realistic to adopt the projected maturity value.

Advocates should also note that insurance policies (unlike pensions) may be used as collateral for a loan, including collateral security for a home loan. This might be useful in terms of making certain that one party or the other is able to secure a mortgage, even if income is not sufficient to support that mortgage.

Advocates must know the difference between a qualifying policy and a non-qualifying policy. A qualifying policy pays no tax on the gain realised on death, maturity, surrender or assignment, provided the policy has not become fully paid. Advocates must note whether any of the policies listed are qualifying or non-qualifying policies.

The most common type of non-qualifying policy is the single premium investment bond.[36] The single premium bond is in one sense the reverse of an endowment policy. The holder invests a premium in year 1. The money is then invested in various funds. The holder is allowed to draw 5 per cent per annum tax free, this representing no more than a return of capital. If the capital appreciates, it can be drawn down or reinvested. The bond may be invested offshore, where it might grow free of tax. It will be liable to tax on encashment. Advocates should note the rule that there should never be a partial surrender of a bond, otherwise all the gain (over and above the tax relief given at 5 per cent per annum) will be treated as falling in one tax year. In general, policy gains are liable to income tax rather than capital gains tax. The limited exception to this is where policies are bought and sold on the second-hand market.

(3) Pensions

Advocates (and clients) prefer to leave the courtroom at the end of the day believing that, one way or another, all issues have been decided. The two parties may still believe in their respective positions, but for the purposes of the law, those disputes have been settled and determined. Advocates practising in the murky netherworld defined by the Welfare Reform and Pensions Act 1999 (WRPA 1999), and the Divorce Etc (Pensions) Regulations 2000,[37] understand that all too often orders are made today carrying seeds that in 10, 15 or 20 years will produce only future disputes.

The Pickering Report on the simplification of pensions legislation was published in July 2002. Not surprisingly, the report recommends simplification of pension sharing. The government responded to the report with the Finance Act 2004, which is intended to enact the recommendations of the Pickering Report. The new regime seeks to simplify: eight different sets of pension rules are being consolidated into one. The new legislation will come into force on 6 April 2006.[38]

Under the new regime, lawyers will need to pay greater attention to the valuations provided by pensions schemes, given the wider range of assets that

---

[36] See discussion by the barrister Peter Duckworth QC in a paper given to the Family Law Bar Association entitled 'Ancillary Relief and Tax: Tips and Traps'.

[37] SI 2000/1123.

[38] For a thorough discussion of the new Act's provisions, see Salter, 'Pensions Law Simplification and the Family Lawyer' [2004] Fam Law 795.

will be held in pension plans. Lawyers must ensure that full details of the assets held in the pension funds are obtained before advising clients after the effective date of the new legislation.

Even a brief account of the pensions industry would require more attention than can be given here, but a brief outline is necessary. Pensions are perhaps best seen as being part of the same general business as life assurance. Most of the major insurance companies provide the personal pensions available in the UK today. Smaller and medium-sized groups also purchase most company pension schemes from large insurance companies.

A company scheme may be insured, where the insurance group sets a premium each year, to be paid by the company, in order that the eventual level of benefit is provided for the employees. The company may instead hand over contributions to a managed fund run by the insurance group. The pension scheme is in allocated units in the fund pro rata with its contribution.

Some pension funds, in particular the large pension funds, manage their own investments. Up until 1988, employees of a company which ran its own pension scheme were forced to join that scheme. After that date, employees were able to make their own arrangements. These are often described as personal portable pensions because they can be taken from job to job. The self-employed worker also has a personal portable pension.

There are two main types of private sector pension arrangements:

(1) defined benefit (or final salary) schemes;
(2) defined contribution or money purchase schemes.

In defined benefit schemes, the employee builds up his entitlement each year he works for the company. Typically the pension is based on two thirds of the final salary after 40 years' employment.

In the defined contribution or money purchase scheme money is contributed each year and invested. When the member retires, his share of the investment is used to buy an annuity to provide him with an income for the remainder of his life. That income may not bear a relationship to his salary in employment. The size of the income will depend on the investment returns earned on the pensioners' money over the years. Personal portable pensions are money purchase pensions.

The advocate or adviser in a case involving pension benefits must have a precise understanding of how and when the pensions are to be valued. David Salter and other members of the Law Society's Pensions Committee have long pointed out the difficulties involved in agreeing a pension valuation.[39] The

---

[39]   See David Salter, 'The Pitfalls of Pension Sharing' [2002] Fam Law.

Pensions Committee has identified what it terms 'the moving target syndrome'. The Divorce Etc (Pensions) Regulations 2000, at reg 3, provides that the court is to carry out its valuation exercise at a date to be specified by the court. This is to be called the valuation date. This date must be no earlier than one year from the date of the petition and no later than the date of the court order. This will be the date inserted in the annex to the pension sharing order. This will be the date of the CETV (cash equivalent transfer value) used by the court at the hearing for evidential purposes or by the parties in negotiations.

The WRPA 1999, s 29(2) provides that the pension debit and pension credit are the specified percentage of the cash equivalent of the relevant benefits on the valuation day. That date is defined, at s 29(7) as 'such day within the implementation period … as the person responsible for the relevant arrangement may specify by notice in writing to the transferor and transferee'. This date will obviously be later than the pension sharing order because the implementation period is defined, at s 34(1), as being the four-month period beginning with the later of the day on which the pension sharing order takes effect, and the day on which the relevant pension sharing documentation is served on the pension arrangement. Therefore the benefits to be valued on the valuation day are those available at the transfer day. Contributions made after the transfer day will not be taken into account. Market fluctuations between the transfer day and the valuation day will be taken into account. The moving target syndrome refers to the difference between the value on the valuation date, that is the value for the purposes of negotiation of the court hearing, and the value available on the date chosen for actual implementation. Advocates in cases involving pension benefits must obviously use the valuation date set out by the Divorce Etc (Pensions) Regulation 2000, reg 3, but must understand that market fluctuations between the valuation date and the implementation date must be taken into account. The risk must either be shared, or borne by one party. Make sure the risk is not borne solely by your party because you did not understand the moving target syndrome.

Advocates must also understand the different characteristics of pension funds. For example, in the case of *Cowan v Cowan*,[40] the trial judge faced a situation where the husband's pension fund was vested, and was now a whole life fixed rate income stream. It would cost £1.19m to purchase an identical income stream. Therefore the figure of £1.19m is useful for comparative purposes, but as Thorpe LJ pointed out (at paragraph 69), 'It is not truly comparable with a cash fund of £1.19m for the obvious reason that the latter is replete with options as to deployment, investment and spending, as well as having the capacity to survive intact after the owner's demise.' In other words, present capital should not be mistaken with the right to financial benefits on retirement. Advocates must present a schedule to the court of benefits to be received under

---

[40]   [2001] 2 FLR 192, CA.

any pension and set out precisely how the benefits are to be received. Any valuations that are used must also, as Thorpe LJ pointed out, 'compare like with like'.

Advocates should consult the publication *At a Glance: Essential Court Tables for Ancillary Relief*, published each year by the Family Law Bar Association, for tables allowing for quick valuation of the value of a lost pension. Section 25B(1)(b) of the MCA 1973 obliges the court in every case to consider the extent of the pension benefits, and the loss of widow's pension rights caused by the divorce. Previous statutory instruments had required the trustees of any pension fund to specify what proportion of the CETV of the scheme was attributable to any pension or other periodical payments to which a spouse of the member would or might become entitled in the event of the member's death. The new Divorce Etc (Pensions) Regulations 2000, provide no equivalent requirement. The table provided by the authors of *At A Glance* will aid courts in seeking to value what the wife will lose by virtue of the divorce.

Sections 25B, 25C and 25D of the MCA 1973 were inserted into the Act (and the minds of litigants, advocates and judges) by the Pensions Act 1995. The effective date is 1 August 1996, with the Act applying to all applicants after that date. The court is empowered to make either a lump sum order, with the amount to be paid from a pension scheme (s 25C) or an attachment order (s 25D). The court will look to s 25C to make its decision: *what* are the financial resources of the parties? what pension arrangements have been made? what has one party lost in pension benefits as a result of the divorce?

Courts have now held that a pension fund is a resource like anything else, and must be included in any list of assets supplied to the court.[41] When the court makes either order, the trustees (or 'persons responsible') may be directed to pay it on the husband's behalf. Payment of periodic payments are taxable in the hands of the recipient, unlike normal periodical payments. The order may also be. The periodical payments order ends on the death of either party.[42]

Advocates must also be aware of those cases where the CETV does not provide an accurate value of the pension. For example, the CETV does not necessarily include discretionary benefits. There are also certain occupations where the CETV bears little relationship to the pension likely to be paid on retirement.[43]

Advocates must also be aware of situations where simply adding the CETV to the assets to be divided is simply inequitable. In the case of *Maskell v Maskell*[44] the parties had assets as follows: (a) £26,000 equity in the former

---

[41]   See Form E, para 2.16; *T v T (Financial Relief: Pensions)* [1998] 1 FLR 107 (Singer J).
[42]   See DJ Bird, *Ancillary Relief Handbook* (Family Law, 4th edn), p 109.
[43]   See discussion in Ellisa Da Costa, 'Pensions – The Maskell Approach' [2002] Fam Law 848.
[44]   [2001] EWCA Civ 858, [2001] 3 FLR 26.

matrimonial home; (b) two policies, worth £10,000 surrender value; (c) the husband's pension, valued at £32,000. The district judge treated the £32,000 pension as if it were available as cash at present, and roughly split all assets on that basis. The Court of Appeal allowed the appeal. Thorpe LJ noted that the district judge had made the error of confusing present capital with rights to benefit upon retirement.

The WRPA 1999 created an additional order with regard to pensions: the court, under s 21 of the Act, may make a 'pension sharing' order. That order provides that one party's shareable rights under a specified pension scheme, or shareable state scheme, may be subject to pension sharing for the benefit of the other party. WRPA 1999, s 29 provides that, for private pensions, the transferor's: shareable rights under the pension will become subject to a debit of the appropriate amount, with the transferee becoming entitled to an equal credit. Similar provisions for state schemes are set out at s 48(1) of the Act. Note that the average state scheme is not shareable. The percentage value to be transferred must be set out in the order, which will be expressed as a percentage of the CETV of the relevant benefits on the valuation day.[45] District Judge Roger Bird points out that a pension sharing order is most appropriate where it was intended that the parties have a clean break, and it was thought desirable to provide the wife with a share of the husband's pension entitlement. The pension sharing order will survive the respondent's death, so that the pension credit transferred to the wife is hers for life.[46]

5.4 THE SPECIAL POSITION OF CHILDREN

In all cases where children are involved, there is the temptation on the part of advocates for the applicant wife with care of the children to seek child maintenance through the back door. Advocates who practice in this area will know that the Child Support Act 1991 (CSA 1991), as amended, takes from courts jurisdiction over maintenance for children, save in exceptional cases. Advocates will know that it is not possible under Sch 1 of the Children Act 1989 to transfer property to the wife to be held in trust for the children. That Schedule only allows for transfer of property to be held on trust for the children, and then to revert to the owners upon the children reaching their majority. Schedule 1 also does not provide a method for applying for child maintenance.

Child support is often sought as well in applications for maintenance pending suit. Advocates presenting to the court a skeleton argument showing expenses for the children and details of their needs will quickly be slapped down by district judges, who will point out that child maintenance is not part of the jurisdiction of the court.

---

45   WRPA 1999, s 29(2).
46   See Bird, above, p 125.

Rather than seek to disguise child maintenance, advocates are better advised to seek top-up orders, or variation of periodical payment orders (see s 8(3A) of the CSA 1991).[47]

Advocates will know the new child support regime was introduced on 3 March 2003 for cases with an effective date on or after that date.[48] The basic scheme of the new Act is that the non-resident parent pays 15 per cent of his net weekly income (up to £2,000 per week) for one child, 20 per cent for two, and 25 per cent for three or more. Part of the income is disregarded for each other child (up to three) living with the non-resident parent. Net weekly income is net of tax and national insurance. Pension contributions are deductible in full. Bonuses, commission, overtime pay are also included. Working Families Tax Credit, Employment Credits and Disabled Person's Tax Credits are also included. Income received from savings, investments, benefits and student grants and loans are excluded.[49]

Where the parents are sharing the care of the children, the rules often cause enormous conflict. The rule is that if the care is shared, the child support otherwise due to a person caring for the child is decreased proportionately to the number of nights in a 12-month period the child stays with the non-resident parent. The rates are set out in the rules: less than 52 nights per year receives no reduction; 52 to 103 nights per year receives one-seventh reduction; 104 to 155 nights per year receives two-sevenths reduction; 156 to 174 receives three-sevenths reduction; more than 175 receives half, and is deducted further by £7 per week per child.

Advocates should have with them at all times the child support tables set out in the publication *At a Glance: Essential Court Tables for Ancillary Relief*, published each year by the Family Law Bar Association. Advocates must always have the appropriate Child Support Agency calculations in order to advise on any financial settlement involving children.

The court hearing ancillary relief proceedings has jurisdiction to hear applications for financial orders concerning children in certain limited circumstances:

(1) when the maximum amount payable under the CSA 1991 has been reached, the court may make a 'topping up' for an amount it considers just under the circumstances of the case;[50]

---

47 See the article by District Judge Stephen Gerlis, 'Read my Lips: No Child Maintenance' at [2003] Fam Law 605.

48 See Roger Bird, *Child's Pay: The Complete Guide to the Child Support Acts* (Sweet and Maxwell, 2nd edn, 1996) ch 2 for a discussion of how to determine effective dates.

49 See Child Support (Maintenance Calculation and Special Cases) Regulations 2000, SI 2000/155.

50 CSA 1991, s 8(6).

(2) additional education expenses: an order may be made to pay the expenses of 'education and training' deemed reasonably necessary;[51]

(3) where a child is disabled or blind;[52]

(4) where the parties have consented, and committed the agreement to writing;[53]

(5) the court is entitled under the MCA 1973 (but not the CA 1989) to make a lump sum capital order in favour of the child;

(6) if the 'child of the family' is a stepchild, or where one of the parties or children is not habitually resident in the UK and hence not subject to the CSA 1991, the court in ancillary proceedings may make an order in favour of that next child.

The court, if it has jurisdiction, is permitted to make any of the MCA 1973 orders – percentage payments, lump sum or property transfer – in favour of a child. The court will consider:

(1) the financial needs of the child;

(2) the income, earning capacity (if any), property and other financial resources of the child;

(3) any physical or mental disability of the child;

(4) the manner in which he was being educated or financed, and the partners' expectations for his education in the future;

(5) all of the considerations above must be made in conjunction with considering the same factor with regard to each parent.

Normally, courts will use the CSA 1991 as a starting point for its calculations.[54]

Advocates will remember that capital provision, or payment adjustment orders, can be made in favour of children even if maintenance for the child will be determined by the Child Support Agency.[55]

5.5 PERIODICAL PAYMENTS OR CLEAN BREAK?

One of the key questions to be answered by both advocates is this: will the parties be asked to achieve a clean break? Will the parties, at the conclusion of the proceedings, have no further obligations to each other?

The difficulty inevitably arises when one party to a reasonably long marriage has much less earning capacity than the other party.

---

[51] CSA 1991, s 8(7).
[52] CSA 1991, s 8(9).
[53] CSA 1991, s 8(5).
[54] See *E v C (Child Maintenance)* [1996] 1 FLR 472; *Gur v RW (Financial Provision: Departure from Equity)* [2003] 1 FLR 666.
[55] See *V v V (Child Maintenance)* [2001] 2 FLR 799. See the discussion in Bird, above, p 136.

As District Judge Roger Bird notes, periodical payments can never be looked at in isolation.[56] DJ Bird believes it logical for courts – and advocates – to divide the reasoning process as follows:

(1) should there be a clean break?
(2) should periodical payments be made and what is the amount?
(3) how long should the payments continue?

With regard to the first question, the court will consider the fairness of a proposed order. Does the party with little earning capacity retain a fair portion of the capital assets? The court will also consider the earning potential of both parties. Can the party with little earning capacity now in fact increase his other capacity to earn in the future?

Two types of cases almost always call for a clean break: the big money case; and the no money case. The former situation allows the court to make a capital division that will serve as a maintenance fund for the non-wage-earning spouse. For the latter situation, courts often state that because there is little prospect of the husband paying periodical payments, it is better to achieve certainty and the avoidance of future litigation.[57]

Young children will usually mean that no clean break is possible. In *SRJ v DWJ (Financial Provision)*,[58] the Court of Appeal held that there is no presumption in favour of a clean break, in particular when there is a small child. The court noted that it would be difficult to achieve a financial clean break when there cannot be a personal clean break between the parties.

If the court makes a clean break order, it will also order that neither party is able to claim against the other under the Inheritance (Provision for Family and Dependants) Act 1975.[59]

5.6   ANCILLARY RELIEF PROCEDURE

Practice in this area has been transformed in the last five years, in particular by the Family Proceedings (Amendment No 2) Rules 1999.[60] This amendment gave effect nationally to the existing pilot scheme rules in relation to ancillary relief which had been applied since 1996 in certain specified courts. The goals of the procedures are to reduce delay, to facilitate settlements, to limit costs incurred by parties, and to provide the court with greater and more effective

---

[56]   See Bird, above, p 34.
[57]   See *Ashley v Blackman* [1988] 2 FLR 278.
[58]   [1999] 2 FCR 176, CA.
[59]   That Act, which allows those who were dependent upon the deceased to claim against the estate if no provision is made for the claimant in the will, includes former wives as potential claimants.
[60]   SI 1999/3491. The amendments came into effect on 5 June 2000.

control over the conduct of the proceedings.[61] Most district judges believe the new system is a huge improvement over past efforts to force parties actively to seek settlement at an early stage of the litigation.[62] Advocates must be prepared to enter substantive negotiations each and every time the matter appears in court. If not, be prepared to say why not.

5.6.1 Pre-action Protocol

Lord Woolf MR in his *Access to Justice* Report of July 1996 recommended that pre-action protocols be developed in all divisions in order 'to build on and increase the benefits of early but well informed settlement which genuinely satisfies both parties to the dispute'. In April 2000, the Lord Chancellor's Ancillary Relief Advisory Committee agreed the Pre-action Protocol for ancillary relief matters. The aim of the protocol is to ensure that disclosure and negotiation take place at an early stage in appropriate cases. The protocol covers all classes of cases. Lawyers for both parties must consider the advantage of disclosing all documents prior to proceedings actually commencing. As noted in the protocol, however:

> '... solicitors should bear in mind the objective of controlling costs and in particular the cost of discovery and that the option of pre-application disclosure and negotiation has risks of excessive and uncontrolled expenditure and delay. This option should only be encouraged where both parties agree to follow this route and disclosure is not likely to be an issue or has been adequately dealt with in mediation or otherwise'.[63]

A solicitor should also consider whether it would be appropriate to suggest mediation to the client as an alternative to solicitor negotiation or court-based litigation.[64] Making an application to the court is not regarded as a hostile step or a last resort. Instead, it should be considered a way of starting the court timetable, controlling disclosure and endeavouring to avoid a costly final hearing.[65]

All parties are directed to bear in mind the overriding objective set out at the Family Proceedings Rules 1991[66] (FPR 1991), r 2.51B: all claims should be resolved and a just outcome achieved as speedily as possible without costs being unreasonably incurred. The needs of any children should also be addressed and safeguarded.[67] In order to do this, parties must clarify claims and identify issues as quickly as possible. Each party must provide full, frank and clear

---

[61]   See *Practice Direction (Ancillary Relief Procedure)* [2000] 1 FLR 997.
[62]   See, for example, District Judge Bird's comments in Law Society Gazette, November, 2001, p 98.
[63]   See *Ancillary Relief Protocol* (the Pre-action Protocol) [2000] 1 FLR 997 at 999, para 2.2.
[64]   Pre-action Protocol, para 2.3.
[65]   Pre-action Protocol, para 2.4.
[66]   SI 1991/1247.
[67]   Pre-action Protocol, para 3.1.

disclosure of facts, information and documents which are contended to be material. If the parties do voluntarily disclose information before the issue of proceedings the parties should exchange schedules of assets, income, liabilities and other material facts, using Form E as a guide to the format of the disclosure.[68] Documents should only be disclosed to the extent that they are required by Form E. Disclosing more documents than that is likely to be seen as excessive and unlikely to reduce costs.

Advocates appearing in court must have a thorough knowledge of the Pre-action Protocol, and must be prepared to respond to questions concerning any aspect of the protocol that has not been followed.

5.6.2   Experts

Parties should also consider whether experts will be required. The Pre-action Protocol notes that:

> 'expert valuation evidence is only necessary where the parties cannot agree or do not know the value of some significant asset. The cost of a valuation should be proportionate to the sums in dispute. Whenever possible, valuations of properties, shares etc should be obtained from a single valuer instructed by both parties. To that end, a party wishing to instruct an expert (the first party) should first give the other party a list of the names of one or more experts in the relevant speciality whom he considers are suitable to instruct. Within 14 days the other party may indicate an objection to one or more of the named experts and, if so, should supply the name for one more expert whom he considers suitable. Where the identity of the expert is agreed, the parties should agree the terms of a joint letter of instruction.'[69]

If the parties are unable to agree an expert, it is unlikely to be cost effective to seek to instruct an individual expert prior to proceedings actually being commenced. As noted in the Pre-action Protocol, 'disagreements about disclosure such as the use and identity of an expert may be better managed by the court within the context of an application for ancillary relief'.[70] In any event, where the parties propose to instruct a joint expert, there is a duty on both parties to disclose whether they have already consulted that expert about the assets in issue.[71]

The FPR 1991, r 2.61C applies Part 35 of the Civil Procedure Rules 1998 (CPR)[72] to ancillary relief proceedings. This means the court must exercise its discretion in accordance with the overriding objective of dealing with cases justly. This means, so far as practicable, the parties must be on an equal footing, the court must ensure that expense is kept to a minimum and the court must

---

[68]   Pre-action Protocol, para 3.5.
[69]   Pre-action Protocol, paras 3.8 and 3.9.
[70]   Pre-action Protocol, para 3.11.
[71]   Pre-action Protocol, para 3.13.
[72]   SI 1998/3132.

deal with each case in a manner that is proportionate to the amount of money in dispute, the complexity of the issues and the financial position of each party.

The CPR regime on experts places a premium on advocates and legal representatives gaining an understanding early on in the case of precisely what issues will require expert help. CPR, r 35.4(1) provides that no party may call an expert or put in evidence an expert's report without the court's permission. When a party applies for permission under the rule he must identify: (a) the field in which he wishes to rely on expert evidence; and (b) where practicable the expert in that field on whose evidence he wishes to rely. If permission is granted, it should only be in relation to the expert names or the field identified. The court may also limit the amount of the expert's fees and expenses that the party who wishes to rely on the expert may recover from any other party.[73]

Expert evidence is always to be given in a written report, unless the court directs otherwise. Each party may put to any of the experts written questions about the report.

If both parties wish to submit expert evidence on a particular issue, the court may direct that the evidence is to be given by one expert only.[74] Where the parties cannot agree who the expert should be, the court may: (a) select the expert from a list prepared or identified by the parties; or (b) direct that the expert be selected in such other manner as the court might direct.

The court may at any stage direct a discussion to be held between experts for the purposes of requiring the experts to identify and discuss the issues in the proceedings and where possible, reach an agreed opinion on those issues.[75] The court may also specify the issues which the experts must discuss. The court may also direct that after discussion the experts must prepare a statement showing: (a) those issues on which they agree; and (b) those issues on which they disagree and a summary of those reasons for disagreement. The content of the discussion between the experts shall not be referred to at the trial unless the parties agree.[76] The Part 35 Practice Direction sets out the requirements of the expert's report:

- Expert evidence should be the independent product of the expert uninfluenced by the pressure of litigation.
- An expert should assist the court by providing objective, unbiased opinion on matters within his expertise, and should not assume the role of an advocate.
- An expert should consider all material facts, including those which might detract from his opinion.

---

[73] CPR, r 35.4(4).
[74] CPR, r 34.7(1).
[75] CPR, r 34.12(1).
[76] CPR, r 35.12(4).

- An expert should make it clear when a question falls outside of his expertise, and when he is not able to reach a definite opinion, for example because he has insufficient information.
- If, after producing a report, an expert changes his view on any material matter, such change of view should be communicated to all the parties without delay and when appropriate to the court.

Obviously advocates should note these requirements and frame any cross-examination of the experts around these requirements.

The parties should note, as HHJ Godfrey Gypps has often stated, that there really is no need to go through the expense of using expert evidence for something as simple as valuing the former matrimonial home. Judge Gypps recommends starting with an estate agent's letter and seeking expert advice only if absolutely necessary. Similarly, if there are questions regarding a party's health, a simple letter from a general practitioner may suffice. It may well be that in a case involving a small family business, so long as fraud and non-disclosure are not in issue, the accountants who have been handling tax matters for the business may be in a position to provide both parties with an analysis of the business.

If a joint expert has reported and your client disagrees with its conclusions, your client has the absolute right to seek further expert advice. The client must know, however, that the expert will be at the client's own cost, regardless of the outcome of the case. The Note by Lord Woolf MR in the case of *Daniels v Walker*,[77] must be followed:

> 'In a case where there is a substantial sum involved, one starts, as I have indicated, from the position that wherever possible a joint report is obtained. If there is disagreement on that report, then there would be an issue as to whether to ask questions or whether to get your own expert's report. If questions do not resolve the matter and a party, or both parties, obtain their own experts reports, then that will result in a decision having to be reached as to what evidence should be called. That decision should not be taken until there has been a meeting between the experts involved. It may be that agreement could then be reached; it may be that agreement was reached as a result of asking the appropriate questions. It is only as a last resort that you would accept that it is necessary for oral evidence to be given by the experts before the court. The expense of cross-examination of expert witnesses at the hearing even in a substantial case can be very expensive.'

Therefore parties are instructed to first put questions to the jointly instructed expert, if need be, drafted by another expert of the client's own choosing. The second step would be to instruct your own expert to report, or to at least to produce a summary. The third and final step would be to apply for permission to use your own expert's report. If granted, the two experts will have to meet

---

[77]   [2001] 1 WLR 1382, CA.

and discuss differences, and to see if they could reach an agreed opinion. If not, oral evidence would be required from both experts.

Advocates at first directions appointments should always timetable, if possible, the following: the instructions to be sent to the experts; the report to be delivered; the questions to be delivered to the experts; the replies to the questions from the experts; the discussion between any experts (if there is more than one expert); and the filing of any joint statements by the experts.

As noted above, once there has been an expert's opinion placed before the court, any court disagreeing with that expert must in the judgment state clearly the reason for disagreeing with that expert evidence. Similarly, a court must provide reasons for rejecting the evidence of one expert and accepting that of another.[78]

5.7   THE ADVOCATE AND THE FIRST DIRECTIONS APPOINTMENT

At the first directions appointment the advocate must be in a position, at the very least, to engage in limited or preliminary settlement negotiations, or be able to tell the court why he is not. In order to discuss settlement, the advocate must have disclosure, at the least, of the following:

- a valuation of the former matrimonial home;
- a valuation of all other properties;
- account statements for all bank accounts for at least the last 12 months;
- surrender value quotations for all policies, including the CETV of all pensions;
- 12 months' accounts for any relevant business or partnership or other relevant documentation, though it would be preferable to have the two years' accounts that are required to be disclosed with the Form E;
- evidence of income;
- a valuation of pension rights.

If further documentation is required, advocates must be prepared to argue for production of those documents at the first directions appointment.[79] There is a continuing duty on both parties to disclose documents required by the rules and Form E, so a party that had been unavoidably prevented from sending any document required by Form E at the time of filing and serving of the documents must at the earliest opportunity, serve copies of this new document on the other party, and file a copy of the document with the court, together with a statement explaining the failure to send it with the Form E.[80] After the first directions

---

[78]   See *Evans v Evans* [1990] 1 FLR 319, per Booth J regarding the decision to prefer one accountant's evidence over another.
[79]   FPR 1991, r 2.61B.
[80]   FPR 1991, r 2.61B(5).

appointment, a party is not entitled to production of any further documents, except with the permission of the court[81].

Rule 2.61D of the FPR 1991 sets out the parameters of the first directions appointment: the first appointment must be conducted with the objective of defining issues and saving costs. The district judge must determine the extent to which questions should be allowed to be posed; and should determine which documents must be produced. The court also must give directions about valuing assets and obtaining and exchanging expert evidence. The court must consider whether evidence or further chronologies or schedules should be filed.

Advocates should also consider whether an interim order is required. If no agreement is reached on interim maintenance, the advocate must seek to set down such hearing at the first available opportunity.

Advocates at the first appointment must set out in skeleton form the answers to the following questions:

- A brief background to the case, including length of marriage, income of the parties and rough estimate of the amount of capital to be divided.
- Whether the Form E disclosures have been complete.
- Whether documents due to be disclosed under Form E have been in fact disclosed.
- What are the likely issues in the ancillary relief application?
- What are the issues for this first directions appointment: that is, will one side contend that full disclosure has been provided, or will one party be seeking additional disclosure beyond that provided by the rules under Form E?
- What will be the next step after the first appointment? Will the court be asked to set the matter down for a financial dispute resolution appointment, a further directions appointment, an appointment for the making of an interim order, an appointment for a final hearing, or an adjournment for mediation, an adjournment for private negotiation, or an adjournment generally. The latter option is available only in exceptional circumstances.

The framing of the issues requires careful analysis. District Judge Godfrey Gypps (as he then was) was extremely critical of those issue statements he often saw in first directions appointments. He cites the following as sadly typical: 'What is the home worth?' 'Should it be sold?' 'If so, how should the proceeds be split?' 'Should there be a clean break?'

All issue statements should be framed in terms of the facts of the individual case, for example.

---

[81]   FPR 1991, r 2.61D(3).

'Should the wife with seven years' experience in the computer industry be seen to have no prospects for earning any income at all, as noted in her Form E?'

'Should the wife and the two children, ages seven and nine, be forced to leave the former matrimonial home so that it might be sold in order to provide housing for both parties, in a case where the wife has no income capacity, and the husband has, during the past three years, earned £70,000 per annum?'

'In a marriage that lasted seven years, does the fact that the wife owned 80 per cent of the assets that the couple owned at the time of the marriage constitute a special contribution by the wife that justifies a departure from the yardstick of equality?'

Judge Gypps put it like this:

'A statement that needs oral explanation is a poor statement. Statements should not be so brief that they paint no useful picture. All statements must state what is agreed, and isolate what is factually in dispute.'[82]

District Judge Stephen Gerlis has his own name for FDAs: 'further darn adjournments'.[83] District Judge Gerlis, as well as many other district judges from around the country, believe that many advocates are not fully prepared for first direction appointments and often seek an adjournment at the last minute. Some courts are simply refusing to adjourn, and considering costs orders against those parties not fully prepared. District Judge Gerlis notes that solicitors and counsel should consider r 2.51B of the FPR 1991, which applies the 'overriding objective' to family proceedings. This means the court must be concerned with its own resources, not only in relation to the case under adjudication, but to all other cases the court has to deal with. If first direction appointments are adjourned, it means that other cases will not be heard as quickly as they might. District Judge Gerlis' view is that solicitors who are not prepared should be debarred from further involvement in the proceedings. Clients who fail to turn up for the first appointment or who are guilty of unreasonable delay in preparing documents that should have been prepared by the first directions appointment, will be likely to be assessed for costs.

5.8   THE ADVOCATE AND THE FINANCIAL DISPUTE RESOLUTION APPOINTMENT

Perhaps no innovation contained in the pilot scheme has received more praise, and more criticism, than the new Financial Dispute Resolution Appointment (FDR) regime. The idea is in one sense an admission that the law in this area is wholly unpredictable. Therefore the primary goal of the FDR is to test each party's theory of the case. The contentions of each party will be put before a

---

[82]   HHJ Godfrey Gypps, in a paper submitted to the 2002 Family Law Conference. HHJ Gypps sits at the Southend County Court and is a Visiting Fellow at the University of Essex. He is a member of the Judicial Studies Board District Judges Tutor Team.

[83]   See 'Talking Shop – FDAs' [2002] Fam Law 702.

judge who will then render a decision which is not binding on the parties. The decision by this judge is an aid for prediction. Is it likely that a different district judge hearing the same arguments will give a decision wholly at odds with the first judgment? Those who criticise the regime say that the FDR never affords enough time for the arguments to be put in a meaningful way, and that the 'judgment' given by the judge at the FDR unduly coerces the parties to settle on those terms; those who support it say that any effort at providing more certainty in this area of law is to be applauded. Apparently the ayes have it, because the FDR is now a settled part of any advocate's life at the Family Bar.

Advocates in an FDR must be concise, remembering the old admission by the scientist Pascal that he would have written a shorter argument if only he had the time. The arguments must be fully presented, however, because the client who has just heard the district judge dismiss them will want to feel his advocate has done justice to the claim.

Advocates must note FPR 1991, r 2.61E (as amended), which set outs the purpose of the FDR and the basic procedure to be followed. No later than seven days prior to the appointment the applicant must file with the court details of all offers and proposals, and responses to those proposals. The FDR appointment will be heard by a judge who will not hear the substantive trial of the matter, should one be necessary.

But the rules do not set out the manner and method of the judge's role in the FDR. Some judges simply act as arbiters, and seek to give indications as to disputed facts or disputed contentions regarding the law. Others act more as mediators, attempting to engage in substantive discussions with counsel about settlement offers that are on the table.

All of this came up for review by the Court of Appeal in the case of *Rose v Rose*.[84] In that case, after a lengthy FDR where Bennett J had, in effect, conducted a mini-trial of the issues and then given 'judgment', counsel for both parties were directed by the judge to continue their negotiations. At approximately 4 pm, both counsel appeared in front of the judge and stated that terms had been agreed. Both counsel then stated that an order would be drawn up.

The judge indicated that he would be very happy to record that the settlement had occurred, and would be available the next week to approve the order. Of course a dispute ensued during the drafting, and it was argued that no settlement had been made at the FDR. The husband contended his case had not been 'fully presented.' He wished to resile from any agreement that had been made, contending any agreement was made under duress. The basis of the duress

---

[84]   [2003] EWCA 505, [2002] 1 FLR 978.

was in fact Bennett J's mini-judgment on the issues that were presented to him. In other words, the husband felt compelled to accept the decision made by this High Court judge, when in fact after some contemplation he realised that he would have had a reasonable chance of success with another High Court judge.

Nicholas Mostyn QC, on behalf of the husband, criticised the manner in which the FDR had been conducted. On this view, the judge should act as a mediator, and attempt to resolve disputes, not seek to sit in judgment and seek to predict what the next judge will do at the substantive hearing.

The Court of Appeal held that the parties had reached agreement, and that the agreement had been made an order of the court. The Court of Appeal held that the product of the FDR was therefore an unperfected order of the court, not merely a contractual agreement between the parties.[85] Whether the FDR was designated a hearing or a meeting was of purely semantic significance, the court held, and was of no legal importance. The court held that the FDR was a hearing in the sense that the attendance of the parties was obligatory, that they were obliged to use their best endeavours to reach agreement on the matters in issue, that the appointment was presided over and controlled by the judge, and that at its conclusion one of three possible orders would result:

(1) an order adjourning the appointment;
(2) a consent order disposing of the case; or
(3) directions to proceed to a final hearing.

The Court of Appeal also refused to accept that Bennett J had been wrong to give judgment on the various issues before him. Thorpe LJ on behalf of the court recognised that a great variation existed in how judges conducted FDR's. Thorpe LJ put it like this:

> 'It would be unhelpful to impose any restrictions on the exercise of the judicial discretion in this innovative and elastic field. However I would strenuously reject any criticism of the manner in which Bennett J conducted this FDR on 3 August 2001. Indeed I would say that his conduct of the hearing might stand as illustrative of one classic method. The art of mediation depends upon qualification and training. Years of experience in a specialist litigation field are no substitute for that training and qualification. Very few of the judges whose duty it is to conduct FDR hearings will have had any training and qualification as mediators. However, those who have long experience in a specialist field of litigation are supremely well qualified to offer what is widely known as early neutral evaluation. That is

---

85 For the legal consequences of this, see *de Lasala (Ernet Ferdinantd Perez) v de Lasala (Hannelore)* [1980] AC 546 (contractual agreement which had not been elevated into an order of the court); *Edgar v Edgar* [1980] 1 WLR 1410, [1981] 2 FLR 19. In those cases, a party had to establish exceptional circumstances to be released from his agreement. On the other hand, if there is a valid consent order a party may only be released by showing misrepresentation, mistake, material non-disclosure or a subsequent fundamental and unforeseen change of circumstance. See *Barder v Caluori* [1988] AC 20, sub nom *Barder v Barder (Caluori Intervening)* [1987] 2 FLR 480. See discussion by Thorpe LJ in *Rose* [2002] 1 FLR 978 at 990.

precisely what Bennett J offered, having prepared himself by extensive pre reading and drawing on the expert submissions of leading counsel both written and oral. In many cases the neutral evaluation will be supplemented by an objective risk analysis of the costs incurred, and the costs to be incurred by proceeding to full trial, against the value of what is truly in issue, drawn from a comparison of the applicant's lowest target and the respondent's highest offer. Beyond those methods there may be dangers in judges over estimating their ability to bring about a compromise by the use of other forms of mediation for which they have received no training.'[86]

District Judge Million of the Principal Registry advises that parties who have reached agreement at the FDR, but do not seek to have an order perfected until there is further drafting, should draft heads of agreement, and then ask the court to make the following order:

(1) By consent, the heads of agreement dated [   ] are made an order of the court in terms to be perfected by the court;

(2) The parties are to draft the agreed proposed terms of the perfected final order, and lodge a written copy of the terms with the court by 4 pm on [date];

(3) the applications for financial ancillary relief are listed for mention before [judge] on [date];

(4) the mention date may be vacated if before then the perfected final order is made.[87]

5.9   ANCILLARY RELIEF APPEALS

There has during the last several years been some uncertainty as to the standard of review by circuit judges (or High Court judges) of decisions by district judges. The Court of Appeal in *Cordle v Cordle*[88] held that circuit judges hearing appeals from district judges should allow the appeal only when the decision of the district judge was 'plainly wrong'. This of course is the same test applied by the Court of Appeal when hearing appeals from the circuit court or from the High Court. The decision in *Cordle* was immediately criticised, not least because the argument really had not been raised in oral argument on appeal in that case. But more importantly, the decision clearly ran afoul of r 8.1 of the FPR 1991. Rule 8.1(3), which was not discussed in *Cordle*, stated that at the time of hearing an appeal to which the rule applies, the judge may exercise his own discretion in substitution for that of the district judge. That provision was not mentioned in *Cordle*.

In any event, shortly after *Cordle* had been handed down, the rules were amended by statutory instrument. The Family Proceedings (Amendment) Rules

---

86   [2002] 1 FLR 978 at 988.

87   The suggestions were made in talk delivered by DJ Million at the Family Law Conference on Property and Finance, on 11 June 2003.

88   [2001] EWCA Civ 1791, [2002] 1 FLR 207.

2003,[89] r 14 puts ancillary relief appeals on the same basis as appeals in non-family cases, which are governed by CPR, r 52.11. Rule 8.1(3) of FPR 1991 now reads as follows:

'3   On any appeal to which paragraph 2 applies—

(a)   the appeal shall be limited to a review of the decision of the District Judge unless the Judge considers that in the circumstances of the case it would be in the interests of justice to hold a rehearing;

(b)   oral evidence or evidence which was not before the District Judge may be admitted if in all the circumstances of the case, it would be in the interests of justice to do so, irrespective of whether the appeal may be way of review or rehearing.'

Therefore appeals from district judges to circuit judges, or appeals from district judges in the Principal Registry to the High Court, will be governed by the standards set out by Lloyd Fraser of Tullybelton in *G v G (Minors: Custody Appeal)*:[90] the judge should only interfere when he considers that the district judge has not merely preferred an imperfect solution that is different from an alternative imperfect solution, but has exceeded the generous ambit within which a reasonable disagreement is possible.[91]

It is not yet clear when (or what type) of additional evidence will be permitted. The barrister Robin Spon-Smith argues that it is likely that circuit judges will use the same standard that the Court of Appeal uses when deciding to remit a case for rehearing by the same or another judge. Had there been inadequate findings of fact made by the district judge, or was the decision of the district judge unjust because of some procedural or other irregularity? A rehearing may also be appropriate if there is a significant change of circumstances in the interim since the district judge's decision.

Mr Spon-Smith also argues that the *Ladd v Marshall*,[92] standard will apply for the admission of new evidence. Fresh evidence will not be admitted on an appeal unless either it was not available at the trial to the party seeking to use it, or that reasonable diligence would not have made it available. The evidence must also have formed a determining factor in, or would have had an important influence on, the result reached by the district judge. See *Gillingham v Gillingham*,[93] for an application of that standard, in light of the 'overriding objective of dealing with a case justly'.

It also must be noted that the new rule has no application to Children Act cases. The new rule only governs appeal of ancillary relief applications. In appeals from district judges in proceedings under the Children Act 1989, r 4.22 of the FPR 1991 continues to apply. These rules do not address the question of whether

89   SI 2003/184.
90   [1985] FLR 894.
91   See the article by Robin Spon-Smith [2003] Fam Law 428.
92   [1954] 1 WLR 1489, CA.
93   [2001] EWCA Civ 906, [2001] All ER (D) 52 (June).

the appeal is a review or a rehearing. In the case of *Re W, Re A, Re B (Change of Name)*[94], the Court of Appeal did state in dicta that all appellate hearings, whether from a district judge to circuit judge or from circuit judge to the Court of Appeal, should be governed by the same *G v G* standard.

5.10   THE PROCEEDS OF CRIME ACT 2002

Advocates appearing for clients who may have committed criminal offences, in particular with regard to property or assets held by that party, must understand and apply the provisions of the Proceeds of Crime Act 2002. The Act imposes onerous duties on advocates who discover that their clients have committed fraudulent or criminal acts with regard to property that is the subject of the litigation.

Section 340(3) of the Proceeds of Crime Act 2002 provides that property is criminal property if: (a) it constitutes a person's benefit from criminal conduct or it represents such benefit (in whole or in part and whether directly or indirectly) and (b) the alleged offender knows or suspects that it constitutes or represents such a benefit. So for example, property that represents a benefit of the non-payment of tax constitutes criminal property for the purposes of the Act. Therefore a barrister who advises a client in respect of how to enforce rights in respect of certain property may well be 'concerned in an arrangement which facilitates the acquisition of criminal property'. See s 328(1) of the Proceeds of Crime Act 2002, which provides that a person commits an offence if he enters into or becomes concerned in an arrangement which he knows or suspects facilitates (by whatever means) the acquisition, retention, use or control of criminal property by or on behalf of another person.

The General Council of the Bar has stated in guidance to barristers that where the barrister knows or suspects that as a result of following his advice, his client may acquire criminal property, the barrister could be said to be concerned in such an arrangement. Similarly, where the parties to litigation agree a settlement where the subject matter of the litigation is (at least in part) criminal property, this too could be said to be an arrangement within the meaning of the Proceeds of Crime Act 2002.

Advocates should note that s 328(2) of the Act provides defences. The most pertinent of those is s 328(2)(a), which provides, in part, that a person does not commit an offence if he makes an authorised disclosure under s 338 and (if the disclosure is made before he does the act mentioned in subsection (1)) he has the appropriate consent. The disclosure is to be made to the National Criminal Intelligence Service (NCIS). The Bar Guidance states that where a member of the Bar is instructed to advise/appear in court in circumstances

---

94   [1999] 2 FLR 930, CA.

where he will become involved in an arrangement as described in s 328, he must consider whether he should make a disclosure to the NCIS before continuing to act. Where the barrister considers that he should make disclosure, he should inform his client of his duty to make a disclosure to the NCIS and to seek the client's consent before continuing to act. However, the barrister should *not* make the disclosure to the client if by doing so the disclosure is likely to prejudice any investigation which might be conducted following the disclosure. Barristers and solicitors are given a defence under s 332(2)(c) if the disclosure is to be required in connection with the giving by the adviser of legal advice to the client. But s 333(4) provides that the exemption does not apply if the disclosure to the client is made with the intention of furthering a criminal purpose. Similarly, s 342 of the Act provides that if a person knows or suspects that a confiscation investigation or money laundering investigation is being or is about to be conducted, he commits an offence if he makes a disclosure which prejudices the investigation. Again, a legal advice exemption is made by the Act,[95] but if the disclosure is made with the intention of furthering a criminal purpose, the exemption is not allowed.[96]

Advocates must know and understand the judgment of the President of the Family Division in the case of *P v P (Ancillary Relief: Proceeds of Crime)*.[97] In that case, the wife's solicitors became concerned that s 328 covered correspondence of the husband's about his business affairs. The President held that the s 328 duty to disclose to the NCIS covered *both* sets of lawyers – the court held that unless the solicitor has an 'improper intention', the solicitor is free to inform his client and his opponents of his disclosures.[98]

5.11 COSTS

Many district judges I spoke to expressed dismay about the lack of preparation of beginning advocates for questions involving costs. The following was typical: 'It will be 16.30, late in the afternoon and I've given a difficult judgment, and then it occurs to the winner's advocate to make an argument about costs, with no schedule available, no real understanding about the offers or counter offers, no application of the rules, and only a vague understanding of why I should make the order.' As that district judge said, the better bet is to ask for a short adjournment to set your schedules in order, or, better yet, to anticipate the result (either way) and have your arguments prepared.

95 See Proceeds of Crime Act 2002, s 342(3)(c).
96 David Burrows queries whether the disclosure principle of MCA 1973, s 25(1) conflicts with the right of citizens not to incriminate themselves. See 'Money Laundering: Four Disclosures and a Privilege' [2004] 34 Fam Law 210.
97 [2004] 1 FLR 193.
98 See Phillip Moor and Christopher Frazer [2003] Fam Law 885, for a discussion of the case. Note, also, that 'suspicion' is all that is required to trigger the duty to disclose to the NCIS. See also Watters and Levy, 'Divorce and Revenue Investigations' [2004] Fam Law 26.

Considerable confusion has existed about costs in family cases, only some of which has been cleared up by the President's judgment in the case of *Norris v Norris, Haskins v Haskins*. [99] In that case, the court held that costs in family cases should be governed both by the procedures set out in CPR, r 44.3 and The FPR 1991, r 2.69. The general rule in all civil cases is set out in CPR, r 44.3(2): the unsuccessful party will pay unless the court makes a different order. *That rule does not apply in family cases.* Rule 10.27(1)(b) of the FPR 1991 specifically provides that the normal costs rule does not apply in family proceedings.

But FPR 1991, r 2.69 provides the method for most costs orders in ancillary relief cases. That rule gives statutory authority to the rule first set out by the Court of Appeal in the case of *Calderbank v Calderbank*.[100] The rule, in short, provides that either party may at any time make a written offer to the other party which is expressed to be 'without prejudice except as to costs'. Where an offer is made, the court is not to be told. If the court's award is more advantageous than the offer, the court must, unless it considers it unjust to do so, order that the other party pay any costs incurred after the date beginning 28 days after the offer was made.

Factors for the court's consideration are set out at r 2.69D of the FPR 1991: In considering whether it would be unjust to make a costs order, the court must take into account all the circumstances of the case, including the terms of any offers; the stage in the proceedings when any offers were made; the information available to the parties at the time when the offer was made; the conduct of the parties with regard to the giving or refusing to give information for the purposes of enabling the offer to be made or evaluated; and the respective means of the parties.

In October 2004, the Department of Constitutional Affairs (DCA) published a consultation paper that contains within it a likely change in the costs regime in ancillary relief cases.[101] If these proposals are adopted, and all indicators are that they will be, the costs regime will be moved away from the 'costs follow the event' approach in civil litigation. The DCA proposal is that courts should consider costs as part of the overall settlement of the parties' financial affairs. The proposed amendments are designed to establish the principle that, in the

---

99   [2003] EWCA Civ 1084, [2003] 2 FLR 1124. See, in particular, Nicholas Mostyn QC's judgment in the case of *GW v RW (Financial Provision: Departure from Equality)* [2003] 2 FLR 108, where the deputy judge of the High Court noted that in high wealth cases, it would be better to start from a standpoint that there will be no order for costs, that is, each party will bear his or her own costs, unless a party is guilty of unreasonable conduct. The President did not follow that rule in *Norris*. It would appear, however, that the Department of Constitutional Affairs will follow Mostyn QC's path; see discussion above.

100   [1976] Fam 93, [1975] FLR 113.

101   See 'Costs in Ancillary Relief Proceedings and Appeals' in Fam Proceedings Consultation Paper (CL(L) 29/04), containing proposals to amend the Family Proceedings Rules 1991 (SI 1991/1247) (FPR).

absence of litigation misconduct, the approach of the court should be to treat the costs as part of the parties' reasonable needs. Costs will have to be paid from the matrimonial 'pot', with the court then dividing the remainder between the parties.

The applicant in all ancillary relief proceedings must file an open offer with the court no less than 14 days before the date fixed for the final hearing. Respondents must reply with a counter offer not more than seven days after service of this open offer. See FPR 1991, r 2.69E.

Advocates must understand the current rules surrounding offers made under *Calderbank*. A *Calderbank* offer cannot be effective until there has been full disclosure by the offeror. By extension, this also applies to an open offer.[102] Applicants in ancillary relief proceedings also risk failure of costs application where no counter offer is made. Singer J has suggested that at least three weeks is a reasonable period for a response to a *Calderbank* offer.[103]

District Judge Gypps (as he then was) has noted in talks to the Family Bar that he was surprised at how often the rules set out above are overlooked. He became used to seeing cases where no offers were made at all.

Judge Gypps believes offers should be as simple as possible. The more sophisticated the proposal, in his view, the more difficult it is for the advocate or the court to see quickly whether it has been beaten. The same goes for any statement of the valuation or other basis on which the offer is made.

An offer must also specify the costs basis on which it is made.

Judge Gypps recommends that advocates place the other side on notice as early as possible that costs will be sought. A separate skeleton should be prepared. The costs must be quantified, if possible.

The possible orders that are available are set out at CPR, r 44.3(6). Orders might be made providing for:

(1) a proportion of another party's costs;
(2) a stated amount in respect of another party's costs;
(3) costs from or until a certain date only;
(4) costs incurred before proceedings began;
(5) costs relating to particular steps taken in the proceedings;
(6) interest on costs from or until a certain date, including a date before judgment.

Each party intending to claim costs must prepare a written statement of the costs he intends to claim, showing separately in the form of a schedule:

---

[102] See *H v H (Clean Break: Non-disclosure: Costs)* [1994] 2 FLR 309.
[103] See *A v A (Costs Appeal)* [1996] 1 FLR 14, FD.

(a) the number of hours claimed;

(b) the hourly rate;

(c) the grade of fee earner;

(d) the amount and nature of any disbursements to be claimed, other than counsel's fee for appearing at the hearing;

(e) the amount of solicitor's costs to be claimed for attending at hearing;

(f) fees of counsel in respect of the hearing;

(g) any VAT to be claimed on these amounts.

Note that it is imperative that a judge consider a summary assessment of costs at the conclusion of the hearing, and that adjournment for a detailed assessment of costs runs contrary to the stated purposes of the CPR 1998.

Courts cannot summarily assess costs payable to a publicly funded party. (See Costs Practice Direction, paragraph 13.9.). The amount of costs payable by a publicly funded party is subject to s 11 of the Access to Justice Act 1999, which provides that 'except in prescribed circumstances, costs ordered against an individual in relation to any proceedings or part of proceedings funded for him shall not exceed the amount (if any) which is a reasonable one for him to pay having regard to all the circumstances including: (a) the financial resources of all the parties to the proceedings and (b) their conduct in connection to which the proceedings relate'. Regulations 8 to 13 of the Community Legal Service (Costs) Regulations 2000[104] provide the procedure for seeking costs against a funded client, as well as the Legal Services Commission (LSC). A party seeking an order for costs against a LSC funded client may at any time file and serve on the LSC funded client a statement of resources. If that statement is served seven or more days before a date fixed for a hearing at which an order for costs may be made, the LSC funded client must also make a statement of resources and produce it at the hearing. If the court decides to make an order for costs against a LSC funded client to whom costs protection applies, it may either: (a) make an order for costs to be determined; or (b) make an order specifying the costs payable.

A 'costs order to be determined' means an order to which s 11 of the Access to Justice Act 1999 applies. The amount of the costs is to be determined by a costs judge or a district judge. The original court, however, may make a finding of facts regarding the conduct of the case, as well as finding the amount of actual or full costs. A 'costs order specifying the costs payable' means an order for costs to which s 11 applies and which specifies that amount which the LSC funded client is to pay. The court will not do that unless it is satisfied that it has sufficient information before it to decide what amount is a reasonable amount for the LSC funded client to pay in accordance with s 11 of the Access to Justice Act.

---

[104] SI 2000/441.

It is possible, of course, to seek costs orders for interlocutory hearings. If the order is silent as to costs, that means no one is entitled to costs. If costs for the hearing are 'reserved', it means the judge at final hearing has the discretion to award those costs to the successful party.

Where a court is assessing the amount of costs, it will assess them either on the standard basis or the indemnity basis. Standard basis means the court will only allow costs which are proportionate to the matters in issue. The court will resolve any doubt which it may have as to whether costs were reasonably incurred or reasonable and proportionate in favour of the paying party (see CPR, r 44.4). If the costs are assessed on an indemnity basis, the court will resolve any doubt which it may have in favour of the receiving party. An award of costs on the indemnity basis is only justified where a paying party has been responsible for conduct which is unreasonable to a high degree. The conduct must 'not be merely wrong or misguided in hindsight'.[105]

Costs that are incurred because of the conduct of the litigants must be distinguished from costs that are wasted because of the conduct of the lawyer. Section 51 of the Supreme Court Act 1981 provides that a court may disallow or order the lawyers concerned to meet the whole of any 'wasted costs or such part of them as may be determined'. 'Wasted costs' means any costs incurred by a party as a result of any improper, unreasonable or negligent act or omission on the part of any legal or other representative or any employee of such a representative; or which, in the light of any such act or omission, the court considers it is unreasonable to expect that party to pay.

In the case of *Medcalf v Mardell*,[106] the House of Lords confirmed the general rule first set out in *Ridehalgh v Horsefield*:[107]

> 'As a general rule allegations of breach of duty relating to the conduct of the case by a barrister or a solicitor with a view to the making of a costs order should be confined strictly to questions which are apt for summary disposal by the court. Failure to appear, conduct which leads to an otherwise avoidable step in the proceedings or the prolongation of a hearing by gross repetition or extreme slowness in the presentation of evidence or argument are typical examples. The factual basis for the exercise of the jurisdiction in such circumstances is likely to be found in facts which are within judicial knowledge because the relevant events took place in court or are facts that can easily be verified. Wasting the time of the court or an abuse of its processes which results in excessive costs to litigants thus can be dealt with summarily on agreed facts or after a brief inquiry if the facts are not all agreed.
>
> Save in the clearest case, applications against the lawyers acting for an opposing party are unlikely to be apt for summary determination, since any hearing to investigate the conduct of a complex action is itself likely to be expensive and time consuming.'

---

[105] See *Kiam v MGN Ltd (No 2)* [2002] EWCA Civ 66, [2002] 1 WLR 2810, CA.
[106] [2002] 3 All ER 721.
[107] [1994] Ch 204.

The Lords also noted that a judge who is invited to make or contemplate making a wasted costs order must make full allowance for the inability of the respondent lawyer to tell the whole story. (The lawyer cannot waive the client's legal privilege regarding information received by the lawyer from the client, nor regarding advice given by the lawyer to the client. Therefore the lawyer may not be able to refute some of the allegations made against him by the other side regarding the conduct of the litigation.) Where there is room for doubt, the respondent lawyers are entitled to the benefit of the doubt. It is only when, with all allowances made, a lawyer's conduct of proceedings is quite plainly unjustifiable will it be appropriate to make a wasted costs order.

FPR 1991, r 8.1(2) and (3) provide for an appeal against an order for costs only, as distinct from appealing against the order as a whole.

5.12   CASE LAW MADE UNDER MCA 1973

Advocates are reminded that comparing fact situations in ancillary relief cases is of little help to a district judge. Nevertheless, the broad principles set down in the following cases are useful for the beginning advocate. Again, the cases have been selected in part bacause the court in each case must address conflicting narratives that often recur in ancillary relief matters. If cases are otherwise unreported, they are available on LAWTEL.

P v P

Fam Div [2004] EWHC 2277 (Fam)(Baron J)

In a claim for financial provision on divorce, where the parties had made equal but different contributions to the marriage, the capital assets were divided with broad equality between the parties.

McFarlane v McFarlane : Parlour v Parlour

CA [2004] EWCA Civ 872 (Thorpe LJ, Latham LJ, Wall, LJ)

When a husband's income substantially exceeds the expenditure of himself and his former wife, the surplus could properly be shared between them by means of a periodical payments order for an extendable period with a view to achieving a clean break at the end of that period. The court should always seek to achieve fairness.

D v D (Financial Provision: Periodical Payments)

Fam Div [2004] EWHC 445 (Fam) (Coleridge J)

Courts should strive to divide assets equally where it is not unjust to do so.

Phillip Anthony Roberts (Trustee in Bankruptcy of Peter John Nunn) (Appellant/Applicant) v (1) Peter Jon Nunn (2) Lorna Tiffany (Respondents)

Ch D (Bankruptcy Ct) [2004] 1 FLR 1123 (Nicholas Strauss QC)

A consent order made between the parties to divorce proceedings had been made without jurisdiction and was therefore ineffective to impose a trust on one-half of the pension fund in issue.

R v R

Fam Div [2003] EWHC 3197 (Fam) (Wilson J)

In ancillary proceedings the court made a lump sum order against the former husband which included the monthly payments on a 20-year mortgage to enable the former wife to purchase a house and ordered that the obligation to pay the instalments should be secured against the husband's shares in a family farming company.

W v W (Financial Provision: Form E)

Fam Div [2003] EWHC 2254 (Fam) (Nicholas Mostyn QC)

Where, in proceedings for financial provision following divorce, a party deliberately filled in 'Form E' falsely, or misrepresented facts, then he could expect to be censured or penalised in costs.

Daniel Norton Idris Pearce v Ursula Helene Pearce

CA [2003] EWCA Civ 1054, [2004] 1 WLR 68, [2003] 2 FLR 1144 (Dame Elizabeth Butler-Sloss (President), Thorpe LJ, Mantell LJ)

A judge was wrong when increasing a periodical payments order, and capitalising it under s 31(7A) and (7B) of the Matrimonial Causes Act 1973, to add a substantial sum over the figure given by application of the Duxbury tables in reliance on *Cornick v Cornick (No 3)* (2001) 2 FLR 1240, which was wrong on that issue.

P v T

CA [2003] EWCA Civ 837 (Thorpe LJ, May LJ, Bodey J)

It was not wrong for the court to augment the periodical payments order for a child to include an allowance for the mother, especially if the mother had to

give up work. A more generous approach to the calculation of the mother's allowance was not only permissible but realistic.

C v C (Variation of Post-Nuptial Settlement: Company Shares)

Fam Div [2003] EWCA 1222 (Fam), [2003] 2 FLR 493 (Coleridge J)

A wife who had helped with her former husband's business was given shares in the company following their divorce in the circumstances of the case; however the husband retained the majority of shares as the matrimonial home was to be transferred to the wife leaving him without any substantially safe assets.

Christopher Philip Ranson v Penelope Ann Ranson

CA [2001] EWCA Civ 1929 (Thorpe LJ, Robert Walker LJ, Sir Martin Nourse)

Where defects in the title caused doubt over the capital value of an asset, payment of a lump sum by instalments funded by rental income pending sale was more appropriate than requiring immediate payment of the whole lump sum. The Human Rights Act 1998 restricted the appointment of a receiver in ancillary relief proceedings.

Beverly Ann Cordle v Sidny Clifford Cordle

CA [2001] EWCA Civ 1791 (Dame Elizabeth Butler-Sloss (President), Thorpe LJ)

It was necessary to reform the practice of appeals from a district judge to a circuit judge in ancillary relief proceedings so that any such appeal would only be allowed if there was a procedural irregularity or if, in the balancing exercise, the district judge failed to take into account relevant matters, took into account irrelevant matters or was plainly wrong.

Waite v Waite

CA [2001] EWCA Civ 1186 (Thorpe LJ, Hale LJ, Astill J)

The Court of Appeal was very hesitant to enforce a suspended order for committal for breach of a court order where the applicant was himself in breach of the order on the which the application to commit was based.

V v V

Fam Div [2001] 2 FLR 799 (Wilson J)

A consideration of the court's jurisdiction to determine the level of child maintenance in an application for the husband to pay lump sums for the benefit of the children or to vary an order for periodical payments where the husband had agreed to pay maintenance at half the level considered appropriate by the court.

Sarita Joan Pasha v Mohammed Tariq Pasha

CA (5 March 2001, unreported) (Thorpe LJ, Hale LJ)

In a dispute between a married couple over both a lump sum and periodical payments to be made by the husband, the circuit judge had correctly directed himself as to his function in conducting an appeal from the decision of a district judge but had wrongly regarded himself as free to re-evaluate essential findings that had neither been challenged nor were in dispute.

Minaz Dharamshi v Anisha Dharamshi

CA (5 December 2000, unreported) (Aldous LJ, Schiemann LJ, Thorpe LJ)

Husband's appeal in relation to a lump sum ordered to be paid by him in ancillary proceedings dismissed in the light of the decision in *White v White* (2003) 3 WLR 1571. * Leave to appeal to the House of Lords refused.

Secretary of State for Social Security v (1) Robert John Foster (2) Elizabeth Joan Foster

CA (4 December 2000, unreported) (Ward LJ, Brooke LJ, Sir Christopher Slade)

An agreement made by consent during divorce proceedings that the father make periodical payments towards the school fees of the children, amounted to a maintenance order for the benefit of the CSA 1991. Accordingly, the Child Support Agency had no jurisdiction to make a maintenance assessment of the father whilst that maintenance order was in force.

A v A (Maintenance Pending Suit: Payment of Legal Fees)

Fam Div (1 November 2000, unreported) (Holman J)

A wife's application for monthly periodical maintenance payments to include a sum allocated for the payment of her legal fees was granted.

Timothy Stewart Dorney-Kingdom v Phillipa Mary Dorney-Kingdom

CA (15 June 2000, unreported) (Dame Elizabeth Butler-Sloss (President), Thorpe LJ, Smith J)

In any case where there was a determination that the primary carer had no entitlement to periodical payments on her own account, then any form of order that was not an agreed order for maintenance plainly circumvented the statutory prohibition. One of the purposes of the CSA 1991 was to deprive the courts of jurisdiction to make discretionary determination as to the extent of a father's liability to maintain his children in a dissolved marriage.

Sandra Elizabeth Jones v William Trebor Jones

CA (30 March 2000, unreported) (Dame Elizabeth Butler-Sloss (President), Thorpe LJ, Mance LJ)

The circuit court judge was wrong in law in declaring that he was unable to extend a periodical payment order and was wrong in finding that he had no jurisdiction to make an order pursuant to s 37 of the MCA 1973 in favour of the claimant wife to extend the time period of her periodical payment order. Accordingly, the matter was remitted to a district judge to set out new terms for an extension of the original order.

DWJ (Applicant) v SRJ (Respondent)

CA (28 October 1998, unreported) (Peter Gibson LJ, Hale J)

Judge had been wrong to order a clean break as opposed to an order for periodical payments in the case of an older wife with dependent children following a 27-year marriage.

R v Secretary of State for Social Security, ex parte Harris

QBD (1 July 1998, unreported) (Scott Baker J)

Once an application for an assessment under the CSA 1991 had been properly made the parent against whom the assessment was made could not terminate the assessment even if the person with care was no longer on benefit.

Stephanie Marjorie Burrow v Adrian Richard Burrow

Fam Div (8 April 1998, unreported) (Cazalet J)

The new provisions of ss 25B, 25C and 25D of the MCA 1973 were a discretion to be awarded by the judge in accordance with the established criteria under s 25 of the 1973 Act and made no statutory provision which raised an entitlement to the earmarking of a pension fund. There was no inconsistency in not allowing a wife to earmark a claim against the pension annuity fund whilst permitting her to maintain a claim against one-half of the capital fund.

White v White

HL [2001] 1 AC 596

Courts should not deviate from yardstick of equality unless there is good reason to do so. Courts should focus not primarily on 'needs' but on fairness.

Cowan v Cowan

CA [2001] 2 FLR 192

Courts must always, when seeking to divide assets, compare 'like with like'.

Lambert v Lambert

[2003] 1 FLR 139

Courts should not engage in intricate analysis regarding division of assets. Court should aim to achieve fairness.

H-J v H-J

Fam Div [2002] 1 FLR 415

Court should use rough measure of equality when seeking to achieve fair division of assets.

Chapter 6

APPEALS

6.1 INTRODUCTION

Appeals in family cases present difficult and unique problems for advocates. Trial judges in family courts are granted broad discretion to make both fact-finding decisions and (crucially in cases about children) predictions about future events. The granting of this discretion to trial judges means appeals of their decisions must be discouraged, in particular appeals in close cases where, in actuality, the decision might have gone either way on the evidence. If appeals were readily available, the granting of a broad discretion to fact-finders would be meaningless. The difficulty of a discretionary jurisdiction, however, is that there are very few 'bright line' rules of guidance for either advocates or judges. When is a judgment beyond the discretion of the fact-finder? When is a decision so unreasonable that no rational judge, hearing the evidence, could reach such a conclusion?

'It is an exercise in line-drawing', one leading QC said. 'You have to convince the appellate judge that the fact-finder not just got it wrong, but got it grossly wrong.'

Lord Justice Thorpe, in an interview with the author, addressed the problem like this:

> 'In appeals in family cases, what is in question on most occasions is not whether the judge got the law right, but whether he has exercised his or her discretion permissibly. It is difficult for an appellant to show that a conscientious exercise by the fact-finder has produced a result that is outside that judge's discretion. An appellate judge reading a skeleton argument must be struck immediately with something that is wrong, fundamentally wrong, with the judgment below.'

This 'fundamentally wrong' standard is embodied in innumerable cases decided by the Court of Appeal, and any advocate deciding whether to seek permission to appeal must seek to understand and apply this standard.

6.2 PRACTICE AND PROCEDURE

The decision by the advocate with regard to applying for permission to appeal must be made immediately after conclusion of the case. Advocates considering

appeal must of course first take note of the procedures set out at CPR PD 52: Appeals, and should also note the Practice Direction: (CPR PD 52: Appeals).[1]

The Court of Appeal, per Lord Woolf MR, in 1998 issued a Practice Direction setting out the practice and procedure for dealing with applications for leave to appeal to the Court of Appeal. That direction has been superseded by the Civil Procedure Rules 1998 (CPR), but that direction contained within it, however, matters of a more substantive nature. Those observations by Lord Woolf remain vital reading for appellant advocates. The court's experience, according to the Direction, at paragraph 7, '... is that many appeals and applications for leave to appeal are made which are quite hopeless. They demonstrate basic misconceptions as to the purpose of the civil appeal system and the different roles played by the appellate courts and courts of first instance.'[2]

> 'Courts of first instance can help to minimise the delay expense which an appeal involves. Where the parties are present for delivery of judgement, it should be routine for the judge below to ask whether either party wants leave to appeal and to deal with the matter then and there. However, if the court of first instance is in doubt whether an appeal would have a real prospect of success or involves a point of general principle, the safe course is to refuse leave to appeal.'[3]

Therefore in any case outside the family proceedings court where the advocate believes appeal may be appropriate, the advocate should immediately seek permission from the trial judge for permission to appeal.[4] This is likely to be summarily denied, but the requirement to seek permission from the trier of fact remains a vital first rule of appellate advocacy. The standard is this: whether there is a real prospect of success in the Court of Appeal, or whether the appeal involves a point of principle.

The Court of Appeal, in the case of *Re B (A Child)*,[5] has now held that where the applicant for permission to appeal contends the judge gave insufficient reasons, or made a material omission in the judgment, the applicant at the permission shearing should draw this to the judge's attention. The advocate must do this, according to Thorpe LJ, in part because of the advocates duty to assist the court to achieve the overriding objective of doing justice in each case (see CPR, r 1.3), and in some cases it may follow from the advocate's duty not to mislead the court. The advocate must raise the matter rather than allow the order to be drawn. 'It was unsatisfactory', Thorpe LJ wrote, 'to use an omission by a judge to deal with a point in a judgment as grounds for an

---

1   29 March 2000.
2   See *Practice Direction: Court of Appeal (Civil Division) Leave to Appeal and Skeleton Arguments (17 November 1998)* [1999] 1 WLR 2. The Practice Direction also gives directions with regard to filing of bundles and skeleton arguments.
3   See Practice Direction, above.
4   Permission is not necessary for appeal from a family proceedings court, though it may well soon become a requirement, as more and more district judges (magistrates' court) replace lay justices.
5   [2003] EWCA Civ 88, [2003] 2 FLR 1035.

application for appeal if the matter had not been brought to the judge's attention where there was a ready opportunity so to do'.[6]

If the trial judge has given a reserved judgment, the applicant for permission must set up an oral hearing. At the oral hearing, the advocate must point out to the judge the alleged insufficient reasoning and explanation given. At the permission hearing before the Court of Appeal, it is open to the Court of Appeal to remit the matter to the trial judge and ask for additional reason in the areas where the applicant contends the judgment is deficient.

Appeals from interim orders made by the family proceedings court must be made to the High Court within seven days.[7] Appeals of final orders from the family proceedings court to the High Court must be made within 14 days.[8] Appeals from a district judge to a county court judge in chambers must be made within 14 days.[9] Appeals from the county court or the High Court to the Court of Appeal must be made within 14 days, unless that time has been extended by the trial court.[10] A petition from the Court of Appeal to the House of Lords must be made within 28 days.[11]

6.3 REVIEW, REHEARING OR APPEAL?

The first decision to be made by an advocate advising on appeal is whether to seek an appeal of the hearing by a higher court, or to refer the matter back to the trial court for a review or for rehearing. If the error is merely a mistake in the drafting of the order, an appeal will almost always be unnecessary. County courts are allowed to vary an order which does not accurately embody the intention of the court (or more likely, the intention of the parties).[12] Often referred to as the 'slip rule', this provision allows for the court, upon application, to vary an order that essentially contains within it a mistake. The court will need to know that both parties agree to the variation. The High Court, too, in the exercise of its inherent jurisdiction, will correct errors in drafting without the necessity of a formal rehearing, or an appeal to a higher court.

Advocates must note that family proceedings courts have no power to order a rehearing except where the court subsequently ascertains that a respondent had not been served with notice of the hearing. In that situation the court may give directions for a rehearing, after first setting aside the original order.

---

[6] See [2003] 2 FLR at 1040. See also *Re T (Contact: Alienation)* [2003] 1 FLR 531.

[7] Family Proceedings Rules 1991 (FPR 1991), SI 1991/1247, r 4.22(3).

[8] FPR 1991, r 4.22(3).

[9] FPR 1991, r 4.22(3); CCR Ord 37, r 6.

[10] CPR, Part 52.4(2).

[11] CPR, Sch 1; RSC Ord 59; House of Lords Directions as to Procedure Direction 2.1. Note that Direction 25.3 also extends the time if the applicant is applying for public funding.

[12] CPR 1998, r 40.12.

Magistrates may not use the 'slip rule' in order to correct an order, even where all parties agree the original order was made in error.[13]

Orders made without notice should almost never be appealed to a higher court. Instead, the aggrieved party should seek to have the court of first instance list the matter for a hearing on notice.[14] Interim orders, or interlocutory orders, even if made on notice are also usually not amenable to appeal, but there are exceptions, primarily in public law cases involving children where there have been split hearings, or in cases where judges have made interim orders changing the residence of a child, or disturbing in a serious way the child's settled lifestyle.[15]

The advocate must also determine whether an application for a rehearing is required or whether the matter must go before a higher court. A rehearing is appropriate when further evidence has subsequently become available which undermines the basis of the court's original decision.[16] Courts have therefore agreed that rehearing may well be appropriate in the following circumstances:

(1) where there has been default or misconduct by an officer of the court;
(2) where one party to the proceedings has been absent;
(3) where there has been a fraud by a party that materially affects the outcome of the case;
(4) where subsequent evidence has been made available, and there has been no fault on the part of the aggrieved party in failing to adduce the evidence which has now come to light;
(5) the revelation that a witness has perjured himself, or that a witness now accepts he or she has made a mistake;
(6) where surprise has caused a miscarriage of justice;
(7) where counsel has made any grievous mistake;
(8) where there has been a misunderstanding by both parties at first instance.[17]

---

13   Family Proceedings Court (Children Act 1989) Rules 1991, SI 1991/1395, r 33a.
14   An interlocutory order is an order which does not entirely determine the proceedings. Where the application is for leave to an appeal from an interlocutory order, additional considerations arise: (a) the point may not be of sufficient significance to justify the costs of an appeal; (b) the procedural consequences of an appeal may outweigh the significance of the interlocutory appeal; (c) it may be more convenient to determine the point at or after the trial. In all such cases, leave to appeal should be refused. See *Wea Records Ltd v Visions Channel 4 Ltd* [1983] 2 All ER 589, [1983] 1 WLR 721, CA where Lord Donaldson noted that 'ex parte orders are essentially provisional in nature.' See also *Re P (A Minor) (Ex parte interim residence order)*, [1993] 2 FCR 417, [1993] 1 FLR 915 'I have no hesitation in saying that, where an ex parte order has been made in the county court and the absent party wishes to challenge such an order, it is quite clear that the appropriate course on the rules is to apply to the judge who made the *ex parte* order and ask him to rescind or vary it.' See discussion in *Family Court Practice 2004* (Family Law, 2004), p 652.
15   See *Re M (Judge's Discretion)* [2001] EWCA Civ 1428, [2002] 1 FLR 730; see also *Re J (a minor) (interim custody: appeal)* [1989] 2 FLR 304; but see *Re M (Interim Order: Domestic Violence)* [2000] 2 FLR 377.
16   CPR, Sch 2; CCR Ord 37.
17   See discussion in Family Court Practice 2004, pp 1581, 2379. see also CCR Ord 37, r 1(3); *Beale v Taylor* [1967] 3 All ER 253, [1967] 1 WLR 1193. The Rules require the application

6.4   THE APPLICATION FOR PERMISSION TO APPEAL

If the advocate determines that a rehearing is not appropriate, the advocate in almost all family proceedings must then consider the test set out by the House of Lords in the case of *G v G*.[18] In order to allow any appeal, the appellate court must be satisfied that either:

- the judge erred as a matter of law; or
- the judge relied on evidence he should have ignored, or ignored evidence which he should have taken into account; or
- the judge's decision was plainly wrong.

Almost all appeals in family proceedings, no matter which court is hearing the appeal, are decided by reference to *G v G*. But within *G v G* there are radically different standards of review by the Court of Appeal. Advocates must understand the different approaches by the Court of Appeal or the High Court, based on the type of error alleged.

The first category set out in *G v G* is 'an error in law'. If an appellant contends that the trial court judge applied the wrong legal rule, the appellate court will not defer to the trial court's ruling. The difficulty here is whether to characterise a particular decision by the trial court as a question of law or a question of fact. Most times the advocate will determine that it is a mixed question of law and fact, that is, that the court made an error in law because it refused to accept that a particular fact mandated a decision for that advocate's client. It is not an error in law if the judge has considered evidence and rejected it. It is correct to characterise an appeal on the grounds that there was no evidence to support the finding as an appeal in law, but it is not correct to make the same argument when there is in fact some evidence for the opposing proposition.[19]

A pure question of law most often occurs when there are competing approaches to a problem taken by two or more High Court judges. Pure questions of law also arise from novel questions that present themselves based on novel sets of facts, or where a provision of a statute is being interpreted by the Court of Appeal for the first time. The advocate for the appellant should be keen to characterise the error by the court below as an error in law, if at all possible.

The second area of enquiry mandated by *G v G* is essentially a question of evidence: that the judge relied on evidence that he should have ignored, or ignored evidence he should have taken into account. Almost invariably, what this area

---

be made on notice and not more than 14 days after the date of the trial. The application should be made to the judge who made the original decision. Note that the application does not operate as a stay of the original order. An application for stay must be applied for separately.

18   [1985] 2 All ER 225, [1985] 1 WLR 647, HL.

19   See in this regard Practice Direction, above, para 1.

of enquiry involves is a recitation of the final submissions made by the advocate at trial. If the advocate reads his skeleton argument on appeal and recognises his closing submissions, it is almost a guarantee that the appeal will fail.

The most fruitful area of enquiry here would be expert evidence, where the court below has improperly relied on or improperly rejected evidence that would fundamentally alter the judgment of the case. In particular in children's cases, the role of expert evidence is key to understanding the decision made by the judge at first instance.

The evidence of experts is discussed in detail elsewhere in the text. However, note should be made here of the particular role of expert evidence in determining whether an aggrieved party should seek permission to appeal.

Where a trial court has rejected expert evidence, the trial court must give specific reasons for doing so.[20] Similarly, where a court relies on an expert's opinion, that expert's opinion must be based on evidence found by the trial court judge to be true. It is often the case that experts assume certain facts to be true where in fact no fact-finding decision has been made. As noted in the section above regarding cross-examination of experts, advocates must always seek to understand the basis on which each expert has stated his or her opinion. If the court fails to do that, then the advocate of the aggrieved party must question whether an appeal is appropriate.

The Court of Appeal's Practice Direction of 17 November 1998 notes that the court will rarely interfere with a decision based on the judge's evaluation of oral evidence as to the primary facts or if an appeal would involve examining the fine detail of the judge's factual investigation. Leave is more likely to be appropriate where what is being challenged is the inference which the judge has drawn from the primary facts, or where the judge has not received any particular benefit from having actually seen the witnesses, and it is properly arguable that materially different inferences should be drawn from the evidence.[21]

The remaining ground for appeal identified in *G v G* is when the judge's decision is 'plainly wrong.' This might best be characterised as a catchall provision for those errors made by the judge at first instance that are 'unreasonable,' as that term has been defined by the High Court and the Court of Appeal in innumerable judicial review cases.[22] No reasonable judge, hearing the same facts, could possibly come to the same conclusion. Obviously there are no bright lines here. Lord Justice Thorpe's dictum must be kept in mind: is the judgment simply 'fundamentally wrong?'

---

20   See *Re B (Split Hearings: Jurisdiction)* [2000] 1 FLR 334, CA; see also *Bolitho v City & Hackney Health Authority* [1998] AC 232, HL.
21   Practice Direction, above, Note, para 14.
22   See *Associated Provincial Picture Houses v Wednesbury Corporation* [1948] 1 KB 223.

Advocates often use this argument when appealing decisions made by lay justices in the family proceedings court. In part, this is the result of these lay justices using a standard form that does not necessarily fit the fact situation in each case. It is also a result, it must be said, of the inability of many lay justices to understand the standard forms. It is rare for the Court of Appeal to find that a circuit judge or High Court judge got it 'plainly wrong'. The appeal that simply suggests the judge got the facts wrong, or argues that different conclusions from the facts should have been reached, will almost never succeed.

In his interview with the author, Lord Justice Thorpe pointed out two fundamental areas of enquiry for any advocate approaching an appeal:

(1) Has the trial judge made an impermissible finding that leads to an incorrect result?
(2) Has there been an erroneous exercise of discretion where the court has reached an irrational result?

In Lord Justice Thorpe's view, advocates should approach appeals by determining the following:

(1) Is this case in an area where the legal approach is confused, either because of conflicting High Court decisions, or because the area has not been addressed by the Court of Appeal?
(2) Is the case in an area where a new statute has changed the court's approach?
(3) Is this case in an area of law capable of evolution simply because the principles on which the rules were based are no longer relevant or appropriate?

Very few family law decisions that are 'principled' decisions have a shelf-life of more than one generation, according to Lord Justice Thorpe. 'Most principles in family law are actually founded upon social policies or social assumptions made by the judges. Those assumptions as to child development or child help have to be reviewed from time to time.'

The difficulty, of course, is finding those fact situations that present opportunities to challenge those social policies or assumptions.

Some cases, particular in this area of law, simply require appellate court analysis because of the novelty of the facts. The obvious example is the case of the conjoined twins.[23] In cases where no other trial judge has had to face the situation previously, almost invariably the Court of Appeal will be asked to provide a final answer. In those cases the Court of Appeal, Thorpe LJ noted, is in one sense simply making certain the public retains faith in the justice system.

---

[23] *Re A (Children), sub nom Re A (Conjoined Twins: Medical Treatment)* [2001] Fam 147, [2004] 4 All ER 961, [2001] 1 FLR 1.

Rule 52.3 of the CPR sets out the circumstances where permission to appeal is required. Advocates should as a rule make an immediate oral application for permission to appeal at the hearing at which the order to be appealed against is made. If no application is made at the trial court, or if the application is refused, the applicant may seek permission from the Court of Appeal. Application for permission to appeal from a decision that was itself an appeal (for example, an appeal of a circuit judge's decision in an ancillary relief case) must always be made to the Court of Appeal.[24]

The documents to be included on appeal are set out at PD 52, para 5.6:

(1)   two additional copies (and the original) of the appellant's notice of appeal;
(2)   one copy of the notice for each respondent;
(3)   one copy of the skeleton to accompany each copy of the notice of appeal;
(4)   a sealed copy of the order being appealed;
(5)   a copy of the permission denial;
(6)   all statutes to be relied on by the appellant.

The appellant must also include in the appeal bundle the following documents:

(a)   a sealed copy of the appellant's notice;
(b)   a sealed copy of the order appealed against;
(c)   a copy of the order refusing or granting permission to appeal;
(d)   any affidavit or skeleton in support;
(e)   a copy of the skeleton;
(f)   a transcript or note of judgment.

All documents not directly relevant to the appeal should be excluded. Where the appellant is represented by solicitors and counsel, the appeal bundle must contain a certificate, signed by counsel or solicitor, certifying that the advocate has read and understood PD 52, r5.6, and that the bundle complies with the Rules.

6.5   THE SKELETON ARGUMENT

Lawyers facing an appeal must still respond to the same three questions as the advocate at trial: Who is the client? What does the client want? And most importantly, why should the court give you what you seek? On appeal, the importance of question number three is heightened. Why should the appellate court overrule the decision of a judge given broad discretionary power?[25]

---

[24]   CPR PD 52, r 4.9.
[25]   The relatively narrow subject of appellate advocacy has attracted little academic attention. There are two helpful texts, both from the US: Fontham, Vitiello and Miller, *Persuasive, Written and Oral Advocacy in Trial and Appellate Courts* (Aspen Law and Business, 2002); and Clary, Paulsen and Vanselow, *Advocacy on Appeal* (West Group, 2001).

The framing of the issue on appeal therefore takes on vital importance. Advocates must keep in mind Lord Justice Thorpe's categories as set out above. Why is this case likely to prompt the Court of Appeal to act? Does it involve an error in approach by the fact-finder? Did that error make a difference in the outcome? Does the case present novel facts?

Advocates very often seek to drag up every potential legal issue available, and throw each issue at the court on appeal, hoping at least one might stick. The assumption here is that the bad issues do not detract from the good. *That assumption is wrong.*

Lord Justice Thorpe put it like this:

> 'An advocate presenting a skeleton to the court must present something close to a "high trump". The advocate must simply play the card. It's better not to dilute the skeleton by playing a lot of low value cards. The reader perceives those to be low value, and that leads the reader to question whether the trump was really a trump.'

This would seem particularly true in family appeals. The appellate jurisdiction is not favoured, and appellate courts do not sit simply to give litigants a second bite of the apple. There will be one, or perhaps at most two, issues that will prompt the Court of Appeal in any case to act.

The advocate's skeleton should, in summary form, inform the court immediately of three things:

(1)   the issue that makes this an appealable case;
(2)   the legal standard that will apply to the appeal;
(3)   the result or order sought by the appellant.

Lord Justice Thorpe noted the importance of the skeleton argument of the appellant. 'It is the document the judge will seek to read first, and, other than the judgment, will be the most important document in the bundle.' The appellant must make clear as quickly as possible that an error in principle has been committed, and, crucially, that the error either determined the outcome, or played such a major role in the outcome it cannot be ignored.

Thorpe LJ put it like this: 'The appellant has to tell us whether the error mattered. Would the case have been decided the same way in any event? If so, the court is unlikely to grant permission to appeal.'

The Court of Appeal in 1999 set out in a Practice Direction the following purpose of the skeleton:

> '... to identify and summarise the points, not to argue them fully on paper. A skeleton argument should therefore be as succinct as possible. In the case of a normal length appeal against a final order (ie an appeal in the range of one to two days) skeleton arguments should not normally exceed 10 pages in the case of an appeal on law and 15 pages in the case of an appeal on fact.'

The current Practice Direction provides that the appellant's skeleton should be accompanied by a chronology, agreed, if possible, with the respondent.[26]

The Court of Appeal, at PD 52, r 5.10, sets out the appropriate use of legal authorities. The skeleton argument must state, in respect of each authority cited:

(1) the propositions of law that the authority demonstrates;
(2) the parts of the authority that support the proposition.

If more than one authority is cited, the advocate must tell the court why. If the skeleton does not comply with the rules, or is filed late, the Court of Appal has jurisdiction to disallow costs of preparing the skeleton.[27]

6.6   FRAMING THE ISSUE FOR THE GROUNDS OF APPEAL

Nothing is more important in an appeal than framing the issue for the court. The *only* advantage the appellant has is the first chance to tell the court precisely what the issue is, why the court below got it wrong, and why this court can easily now get it right.

The issue is in fact the answer to the Court of Appeal's initial question: what is this litigant doing here in the first place?

The appellant's grounds of appeal should be simple, concise, and should state the issue in terms of the facts of the case. The issue should be stated as narrowly as possible in order to win your case. You need not claim the case will change existing law if that is not necessary for your client to prevail.

Never frame in general terms: 'The court below was wrong in principle when it made a care order in favour of the local authority.' 'The court's decision to terminate contact was an abuse of the court's discretion.' 'The court was wrong in principle when it ordered the husband to transfer all his interest in the family home to the wife.' This tells the court nothing about this particular appeal.

Instead, each issue must be framed to follow the facts: 'The court below was wrong in principle when it rejected the recommendation of a child psychiatrist and the guardian and made care orders with a care plan for adoption in a case where the court accepted that the child's closest attachment was with his father.' 'The court's decision to terminate contact was wrong in principle when the court relied solely on evidence by the mother, not confirmed by anyone else, and not confirmed by the child in any interview, that the child was complaining of being touched inappropriately by the father.' 'The court was wrong in principle when after a five-year-marriage it ordered the assets of

---

26   See CPR PD 52, r 5.10 for further direction on the content of skeleton arguments.
27   CPR PD 52, r 5.10(6).

the parties divided 100 per cent to the wife, 0 to the husband, leaving the husband nowhere to live, and with no assets in order to invest in a new property, either now or in the future.'

A good test with regard to the issue you have framed is this: After you have drafted your issue statement, see if it might easily be turned into the holding of the court. 'We therefore allow the appeal because ...' If not, then the issue is framed too generally.

Fontham, Vitiello and Miller, in their text on appellate advocacy, give six effective rules for framing the issue in a case:

(1) The issue must be stated in terms of facts of the case.
(2) The statement must eliminate all unnecessary detail.
(3) It must be readily comprehensible on first reading.
(4) It must avoid self-evident propositions.
(5) It must be so stated that the appellant has no choice but to accept it as an accurate statement of the question.
(6) It should be subtly persuasive.[28]

6.6.1   The factual background

The Court of Appeal (or the High Court judge, if this is an appeal from the family proceedings court) will obviously have before it the judgment or reasons that have prompted the appeal. Therefore any statement of facts by the appellant in the skeleton must cite to the judgment, or cite to the record in the case below. Each statement of fact put forward by the appellant must either be found as true by the court below, or be an agreed fact, or at least be a part of the evidence below and not challenged by the respondent to the appeal. The statement of facts should not be argumentative, and where there are disputes about facts (in particular disputes about facts not dealt with by the court in its judgment) the appellant must always disclose to the court the nature of the dispute.

The appellant should identify the parties, the procedural position of the case, the standard of review, and the orders sought, all within the first paragraph of the skeleton:

> 'The Appellant London Borough of >>>>>>>>> seeks to appeal an order made by HHJ ——— on .... .. 2002 at the ....County Court within care proceedings regarding the child (name and dob). On that date the Learned judge made a supervision order in favour of the local authority. It is contended on behalf of the local authority the court was wrong in principle when it made this order, instead of a care order, in a case where the court also found the father had committed numerous acts of sexual abuse with the child, and where the two experts in the case, as well as the child's guardian, had recommended the child

---

28   See Fontham, Vitiello and Miller, above, p 58.

be removed from the care of the parents. The brief factual background is as follows.'

The court should also have before it, as a separate document, an appellant's chronology, again with each fact cited to the judgment, or to the record of the case.

Appellants must remember that they seek to tell a story. That does not mean the story is told in a manner that keeps the reader waiting to the end to discover who did it, nor do you seek to tell the story of the dispute only from the perspective of the appellant. Instead, the story you seek to tell is this: A and B have a dispute; A and B placed their dispute in the hands of a judge, and the judge made a decision; that judge, however, has made an error that means her decision that was meant to end the dispute cannot stand. In other words, you seek to tell the story from the perspective of the Court of Appeal. That perspective means the dispute is seen against the background of what *should* have been done. The background, in other words, is the 'law' that applies to this case. The story's elements all relate to the crucial error that was made: the reason, in the end, that the story is being told in the first place.

You should strive to omit all facts not absolutely relevant to the story of the appeal. That means the appellant must ruthlessly edit the factual outline, making certain the Court of Appeal is not sent down some back road leading nowhere, when what you seek is to keep the court focused only on the error you want to have corrected.

Do not seek to argue the case when you set out the factual background. But do not lose sight of your argument. That means you do not place before the court a fact not directly relevant to the court's decision, and you seek to relate each fact you do set out to the eventual decision to be made by the Court of Appeal.

6.6.2 Analysing legal precedent

Appellate courts exercising family law jurisdiction are interested in legal principles. The Court of Appeal hearing a family case will not be interested in a recitation of facts in previous cases that are similar to the facts in this case. This is not true of appellate jurisdiction in other areas of law, where advocates are seeking to compare factual situations in order to argue that the trial court applied the wrong rule. Family law almost invariably is based on broad issues: the best interests of the child; the needs and assets of the parties; the future conduct of the parties. These broad principles are not given substantive content by comparing fact situations in previously decided cases, because fact situations in these types of cases are infinite and, in the end, not comparable. Therefore skeleton arguments should not contain a serial digest of factual outlines of previous cases from the Court of Appeal.

It is also wholly wrong for the advocate to list a string or cases, and then say nothing about how those cases support the legal propositions that are contended to apply. Each case cited should:

(1) be a case from the House of Lords, Court of Appeal or the High Court;
(2) be a case where the Court of Appeal (if from that court) has made a judgment of the court;
(3) be a case where the principle is clearly enunciated by the House of Lords in the leading speech, or by the Court of Appeal in the leading judgment given;
(4) be a case that states a principle the advocate seeks to apply in the instant case.[29]

Advocates should use the minimal number of cases necessary to make the advocate's point. The Court of Appeal does not hand out bonus points based on cases cited. Never cite more than one case for each legal proposition. In most areas, the Court of Appeal will know the leading case. Cite that case, the principle involved, and move on to your substantive argument. Advocates should note the Practice Direction of 9 April 2001.[30] By that direction, the court requires advocates to state, in respect to each authority cited, the proposition of law that the authority demonstrates, and the parts of the judgment that support that proposition. Advocates must explain why they cite more than one authority for any proposition.

That being said, it is right to cite (perhaps in a footnote) any supportive secondary authorities such as treatises, annotations or law review articles that support the appellant's position. The Court of Appeal will want to know what is the generally held view of trial practitioners regarding the topic under consideration. The best way to do that is to cite well-known texts, particularly those used by judges and advocates in court.

Whenever any case or statute is cited in a skeleton argument, a copy should be provided in a separate bundle for the Court of Appeal. The best way to do this is to provide a legal bundle that is numbered consecutively from 1 to the

---

[29] Advocates will know that not every opinion expressed by a judge forms a judicial precedent. In order for an opinion to be considered a precedent, two things must concur:
(a) it must be an opinion by the judge;
(b) it must be an opinion the format of which is necessary for the decision in a particular case. In other words, the opinion must not be obiter dictum.
 The best discussion of what the ratio decidendi of a case is remains Lord Goodhart's essay, 'Determining the Ratio Decidendi of a Case' (Cambridge, 1931). Lord Goodhart takes issue with the commonly accepted notion of the ratio, and he points out that advocates must always beware of an appellate court misstating what its decision actually means. He also points out that discovering the ratio is not done by simply applying the legal principles to a set of facts. Law, sadly, is more complicated than that. He concludes that the 'principle of the case is found by taking account of: a) the facts treated by the judge as material; and b) his decision as based on those facts. In finding the principle it is also necessary to establish what facts are considered immaterial, for the principle may depend as much on exclusion as inclusion.' Goodhart, above, p 25.

[30] [2001] 1 WLR 1001, [2001] 2 All ER 510, [2001] Fam Law 794.

end. Nothing is more likely to disrupt the flow of oral argument than searching through bundle A, bundle B and bundle C for a cite to a legal proposition, or to force the panel to search through loose photocopies of cases scattered before them, when it would be a simple matter to have all legal documents collected together in one bundle, numbered consecutively, with a page of contents showing the case name and the page number in the bundle where the case may be found. In that way the panel might simply be directed to a certain page in the legal bundle. Advocates should provide one legal bundle for each Lord Justice of Appeal sitting on the panel, and of course one bundle for each opponent. Again, the flow of argument is disrupted if you have to hand up copies.

Advocates must deal fairly and effectively with unfavourable precedent. Advocates will know there is a duty to give to the court any unfavourable precedent that exists, in particular if that precedent is not cited by opposing counsel. Advocates should first examine the supposedly unfavourable decision by the Court of Appeal to determine the following:

(1) What is the precise holding of the case? Is the proposition being put forward by your opponent actually only dicta, or is it the actual holding or reason for the court's decision?

(2) Make certain the case involved was not at a significantly different procedural posture than your case.

(3) Look to see if there are material facts that are distinguishable.

(4) Make certain the unfavourable precedent is by a court of higher jurisdiction. If you are appealing a decision of the family proceedings court to the High Court, a judgment by a fellow High Court judge may very well be persuasive, but it would not be controlling authority.

(5) Make certain that the unfavourable precedent is not against the weight of authority or the modern trend of authority. To that end, make certain that the unfavourable precedent is not old and outdated.

(6) Make certain that the unfavourable precedent has not been overruled or modified by a subsequent decision.

(7) If the unfavourable precedent has a dissent, look for the reasons for that dissent, and be prepared to argue that the dissent is more persuasive

(8) If all else fails, you must argue that the unfavourable precedent was wrongly decided and created bad law.

Professor Bradley Clary, Director of Legal Writing at the University of Minnesota Law School, has usefully set out in his text *Advocacy on Appeal* the following key objectives for advocates preparing an appeal:

(1) Understand your audience

Appellate courts are not trial courts; and they are decidedly not juries. Emotional appeals will not be likely to impress. Any narrative that is given

by the advocate must be firmly anchored in a legal argument. Therefore it makes no sense to make an emotional appeal based on an interpretation of facts that was rejected by the trial court judge.

(2) Develop a theme on appeal

Legal arguments are obviously designed to seek to persuade the court to rule in your favour. Professor Clary, however, notes that the theme of an appeal should give the Court of Appeal not only a legal argument, but a *reason* to rule in your favour. The theme may be that the client was the victim of a fraudulent scheme; the theme may be that a fiscally responsible local authority had to make difficult decisions about allocating limited resources; the theme may be that a child has wrongly been taken from her family, and a father wrongly branded as a sexual abuser, because of unlawful findings of sexual abuse based on errors made by experts advising the court. The advocate's goal, obviously, is to convince the court that simple fairness and justice compel a ruling for the advocate's client. Experienced advocates (and experienced judges on the Court of Appeal) soon come to understand that legal analysis can be made to serve either to confirm or overrule a judgment of the trial court. If the appellate court comes to the conclusion that there are public policy reasons for supporting one side or the other, that appellate court will find the appropriate legal analysis to make such a ruling. It is therefore the advocate's job, in the appropriate case, to seek to put forward the public policy arguments that favour his or her client's position.

(3) Keep the argument simple

The appellate court comes to the case fresh. The judges on the Court of Appeal have not lived with the case for 15 days at trial; they did not read 10 lever arch files of statements; they did not hear the day of submissions, nor did they hear the half-day judgment. Therefore advocates seeking to convince the Court of Appeal must break complicated arguments into smaller, more digestible parts that build upon one another. Advocates must seek to eliminate extraneous details. Advocates must learn that if the argument cannot be articulated in a relatively simple fashion, that advocate's chances of success are severely diminished. It is almost always wrong for the advocate seeking to have the Court of Appeal overrule the trial court to argue that the case is complex. Rather, this advocate must seek to show that the case in fact is really quite simple, and that the reasons your client should prevail are equally simple. (Likewise, it is almost always right for the respondent to argue that the case is exceedingly complex, and that the trial court judge – and only the trial court judge – was in a position to hear all arguments, consider all witness statements and expert's reports, and has come to a conclusion that is within the range of reasonable decisions trial court judges are allowed to make.)

(4) Provide a logical affirmative analysis for the court to rule in your favour

This is nothing more than saying you must have an appropriate theory of the case in order to prevail. This cannot simply be a point-by-point attack on your opponent's argument. Rather, your argument should articulate a rule of law with reasonable limits that will work in other cases.

(5) Be fair and maximise your credibility

You maximise credibility by accurately and fairly reciting facts and the applicable law, by conceding losing arguments, by avoiding *ad hominem* attacks, by avoiding hyperbole, and by carefully proof reading and cite checking your skeleton argument.[31]

It is *always* an error to describe an opponent's argument as 'outrageous,' or 'ridiculous.' Far better to show the court the opponent's argument is flawed by giving a straightforward and sound analysis of the law and facts.

6.6.3   Respondent's skeleton argument

Once permission to appeal has been granted, or where oral argument has been set down, the rules allow for the respondent to file a skeleton argument in reply to the appellant's. The judges have now read the judgment, the skeleton argument on behalf of the appellant, and are very likely to have read some of the evidence. It makes no sense for the respondent to set out in preliminary form all of the facts of the case, and to go through the judgment in any detailed way.

But the rule that the respondent should respond to arguments put forward by the appellant does not mean that the respondent should accept the issues as framed by the appellant. Instead, the respondent should provide an affirmative analysis of why the trial court correctly decided the case. If the respondent does nothing more than repeat the issue as framed by the appellant, the appellant in many cases is more than halfway home.

The rule here is related to the rule regarding cross-examination: advocates conducting cross-examination should not simply repeat the evidence given on direct examination. Obviously some repetition is inevitable as the respondent seeks to refute the appellant's arguments. That being said, the better way is to frame the issue in a way that is favourable to the respondent, and more likely to convince the Court of Appeal that the trial court correctly exercised its discretion. Respondents must seek first and foremost to defend the judgment of the court below. The issue therefore ordinarily should be framed precisely as the judge below framed it. If the Court of Appeal accepts that framing, the respondent is likely to succeed.

---

31   See Clary et al, above, p 54.

6.7 ORAL ARGUMENT

Any advocate appearing before an appellate bench has three goals on oral argument:

(1) discover and address the concerns of the court;
(2) personalise the theme of the appeal, that is, show the court why it is just and fair that your client should prevail, and that a fair legal analysis should mandate such a result; and, crucially,
(3) answer your opponent.

The days when the Court of Appeal might be expected to sit for 10 days and allow advocates to meander through a series of lectures to the bench regarding the appropriate law are now ancient history. The Court of Appeal now limits oral arguments, save in the rarest of cases. The most important goal of oral argument is therefore to understand precisely what the court's concerns are, and to have answers ready for those concerns.

Planning is crucial. It always helps to allow colleagues to read your skeleton arguments, in particular, to read the skeleton argument without having any prior understanding of what the facts of the case might be. The questions raised by your colleague will be likely to be questions on the mind of the appellate judges. Advocates should always seek to anticipate the weak links of the case, and have prepared responses to those difficulties.

Because oral arguments are now relatively brief,[32] advocates must focus during those few minutes or hours on the client, and on the reasons why fundamental fairness compels a result one way or the other. This is not an emotional appeal to the fact-finder's conscience. Rather, this is an effort made by the advocate on appeal to show that this is not simply a dry, narrow legal issue. This is an issue that affects real people.

Oral argument is also an opportunity to address your opponent's arguments. The advocate must seek to determine, however, whether the appellate bench actually wishes to hear an effort to destroy one of the points made by the other side. If the court clearly does not find the other side's argument persuasive on an issue, there is no need for the advocate to waste precious time on oral argument seeking to further destroy that point. This is not a debate where points are scored. It is far more important to keep the court's interest focused on the reason why your client should prevail.

---

[32] Advocates at the Bar should always remember, when being critical of the new regime of shorter oral arguments, the rule at the US Supreme Court: each advocate is given 30 minutes for oral argument. When the red light goes on, indicating the end of time, Chief Justice Rehnquist has been known to rise and walk out of the courtroom, leaving counsel at the lectern in full flow. The rule serves to concentrate the minds of advocates on ruthless editing of their arguments: only the most important points need be addressed.

The advocate for the appellant need not introduce himself or herself, but the advocate should introduce all opposing counsel. For example:

> 'I do appear on behalf of the Appellant parents, Mr and Mrs A; Mr Ablelawyer appears on behalf of the Respondent London Borough of .... Mrs Childlawyer appears on behalf of the children, through their Guardian.'

The advocate should then immediately identify the order sought to be appealed, and identify why the trial court got it wrong.

> 'It is contended on behalf of the Appellants that the order made by HHJ .... at the .... County Court on 7th March 2003 was wrong in principle. Each of the errors, we contend, compel this court to set aside the care orders made by the court and direct there be a rehearing. The case concerns a father who has never been found by a court to have sexually abused any child, yet is considered by every expert who gave evidence in this case to be a sex abuser who should not be allowed to care for a child. We contend on his behalf he has been tried by the experts, but not by the courts. It is therefore contended that the Learned judge below was wrong in principle when he concluded that this man's child must be removed permanently from the care of her parents because the father required 'years of cognitive therapy' to address the father's alleged acts of sexual abuse against minors, in a case where no conclusive findings of fact regarding any alleged acts of sexual abuse had ever been made against the father. It is further contended judge .... was wrong in principle when he followed the advice of experts who supported the permanent removal of the child when those experts agree their conclusions were inescapably coloured by their unanimous view that the father committed at least five separate acts of sexual abuse in the past, in a case where no judge had ever found that the father had committed any acts of sexual abuse. It will also be contended that the judge's decision to order the permanent removal of the child from the care of her parents was disproportionate to the risk of harm that child faced in a case where the Court accepted the experts' conclusion that but for the risk of sexual abuse the risk of harm to the child was manageable and low. Because the Learned judge's decision to order the permanent removal was disproportionate to the risk of harm the child faced, that judge's decision violated rights of the parents and the child protected by Article 8 of the European Convention on Human Rights.'

It is likely that just after the appellant's advocate has stated the grounds of appeal, one Lord Justice or another will interrupt with a question. In the unlikely event of that not occurring, the advocate would then go forward to address, in order, each of the errors alleged.

But it is likely the court will indicate fairly quickly the precise area of enquiry it has with regard to the appellant's argument. *Always stop and answer the question*. It is never correct to defer the answer to later, to state that you have already answered the question, or to waffle with regard to addressing the question. It is not correct to seek to continue your sentence or your thought. Answer the question. If the answer to the question is 'I don't know,' then the response should be 'I do not know.' (Advocates who are forced to give this response will likely understand that their chances of success have just been

diminished considerably.) Nothing irritates a judge more than to have an advocate fail to respond directly to a question put in oral argument.

The Honourable Paul Michel, for more than two decades a judge on the United States Court of Appeal for the Second Circuit, puts it like this:

> 'In appellate argument, rhetoric is overrated. Success seldom depends on eloquence. It turns instead on identifying the inevitable, sceptical questions, and preparing effective answers.'[33]

The best advocates have anticipated these questions and have prepared appropriate responses to them. Nevertheless, even the best advocates sometimes are blindsided by questions that had not been considered prior to oral argument. Professor Clary lists several areas of questions that always should be anticipated:

(1) What do you want the court to do?
(2) Can the court reach the result you want consistent with existing law?
(3) What is your best authority.
(4) What legal rule do you advocate.
(5) How broadly applicable is the rule you advocated? At what point would the rule no longer make sense?
(6) To overrule the trial court do we have to find that any of the court's factual determinations were wrong?[34]

When answering the court's questions:

* stop and answer immediately;
* be direct;
* seek clarification if necessary;
* use yes or no responses, and then explain;
* use the questions that have been directed to your opponent;
* never become confrontational;
* never assume the questions are hostile;
* anticipate the most difficult questions;
* read the court and seek to understand when it is best to back down and when it is best to stand your ground;
* seek to make an effective transition from the question back to your client's argument.

Maintain eye contact with any judge asking a question. Respond directly to that judge, and then seek to include other judges as you make the transition from the question to the theme of your case. An oral argument is a conversation

---

[33] See the Honourable Paul Michel, 'Effective Appellate Advocacy' (1998) 24 *Litigation Journal* 19, 22.
[34] Clary et al, above.

with the court. Always remember that when making conversation it is extremely rude to avoid eye contact. Rudeness always lessens your credibility.

Advocates must also listen carefully to the court's questions directed at the opponent. These questions are sometimes, but not always, clues to what the court may perceive as weaknesses in the opponent's position. If possible the advocate should seek to exploit them. The advocate should refer specifically to critical questions asked of the advocate's opponent. The advocate should then give specific responses to those questions.

6.7.1   Style and demeanour

One High Court judge stated to me that, for him, the most distracting habit for advocates was placing their hands in their pockets and fiddling with change or keys. Another judge said it was even more distracting when advocates constantly touch their hair, usually in an effort to keep the wig on straight. Judges are interested in the substance of the argument. Everything else becomes a distraction and an annoyance. Advocates should stand before the podium with hands to their side for relaxed, natural gestures. Do not hold a pen in your hand. There is nothing much worse than pointing a pen at a judge while trying to make a point, save maybe throwing it at him after you have finished.

Irving Younger used to admonish students to make certain, just before walking into a courtroom for the first time, to hold up their hands and to look at them carefully. Turn them over. Touch your nose with them. Run your fingers through your hair (if that is possible). Now place your hands by your side, and when you walk into a courtroom and begin to speak, never use them ever again.

Advocates must also make certain never to react visibly or audibly to an opponent's argument. Advocates must always sit at attention. Do not lean back in the chair, and minimise any conversations you have with solicitors sitting behind you. Use a pad in order to pass notes for communication. Always stand when addressing or being addressed by the court. If your client is in attendance, that client does not sit with counsel, and the client is not introduced to the appellate court.

Perhaps one rule given to me by a High Court judge bears repeating, even if it seems a brutally obvious point: appellate courts do not want to hear cute or funny or familiar arguments. An appellate court demands formality. Know that if you do crack a joke in court that makes a Lord Justice of Appeal laugh, you may well be the first advocate in legal history to do so. It is an accomplishment not worth the risk.

Appendix 1

PRACTICE DIRECTION (5 JUNE 1992)

Court Work – General

Citations: [1992] 2 FLR 87, [1992] 1 WLR 586, [1992] 3 All ER 151

Family Division: Distribution of Business

Distribution and transfer between the High Court and county courts of family business and family proceedings.

1 These directions are given under s 37 of the Matrimonial and Family Proceedings Act 1984 by the President of the Family Division, with the concurrence of the Lord Chancellor, and apply to all family proceedings which are transferable between the High Court and county courts under ss 38 and 39 of that Act. They supersede the Practice Direction given on 6 April 1988, save in respect of family proceedings concerning children pending immediately before 14 October 1991. They do not apply to:

> (a) proceedings under the Children Act 1989 or under the Adoption Act 1976, which are governed by the Children (Allocation of Proceedings) Order 1991;
> (b) an application that a minor be made or cease to be a ward of court, or to proceedings under Part III of the Matrimonial and Family Proceedings Act 1984, which may be heard and determined in the High Court alone.

2 (1) Family proceedings to which these directions apply (including interlocutory proceedings) shall be dealt with in the High Court where it appears to the court seised of the case that by reason of the complexity, difficulty or gravity of the issues they ought to be tried in the High Court.

(2) Without prejudice to the generality of sub-para (1), the following proceedings shall be dealt with in the High Court unless the nature of the issues of fact or law raised in the case makes them more suitable for trial in a county court than in the High Court:

> (a) petitions under s 1(2)(e) of the Matrimonial Causes Act 1973 which are opposed pursuant to s 5 of that Act;
> (b) petitions for presumption of death and dissolution of marriage under s 19 of the Matrimonial Causes Act 1973;
> (c) proceedings involving a contested issue of domicile;
> (d) applications under s 5(6) of the Domicile and Matrimonial Proceedings Act 1973;
> (e) applications to restrain a respondent from taking or continuing with foreign proceedings;
> (f) suits in which the Queen's Proctor intervenes or shows cause and elects trial in the High Court;
> (g) proceedings in relation to a ward of court –
>> (i) in which the Official Solicitor is or becomes the guardian ad litem of the ward or of a party to the proceedings;

(ii) in which a local authority is or becomes a party;

(iii) in which an application for blood tests is made;

(iv) in which an application is opposed on the grounds of want of jurisdiction;

(v) in which there is a substantial foreign element;

(vi) in which there is an opposed application for leave to take the child permanently out of the jurisdiction or where there is an application for temporary removal of a child from the jurisdiction and it is opposed on the ground that the child may not be duly returned;

(*h*) interlocutory applications involving –

(i) *Mareva* injunctions;

(ii) directions as to dealing with assets out of the jurisdiction;

(*i*) petitions in respect of declarations under Part III of the Family Law Act 1986.

3 (1) Proceedings in the county court for an order within sub-para (2) shall be heard and determined in the High Court where either the county court or any party to the proceedings considers that any such orders, if made, should be recognised and enforced in Scotland or Northern Ireland under Part I of the Family Law Act 1986.

(2) The orders referred to in sub-para (1) are those made by the county court in the exercise of its jurisdiction relating to wardship so far as it determines the living arrangements of a child or provides for the education of, or contact with, a child.

4 In proceedings where periodical payments, a lump sum or property are an issue the court shall have regard in particular to the following factors when considering in accordance with para 2(1) above whether the complexity, difficulty or gravity of the issues are such that they ought to be tried in the High Court:

(*a*) the capital values of the assets involved and the extent to which they are available for, or susceptible to, distribution or adjustment;

(*b*) any substantial allegations of fraud or deception or non-disclosure;

(*c*) any substantial contested allegations of conduct.

An appeal in such proceedings from a district judge in a county court shall be transferred to the High Court where it appears to the district judge, whether on application by a party or otherwise, that the appeal raises a difficult or important question, whether of law or otherwise.

5 Subject to the foregoing, family proceedings may be dealt with in a county court.

6 Proceedings in the High Court which under the foregoing criteria fall to be dealt with in a county court or a divorce county court, as the case may be, and proceedings in a county court which likewise fall to be dealt with in the High Court shall be transferred accordingly, in accordance with rules of court, unless to do so would cause undue delay or hardship to any party or other person involved.

Sir Stephen Brown P

Appendix 2

BEST PRACTICE NOTE (JANUARY 1995)

Court Work – General

Form of Directions; Certificate of Time Estimate; Welfare Reports

Note: the following materials are taken from the *Children Act Advisory Committee Annual Report 1993/94*, and are reproduced with the kind permission of the President of the Family Division.

(1) Form of Directions
Form of Directions

Form of Directions

In the

Case Number

Child(ren)'s Number

Directions

The full name(s) of the child(ren)	Boy or Girl	Date of Birth

The Application

☐ The Court orders that

be joined as [a] part[y][ies] to the proceedings

☐ The Court grants leave to

, the [1st] [2nd] [3rd] applicant, to withdraw the application for   in respect of the child[ren]

Statements

☐ The Court orders that

the oral evidence which the parties shall be entitled to bring to the final hearing of this matter shall be limited to those witnesses whose statements have been filed at court and served on all other parties by the following dates:

Applicant's evidence   ....

1st Respondent   ....

2nd Respondent   ....

No further statements may be lodged with the court without the leave of the court

Reports

☐ The Court orders that

[all parties]   nominate their experts
in the field[s] of   by

☐ The Court requires

[the experts]   jointly to examine the child[ren] by

☐ The Court orders that

the parties consult for the purpose of jointly instructing [an] expert[s] in on the following matters

The parties must consult by 4 pm on and the report[s] of the [expert[s]] must be lodged at the court office by

☐ The Court orders that

the expert witnesses meet to discuss the areas of dispute revealed by the report[s] of [the expert witnesses]

This meeting shall be within days of the report[s] being filed at the court office and disclosure of them to

Within days of that meeting, and no later than the solicitors for must file at the court office a statement agreed by the parties.

The statement must state the issues which are agreed and those which are not agreed.

☐ The Court orders that

the [Guardian ad litem] [Court Welfare Officer] file a report [on the matter of].

The report must be filed by 4 pm on

The [Guardian ad litem] [Court Welfare Officer] must attend the [final hearing] [next directions hearing].

☐ The Court grants leave to

to disclose to
the following papers

☐ The Court orders that

any reports which result from this disclosure must be filed at the court office and disclosed to [all the parties].

☐ The Court directs that

the   serve and lodge a statement
according to [Family Proceedings Rules 1991 r 4.17(1)] [Family Proceedings Courts (Children Act 1989) Rules 1991 r 17(1)] [in support of] [in answer to] the application. The statement must be lodged at the court office by 4 pm on

Reports continued overleaf

The statement must be limited to
  findings of the report[s] with which [he] [she] [they] do not agree
  relevant matters not covered by the report[s]
  the matter of

Further Directions

☐ The Court directs that   this application be listed for [further discussion] [a final hearing]
before   at   on

[Notice The child[ren] must [not] attend [in person] [with [his] [her]
[their] solicitor]

The time estimate is days

☐ The Court grants   liberty to the [parties] [Guardian ad litem] [Court Welfare Officer]
to apply for urgent further directions

Notice 24 hours' notice must be given to the Court.

Documents

☐ The Court directs that   the [applicant][respondent] prepare a precise chronology comprising
  a summary of the history of the case
  a schedule of the lodgement of the statements
  a summary of the issues to be resolved between the parties

The chronology must be lodged with the court office and served
on the parties by 4 pm on

☐ The Court directs that   a bundle of papers for the court be prepared. The bundle must
contain the chronology and the issues; all exhibits, reports and
authorities; the statements lodged by all parties. The bundle must
be paginated and indexed. All parties must agree the contents of
the bundle. The [applicant] [respondent] [local authority] must
lodge the bundle with the court office by 4 pm on

Interim orders

☐ The Court orders that   between the date of this order and the next hearing the child[ren]
be [placed] [remain] [under the supervision of] [in the care of]

Notice This interim [care] [supervision] order may be
renewed ex parte for 28 days if all the parties consent in writing.

An application for renewal must be lodged at least 48 hours before
the date on which the interim order ends. The application must
be accompanied by written confirmation that the circumstances
of the child[ren] have not changed.

[This interim order is subject to [a] [specific issue] [prohibited
steps] order [that]
[the child[ren] reside[s] with the [applicant] [respondent] [and]
the child[ren] have contact with the [applicant] [respondent]
[according to Schedule [ ] which is attached]]

☐ The Court orders that   between the date of this order and the next hearing the [applicant]
[respondent] pay, or cause to be paid, to the [applicant] [respondent]
for the child[ren] periodical payments of £ a year.

This sum is to be paid to the [applicant] [respondent] at £
a [week] [month] until further order of the Court.

Costs

☐ The Court orders that   the [applicant] [respondent] pay the costs of this
directions hearing
  the costs of the [applicant] [respondent] [ ] be taxed
on a standard basis under the Legal Aid in Family Proceedings
(Remuneration) Regulations 1991.

Ordered by   [Mr] [Mrs] Justice [His] [Her] Honour Judge
District Judge [of the Family Division]
Justice[s] of the Peace   [Clerk of the Court]
[Assistant Recorder]

on

(2) Certificate of Time Estimate

Certificate of Time Estimate   **Form**

The Court

To be completed by the court

Date issued.

Case Number

The full name(s) of the child(ren)   Child(ren)'s Number(s)

	Hours	Minutes		Hours	Minutes
Judge's preliminary reading time			Expert Witnesses		
Counsel opening			Name		
[Witness as to fact] [Parties]			Examination in chief		
Name			Cross examination		
Examination in chief			Name		
Cross examination			Examination in chief		
Name			Cross examination		
Examination in chief			[Guardian ad litem][Court Welfare Officer]		
Cross examination			Evidence		
Name			Cross examination		
Examination in chief			Counsel's closing speeches		
Cross examination			Number of counsel		
Name			Judgment		
Examination in chief			Total carried over		
Cross examination			**Total estimate**		
Total carried over					

We, the undersigned counsel and solicitors for all parties in this application, certify that our estimate of the time needed to dispose of this application is given above.

Signatures of counsel and solicitors
Solicitors may sign on behalf of counsel but they must certify that they do so with the authority of counsel.

Signed	Signed
Name	Name
Counsel Solicitor for [Applicant] [Respondent]	Counsel Solicitor for [Applicant] [Respondent]
Signed	Signed
Name	Name
Counsel Solicitor for [Applicant] [Respondent]	Counsel Solicitor for [Applicant] [Respondent]

(3) Welfare Reports

Best Practice Note for the Judiciary and Family Proceedings Courts when Ordering a Court Welfare Officer's Report

1 A welfare report may only be ordered pursuant to Section 7 of the Children Act 1989 ie when a court 'considering any question with respect to a child under [the] Act 'requires a report' on such matters relating to the welfare of that child as are required to be dealt with in the report'. A report may not be ordered for any other purpose.

2 Before a welfare report is ordered consideration should be given to the court's power to refer parties to mediation (with the consent of the parties). This may be a mediation service or the court welfare officer, depending on local arrangements. It is important that this should not be confused with a welfare report and that any court welfare officer who may have been involved in any privileged mediation proceedings should not be the officer who undertakes the preparation of a welfare report.

3 The ordering of a welfare officer's report is a judicial act requiring inquiry into the circumstances of the child. A report should never be ordered when there is no live issue under the Children Act before the court; for example, a report must not be ordered when no formal proceedings have yet been instituted. Furthermore, save in exceptional circumstances, a report should not be ordered in response to a written request by the parties.

4 Although the exact procedures in different courts vary, there will always be some kind of preliminary appointment or hearing before the district judge, justices' clerk or family proceedings court in children's cases. This is normally the occasion on which a welfare report should be ordered. The attendance of the parties and their solicitors is required at this time to enable the court properly to inquire into the issues to be covered in the report. When a court welfare officer is present, or otherwise available, the court may consider inviting the parties to have a preliminary discussion with him or her.

5 When a welfare report is ordered the judge, district judge or justices' clerk should explain briefly to the parties what will be involved and should emphasize the need to co-operate with the welfare officer and specifically to keep any appointments made. In particular, when the principle of contact is in dispute the parties should be told that the welfare officer will probably wish to see the applicant parent alone with the child. It should also be emphasised that the report, when received, is a confidential document and must not be shown to anyone who is not a named party to the application.

6 The order for the report should specify the time by which the report should be filed and, if possible, indicate the date of the substantive hearing. The solicitors for the applicant should be handed a pro forma in the form of the model attached and asked to complete details such as name, address and telephone number on the front of the form. The judge, district judge or justices' clerk should complete the rear of the pro forma which sets out the reasons for the report and the concern of the court; this should set out succinctly the issues on which the officer is being asked to report. This part of the form should specify any documents which are to be sent to the welfare officer. This form must be fully completed and attached to the court file before the court disposes of the case.

7 An addendum report may be ordered eg for the purpose of testing an agreement between the parties or where there has been a substantial change in circumstances. However, an addendum report should not be ordered merely because of a delay or adjournment in the listing of the substantive hearing.

8 The court will not order both a welfare report and Section 37 report.

9 It should be noted that the court welfare officers do not travel outside the United Kingdom; International Social Services are available to meet this need.

10 A court welfare officer will not attend a hearing unless specifically directed to do so by the court (Family Proceedings Rules 1991 rule 4.13 and Family Proceedings Courts (Children Act 1989) Rules 1991 rule 13). When such a direction is given the court should ensure that the officer gives evidence as soon as possible after the case has opened (and in any event on the first day) and is released after that evidence has been completed.

Best Practice Note to Court Staff when Welfare Reports have been Ordered

1 Staff should ensure that the pro forma on the court file has been fully completed by the solicitors and the judge, district judge or justices' clerk on the day that a welfare report is ordered. When this has not been done the file should be immediately referred back to the judge or, when he or she is not immediately available, to another family judge or authorised clerk.

2 A copy of the order and of the pro forma should be sent by the court to the court welfare office within whose area the child lives within 48 hours of the order being made. Copies of all documents specified on the pro forma should accompany the order. The pro forma should be date stamped with the date of despatch.

3 When a welfare report is received, it should immediately be date stamped and copies should be sent by the court to the solicitors for the parties immediately (or faxed when there is less than 7 days before the hearing) usually without reference back to the judge. Where a party acts in person a letter should be sent by the court inviting that party to call to collect the report.

4 When a hearing date (or change of date) is being considered and it appears that the parties will require the court welfare officer to attend, he or she should be consulted before the date is fixed.

Welfare Report Referral
About this form

- The solicitor for the applicant must fill in Part 1 (below)

- A judge or a justices' clerk will fill in Part 2 (overleaf)

- The court office will then send a copy of this form and any other papers to the court welfare office within whose area the child lives. This will be done within 48 hours.

For the use of the court office
Court
Case Number
Name of judge or clerk to the justices
Date of case review
Date of final hearing
Report ordered on
This form sent on
Report to be filed by

Part 1
The Applicant

Full name (surname in BLOCK LETTERS)
Date of birth & Relationship to the child
Address

Date of Birth .	Relationship

Daytime Telephone Number

The Applicant's Solicitor
Name and Reference
Address

Home	Work

	Ref.

Telephone & FAX numbers

Telephone	FAX

The Respondent

Full name (surname in BLOCK LETTERS)
Date of birth & Relationship to the child
Address

Date of Birth	Relationship

Daytime Telephone Number

The Respondent's Solicitor
Name and Reference
Address

Home	Work

	Ref.

Telephone & FAX numbers

Telephone	FAX

Other relevant parties

Full name (surname in BLOCK LETTERS)
Date of birth
Address

Children

	Name	Date of Birth	Residing with	School Attended
1				
2				
3				
4				

Part 2

The nature of the application

For example: residence, contact, parental responsibility, prohibited steps, specific issue, (or other)

The welfare report

Give, in detail
- *the reason(s) for the Court ordering the report*
- *particular areas of concern which are to be reported on.*

About the parties

Were they interviewed at court?   No ☐ Yes ☐   The Family Court Welfare Officer *(name)*

Was a settlement or mediation attempted?   No ☐ Yes ☐   The Family Court Welfare Officer *(name)*

Have the parties been given copies of the information leaflet?   No ☐ Yes ☐

Are there any dates when the parties will **not** be available?   No ☐ Yes ☐   The dates _____

Will an interpreter be needed?   No ☐ Yes ☐   The language(s) *(including signing)*

Are there any issues of culture or religion which the Family Court Welfare Officer should be aware of?   No ☐ Yes ☐   The issue(s) _____

Are other papers attached to this form? *For example: statements, directions*   No ☐ Yes ☐   The papers are **the Court Order** + _____

Is there a Child Protection issue?   No ☐ Yes ☐

The Court Welfare Officer is
Give the name and address

Part 2 completed by

Name: Date:

[District] Judge   Justices' Clerk
☐   ☐

Appendix 3

PRACTICE DIRECTION (31 JANUARY 1995)

Court Work – General

Citations: [1995] 1 FLR 456, [1995] 1 WLR 332, [1995] 1 All ER 586

Case Management

1 The importance of reducing the cost and delay of civil litigation makes it necessary for the court to assert greater control over the preparation for and conduct of hearings than has hitherto been customary. Failure by practitioners to conduct cases economically will be visited by appropriate orders for costs, including wasted costs orders.

2 The court will accordingly exercise its discretion to limit –

(*a*) discovery;
(*b*) the length of opening and closing oral submissions;
(*c*) the time allowed for the examination and cross-examination of witnesses;
(*d*) the issues on which it wishes to be addressed;
(*e*) reading aloud from documents and authorities.

3 Unless otherwise ordered, every witness statement or affidavit shall stand as the evidence in chief of the witness concerned. The substance of the evidence which a party intends to adduce at the hearing must be sufficiently detailed, but without prolixity; it must be confined to material matters of fact, not (except in the case of the evidence of professional witnesses) of opinion; and if hearsay evidence is to be adduced, the source of the information must be declared or good reason given for not doing so.

4 It is a duty owed to the court both by the parties and by their legal representatives to give full and frank disclosure in ancillary relief applications and also in all matters in respect of children. The parties and their advisers must also use their best endeavours:

(*a*) to confine the issues and the evidence called to what is reasonably considered to be essential for the proper presentation of their case;
(*b*) to reduce or eliminate issues for expert evidence;
(*c*) in advance of the hearing to agree which are the issues or the main issues.

5 (*ceased to have effect – see President's Direction of 10 March 2000*)

6 In cases estimated to last for five days or more and in which no pre-trial review has been ordered, application should be made for a pre-trial review. It should when practicable be listed at least three weeks before the hearing and be conducted by the judge or district judge before whom the case is to be heard and should be attended by the advocates who are to represent the parties at the hearing. Whenever possible, all statements of evidence and all reports should be filed before the date of the review and in good time for them to have been considered by all parties.

7 Whenever practicable and in any matter estimated to last five days or more, each party should, not less than two clear days before the hearing, lodge with the court, or the Clerk of the Rules in matters in the Royal Courts of Justice in London, and deliver to other parties, a chronology and a skeleton argument concisely summarising that party's submissions in relation to each of the issues, and citing the main authorities relied upon. It is important that skeleton arguments should be brief.

8 *(ceased to have effect – see President's Direction of 10 March 2000)*

9 The opening speech should be succinct. At its conclusion other parties may be invited briefly to amplify their skeleton arguments. In a heavy case the court may in conjunction with final speeches require written submissions, including the findings of fact for which each party contends.

10 This practice direction which follows *Practice Direction (Civil Litigation: Case Management)* [1995] 1 WLR 262 handed down by Lord Taylor of Gosforth CJ and Sir Richard Scott V-C to apply in the Queen's Bench and Chancery Divisions, shall apply to all family proceedings in the High Court and in all care centres, family hearing centres and divorce county courts.

11 Issued with the concurrence of the Lord Chancellor.

Sir Stephen Brown P

Appendix 4

HANDBOOK OF BEST PRACTICE IN CHILDREN ACT CASES

INTRODUCTION

When writing its final report, the Committee thought it might be helpful to gather together in a separate document the guidance available on best practice in Children Act proceedings with a view to providing a useful tool for the conscientious but busy practitioner. Some of this material is newly written and some is a compendium of guidance from our earlier reports updated both by experience and authoritative reported decisions. It follows that some of this guidance is firmly authoritative (deriving from binding decisions or practice directions) whilst much remains advisory, but based on accumulated experience of what works best.

The basic message of this Handbook is that the earlier matters are considered and acted upon by the parties and their advisers, and the more that can be done jointly with other parties, the better the court process can serve the interests of children. Work done in preparation, and in liaison with other parties, is rarely wasted and indeed is almost always productive in terms of avoiding, or at least reducing, the trial process which is after all both the most costly and certainly the most stressful part of the whole proceedings.

We hope that all practitioners (and not just the lawyers) will find this Handbook useful as we try to translate into practice in each case the obligation to promote the welfare of the children with whom we are dealing. We have set out this Handbook with a view primarily to ease of reference in the hope that it will find widespread use in practice.

SECTION 1 – PREPARATION FOR COURT IN CARE PROCEEDINGS

Local authority solicitors

1 At the earliest stage, when first consulted, focus on:

(*a*) the issues;
(*b*) the legal framework;
(*c*) the evidence needed to support an application;
(*d*) the proposed care plan;
(*e*) the appropriate level of court; and
(*f*) the likely time scale for concluding the court case in the light of:
    (i) the complexities involved, and
    (ii) the ages and needs of the children.

2 If counsel is to be instructed, do so at an early stage. Consider together the preparation for trial and whether transfer to the care centre is appropriate.

All parties and their legal advisers

3 By the first directions hearing, consider whether the issues of fact are stark enough to justify a split hearing, with an early resolution of factual disputes to enable a definitive care plan to be formulated and to enable the guardian ad litem to make recommended actions as to outcome. For example, this is likely to arise in cases of alleged non-accidental injury where different persons are in the frame as possible perpetrators and/or accomplices, and in cases of sexual abuse.

4 Use directions hearings imaginatively. Anticipate problems and address them in advance.

    (*a*) Ensure strict compliance with timetables for filing evidence and documents.
    (*b*) Inform the court, as a matter of urgency, if the timetable cannot be met for any reason.
    (*c*) Be prepared in advance with dates and availability of witnesses and time needed to adduce evidence.
    (*d*) Liaise with other parties to ensure that all issues are addressed at an early stage, for example:
        (i) whether transfer to the care centre would be appropriate;
        (ii) which other persons are seeking party status;
        (iii) issues of disclosure and confidentiality; or
        (iv) any assessments or experts' reports sought by any party.
    (*e*) Fix the final hearing, even if only provisionally.

5 All parties, and in particular the guardian ad litem, have a duty to:

    (*a*) advise the court on the timetable appropriate to the issues and timescale of the child concerned;
    (*b*) keep the timetable under constant review throughout the preparation for the hearing; and
    (*c*) bring to the attention of the court promptly any significant developments and seek further directions.

Instruction of experts

6 See **Section 5** below.

The care plan

7 Ensure that the issues raised by the local authority are clearly set out with a fully researched care plan, to enable the parties to know what case they have to meet.

8 If permanent placement in an alternative family is the plan, prepare the ground as far as possible without pre-empting the court's decision.

9 If the plan is for an adoptive placement, the court will be handicapped in assessing the plan and the timescale, unless the child concerned has already been considered and approved by the adoption and fostering panel, and potential suitable adoptive families have been identified. It is not good practice to await the making of a care order before obtaining such information, because the court is deprived of important background information and significant delay can occur in placing the child in the event of the court approving the plan.

10 If the plan involves a specialist placement with therapy and/or further assessment, identify the placement and any professionals involved, together with the timescale and the availability of appropriate funding.

11 If the plan depends upon the finding of facts or determination of particular issues by the court, state why and set out clear alternative proposals.

12 If no firm proposal can be made, that should be made clear and explained.

****

Note—Paragraphs 13–20: '*Preparing the Evidence*'; paragraph 21: '*The Court*'; paragraphs 22–32: '*Section 2 – Renewal of Interim Care Orders*'; and paragraphs 33–35: '*Section 3 – First Appointments in Public Law Cases in the County Courts: The Role of the Court*' have been omitted on the basis that their substance has in part been superseded by the public law protocol (as to which see *Protocol for Judicial Case Management in Public Law Children Act Cases (June 2003)*.

SECTION 4 – PRIVATE LAW CASES

Introduction

36 The following is a brief guide to best practice in applications made under section 8 of the Children Act. This guidance may need to be tailored to deal with cases involving unrepresented litigants.

37 Specific good practice for cases involving allegations of sexual abuse is set out in the Annex to this section.

Before proceedings

38 Consider whether the dispute between the parties could be resolved in any way other than litigation. Most areas have a mediation service which would be able to attempt to deal with disputes by way of negotiation and agreement. There is rarely anything to be lost, and normally much to be gained, by mediation.

39 At the earliest stage, if it becomes clear that negotiated or mediated settlement will not be possible, focus on:

(*a*) the issues, including the question of how crucial facts are to be proved;
(*b*) the legal framework; and
(*c*) the evidence needed to support the case to be put forward.

Issue of proceedings

40 Ensure that form C1 contains all relevant information, including a brief outline of the case (but not a detailed statement by the applicant).

41 To prevent unnecessary delay at the first directions appointment, prepare at least draft statements by:

(*a*) the applicant, and
(*b*) any witnesses who it is known will have to give evidence.

The first directions appointment

The role of the court

42 The court will fix a first directions appointment when an application is issued. The task of the court at the first appointment is to:

(*a*) investigate the issues;

(*b*) inquire into the possibility of settlement; and

(*c*) give directions in any case which has to proceed.

43 When giving directions, the court will normally:

(*a*) consider the appropriate tier of court;

(*b*) order the filing of witness statements;

(*c*) consider whether there are circumstances justifying sequential rather than simultaneous exchange;

(*d*) express times for filing (for example, of witness statements or the court welfare officer's report) by fixing a date, eg 'by 28 April 1997' and not 'within 14 days'; and

(*e*) include in the order the date for the next appointment and, even if only provisionally, the final hearing.

44 An order should not provide for an application to be adjourned generally unless the parties consider that it will not be necessary to return to court. In that event the order should also provide for the application to stand dismissed if not restored by a certain date.

45 The order should provide that any letter of instructions to experts (to be joint instructions wherever possible) is to be filed at court.

46 A paginated bundle of documents and chronology should be normal practice except in the simplest case.

The role of the parties

47 Parties and their legal representatives must attend directions appointments unless specifically excused.

48 A party's legal representative must have both sufficient knowledge and authority to take any necessary decisions.

49 Use the first appointment imaginatively, anticipating problems and addressing them in advance, and dealing with questions of expert evidence. (See **Section 5**)

50 When it is to be suggested that there should be contact at a contact centre or supervised contact by an individual, make enquiries to ensure that the centre or individual will be available to provide the service.

Welfare reports

51 Parties should have access to a court welfare officer, or other person qualified to assist them, at or before the first appointment. Some courts achieve this by requiring a court welfare officer to attend the first appointment, others by referring the parties to the welfare officer before the date of the first appointment. Ask about the practice of the local court if you are in any doubt.

52 If a welfare officer has attempted to mediate between the parties, he should not be involved in the case in any other way.

53 When ordering a welfare report, the guidance as to best practice under 'Welfare Reports' at *Best Practice Note of January 1995* should be followed. In particular:

(a) the request for a report should state the issue giving rise to the request;

(b) addendum reports should not normally be ordered, and should not be necessary for the hearing if timetabling has been effective;

(c) any request for the court welfare officer to attend the final hearing should be examined carefully, and not granted as a matter of course;

(d) when a court requires the court welfare officer to attend a hearing, enquiry should be made to ensure that he is available; and

(e) the court hearing the case should allow the officer to give evidence first and then to be released.

Final directions appointments or pre-trial reviews

54 The final directions appointment, or pre-trial review, should be timetabled to take place when any welfare report and all evidence has been filed.

55 The applicant's solicitor must prepare an agreed and paginated bundle of documents, containing an index and a chronology, not less than 24 hours before the hearing.

56 The court will expect the parties' advisers to have addressed the question of what evidence can be agreed and what is in dispute. An order will be made accordingly.

57 The counsel or solicitor who will attend the final hearing should attend the pre-trial review. If this is not possible, the person attending must be thoroughly conversant with the case and competent to make any necessary concessions or admissions and to advise the lay client in respect of settlement.

The final hearing

58 Except by direction of the court, children should not attend a hearing.

59 Consider how the decision of the court is to be communicated to the children. In some cases, particularly where the court's decision is contrary to the reported wishes of the child, it may be appropriate for the court welfare officer to see the child to explain what has happened.

Annex: Flawed sexual abuse investigation

Despite the guidance in *B v B (Sexual Abuse: Procedural Delay)* [1994] 1 FLR 323 and *Re A and B (Minors) (No 2)* [1995] 1 FLR 351, problems continue to occur in private law cases where allegations of sexual abuse of a child are investigated by the police and/or social services. Frequently the cases involve an application for contact with a child, where the primary carer has refused contact on the ground that the child has been sexually abused by the applicant. Such cases cause particular difficulties where the applicant denies the allegation, and alleges that the other parent has either invented the sexual abuse or has brainwashed the child into believing that sexual abuse has occurred. The parent opposing contact may be obstructive and use delaying tactics in order to prevent contact taking place, even under supervision. If such cases are not strictly timetabled, resulting delays can achieve the object of frustrating resumption of contact, even if the court finds that sexual abuse is not proved. Good practice requires as follows:

(a) The legal representatives have a duty, irrespective of whether or not delay might be tactically of advantage to their client, to ensure that a case does not drift and is resolved with the minimum of delay.

(*b*) The timetable must be strictly controlled by the court and must never be left to the parties. As in public law cases, the court must monitor the procedural steps ordered, building in reviews of progress and setting stringent time limits and return dates.

(*c*) When the local authority is involved with a concurrent, but independent investigation, the principal co-ordinating agency for the determination of issues is the court, using section 7 of the Children Act 1989 which enables the court to require the local authority to report to the court on the nature, progress and outcome of the child protection investigation. Section 7 should be used to keep the parties informed of progress and material available.

(*d*) The local authority should make available a social worker to give evidence on the report and to be cross examined if so required.

(*e*) Any joint child abuse interview conducted by police and social services must follow the memorandum of good practice. Otherwise not only is the resulting interview of no forensic value, but it may impede or contaminate any further assessment of the child ordered by the court.

(*f*) The court has power to compel discovery of documents held by local authorities or the police, eg videos of interview with the child. If any arguments arise as to confidentiality, or public interest immunity, they should be determined at an early stage at a directions hearing.

(*g*) Although the court cannot compel a prosecuting authority to reach decisions speedily, the court can and should bring to the attention of the authority the need for a timely decision on criminal prosecution.

(*h*) Even when there is a police investigation, there is no good legal or social work reason why the social worker should not make contact with the parent under investigation, so that information can be given and exchanged which is relevant to the welfare of the child. The social worker should make it clear that until the police investigation is complete, the specific allegation cannot be discussed. Many parents under police investigation suffer a sense of grievance when no reason is given for denial of contact, with the result that the parent perceives the local authority as pursuing investigations with a closed mind and a presumption of guilt.

(*i*) The issue whether or not a child has been sexually abused is for decision by the court and it is essential that other agencies await that decision before introducing management, counselling or therapy that pre-judges the issue. Therefore, the welfare of the child demands speedy resolution of issues.

(*j*) If leave is sought to instruct an expert, it is essential to define the issues, to establish the area of expertise required and the proposed timetable, to consider joint instruction and to follow the guidance in **Section 5**. In deciding whether to grant leave for a child to be assessed the court should consider carefully the issues, and whether the court is likely to be assisted in determining whether sexual abuse has been established, as opposed to outcome, by the contribution from an expert in the field of psychological medicine.

(*k*) There is often a tension between a positive clinical finding of sexual abuse, and judicial findings that abuse has not occurred. In contested cases clinical methods will inevitably be subjected to scrutiny. Any investigation which focuses attention on the statements of the child runs the risk of producing a false result if what the child says is unreliable or if the child's primary caretaker is unreliable, particularly where the allegation emerges in bitterly contested section 8 proceedings. The dangers of a false conclusion are enhanced if the alleged perpetrator is excluded from clinical investigation. It is vital to approach a child abuse investigation with an open mind.

(*l*) Where possible directions appointments should be heard by the judge who is likely to determine the substantive issues.

(*m*) In cases in which there is a stark factual issue to be determined the court will need to consider carefully whether it is appropriate to obtain a section 7 report clarifying the issues before ordering a welfare report, whether factual issues need to be determined by the court before a welfare report is ordered as to outcome, or whether a report should be ordered at an early stage in the proceedings. Each case needs to be considered on its merits, and the court welfare service should be invited to make representations.

SECTION 5 – EXPERTS AND THE COURTS

Introduction

60 The guidance in this section applies equally to public and private law cases in which experts are instructed.

61 It is of critical importance to distinguish the respective functions of expert and judge.

(*a*) The expert forms an assessment, and expresses an opinion within the area of his expertise. This may include an opinion on the issues in the case, but the judge decides particular issues in individual cases.

(*b*) It is not for the judge to become involved in medical controversy, except in the rare case where such controversy is an issue in the case.

62 The court depends on the skill, knowledge, and above all, the professional and intellectual integrity of the expert witness.

Leave to instruct experts

The role of the instructing parties

63 Applications for leave to instruct experts should be considered by each party at the earliest possible stage of the proceedings in order to avoid serial applications by different parties seeking to counter opinions from experts which do not support their case. Such applications are likely to be refused – see *H v Cambridgeshire County Council* [1997] 1 FCR 569.

64 Advocates who seek such leave have a positive duty to place all relevant information before the court at the earliest opportunity. Applications are unlikely to succeed unless they specify:

(*a*) the category of expert evidence sought to be adduced;

(*b*) the name of the expert;

(*c*) his availability for reporting, meeting with other experts and attendance at court;

(*d*) the relevance of the expert evidence to the issues in the case;

(*e*) whether evidence can properly be obtained by both parties jointly instructing one expert; and

(*f*) whether expert evidence may properly be adduced by one party only, eg the guardian ad litem.

The role of the court

65 The court has a positive duty to enquire into the information provided by the party or parties seeking leave to instruct an expert.

66 The court should never make a generalised order for leave to disclose papers to an expert. The order should specify:

(*a*) the area of expertise;

(*b*) the issues to be addressed;

(*c*) the identity of the expert;

(*d*) the date by which the letter of instruction is to be sent;

(*e*) the documents to be released to the expert;

(*f*) the date for filing the expert's report with the court;

(*g*) a provision for experts of like discipline to communicate (as discussed below) to agree facts and define issues, together with responsibility for fixing the agenda and chairing the meeting; and

(*h*) the availability of the expert to give oral evidence, if required.

67 Expert reports based solely upon leave to disclose documents in a 'paper exercise' are rarely as persuasive as those reports based on interviews and assessment as well as the documentation. *Re C (Expert Evidence: Disclosure Practice)* [1995] 1 FLR 204 provides guidance on experts, in contested cases, meeting in advance of the hearing. It should be a condition of appointment of any expert that he should be required to hold discussions with other experts instructed in the same field of expertise, in advance of the hearing, in order to identify areas of agreement and dispute, which should be incorporated into a schedule for the court. Such discussion should be chaired by a co-ordinator, such as the guardian ad litem if there is consent so to act. In advance of the meeting, the co-ordinator should prepare and circulate to all experts a schedule of issues and questions to be addressed at the meeting. The schedule should be prepared in co-operation with all parties, so that all relevant matters are considered by the experts.

68 Problems may arise when an expert's conclusion is unfavourable to the instructing party's case. The court may need to give consideration as to how that expert's evidence is to be adduced.

Letters of instruction and provision of information to experts

69 The letter of instruction should:

(*a*) define the context in which the opinion is sought;

(*b*) set out specific questions for the expert to address;

(*c*) identify any relevant issues of fact to enable each expert to give an opinion on each set of competing issues;

(*d*) specify any examinations to be permitted;

(*e*) list the documents to be sent to the expert, which should be presented in a sorted bundle and include an agreed chronology and background history; and

(*f*) require, as a condition of appointment, that the expert must, in advance of the hearing, hold discussions with other experts appointed in the same field of expertise, and produce a statement of agreement and disagreement on the issues by a specified date.

70 Always disclose the letter of instruction to the other parties, and invite them to contribute to defining the appropriate issues, relevant documentation, history, and

questions to be addressed. Include the resulting letter in the bundle of documents for use in court.

71 Doctors who have clinical experience of a child before the commencement of proceedings should have all clinical material made available for inspection by the court and other experts, eg medical notes, hospital records, x-rays, photographs, and correspondence.

72 It is the instructing solicitor's duty to ensure that an expert who is to give oral evidence is kept up to date with relevant developments in the case.

73 It is the duty of the advocate calling an expert to ensure that the witness, in advance of giving oral evidence, has seen all fresh relevant material, and is aware of new developments.

Duties of experts

74 The role of the expert is to provide independent assistance to the court by way of objective, unbiased opinion, in relation to matters within his expertise. Expert evidence presented to the court must be, and be seen to be, the independent product of the expert, uninfluenced by the instructing party.

75 Acceptance of instructions imposes an obligation to

(*a*) comply with the court's timetable and
(*b*) notify the instructing solicitors promptly if there is any risk that the timetable cannot be adhered to.

76 Experts should not hesitate to seek further information and documentation when this is required. Such requests should form part of the court bundle.

77 In his report, an expert should:

(*a*) state the facts or assumptions on which his opinion is based, and not omit to consider material facts which detract from his concluded opinion;
(*b*) make it clear when a particular aspect of the case is outside his expertise;
(*c*) indicate, if appropriate, that his opinion is not properly researched because of insufficient data, and is therefore provisional; and
(*d*) inform the other parties, and, when appropriate, the court if at any time he changes his opinion on a material matter.

78 If an opinion is based, wholly or in part, on research conducted by others, the expert must:

(*a*) set this out clearly in the report;
(*b*) identify the research relied on;
(*c*) state its relevance to the points at issue; and
(*d*) be prepared to justify the opinions expressed.

79 It is unacceptable for any expert in a child case, whose evidence is relevant to the outcome, to give evidence without having read, in advance, the report of the guardian ad litem.

Assisting the experts

80 Legal advisers for the parties should co-operate, at an early stage in the preparation for trial, to ensure availability of the experts to give evidence in a logical sequence.

81 It is helpful to timetable experts, in a difficult case, to give evidence one after another, so that each can listen to the evidence of other experts, and comment on that evidence.

82 Child proceedings are non-adversarial, and it is not necessary that witnesses are called in conventional order.

83 Where it becomes clear that an expert's opinion is uncontentious, and that the expert will not be required to attend court, he must be notified at the earliest opportunity. Whenever attendance at court is necessary, the court must always try to accommodate the expert by interposing the evidence at a given time.

84 In order that all relevant matters are fully considered at the appropriate time in advance of the hearing, it is essential that advocates who will appear at the hearing are involved at the earliest stage in order to consider how the case should be prepared and progressed.

The Expert Witness Group

85 The Expert Witness Group has been active in developing an 'Expert Witness Pack', which it hopes to have published in the autumn of 1997. The pack, which will be available for purchase and will be cited in bibliographies, etc, will include several pro formas and:

(a) draft letters of instruction and acceptance;
(b) a checklist for both solicitor and expert;
(c) guidelines and a model curriculum vitae for expert witnesses; and
(d) a model format for experts' reports.

86 Further information about the Expert Witness Group and the Expert Witness Pack may be obtained from: Dr Eileen Vizard, Consultant Child and Adolescent Psychiatrist, Camden and Islington Community Health Services NHS Trust, Simmons House Adolescent Unit, St. Luke's-Woodside Hospital, Woodside Avenue, London N10 3HU (Telephone: 0181 219 1883).

SECTION 6 – APPEALS FROM THE FAMILY PROCEEDINGS COURTS UNDER SECTION 94 OF THE CHILDREN ACT 1989

87 Appeals lie to a single judge of the Family Division unless the President otherwise directs. The procedure on appeal is set out in Rule 4.22 of the Family Proceedings Rules 1991.

88 Despite guidance in reported cases, problems continue to arise in the preparation and determination of such appeals.

89 Compliance with the rules and good practice requires the following.

(a) The merits of an appeal must be carefully and expeditiously considered. Dissatisfaction with the decision of the family proceedings court will not justify an appeal, unless the court erred in the exercise of discretion within the meaning of *G v G* [1985] FLR 894. An appeal is not a rehearing.

(b) Time limits are strict. An appeal must be commenced by filing and serving the notice of appeal on all parties and on any guardian ad litem within 14 days of the decision, unless the appeal is against an interim care order or interim supervision order, in which event the time limit is 7 days. The period for service may be altered by the High Court on application, to a longer or shorter period,

under Rule 4.22(3)(*c*). The High Court will not grant an extension of time without good reason and advocates must be prepared to justify such applications.

(*c*) The documents set out in Rule 4.22(2) must be filed in the nearest district registry which is a care centre to the court in which the order appealed from was made. Good practice requires that all reports and witness statements filed in the proceedings should be filed for the appeal in addition to the documents identified in Rule 4.22(2).

(*d*) The family proceedings court must as a matter of urgency supply to the appellant a typed copy of the notes of evidence and of the reasons for the decision. It is detrimental to the welfare of the child concerned if there is any delay in the production of these documents.

(*e*) Strict time limits are laid down for a respondent who wishes to cross appeal, or to seek a variation, or an affirmation of the decision on grounds other than those relied upon by the family proceedings court. Within 14 days of receipt of the notice of appeal the respondent must file and serve on all parties to the appeal, a notice in writing setting out the grounds relied on. No notice may be filed or served in an appeal against an order under section 38.

90 The appeal should be set down promptly. Where it is unlikely that a case can be listed without delay on Circuit, arrangements will be made for the appeal to be heard in London.

91 In advance of the hearing the appellant must file a paginated bundle with a chronology and in all save the most simple cases, each party must file a skeleton argument. There is a duty upon advocates to file in advance an accurate time estimate of the length of hearing, and to keep the court informed of any change to that estimate.

92 Any application for a stay pending appeal must be made to the High Court. The family proceedings court has no power to grant a stay.

SECTION 7 – DISCLOSURE OF LOCAL AUTHORITY DOCUMENTS

Early consideration

93 Crown Prosecution Service and defence solicitors should give early consideration whether disclosure of records held in the possession of a local authority may be required. The appropriate time for such consideration will be at the commencement of the 4 weeks period (custody cases) or 6 weeks period (bail cases) between committal or transfer and the plea and directions hearing.

94 The parties should inform the judge of the steps that have been taken so that, if necessary, directions may be given and noted on the questionnaire.

95 Requests by the Crown Prosecution Service or the defence solicitor for disclosure should:

(*a*) be made in writing to the legal services department of the local authority who will nominate a lawyer to deal with the matter;

(*b*) provide specific details of the information required and an explanation as to why it is relevant to the proceedings, identifying as precisely as possible the category and nature of the documents for which disclosure is sought and

(*c*) be accompanied by a copy of the indictment or of the schedule of charges upon committal.

96 If the defence solicitors request information, they should notify the Crown Prosecution Service of the request and vice versa.

97 Case records will be examined by legal services and the appropriate officer to identify whether they contain the information which is sought.

98 Information which is disclosed to the defence solicitors will also be disclosed to the Crown Prosecution Service and vice versa.

99 If the case records do *not* contain the requested information, the requester will be so informed by legal services which, subject to relevance and the principle of confidentiality, may be able (but is not bound) to provide a summary of the type of information which is on file.

100 If the requester is not satisfied with the response, legal services, after appropriate consultation, will provide the name of a person to be witness summonsed to attend court with the records.

101 Where the case records do contain the information requested, legal services will disclose it so long as it is not protected by public interest immunity, legal privilege or statutory confidentiality.

102 If the local authority wishes to assert protection from disclosure for the records requested or any of them, legal services, after appropriate consultation, will provide the name of a person to be witness summonsed to attend court with the records.

103 If the local authority wishes to make representations as to why the records requested should not be disclosed, it will inform:

    (*a*) the requester;
    (*b*) the opposing party's representative and
    (*c*) the court listing officer,

and a convenient date for listing, before a judge will be set.

104 The local authority should provide a skeleton argument and serve it on the parties and the court.

105 At the hearing:

    (*a*) the witness must produce the records to the judge;
    (*b*) files must be flagged to identify the documents for which immunity from disclosure is sought;
    (*c*) representations will be made on behalf of the parties; and
    (*d*) the judge will give appropriate directions.

106 Whenever possible, the hearing will be before the judge who will be conducting the trial. If the trial judge has not been nominated, then the hearing judge may determine the issue of disclosure.

107 The judge will give his decision in court or chambers, in the presence of the parties' representatives.

108 The judge may also give direction as to the custody of the records pending trial and as to any copies to be obtained on behalf of the parties.

109 The hearing referred to above should take place not less than 4 weeks before trial.

110 Where the requester has reasonable grounds to believe that a witness or a defendant has been involved with social services, information may be obtained by writing to the relevant department stating the witness's or defendant's name, date of birth and address.

Confidentiality of records

111 The court will normally conduct the hearing at which public interest immunity is claimed in chambers, where the local authority may be represented by a solicitor.

112 When records are disclosed to the parties by order of the court, it is on the undertaking that:

- (*a*) they will only be used for the purpose of the criminal proceedings before the court; and
- (*b*) their contents are revealed only to the parties and their legal representatives. (Leave of the court must be obtained for wider disclosure, eg to an expert witness.)

Costs

113 An officer of the local authority who necessarily attends court for the purpose of the proceedings otherwise than as a witness may be allowed expenses (Regulation 18(2) within Costs in Criminal Cases (General) Regulations 1986).

114 The court has no power to order payment from central funds of the cost of a search or legal costs.

115 If the court rules that the application for disclosure is frivolous or by way of a fishing expedition, it may order that costs be paid by the applicant or his legal advisers.

****

Appendix 5

PRESIDENT'S DIRECTION (17 DECEMBER 1997)

Injunctions and Contempt of Court

Citations: [1998] 1 FLR 496, [1998] Fam Law 109

Family Law Act 1996, Part IV

The procedure formulated in the President's Directions of 23 January 1980 and 7 March 1991, in relation to orders made under the Domestic Violence and Matrimonial Proceedings Act 1976, shall apply in respect of orders made under Part IV of the Family Law Act 1996, as follows:

(1) Where at a hearing which has been held in private, an occupation or non-molestation order is made to which a power of arrest is attached and the person to whom it is addressed was not given notice of the hearing and was not present at the hearing, the terms of the order and the name of the person to whom it is addressed shall be announced in open court at the earliest opportunity. This may be either on the same day when the court proceeds to hear cases in open court or where there is no further business in open court on that day at the next listed sitting of the court.

(2) When a person arrested under a power of arrest cannot conveniently be brought before the relevant judicial authority sitting in a place normally used as a courtroom within 24 hours after the arrest, he may be brought before the relevant judicial authority at any convenient place but, as the liberty of the subject is involved, the press and public should be permitted to be present, unless security needs make this impracticable.

(3) Any order of committal made otherwise than in public or in a courtroom open to the public, shall be announced in open court at the earliest opportunity. This may be either on the same day when the court proceeds to hear cases in open court or where there is no further business in open court on that day at the next listed sitting of the court. The announcement shall state (a) the name of the person committed, (b) in general terms the nature of the contempt of the court in respect of which the order of committal has been made and (c) the length of the period of committal.

Issued with the concurrence of the Lord Chancellor.

Sir Stephen Brown
President

Appendix 6

PRESIDENT'S DIRECTION (25 MAY 2000)

Ancillary Relief

Citations: [2000] 1 FLR 997

Ancillary Relief Procedure

1 *Introduction*
1.1 The Family Proceedings (Amendment No 2) Rules 1999 make important amendments to the Family Proceedings Rules 1991 as from 5 June 2000. The existing 'pilot scheme' rules in relation to ancillary relief which have applied since 1996 but only in specified courts will become, with significant revisions, of general application. In the same way as the pilot scheme, the new procedure is intended to reduce delay, facilitate settlements, limit costs incurred by parties and provide the court with greater and more effective control over the conduct of the proceedings.

2 *Pre-application Protocol*
2.1 The 'Pre-application protocol' annexed to this Direction outlines the steps parties should take to seek and provide information from and to each other prior to the commencement of any ancillary relief application. The court will expect the parties to comply with the terms of the protocol.

3 *Financial Dispute Resolution (FDR) Appointment*
3.1 A key element in the new procedure is the Financial Dispute Resolution (FDR) appointment. Rule 2.61E provides that the FDR appointment is to be treated as a meeting held for the purposes of discussion and negotiation. Such meetings which were previously described as meetings held for the purposes of conciliation have been developed as a means of reducing the tension which inevitably arises in matrimonial and family disputes and facilitating settlement of those disputes.

3.2 In order for the FDR appointment to be effective, parties must approach the occasion openly and without reserve. Non-disclosure of the content of such meetings is accordingly vital and is an essential prerequisite for fruitful discussion directed to the settlement of the dispute between the parties. The FDR appointment is an important part of the settlement process. As a consequence of *Re D (Minors) (Conciliation: Disclosure of Information)* [1993] Fam 231, sub nom *Re D (Minors) (Conciliation: Privilege)* [1993] 1 FLR 932, evidence of anything said or of any admission made in the course of an FDR appointment will not be admissible in evidence, except at the

trial of a person for an offence committed at the appointment or in the very exceptional circumstances indicated in *Re D.*

3.3 Courts will therefore expect:

> parties to make offers and proposals;
> recipients of offers and proposals to give them proper consideration;
> that parties, whether separately or together, will not seek to exclude from consideration at the appointment any such offer or proposal.

3.4 In order to make the most effective use of the first appointment and the FDR appointment, the legal representatives attending those appointments will be expected to have full knowledge of the case.

4 *Single joint expert*

4.1 The introduction of expert evidence in proceedings is likely to increase costs substantially and consequently the court will use its powers to restrict the unnecessary use of experts. Accordingly, where expert evidence is sought to be relied upon, parties should if possible agree upon a single expert whom they can jointly instruct. Where parties are unable to agree upon the expert to be instructed, the court will consider using its powers under Part 35 of the Civil Procedure Rules 1998 to direct that evidence be given by one expert only. In such cases parties must be in a position at the first appointment or when the matter comes to be considered by the court to provide the court with a list of suitable experts or to make submissions as to the method by which the expert is to be selected.

5 This Direction shall have effect as from 5 June 2000 and replaces *Practice Direction: Ancillary Relief Procedure: Pilot Scheme* [1997] 2 FLR 304 dated 16 June 1997.

6 Issued with the approval and concurrence of the Lord Chancellor.

Dame Elizabeth Butler-Sloss
President

PRE-APPLICATION PROTOCOL

1 *Introduction*
1.1

> 1.1.1 Lord Woolf in his final *Access to Justice* Report of July 1996 recommended the development of pre-application protocols:
> 'to build on and increase the benefits of early but well informed settlement which genuinely satisfy both parties to dispute'
> 1.1.2 Subsequently, in April 2000 the Lord Chancellor's Ancillary Relief Advisory Committee agreed this Pre-application Protocol.

1.2 The aim of the pre-application protocol is to ensure that:

> (*a*) pre-application disclosure and negotiation takes place in appropriate cases;
> (*b*) where there is pre-application disclosure and negotiation, it is dealt with:
> > (i)   cost-effectively;
> > (ii)   in line with the overriding objectives of the Family Proceedings (Amendments) Rules 1999;
> (*c*) the parties are in a position to settle the case fairly and early without litigation.

1.3 The court will be able to treat the standard set in the pre-application protocol as the normal reasonable approach to pre-application conduct. If proceedings are

subsequently issued, the court will be entitled to decide whether there has been non-compliance with the protocol and, if so, whether non-compliance merits consequences.

2 *Notes of guidance*

Scope of the Protocol

2.1 This protocol is intended to apply to all claims for ancillary relief as defined by FPR 1991, r 1(2). It is designed to cover all classes of case, ranging from a simple application for periodical payments to an application for a substantial lump sum and property adjustment order. The protocol is designed to facilitate the operation of what was called the pilot scheme and is from 5 June 2000 the standard procedure for ancillary relief applications.

2.2 In considering the option of pre-application disclosure and negotiation, solicitors should bear in mind the advantage of having a court timetable and court-managed process. There is sometimes an advantage in preparing disclosure before proceedings are commenced. However, solicitors should bear in mind the objective of controlling costs and in particular the costs of discovery and that the option of pre-application disclosure and negotiation has risks of excessive and uncontrolled expenditure and delay. This option should only be encouraged where both parties agree to follow this route and disclosure is not likely to be an issue or has been adequately dealt with in mediation or otherwise.

2.3 Solicitors should consider at an early stage and keep under review whether it would be appropriate to suggest mediation to the clients as an alternative to solicitor negotiation or court-based litigation.

2.4 Making an application to the court should not be regarded as a hostile step or a last resort, rather as a way of starting the court timetable, controlling disclosure and endeavouring to avoid the costly final hearing and the preparation for it.

First letter

2.5 The circumstances of parties to an application for ancillary relief are so various that it would be difficult to prepare a specimen first letter. The request for information will be different in every case. However, the tone of the initial letter is important and the guidelines in para 3.7 should be followed. It should be approved in advance by the client. Solicitors writing to an unrepresented party should always recommend that he seeks independent legal advice and enclose a second copy of the letter to be passed to any solicitor instructed. A reasonable time-limit for a response may be 14 days.

Negotiation and settlement

2.6 In the event of pre-application disclosure and negotiation, as envisaged in para 2.2 an application should not be issued when a settlement is a reasonable prospect.

Disclosure

2.7 The protocol underlines the obligation of parties to make full and frank disclosure of all material facts, documents and other information relevant to the issues. Solicitors owe their clients a duty to tell them in clear terms of this duty and of the possible consequences of breach of the duty. This duty of disclosure is an ongoing obligation and includes the duty to disclose any material changes after initial disclosure has been given. Solicitors are referred to the *Good Practice Guide for Disclosure* produced by the Solicitors Family Law Association (obtainable from the Administrative Director, 366A Crofton Road, Orpington, Kent BR2 8NN).

3 *The Protocol*

General principles

3.1 All parties must always bear in mind the overriding objective set out at FPR 1991, r 2.51B and try to ensure that all claims should be resolved and a just outcome achieved as speedily as possible without costs being unreasonably incurred. The needs of any children should be addressed and safeguarded. The procedures which it is appropriate to follow should be conducted with minimum distress to the parties and in a manner designed to promote as good a continuing relationship between the parties and any children affected as is possible in the circumstances.

3.2 The principle of proportionality must be borne in mind at all times. It is unacceptable for the costs of any case to be disproportionate to the financial value of the subject matter of the dispute.

3.3 Parties should be informed that where a court exercises a discretion as to whether costs are payable by one party to another, this discretion extends to pre-application offers to settle and conduct of disclosure (r 44.3, para 1 of the Civil Procedure Rules 1998).

Identifying the issues

3.4 Parties must seek to clarify their claims and identify the issues between them as soon as possible. So that this can be achieved they must provide full, frank and clear disclosure of facts, information and documents which are material and sufficiently accurate to enable proper negotiations to take place to settle their differences. Openness in all dealings is essential.

Disclosure

3.5 If parties carry out voluntary disclosure before the issue of proceedings the parties should exchange schedules of assets, income, liabilities and other material facts, using Form E as a guide to the format of the disclosure. Documents should only be disclosed to the extent that they are required by Form E. Excessive or disproportionate costs should not be incurred.

Correspondence

3.6 Any first letter and subsequent correspondence must focus on the clarification of claims and identification of issues and their resolution. Protracted and unnecessary correspondence and 'trial by correspondence' must be avoided.

3.7 The impact of any correspondence upon the reader and in particular the parties must always be considered. Any correspondence which raises irrelevant issues or which might cause the other party to adopt an entrenched, polarised or hostile position is to be discouraged.

Experts

3.8 Expert valuation evidence is only necessary where the parties cannot agree or do not know the value of some significant asset. The cost of a valuation should be proportionate to the sums in dispute. Wherever possible, valuations of properties, shares, etc should be obtained from a single valuer instructed by both parties. To that end, a party wishing to instruct an expert (the first party) should first give the other party a list of the names of one or more experts in the relevant speciality whom he considers are suitable to instruct. Within 14 days the other party may indicate an

objection to one or more of the named experts and, if so, should supply the names of one or more experts whom he considers suitable.

3.9 Where the identity of the expert is agreed, the parties should agree the terms of a joint letter of instructions.

3.10 Where no agreement is reached as to the identity of the expert, each party should think carefully before instructing his own expert because of the costs implications. Disagreements about disclosure such as the use and identity of an expert may be better managed by the court within the context of an application for ancillary relief.

3.11 Whether a joint report is commissioned or the parties have chosen to instruct separate experts, it is important that the expert is prepared to answer reasonable questions raised by either party.

3.12 When experts' reports are commissioned pre-application, it should be made clear to the expert that they may in due course be reporting to the court and that they should therefore consider themselves bound by the guidance as to expert witnesses in Part 35 of the Civil Procedure Rules 1998.

3.13 Where the parties propose to instruct a joint expert, there is a duty on both parties to disclose whether they have already consulted that expert about the assets in issue.

3.14 If the parties agree to instruct separate experts the parties should be encouraged to agree in advance that the reports will be disclosed.

Summary
3.15 The aim of all pre-application proceedings steps must be to assist the parties to resolve their differences speedily and fairly or at least narrow the issues and, should that not be possible, to assist the court to do so.

Appendix 7

PRACTICE NOTE (2 APRIL 2001)

Children

Citations: [2001] 2 FLR 155

Official Solicitor: Appointment in Family Proceedings

1 This Practice Note supersedes *Practice Note (Official Solicitor: Appointment in Family Proceedings)* (4 December 1998) [1999] 1 FLR 310 issued by the Official Solicitor in relation to his appointment in family proceedings. It is issued in conjunction with a Practice Note dealing with the appointment of officers of CAFCASS Legal Services and Special Casework in family proceedings. This Practice Note is intended to be helpful guidance, but always subject to Practice Directions, decisions of the court and other legal guidance.

2 The Children and Family Court Advisory and Support Service (CAFCASS) has responsibilities in relation to children in family proceedings in which their welfare is or may be in question (Criminal Justice and Court Services Act 2000, s 12). From 1 April 2001, the Official Solicitor will no longer represent children who are the subject of family proceedings (other than in very exceptional circumstances and after liaison with CAFCASS).

3 This Practice Note summarises the continuing role of the Official Solicitor in family proceedings. Since there are no provisions for parties under disability in the Family Proceedings Courts (Children Act 1989) Rules 1991, the Official Solicitor can only act in the High Court or in a county court, pursuant to Part IX of the Family Proceedings Rules 1991. The Official Solicitor will shortly issue an updated Practice Note about his role for adults under disability who are the subject of declaratory proceedings in relation to their medical treatment or welfare.

Adults under disability

4 The Official Solicitor will, in the absence of any other willing and suitable person, act as next friend or guardian ad litem of an adult party under disability, a 'patient'. 'Patient' means someone who is incapable by reason of mental disorder of managing and administering his property and affairs (Family Proceedings Rules 1991, r 9.1). Medical evidence will usually be required before the Official Solicitor can consent to act and his staff can provide a standard form of medical certificate. Where there are practical difficulties in obtaining such medical evidence, the Official Solicitor should be consulted.

Non-subject children

5 Again in the absence of any other willing and suitable person, the Official Solicitor will act as next friend or guardian ad litem of a child party whose own welfare is not the subject of family proceedings (Family Proceedings Rules 1991, r 2.57, r 9.2 and r 9.5). The most common examples will be:

(a) a child who is also the parent of a child, and who is a respondent to a Children Act 1989 or Adoption Act 1976 application. If a child respondent is already represented by a CAFCASS officer in pending proceedings of which he or she is the subject, then the Official Solicitor will liaise with CAFCASS to agree the most appropriate arrangements;

(b) a child who wishes to make an application for a Children Act 1989 order naming another child (typically a contact order naming a sibling). The Official Solicitor will need to satisfy himself that the proposed proceedings would benefit the child applicant before proceeding;

(c) a child witness to some disputed factual issue in a children case and who may require intervener status. In such circumstances the need for party status and legal representation should be weighed in the light of *Re H (Care Proceedings: Intervener)* [2000] 1 FLR 775;

(d) a child party to a petition for a declaration of status under Part III of the Family Law Act 1986;

(e) a child intervener in divorce or ancillary relief proceedings (r 2.57 or r 9.5);

(f) a child applicant for, or respondent to, an application for an order under Part IV of the Family Law Act 1996. In the case of a child applicant, the Official Solicitor will need to satisfy himself that the proposed proceedings would benefit the child before pursuing them, with leave under Family Law Act 1996, s 43 if required.

6 Any children who are parties to Children Act 1989 or inherent jurisdiction proceedings may rely on the provisions of Family Proceedings Rules 1991, r 9.2A if they wish to instruct a solicitor without the intervention of a next friend or guardian ad litem. Rule 9.2A does not apply to Adoption Act 1976, Family Law Act 1986/1996 or Matrimonial Causes Act 1973 proceedings.

Older children who are also patients
7 Officers of CAFCASS will not be able to represent anyone who is over the age of 18. The Official Solicitor may therefore be the more appropriate next friend or guardian ad litem of a child who is also a patient and whose disability will persist beyond his or her eighteenth birthday, especially in non-emergency cases where the substantive hearing is unlikely to take place before the child's eighteenth birthday. The Official Solicitor may also be the more appropriate next friend or guardian ad litem in medical treatment cases such as sterilisation or vegetative state cases, in which his staff have particular expertise deriving from their continuing role for adult patients.

Advising the court
8 The Official Solicitor may be invited to act or instruct counsel as a friend of the court (amicus) if it appears to the court that such an invitation is more appropriately addressed to him rather than (or in addition to) CAFCASS Legal Services and Special Casework.

Liaison with CAFCASS
9 In cases of doubt or difficulty, staff of the Official Solicitor's office will liaise with staff of CAFCASS Legal Services and Special Casework to avoid duplication and ensure the most suitable arrangements are made.

Invitations to act in new cases
10 Solicitors who have been consulted by a child or an adult under disability (or by someone acting on their behalf, or concerned about their interests) should write to the Official Solicitor setting out the background to the proposed case and explaining why there is no other willing and suitable person to act as next friend or guardian ad

litem. Where the person concerned is an adult, medical evidence in the standard form of the Official Solicitor's medical certificate should be provided.

Invitations to act in pending proceedings
11 Where a case is already before the court, an order appointing the Official Solicitor should be expressed as being made subject to his consent. The Official Solicitor aims to provide a response to any invitation within 10 working days. He will be unable to consent to act for an adult until satisfied that the party is a 'patient'. A further directions appointment after 28 days may therefore be helpful. If he accepts appointment the Official Solicitor will need time to prepare the case on behalf of the child or patient and may wish to make submissions about any substantive hearing date. The following documents should be forwarded to the Official Solicitor without delay:

(*a*) a copy of the order inviting him to act (with a note of the reasons approved by the judge if appropriate);

(*b*) the court file;

(*c*) if available, a bundle with summary, statement of issues and chronology (as required by *President's Direction (Family Proceedings: Court Bundles)* (10 March 2000) [2000] 1 FLR 536).

Contacting the Official Solicitor
12 It is often helpful to discuss the question of appointment with the Official Solicitor or one of his staff by telephoning 020 7911 7127. Enquiries about family proceedings should be addressed to the Team Manager, Family Litigation.

The Official Solicitor's address is:

81 Chancery Lane
London WC2A 1DD

DX 0012 London Chancery Lane
Fax: 020 7911 7105
Email: officialsolicitor@offsol.gsi.gov.uk

Laurence Oates
Official Solicitor

Appendix 8

PRACTICE NOTE (1 MAY 2001)

Court Work – General

Citations: [2001] 2 FLR 158

Official Solicitor: Declaratory Proceedings: Medical and Welfare Decisions for Adults who Lack Capacity

1 This Practice Note supersedes Practice Notes dated June 1996 ((*Official Solicitor: Sterilisation*) [1996] 2 FLR 111) and 26 July 1996 ((*Official Solicitor to the Supreme Court: Vegetative State*) [1996] 2 FLR 375). It combines the guidance given in those earlier Practice Notes, and extends it to a wider range of medical and welfare disputes leading to litigation. This Practice Note deals only with adults who lack capacity. Medical treatment or welfare disputes about children will be dealt with under the Children Act 1989 or the inherent jurisdiction in relation to children (see *Practice Note (Official Solicitor: Appointment in Family Proceedings)* (2 April 2001) [2001] 2 FLR 155 and *CAFCASS Practice Note (Officers of CAFCASS Legal Services and Special Casework: Appointment in Family Proceedings)* (March 2001) [2001] 2 FLR 151).

Jurisdiction

2 The High Court has jurisdiction to make declarations as to the best interests of an adult who lacks decision-making capacity. The jurisdiction will be exercised when there is a serious justiciable issue requiring a decision by the court. It has been exercised in relation to a range of medical treatment issues, in particular sterilisation operations and the continuance of artificial nutrition and hydration. It has also been exercised in relation to residence and contact issues. The jurisdiction is comprehensively reviewed and analysed in *Re F (Adult: Court's Jurisdiction)* [2000] 2 FLR 512.

The need for court involvement

3 Case-law has established two categories of case that will in virtually all cases require the prior sanction of a High Court judge. The first is sterilisation of a person (whether a child or an adult) who cannot consent to the operation: *Re B (A Minor) (Wardship: Sterilisation)* [1988] AC 199, [1987] 2 FLR 314 and *Re F (Mental Patient: Sterilisation)* [1990] 2 AC 1, sub nom *Re F (Sterilization: Mental Patient)* [1989] 2 FLR 376. The second is the discontinuance of artificial nutrition and hydration for a patient in a vegetative state: *Airedale NHS Trust v Bland* [1993] AC 789, 805. Further guidance about sterilisation and vegetative state cases is given below. In all other cases, doctors and carers should seek advice from their own lawyers about the need to apply to the court. In the Official Solicitor's view, applications should be made where there are disputes or difficulties as to either the patient's capacity or the patient's best interests. Guidelines were handed down by the Court of Appeal in *St George's Healthcare NHS Trust v S; R v Collins and Others ex parte S* [1999] Fam 26, 63–65, [1998] 2 FLR 728,

758–760. It was stressed in that case that a declaration made without notice would be ineffective and ought not to be made.

The application

4 Applications should be made to the Family Division of the High Court (principal or district registry). The proceedings are not, however, 'family proceedings' for the purposes of the Civil Procedure Rules 1998, r 2.1(2). The Civil Procedure Rules 1998 will therefore apply.

The claim

5 In the Official Solicitor's view, the Part 8 alternative procedure is the more appropriate and a Part 8 claim form should be used. The claimant should file all evidence with the claim form. The Official Solicitor is unlikely to be in a position to file all his evidence with his acknowledgment of service. A directions hearing should therefore be fixed when the claim form is issued.

6 The relief sought should be declarations that:[1]

    (1) [the patient] lacks capacity to make a decision about ... [specify treatment or welfare decision at issue, eg 'having a kidney transplant' or 'where to live'].

    (2) It is [or is not] in the existing circumstances in the best interests of [the patient] for ... [specify treatment or other issue, eg 'him to undergo below-knee amputation of his left leg' or 'her to have contact with the claimant for at least 2 hours each week'].

1 See appendices below for suggested wording in sterilisation and PVS cases.

The evidence

7 The claimant must adduce evidence going to both capacity and best interests.

    (1) *Capacity*

        The court has no jurisdiction unless it is established that the patient is incapable of making a decision about the matter in issue. The test of capacity to consent to or refuse treatment is set out in *Re MB (Medical Treatment)* [1997] 2 FLR 426, 437. In the Official Solicitor's view, this test can be used for a wide range of decisions. Evidence from a psychiatrist or psychologist who has assessed the patient applying the *Re MB* test to the particular decision in question is generally required. It follows from the terms of the *Re MB* test that global psychometric test results are unlikely to be relevant. The Official Solicitor's experience is that references to the outdated and discredited concept of 'mental age' are of no assistance at all. It is important for the expert assessing capacity to advise whether the patient is likely to develop capacity to make personal decisions about the matter in issue in the future.

    (2) *Best interests*

        In any medical case, the claimant must adduce evidence from a responsible medical practitioner not only (i) that performing the particular operation would not be negligent, but also (ii) that it is necessary in the best interests of the patient: *Re A (Male Sterilisation)* [2000] 1 FLR 549, 555. The court's jurisdiction is to declare the best interests of the patient on the application of a welfare test analogous to that applied in wardship: *Re S (Sterilisation: Patient's Best Interests)* [2000] 2 FLR 389, 403. The judicial decision will incorporate broader ethical, social, moral and welfare considerations (above, at 401). Emotional, psychological and social benefit to the patient will be considered: *Re Y (Mental Patient: Bone Marrow Transplant)* [1997] Fam 110, [1996] 2 FLR 787. The court will wish to prepare a balance sheet listing the

advantages and disadvantages of the procedure for the patient. If potential advantages and disadvantages are to be relied on then the court will wish to assess in percentage terms the likelihood of them in fact occurring: *Re A (Male Sterilisation)* [2000] 1 FLR 549, 560.

The parties

8 The claimant should be the NHS Trust or other body responsible for the patient's care, although a claim may also be brought by a family member or other individual closely connected with the patient. The body with clinical or caring responsibility should in any event be made a party: *Re S (Hospital Patient: Court's Jurisdiction)* [1996] Fam 1, [1995] 1 FLR 1075.

9 The person concerned must always be a party and should normally be a defendant, with the Official Solicitor acting as litigation friend. The Official Solicitor has a standard form of medical certificate if there is any question about whether the person concerned is a 'patient' within the meaning of the Civil Procedure Rules 1998, r 21. If the Official Solicitor does not act as litigation friend, the court will wish to consider whether he should be joined as an ex officio defendant or invited to act as a friend of the court. The Official Solicitor is invariably asked to be involved in sterilisation and vegetative state cases.

The directions hearing

10 Unless the matter is urgent, the claimant should fix a directions hearing for no less than 8 weeks after the date of issue, to allow the Official Solicitor to make initial inquiries. The court should, if appropriate, be asked to hold the directions hearing in private to protect the interests of the patient: the Civil Procedure Rules 1998, r 39.2(3)(*d*). The court will use the directions hearing to:

(1) make orders where necessary to preserve the anonymity of the patient, family and other parties;

(2) set a timetable for the Official Solicitor to conduct inquiries, obtain expert evidence and file his statement or report;

(3) fix a further hearing, to serve either as a final hearing if the matter is unopposed or as a final directions hearing to fix a contested hearing.

The Official Solicitor's inquiries

11 The Official Solicitor's representative will always see the patient, review relevant medical/social work records and interview carers, family members and others close to the patient as appropriate.

12 The Official Solicitor will consider the patient's wishes and feelings, and will inquire as to any earlier views the patient may have expressed, either in writing or otherwise. The High Court may determine the effect of a purported advance statement as to future medical treatment: *Re T (Adult: Refusal of Treatment)* [1993] Fam 95, sub nom *Re T (An Adult) (Consent to Medical Treatment)* [1992] 2 FLR 458, *Re C (Refusal of Medical Treatment)* [1994] 1 FLR 31. A valid and applicable advance refusal of treatment may be determinative. Previously expressed wishes and feelings which do not amount to an effective advance decision will still be an important component in the best interests decision.

The final hearing

13 Any substantive hearing should be before a High Court judge of the Family Division. Cases proceeding unopposed may be disposed of without oral evidence. The final hearing may be in private if necessary to protect the interests of the patient: the Civil Procedure Rules 1998, r 39.2(3)(*d*). If the hearing is in public, there may be orders that the identities of parties and witnesses (other than expert witnesses) should

not be disclosed: the Civil Procedure Rules 1998, r 39.2(4). An order restricting publicity will continue to have effect notwithstanding the death of the patient, unless and until an application is made to discharge it: *Re C (Adult Patient: Publicity)* [1996] 2 FLR 251. The Official Solicitor will invite the court to make an appropriate order in relation to his costs.

Consultation with the Official Solicitor

14 Members of the Official Solicitor's legal staff are prepared to discuss adult medical and welfare cases before proceedings are issued. Inquiries should be addressed to a family litigation lawyer at:

The Official Solicitor
81 Chancery Lane
London WC2A 1DD

Telephone: 020 7911 7127
Fax: 020 7911 7105
Email: inquiries@offsol.gsi.gov.uk

Inquiries about *children* medical and welfare cases should be directed to:

CAFCASS Legal Services and Special Casework
Newspaper House
8–16 Great New Street
London EC4A 3BN

Telephone: 020 7904 0867
Fax: 020 7904 0868/9
Email: legal@cafcass.gsi.gov.uk

Staff of CAFCASS Legal will liaise with the Official Solicitor where it is unclear which office can best represent a child.

Laurence Oates
Official Solicitor

APPENDIX 1: STERILISATION CASES

1 If a sterilisation procedure is necessary for therapeutic as opposed to contraceptive purposes then there may be no need for an application to court: *Re GF (Medical Treatment)* [1992] 1 FLR 293. If, however, any case lies anywhere near the boundary line it should be referred to the court: *Re S (Sterilisation: Patient's Best Interests)* [2000] 2 FLR 389, 405.

The claim

2 The relief sought in relation to an adult should be declarations that:

(1) [The patient] lacks capacity to consent to an operation of … [specify procedure proposed, eg 'tubal occlusion by Filshie clips', or 'laparoscopic sub-total hysterectomy', or 'vasectomy'].
(2) It is in the existing circumstances in the best interests of [the patient] for her/ him to undergo an operation of … [specify procedure as above].

The evidence

3 The court must be satisfied that the patient lacks capacity and that the operation will promote the best interests of the patient, rather than the interests or convenience of the claimant, carers or public. In sterilisation cases, the best interests tests has at least three particular components.

(1) *Likelihood of pregnancy*
An operation must address a current real need. It must be shown that the patient is capable of conception and is having or is likely to have full sexual intercourse. In relation to a young woman who has no interest in human relationships with any sexual ingredient a high level of supervision is an appropriate protection: *Re LC (Medical Treatment: Sterilisation)* [1997] 2 FLR 258. Any risk of pregnancy should be identifiable rather than speculative: *Re S (Medical Treatment: Adult Sterilisation)* [1998] 1 FLR 944.

(2) *Damage deriving from conception and/or menstruation*
The physical and psychological consequences of pregnancy and childbirth for the patient should be analysed by obstetric and psychiatric experts. In the case of a male, these considerations will be different: *Re A (Male Sterilisation)* [2000] 1 FLR 549, 557. Psychiatric evidence as to the patient's likely ability to care for and/or have a fulfilling relationship with a child should be adduced. Evidence as to any child having a disability is likely to be irrelevant: *Re X (Adult Sterilisation)* [1998] 2 FLR 1124, 1129. If the proposed procedure is intended to affect the patient's menstruation, then evidence about any detriment caused by her current menstrual cycle must also be adduced.

(3) *Medical and surgical techniques*
The court will require a detailed analysis of all available and relevant methods of addressing any problems found to be substantiated under (1) and (2) above. This analysis should be performed by a doctor or doctors with expertise in the full range of available methods. The expert should explain the nature of each relevant method and then list its advantages and disadvantages (in particular, morbidity rates, mortality rates and failure rates) for the individual patient, taking into account any relevant aspects of her physical and psychological health. The Royal College of Obstetrics and Gynaecology has published relevant evidence-based clinical guidelines (No 4: *Male and Female Sterilisation*, April 1999 and No 5: *The Management of Menorrhagia in Secondary Care*, July 1999).

APPENDIX 2: PERMANENT VEGETATIVE STATE CASES

1 It is futile to provide medical treatment, including artificial nutrition and hydration, to a patient with no awareness of self or environment and no prospect of recovery: *Airedale NHS Trust v Bland* [1993] AC 789, 869, [1993] 1 FLR 1026, 1040. The purpose of the proceedings is to establish whether the patient is in this condition. It is not appropriate to apply to court to discontinue artificial feeding and hydration until the condition is judged to be permanent. Diagnostic guidelines are not statutory provisions and a precise label may not be of importance. The court's concern is whether there is any awareness whatsoever or any possibility of change: *Re D (Medical Treatment)* [1998] 1 FLR 411, 420 and *Re H (A Patient)* [1998] 2 FLR 36. The approach of the court has been reviewed in the light of the Human Rights Act 1998 and held to be compatible with Convention rights (European Convention for the Protection of Human Rights and Fundamental Freedoms 1950): *NHS Trust A v M; NHS Trust B v H* [2001] 2 WLR 942. There has as yet been no decided case dealing with the discontinuance of artificial feeding and hydration for an adult patient with any (however minimal) awareness of self or environment.

The claim
2 All claims in these cases should be issued in the Principal Registry and will normally be heard by the President of the Family Division unless she releases the case to another Family Division judge. The relief sought should be declarations that:

(1) [The patient] lacks capacity to consent to continued life-sustaining treatment measures and is in the permanent vegetative state.
(2) It is not in the existing circumstances in the best interests of [the patient] to be given life-sustaining medical treatment measures (including ventilation, nutrition and hydration by artificial means) and such measures may lawfully be discontinued.
(3) It is in [the patient's] best interests to be given such treatment and nursing care whether at hospital or elsewhere under medical supervision as may be appropriate to ensure he/she retains the greatest dignity until such time as his/her life comes to an end.

The medical evidence
3 The diagnosis should be made in accordance with the most up-to-date generally accepted guidelines for the medical profession. A review by a working group of the Royal College of Physicians has been endorsed by the Conference of Medical Royal Colleges (*The Permanent Vegetative State*, Royal College of Physicians Publication Unit, 1996; with addendum published in (1997) 31 J R Coll Physns 260). The review concludes that the diagnosis of permanent vegetative state should not be made until the patient has been in a continuing vegetative state following head injury for 12 months or following other causes of brain damage for 6 months. The addendum to the review emphasises that there is no urgency in making the diagnosis and the assessors should take into account descriptions given by relatives, carers and nursing staff who spend most time with the patient. The *International Working Party Report on the Vegetative State* (1996), produced by the Royal Hospital for Neuro-disability, sets out in an appendix a range of vegetative presentations.

4 The claimant should, as a minimum, adduce evidence from (i) the treating physician and (ii) a neurologist or other expert experienced in assessing disturbances of consciousness. Both should deal with the diagnosis and their professional judgment of whether continued treatment would be in the patient's best interests. The duties of doctors making the diagnosis are described in the Royal College of Physicians review.

5 The court will generally wish to see at least two reports from experts, one of whom must be independent of the treating clinical team and claimant. The Official Solicitor will usually commission the second expert report.

Other evidence
6 The claimant should also adduce evidence about the views of family members. The views of family members or others close to the patient cannot act as a veto to an application but they must be taken fully into account by the court: *Re G (Persistent Vegetative State)* [1995] 2 FCR 46, 51.

The final hearing
7 It is usual for the final hearing to be in public, with protection for the identities of parties and witnesses. Even if the matter is unopposed, it may be appropriate for at least one expert to attend to give oral evidence. Family members need not attend if this would cause distress.

Appendix 9

PRESIDENT'S DIRECTION (5 APRIL 2004)

Children

Citations: [2004] 1 FLR 1188

Representation of Children in Family Proceedings Pursuant to Family Proceedings Rules 1991, Rule 9.5

1 The proper conduct and disposal of proceedings concerning a child which are not specified proceedings within the meaning of s 41 of the Children Act 1989 may require the child to be made a party. Rule 9.5 of the Family Proceedings Rules 1991 ('FPR') provides for the appointment of a guardian ad litem ('a guardian') for a child party unless the child is of sufficient understanding and can participate as a party in the proceedings without a guardian, as permitted by FPR r 9.2A.

2 Making the child a party to the proceedings is a step that will be taken only in cases which involve an issue of significant difficulty and consequently will occur in only a minority of cases. Before taking the decision to make the child a party, consideration should be given to whether an alternative route might be preferable, such as asking an officer of the Children and Family Court Advisory and Support Service ('CAFCASS') to carry out further work or by making a referral to social services or possibly, by obtaining expert evidence.

3 The decision to make the child a party will always be exclusively that of the judge, made in the light of the facts and circumstances of the particular case. The following are offered, solely by way of guidance, as circumstances which may justify the making of an order:

    3.1 Where a CAFCASS officer has notified the court that in his opinion the child should be made a party (see FPR r 4.11B(6)).

    3.2 Where the child has a standpoint or interests which are inconsistent with or incapable of being represented by any of the adult parties.

    3.3 Where there is an intractable dispute over residence or contact, including where all contact has ceased, or where there is irrational but implacable hostility to contact or where the child may be suffering harm associated with the contact dispute.

    3.4 Where the views and wishes of the child cannot be adequately met by a report to the court.

    3.5 Where an older child is opposing a proposed course of action.

    3.6 Where there are complex medical or mental health issues to be determined or there are other unusually complex issues that necessitate separate representation of the child.

    3.7 Where there are international complications outside child abduction, in particular where it may be necessary for there to be discussions with overseas authorities or a foreign court.

    3.8 Where there are serious allegations of physical, sexual or other abuse in relation to the child or there are allegations of domestic violence not capable of being resolved with the help of a CAFCASS officer.

    3.9 Where the proceedings concern more than one child and the welfare of the children is in conflict or one child is in a particularly disadvantaged position.

    3.10 Where there is a contested issue about blood testing.

4 It must be recognised that separate representation of the child may result in a delay in the resolution of the proceedings. When deciding whether to direct that a child be made a party, the court will take into account the risk of delay or other facts adverse to the welfare of the child. The court's primary consideration will be the best interests of the child.

5 When a child is made a party and a guardian is to be appointed:

    5.1 Consideration should first be given to appointing an officer of CAFCASS as guardian. Before appointing an officer, the court will cause preliminary enquiries to be made of CAFCASS. For the procedure, reference should be made to *CAFCASS Practice Note (Representation of Children in Family Proceedings Pursuant to Family Proceedings Rules 1991, Rule 9.5)* (6 April 2004) [2004] 1 FLR 1190.

    5.2 If CAFCASS is unable to provide a guardian without delay, or if for some other reason the appointment of a CAFCASS officer is not appropriate, FPR r 9.5(1) makes further provision for the appointment of a guardian.

6 In cases proceeding in a county court, the court may, at the same time as deciding whether to join a child as a party, consider whether the nature of the case or the complexity or importance of the issues require transfer of the case to the High Court.

7 Issued with the concurrence and approval of the Lord Chancellor.

Elizabeth Butler-Sloss
President

Appendix 10

CAFCASS PRACTICE NOTE (6 APRIL 2004)

Children

Citations: [2004] 1 FLR 1190

Representation of Children in Family Proceedings Pursuant to Family Proceedings Rules 1991, Rule 9.5

Introduction
1 This Practice Note is issued in conjunction with the *President's Direction (Representation of Children in Family Proceedings Pursuant to Family Proceedings Rules 1991, Rule 9.5)* (5 April 2004) [2004] 1 FLR 1188 with the President's approval. It supersedes *CAFCASS Practice Note (Officers of CAFCASS Legal Services and Special Casework: Appointment in Family Proceedings)* (March 2001) [2001] 2 FLR 151.

Appointment of CAFCASS officers in private law proceedings pursuant to rule 9.5 Family Proceedings Rules 1991 ('FPR 1991')
2 Where the court has decided to appoint an officer of CAFCASS as guardian the preferred order should simply state that '[name of the child] is made party to the proceedings and pursuant to Family Proceedings Rules 1991, r 9.5 an officer of CAFCASS be appointed as his/her guardian'. It is also helpful for CAFCASS to know whether the court considers there is any reason why any CAFCASS officer who has dealt with the matter so far should not continue to deal with it in the role of guardian.

3 The decision about which particular officer of CAFCASS to allocate as guardian is a matter for CAFCASS.

4 In cases proceeding in the High Court, a copy of the court file, including the order making the rule 9.5 appointment and any information about the record of the court's reasons, should be sent for the attention of The Manager, CAFCASS Legal, 1st Floor, Newspaper House, 8–16 Great New Street, London, EC4A 3BN or by Document Exchange to DX 144 London Chancery Lane. If the appointment of a CAFCASS officer as guardian is urgent then the judge or a member of the Court Service is encouraged, if possible, to telephone on 020 7904 0867 to discuss the matter before an order is made; alternatively, the order and any information about the court's reasons can be faxed to CAFCASS Legal on 020 7904 0868.

5 In cases proceeding in the county court, the order making the rule 9.5 appointment should be faxed to the local CAFCASS office responsible for private law cases unless the case falls within any of the categories identified in paragraph 10 below when it should be referred to CAFCASS Legal following the procedure in paragraph 4 above.

6 In either case CAFCASS will make a decision within five working days of receipt of the papers from the court about whether it will provide an officer of the Service locally

(as will be the case in most county court cases) or from CAFCASS Legal (as will be the case in most High Court cases) to act as guardian. It is the responsibility of the local CAFCASS service manager and CAFCASS Legal to liaise whenever necessary to ensure that the most appropriate CAFCASS officer is appointed as guardian.

7 The CAFCASS office that is to be responsible for the matter will notify the court of the name and professional address and telephone number of the particular officer who will act as guardian. If for whatever reason there is likely to be any significant delay in an officer of the Service being made available CAFCASS will notify the court accordingly to enable the court to consider whether some other proper person should instead be appointed as guardian.

8 If the CAFCASS officer to be appointed as guardian is based at CAFCASS Legal there will normally be no need for a solicitor for the child also to be appointed as the litigation will usually be conducted in-house pursuant to section 15 of the Criminal Justice and Court Services Act 2000.

9 If the CAFCASS officer to be appointed as guardian is based at a local CAFCASS office then legal representation will be provided either through CAFCASS Legal or by the appointment of a local solicitor to act for the child. It is normally the guardian's responsibility to appoint a solicitor pursuant to the combined effect of FPR 1991, rr 9.5(6) and 4.11A(1). A local solicitor can apply for legal aid for the child in the ordinary way enabling the guardian (funded by CAFCASS) and the child's solicitor (funded by the Legal Services Commission) to work together in the same way as they routinely do in specified proceedings.

Cases that should be referred to CAFCASS Legal whether or not involving an appointment pursuant to FPR 1991 rule 9.5 and whether proceeding in the High Court or the county court
10 Whilst the great majority of cases are likely to continue to be referred by courts to local CAFCASS offices the following categories of case should be referred to CAFCASS Legal:

10.1 Cases in which the Children's Divisions of the Official Solicitor or CAFCASS Legal previously acted for the child;

10.2 Exceptionally complex international cases where legal or other substantial enquiries abroad will be necessary or where there is a dispute as to which country's courts should have jurisdiction over the child's affairs (for example, a case in which two children previously the subject of adoption and then care proceedings in two other countries were brought to England illegally and made the subject of further care proceedings here);

10.3 Exceptionally complex adoption cases (for example, where there is a need to investigate a suspected illegal payment or placement; adoption proceedings following a mistake during fertility treatment involving the use of unauthorised sperm; and the circumstances arising in *Flintshire County Council v K* [2001] 2 FLR 476);

10.4 All medical treatment cases where the child is old enough to have views which need to be taken into account, or where there are particularly difficult ethical issues such as the withdrawal of treatment, unless the issue arises in existing proceedings already being handled locally when the preferred arrangement will usually be for the matter to continue to be dealt with locally but with additional advice provided by CAFCASS Legal;

10.5 Any free-standing human rights applications pursuant to section 7(1)(*a*) of the Human Rights Act 1998 in which it is thought that it may be possible and appropriate for any part to be played by CAFCASS or its officers;

10.6 Any additional categories of case for referral to CAFCASS Legal that may from time to time be added to this list.

11 In such cases the referral to CAFCASS Legal should follow a similar procedure to that set out in paragraph 4 above.

Other cases that may be referred to CAFCASS Legal
12 Other family proceedings in which the welfare of children is or may be in question may be referred to CAFCASS Legal where they are exceptionally difficult, unusual or sensitive (for example, a care case in which death threats were made against the child and other professionals necessitating special security measures including false identities for some of those under threat; and an adoption case in which there had been serious misconduct by the local CAFCASS officer originally appointed).

CAFCASS Legal acting as advocate to the court
13 CAFCASS Legal may be invited to act or instruct counsel to appear as advocate to the court in family proceedings in which the welfare of children is or may be in question. (for example in a recent case an issue arose about the extent of the court's powers in Hague Convention proceedings to give directions designed to prevent further abduction pending trial, which led to CAFCASS Legal briefing counsel as advocate to the court).

14 Sometimes it will be more appropriate for the Attorney General or the Official Solicitor to fulfil this role. Reference should be made to the Memorandum on Requests for the appointment of an Advocate to the Court issued by the Attorney General and the Lord Chief Justice on 19 December 2001.

Liaison between CAFCASS Legal and the Official Solicitor
15 In cases in which there is any doubt as to whether CAFCASS or the Official Solicitor should provide representation, staff of CAFCASS Legal will liaise with staff of the Official Solicitor's office to ensure that the most suitable arrangements are made.

Provision of general assistance by CAFCASS Legal
16 CAFCASS Legal is available to provide legal advice to officers of CAFCASS, whether employed or self-employed, in connection with their professional responsibilities.

17 CAFCASS Legal is also available to offer informal advice to judges and other professionals engaged in family proceedings in which the welfare of children is or may be in question without necessarily being appointed as a guardian or advocate to the court (for instance in relation to passport applications for accommodated children).

18 Lawyers at CAFCASS Legal take it in turn to carry a mobile telephone through which they can be contacted any day of the year by the High Court out of hours duty judge if their help is needed, for instance in relation to a medical treatment emergency.

Charles Prest
Director of Legal Services

CAFCASS

Appendix 11

PROTOCOL (JUNE 2003)

Children

Judicial Case Management in Public Law Children Act Cases

Citations: [2003] 2 FLR 719

Foreword

by the President of the Family Division, the Lord Chancellor and the Secretary of State for Education and Skills

After over a decade of otherwise successful implementation of the Children Act there remains a large cloud in the sky in the form of delay. Delay in care cases has persisted for too long. The average care case lasts for almost a year. This is a year in which the child is left uncertain as to his or her future, is often moved between several temporary care arrangements, and the family and public agencies are left engaged in protracted and complex legal wranglings. Though a fair and effective process must intervene before a child is taken from its parents, we believe it is essential that unnecessary delay is eliminated and that better outcomes for children and families are thereby achieved. This protocol sets a guideline of 40 weeks for the conclusion of care cases. Some cases will need to take longer than this, but many more cases should take less.

The causes of delay have become clear from the Scoping Study published by the Department in March 2002, and through the work of the Advisory Committee that finalised this protocol. There is now a real enthusiasm among all the agencies involved for tackling these causes. Other work has begun and the momentum is building. Overt efforts have been made locally, both by Care Centres and by Family Proceedings Courts. Additional judicial sitting days for care work are being found. Measures are being taken to help improve the performance of CAFCASS. This protocol will form the backbone of these other efforts.

The Advisory Committee has involved all of the agencies and organisations that have a significant role to play in the care process and has striven to produce a consensus as to the content of this protocol. We are grateful to all the members of the Committee and to everyone else who engaged with the consultation process.

This protocol has been prepared on the basis that a change in the whole approach to case management and a clarification of focus, among all those involved in care cases, is the best way forward. This protocol is not a fresh start – it is a collation and distillation of best practice – we do ask you to engage it wholeheartedly with all your usual enthusiasm and dedication.

Dame Elizabeth Butler-Sloss
President

Lord Falconer of Thoroton
The Secretary of State for Constitutional Affairs and Lord Chancellor

Rt Hon Charles Clarke MP
Secretary of State for Education and Skills

1

The Application

Day 1 to Day 3

Objective:
LA to provide sufficient information to identify issues/make early welfare and case management decisions

Action:

- LA file Application in Form C1/C3 ***on Day 1*** [1.1]
- Directions on Issue by Court
  - fixing the hearing
  - Appointment of Guardian ***on Day 1*** [1.2]
- Allocation of Guardian by Cafcass ***by Day 3*** [1.2-3]
- Appointment of Solicitor for the child
  - no appointment of Guardian
  - Notification to parties of name of Guardian/solicitor ***on Day 3*** [1.4]
- LA File and serve Documents ***by Day 3*** [1.5]

▶

2

The First Hearing in the FPC

On (or before) Day 6

Objective:
To decide what immediate steps are necessary/contested ICO/preventing delay/appropriate court

Action:

- Parties [2.2]
- Contested Interim Care Orders [2.3]
- Transfer [2.4] and transfer arrangements [2.5]

Initial Case Management and Checklist [2.6] including:
- Case Management Conference
- Final Hearing
- Pre-Hearing Review
- Evidence
- Disclosure
- Core Assessment
- Standard Directions Form

by Day 6

▶ **5 days**

3

Allocation Hearing & Directions

By Day 11 (CC) 15(HC)

Objective:
To make provision for continuous/consistent judicial case management

Action:

Care Centre court officer shall:

- Allocate 1-2 Judges (including final hearing judge) [3.2]
- Attach SDF with proposed date for CMC, Final Hearing and PHR ***by Day 8*** [3.2]:

Judge (at Allocation Hearing) considers:

- Transfer, ICO, CM Checklist, dates for CMC, Final Hearing, PHR, Disclosure, Core Assessment, SDF ***by Day 11*** [3.4]
- Case Management Documents [3.4]

▼ **1 Day** ▼

In High Court:

- Court Officer ***by Day 12*** [3.6]
- Case Management Judge ***by Day 15*** [3.7]

Within 54 days

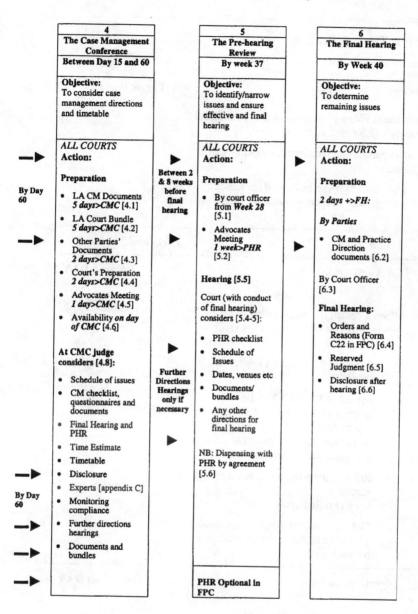

4		5		6
The Case Management Conference		**The Pre-hearing Review**		**The Final Hearing**
Between Day 15 and 60		**By week 37**		**By Week 40**
Objective: To consider case management directions and timetable		**Objective:** To identify/narrow issues and ensure effective and final hearing		**Objective:** To determine remaining issues
ALL COURTS **Action:**		*ALL COURTS* **Action:**		*ALL COURTS* **Action:**
Preparation	**Between 2 & 8 weeks before final hearing**	**Preparation**		**Preparation**
• LA CM Documents *5 days>CMC* [4.1]		• By court officer from *Week 28* [5.1]		*2 days +>FH:* **By Parties**
• LA Court Bundle *5 days>CMC* [4.2]		• Advocates Meeting *1 week>PHR* [5.2]		• CM and Practice Direction documents [6.2]
• Other Parties' Documents *2 days>CMC* [4.3]		**Hearing [5.5]**		By Court Officer [6.3]
• Court's Preparation *2 days>CMC* [4.4]		Court (with conduct of final hearing) considers [5.4-5]:		**Final Hearing:**
• Advocates Meeting *1 day>CMC* [4.5]		• PHR checklist		• Orders and Reasons (Form C22 in FPC) [6.4]
• Availability *on day of CMC* [4.6]		• Schedule of Issues		• Reserved Judgment [6.5]
At CMC judge considers [4.8]:	**Further Directions Hearings only if necessary**	• Dates, venues etc		• Disclosure after hearing [6.6]
• Schedule of issues		• Documents/ bundles		
• CM checklist, questionnaires and documents		• Any other directions for final hearing		
• Final Hearing and PHR		NB: Dispensing with PHR by agreement [5.6]		
• Time Estimate				
• Timetable				
• Disclosure				
• Experts [appendix C]				
• Monitoring compliance				
• Further directions hearings				
• Documents and bundles				
		PHR Optional in FPC		

By Day 60

By Day 60

Days

Where target times are expressed in days, the days are 'court business days' in accordance with the Rules (principles of application para 10)

STEP 1: The Application

Objective   **Target time: by DAY 3**

To provide sufficient information about the Local
Authority's (LA) case to enable:

- The parties and the Court to identify the
  issues
- The Court to make early welfare and case
  management decisions about the child

Action	**Party and Timing**
1.1 **LA Application**	LA **on DAY 1**
When a decision is made to apply for a care or supervision order the **LA** shall: • File with the Court an application in **form C1** • Set out in **form C13** under 'Reasons' a summary of all facts and matters relied upon, in particular, those necessary to satisfy the threshold criteria and/or • Refer in the Reasons to any annexed schedules setting out the facts and matters relied upon • **Not** state that the Reasons are those contained in the evidence filed or to be filed.	
1.2 **Directions on Issue**	Court **on DAY 1**
On the day the application is filed (**DAY 1**) the **Court** shall: • Issue the application • Issue a notice in **form C6** to the LA fixing a time and a date for the First Hearing which shall be not later than on **DAY 6** • Appoint a Guardian (unless satisfied that it is not necessary to do so to safeguard the child's interests)	

Action	Party and Timing
• Inform CAFCASS of the decision to appoint and the request to allocate a Guardian	

1.3	**Allocation of the Guardian by CAFCASS**	CAFCASS **by DAY 3**

Within **2 days** of issue (by **DAY 3**) **CAFCASS** shall inform the Court of:

- The name of the allocated Guardian
  or
- The likely date upon which an application will be made.

1.4	**Appointment of the Solicitor for the Child**	Guardian **on DAY 3**

When a Guardian is allocated the **Guardian** shall on that day:

- Appoint a solicitor for the child
- Inform the Court of the name of the solicitor appointed
- In the event that the Guardian's allocation is delayed and the Court has already appointed a solicitor, ensure that effective legal representation is maintained

Where a Guardian is not allocated within **2 days** of issue, the **Court** shall on **DAY 3**:   FPC   **on DAY 3**

- Consider when a Guardian will be allocated
- Decide whether to appoint a solicitor for the child

In any event on the day the appointment is made the **Court** shall: FPC   **on DAY 3**

Action	**Party and Timing**

- Notify all parties on **form C47** of the names of the Guardian and/or the solicitor for the child who have been appointed.

1.5 LA Documents	**LA by DAY 3**

Within **2 days** of issue (by **DAY 3**) the **LA** shall file and serve on all parties, the solicitor for the child and CAFCASS the following documents:

- The **forms C1 and C13** and any supplementary forms and notices issued by the Court

- Any relevant **court orders** relating to the child (together with the relevant Justices Facts and Reasons in **form C22** and any relevant **judgments** that exist)

- The **initial social work statement (appendix B/3)**

- The **social work chronology (appendix B/2)**

- The **core or initial assessment** reports (**appendix F**)

- Any other **additional evidence** including specialist assessments or reports which then exist and which are relied upon by the LA.

STEP 2: The First Hearing in the FPC

Objective	**Target time: by DAY 6**

To decide what immediate steps are necessary to safeguard the welfare of the child by:

- Determining contested interim care order applications/with whom the child will live

- Identifying how to prevent delay

- Identifying the appropriate Court

- Transferring to the appropriate Court

Action	Party and Timing
2.1 **The First Hearing**	FPC **on DAY 6**

The First Hearing shall take place in the Family Proceedings Court (FPC) on or before **DAY 6**. At every First Hearing the **FPC** shall:

- Consider who should be a **party** to the proceedings (step 2.2)

- Make arrangements for contested **interim care applications** to be determined (step 2.3)

- Consider whether the proceedings should be **transferred** to the Care Centre or another FPC (step 2.4)

- Where the proceedings are not transferred, make **initial case management** decisions (step 2.6).

2.2 **Parties and Service**	FPC **on DAY 6**

At the First Hearing the **FPC** shall:

- Obtain confirmation that all those who are entitled to be parties have been served

- Consider whether any other person should be joined as a party

- Give directions relating to party status and the service of documents upon parties.

2.3 **Contested Interim Care Orders**	FPC **on DAY 6**

In any proceedings where the application for an interim care order (ICO) is not agreed at the First Hearing, the **FPC** shall:

- Decide whether to grant an order and if so what order; or

- List the application for an urgent contested interim hearing in an FPC prior to the Case Management Conference (CMC); and

Action	Party and Timing
• Give such case management directions as are necessary to ensure that the interim hearing will be effective; or • Transfer the proceedings to be heard at the Care Centre.	

Action	Party and Timing
2.4 Urgency and Transfer	**FPC on DAY 6**

At the First Hearing the **FPC** shall:

- Hear submissions as to complexity, gravity and urgency

- Consider whether transfer to another Court is appropriate and in any event determine any application made by a party for transfer

- Give reasons for any transfer decision made and record the information provided by the parties relating to transfer on **form C22** (including any intention to apply for transfer to the High Court)

- Send the court file and the Order of transfer in **form C49** to the receiving court within **1 day** of the First Hearing (by **DAY 7**)

Action	Party and Timing
2.5 Proceedings Transferred to the Care Centre	**FPC on DAY 6**

Where a decision is made to transfer to the Care Centre, the **FPC** shall:

- In accordance with the arrangements set out in the **Care Centre Plan** (CCP) and the **FPC Plan** (FPCP) (**appendix E**), immediately inform the court officer at the Care Centre of the transfer and of the reasons set out on **form C22**

- Obtain a date and time from the court officer for an **Allocation Hearing**/contested interim hearing in the Care Centre which shall be between **3** and **5** days of the decision to transfer (by **DAY 11**)

Action	Party and Timi

- Notify the parties of the Care Centre to which the proceedings are transferred and of the date and time of the Allocation Hearing/contested interim hearing

- Direct the LA or the child's solicitor to prepare a **case synopsis (appendix B/1)** which shall be filed with the Care Centre and served within **2 days** of the First Hearing in the FPC (by **DAY 8**)

- Except as to disclosure of documents, make only those **case management directions upon transfer** as are agreed with the Care Centre as set out in the CCP and the FPCP.

2.6   **Case Management in the FPC**   FPC   on

In any case where the proceedings are **NOT** transferred to the care centre the **FPC** shall at the First Hearing:

- Consider the **case management checklist (appendix A/3)**

- Fix a date and time for a **Case Management Conference** (CMC) in the FPC within **54 days** of the First Hearing (between **DAYS 15 and 60**) unless all of the case management decisions set out at step 4.8 of this protocol can be taken at the First Hearing and the application can be listed for Final Hearing

- Fix a date for the **Final Hearing** or if it is not possible to do so fix a hearing window (either of which shall be not later than in the **3 week** period commencing the **37th WEEK** after the application was issued)

- Consider whether a **Pre Hearing Review** (PHR) is necessary and if so fix a PHR not later than **2 weeks** and no earlier than **8 weeks** before the Final Hearing date/window

Action	Party and Timing

- Give such **case management directions** as are necessary to ensure that all steps will have been taken prior to the CMC to enable it to be effective, in particular:

    - that a **statement of evidence** from each party (including the child where of sufficient age and understanding, but excluding the child's Guardian) is filed and served replying to the facts alleged and the proposals made by the LA in the initial social work statement

    - whether directions as to full and frank **disclosure** of all relevant documents need to be given and in any event give directions where necessary to ensure that the disclosure of relevant documents by the LA occurs within **20 days** of the First Hearing (by **DAY 26**)

    - whether a **core assessment** (**appendix F**) exists or should be directed to be undertaken by the LA before the CMC

    - Record on the **Standard Directions Form (SDF)** (**appendix A/1**) the Court's case management decisions and reasons and serve the directions given on the parties

2.7	The **FPC** shall give a direction at the First Hearing that **no further documents** shall be filed without the Court's permission unless in support of a new application or in accordance with case management directions given at that hearing (the Court will consider directions relating to the filing of comprehensive evidence and documents at the CMC)

STEP 3: Allocation Hearing & Directions

Objective   Target time: by DAY 11

To make provision for continuous and consistent
judicial case management

Action	Party and Timing
3.1 Following Transfer	Care Centre **from DAY 6**

Following transfer to the **Care
Centre** or to the **High Court** all
further hearings in the proceedings
shall be conducted:

- So as to ensure **judicial
  continuity of case
  management** in accordance
  with the protocol;

- By one or not more than 2
  judges who are identified as
  case management judges in the
  CCP (**appendix E/1**), one of
  whom may be and where
  possible should be the judge
  who will conduct the Final
  Hearing

Action	Party and Timing
3.2 Allocation in the Care Centre	Court Officer **by DAY 8**

Within **2 days** of the order
transferring proceedings to the Care
Centre (normally by **DAY 8**) the
court officer shall:

- Allocate one and not more than
  two **case management judges**
  (one of whom may be and
  where possible should be the
  Judge who will conduct the
  Final Hearing) to case manage
  the proceedings in accordance
  with the protocol and the CCP

- Where possible, identify the
  judge who is to be the **Final
  Hearing judge**

Action	Party and Timing

- Upon receipt of the court file from the FPC, attach to the file the **form C22** issued by the FPC, the **case synopsis (appendix B/1)** and a **Standard Directions Form (SDF) (appendix A/1)** and complete the SDF to the extent only of:

  - the names of the **allocated and identified judges**

  - the proposed date of the **CMC** (which shall be within **54 days** of the date of the First Hearing in the FPC ie between **DAYS 15 and 60**)

  - the proposed **Final Hearing** date or hearing window (which shall be not later than in the **3 week** period commencing the **37th WEEK** after the application was issued)

  - the proposed date of the **PHR** (which shall be not later than **2 weeks** and no earlier than **8 weeks** before the Final Hearing/trial window)

- Inform the case management judge in writing:

  - of any other circumstances of **urgency**

  - of any contested interim hearing for an **ICO**

  - of any application to **transfer to the High Court**

  - of the date and time of the **Allocation Hearing** (which shall be between **3 and 5 days** of the First Hearing in the FPC ie by **DAY 11**)

Action	Party and Timing
• Notify the parties of the date, time and venue fixed for the Allocation Hearing, together with the identity of the allocated/nominated judges	

Action	Party and Timing	
3.3 **Section 37 Request for a Report and Transfer to a Care Centre**	Court Officer	**within 2 days of the order of transfer**

Where in any family proceedings a Court decides to direct an appropriate LA to investigate a child's circumstances, the Court shall follow the guidance set out at **appendix G**.

Where, following a section 37 request for a report, proceedings are transferred to the Care Centre:

- The **transferring court** shall make a record of the Court's reasons for the transfer on **form C22** and the **court officer** of the transferring court shall send the court file, the order of transfer in **form C49** and the record of reasons to the Care Centre within **1 day** of the order

- The **court officer** in the care centre shall within **2 days** of the order transferring the proceedings take the steps set out at paragraph 3.2 and shall also:

  - inform the case management judge in writing of the transfer (and such circumstances as are known)

  - request the case management judge to consider giving directions as to the **appointment of a Guardian and/or a solicitor for the child** at or before the Allocation Hearing

Action	Party and Timing
• notify all parties on **form C47** of the names of the Guardian and/or the solicitor for the child when they are appointed	
• inform the LA solicitor or the child's solicitor of the requirement that a **case synopsis (appendix B/1)** be prepared which shall be filed with the care centre and served not later than **2 days** before the date fixed for the Allocation Hearing.	

3.4 **Allocation Hearing**	Case **by DAY 11** Management Judge

The Allocation Hearing in the Care Centre shall take place between **3 and 5 days** of the First Hearing in the FPC (by **DAY 11**). At the Allocation Hearing the **case management judge** shall:

• Consider whether the proceedings should be **transferred to the High Court or re-transferred to the FPC**

• Determine any **contested interim application** for a care or supervision order

• Where **the proceedings have been transferred from a court following a section 37 request** consider:

    • whether directions should be given to appoint a Guardian and/or a solicitor for the child in accordance with steps 1.2 to 1.4 of the protocol

Action	Party and Timing
• whether any directions need to be given for the filing and service of LA documents in accordance with step 1.5 of the protocol	
• Consider the **case management checklist (appendix A/3)**	
• Fix a date and time for a **CMC** which shall be within **54 days** of the First Hearing in the FPC (between **DAYS 15 and 60**)	
• Fix a date for the **Final Hearing** and confirm the identity of the Final Hearing judge or if it is not possible to do so fix a hearing window (either of which shall be not later than in the **3 week** period commencing the **37th WEEK** after the application was issued)	
• Fix a date and time for a **PHR** which shall be not later than **2 weeks** and no earlier than **8 weeks** before the Final Hearing date or window	
• Give such **case management directions** as are necessary to ensure that all steps will have been taken prior to the CMC to enable it to be effective, in particular:	
• that a **statement of evidence from each party** (including the child where of sufficient age and understanding, but excluding the child's Guardian) is filed and served replying to the facts alleged and the proposals made by the LA in the initial social work statement	

Action	Party and Timing

- whether directions as to full and frank **disclosure** of all relevant documents need to be given and in any event give directions where necessary to ensure that the disclosure of relevant documents by the LA occurs within **20 days** of the First Hearing (by **DAY 26**)

- whether a **core assessment (appendix F)** exists or should be directed to be undertaken by the LA before the CMC

• Having regard to the *Practice Direction (Family Proceedings: Court Bundles)* [2000] 1 FLR 536 (**appendix D**), if applicable, give directions to the LA setting out which of the following **case management documents** in addition to the **case management questionnaire (appendix A/2)** are to be filed and served for use at the CMC:

- a **schedule of findings of fact** which the Court is invited to make (in particular so as to satisfy the threshold criteria)

- any update to the **social work chronology (appendix B/2)** that may be required

- the **initial care plan (appendix F)**

- if there is a question of law; a **skeleton argument with authorities**

- a **summary of the background** (only if necessary to supplement the case synopsis)

Action	Party and Timing

- an **advocate's chronology** (only if necessary to supplement the social work chronology or the case synopsis)

- Having regard to **appendix D**, give directions to the LA setting out the form of **bundle or documents index** that the Court requires

- Complete the **SDF (appendix A/1)** to record the Court's case management decisions and reasons.

3.5   Case Management Questionnaire   Court Officer   **on DAY 12**

Within **1 day** of the Allocation Hearing (on **DAY 12**) the **court officer** shall serve on each party:

- the completed **SDF** together with a

- **case management questionnaire (appendix A/2)**.

3.6   Allocation in the High Court   Court Officer   **on DAY 12**

Where an application is transferred to the High Court, the **court officer** shall within **1 day** of the Allocation Hearing (on **DAY 12**):

- In consultation with the Family Division Liaison Judge (or if the proceedings are transferred to the RCJ, the Clerk of the Rules) allocate a judge of the High Court who shall be the **case management judge** (and who may be the judge who will conduct the final hearing) to case manage the proceedings in accordance with the protocol and the CCP

Action	Party and Timing

- If necessary to accord with the CCP, allocate a **second case management judge** in the Care Centre who shall be responsible to the allocated High Court judge for case management of the proceedings

- Where possible, identify a judge of the High Court to be the **Final Hearing judge**

- Attach to the court file the **form C22** issued by the FPC, the **case synopsis (appendix B/1)** and a **SDF (appendix A/1)** and complete the SDF to the extent only of:

  - the names of the **allocated judges**

  - the date of the **CMC** (which shall be within **54 days** of the date of the First Hearing in the FPC ie between **DAYS 15 and 60**)

  - the proposed **Final Hearing** date or window (which shall be not later than in the **3 week** period commencing the **37th WEEK** after the application was issued) Action

    - the proposed date of the **PHR** (which shall be not later than **2 weeks** and no earlier than **8 weeks** before the Final Hearing or window)

- Inform the case management judge in writing of:

  - any other circumstance of **urgency**

  - any contested hearing for an **ICO**

Action	Party and Timing
• Within **1 day** of receipt of the court file and **completed SDF** from the allocated High Court judge (by **DAY 16**), send to each party a copy of the completed SDF together with a **case management questionnaire (appendix A/2)**	Court Officer **on DAY 16**

3.7 **Allocation Directions in the High Court**	Case **by DAY 15** Management Judge

Within **3 days** of receipt of the court file (by **DAY 15**) the allocated **case management judge** shall:

- Consider the **case management checklist (appendix A/3)**

- Complete the **SDF (appendix A/1)** having regard to those matters set out at step 3.4

- Return the court file and the completed SDF to the court officer.

STEP 4: The Case Management Conference

Objective   **Target time: between DAYS 15 and 60**

To consider what case management directions are necessary

- To ensure that a fair hearing of the proceedings takes place

- To timetable the proceedings so that the Final Hearing is completed within or before the recommended hearing window

	Action	Party and Timing
4.1	**LA Case Management Documents** In every case the **LA** shall not later than **5 days** before the CMC prepare, paginate, index, file and serve: • The **case management documents** for the CMC that have been directed at the Allocation Hearing/Directions (step 3.4) and • A **case management questionnaire (appendix A/2)**	LA **not later than 5 days before the CMC**
4.2	**The Court Bundle** Not later than **5 days** before the date fixed for the CMC, the **LA** shall: • For hearings to which the *Practice Direction (Family Proceedings: Court Bundles)* [2000] 1 FLR 536 (**appendix D**) applies or in accordance with any direction given at a First Hearing or Allocation Hearing, file with the Court a **bundle** • Serve on each of the represented parties an **index** to the bundle • Serve on any un-represented party a copy indexed bundle • For hearings to which **appendix D does not apply**, serve on all parties an **index** of the documents that have been filed	LA **not later than 5 days before the CMC**
4.3	**Other Party's Case Management Documents**	All Parties except the LA **not later than 2 days before the CMC**

Action	Party and Timing
Not later than **2 days** before the date of the CMC **each party other than the LA** shall:	

- File with the court and serve on the parties the following **case management documents**

  - a **position statement** which sets out that party's response to the case management documents filed by the LA indicating the issues that are agreed and those that are not agreed. (A Guardian's position statement on behalf of the child should comment on the LA's arrangements and plans for the child)

  - a completed **case management questionnaire (appendix A/2)**

- **Not** file any **other case management documents** without the prior direction of the Court

4.4	**The Court's Preparation** Not later than 2 days before the CMC the court officer shall:	Court Officer **not later than 2 days before the CMC**

- Place the **case management documents of all parties** at the front of the court file and at the front of any bundle that is filed by the LA

- Deliver the court file and bundle to the case management judge who is to conduct the CMC

- Ensure that any arrangements for video and telephone conferencing and with criminal and civil listing officers have been made

Action	Party and Timing
4.5 **Advocates Meeting**	Advocates **on or before the day of the CMC**

Before **the day** fixed for the **CMC** or (where it has not been practicable to have an earlier meeting) not later than **1 hour** before the time fixed for the CMC, the **parties and/or their lawyers** shall:

- Meet to **identify and narrow the issues** in the case

- Consider the **case management checklist (appendix A/3)**

- Consider the **case management questionnaires (appendix A/2)**

- Consider in accordance with the **experts code of guidance (appendix C)** whether and if so why any application is to be made to instruct an **expert**

- Consider whether full and frank **disclosure** of all relevant documents has taken place   All Parties **on DAY 34**

- Draft a composite **schedule of issues (appendix B/4)** which identifies:

  - a summary of the issues in the case

  - a summary of issues for determination at the CMC by reference to the case management questionnaires/case management checklist

  - the timetable of legal and social work steps proposed

  - the estimated length of hearing of the PHR and of the Final Hearing

  - the order which the Court will be invited to make at the CMC

Action	Party and Timing

4.6   Availability

On **the day** of the CMC **the parties** shall complete and file with the Court:

- **witness non-availability form (appendix A/4)**
- A schedule (so far as it is known) of the names and contact details (professional address, telephone, fax, DX and e-mail) of:
    - the lead social worker and team manager
    - the Guardian
    - solicitors and counsel/advocates for each party
    - un-represented litigants
    - any experts upon whose evidence it is proposed to rely

4.7   Conduct of the CMC

The CMC shall be conducted by one of the allocated case management judges or as directed by the FPC case management legal adviser in accordance with the protocol. It is the essence of the protocol that case management through to Final Hearing must be consistently provided by the same case management judges/legal advisers/FPCs.

All advocates who are retained to have conduct of the final hearing shall:

- Use their best endeavours to attend the CMC and must do so if directed by the Court

Action	Party and Timing
• Bring to the CMC details of their own availability for the 12 month period following the CMC	
• Attend the advocates meeting before the CMC	

Action	Party and Timing
4.8 **The Hearing**	Case Management Judge

At the CMC the **case management judge/court** shall:

- Consider the parties' composite **schedule of issues (appendix B/4)**

- Consider the **case management checklist (appendix A/3)**

- Consider the parties' **case management questionnaires (appendix A/2)** and **case management documents** (steps 3.4 and 4.3)

- If not already fixed at the First or Allocation Hearing, fix the date of the **Final Hearing** which shall be not later than in the **3 week** period commencing the **37th WEEK** after the application was issued

- If not already fixed, fix the date and time of the **PHR** which shall be not later than **2 weeks** before and no earlier than **8 weeks** before the Final Hearing

- Give a **time estimate** for each hearing that has been fixed

   Consider whether any hearing can take place using video, telephone or other **electronic means**

- Consider any outstanding application of which notice has been given to the Court and to the parties in accordance with the rules

Action	Party and Timing

- Give all necessary **case management directions** to:

  - **timetable** all remaining legal and social work steps

  - ensure that full and frank **disclosure** of all relevant documents is complete

  - ensure that a **core assessment (appendix F)** or other appropriate assessments materials will be available to the Court

  - ensure that if any **expert** is to be instructed the expert and the parties will complete their work for the Court within the Court's timetable and in accordance with the **experts code of guidance (appendix C)**

  - provide for **regular monitoring** of the Court's case management directions to include certification of compliance at each ICO renewal and the notification to the Court by the Guardian and by each responsible party of any material non compliance

  - permit a **further directions hearing** before the allocated case management judge in the event of a change of circumstances or significant non compliance with the directions of the Court

  - update, file and serve such of the **existing case management documents** as are necessary

  - update, file and serve a **court bundle/index** for the PHR and for the final Hearing

Action	Party and Timing
• ensure that the PHR and Final Hearing will be effective	

STEP 5: The Pre-Hearing Review

Objective	Target time: by WEEK 37

To identify and narrow the remaining issues between the parties and ensure that the Final Hearing is effective

Action	Party and Timing	

5.1   **The Court's Preparation**
 	
The **court officer** shall:
 	
   • In circumstances where **no PHR direction** has been given, send the court file/bundle to the case management judge during **WEEK 28** with a request for confirmation that no PHR is necessary or for a direction that a PHR be listed
 	
   • **Notify** the parties of any **PHR direction** given by the case management judge
 	
   • **List a PHR** where directions have been given by the case management judge (not earlier than **8 weeks** and not later than **2 weeks** before the Final Hearing ie between **WEEKS 29 and 37**)
 	
   • Not later than **2 days** before the PHR:
 	
      • place the **updated case management documents** directed at the CMC (if any) at the front of the court file and at the front of any bundle that is filed by the LA
 	
      • deliver the court file/bundle to the judge/FPC nominated to conduct the PHR
	Court Officer	from **WEEK 28**

Action	Party and Timing
• ensure that any arrangements for video and telephone conferencing and with criminal and civil listing officers have been made	

5.2   Advocates Meeting

Advocates **in the week before the PHR**

In the **week** before the PHR **the advocates** who have conduct of the **Final Hearing** shall:

- Communicate with each other and if necessary meet to **identify and narrow the issues** to be considered by the Court at the PHR and the Final Hearing

- Consider the **pre-hearing review checklist (appendix A/5)**

- **2 days** before the PHR file a composite **schedule of issues (appendix B/4)** which shall set out:

  - a summary of issues in the case

  - a summary of issues for determination at the PHR

  - a draft witness template

  - the revised estimated length of hearing of the Final Hearing

  - whether the proceedings are ready to be heard and if not, what steps need to be taken at the PHR to ensure that the proceedings can be heard on the date fixed for the Final Hearing

  - the order which the Court will be invited to make at the PHR

5.3   Case Management Documents

Advocates **between WEEKS 29 and 30**

No case management documents are to be filed for use at a PHR except:

- Any **updated case management documents** directed by the case management judge at the CMC (step 4.8)

Action	Party and Timing
• The composite **schedule of issues** (appendix B/4)	
• Documents in support of a **new application**.	

5.4 Conduct of the PHR

The **PHR** (or any directions hearing in the FPC which immediately precedes a Final Hearing) shall be listed before the judge/FPC nominated to conduct the Final Hearing. In exceptional circumstances the Court may in advance approve the release of the PHR but only to one of the allocated case management judges.

The **advocates** who are retained to have conduct of the Final Hearing shall:

- Use their best endeavours to secure their release from any other professional obligation to enable them to attend the PHR

- Update the case management documents as directed at the CMC

- Attend the advocates meeting.

### 5.5 The Hearing	Court **at the PHR**

At the PHR the **Court** shall:

- Consider the **pre-hearing review checklist (appendix A/5)**

- Consider the parties' composite **schedule of issues (appendix B/4)**

- Confirm or give a **revised time estimate** for the Final Hearing

- Confirm the **fixed dates, venues and the nominated judge** for the Final Hearing

Action	Party and Timing

- Give such directions as are necessary to **update the existing case management documents** and the Court **bundle/index** having regard to the application of the *Practice Direction* (*Family Proceedings: Court Bundles*) [2000] 1 FLR 536 (**appendix D**)

- Give such directions as are necessary to ensure that the Final Hearing will be effective

---

5.6	**Dispensing with the PHR**	All Parties **before the PHR**

Where the requirements of an advocates meeting have been complied with and all parties certify (in the composite **schedule of issues**) that:

- The proceedings are ready to be heard

- There has been compliance with the directions of the Court and

- There is agreement by all parties to all of the directions proposed having regard to the **pre-hearing review checklist** (**appendix A/5**)

The Court may decide to **dispense with the PHR** or deal with it on paper or by electronic means, including computer, video or telephone conferencing

---

STEP 6: The Final Hearing

Objective   **Target time: by WEEK 40**

To determine the remaining issues between the parties

	Action	Party and Timing
6.1	**The Hearing** • The judge or FPC identified in the allocation directions as confirmed at the PHR Where one of the allocated case management judges or an FPC has heard a substantial factual issue or there has been a 'preliminary hearing' to determine findings of fact it is necessary for the same judge/magistrates who conducted the preliminary hearing to conduct the Final Hearing.	Judge/FPC nominated for the Final Hearing
6.2	**Case Management and Practice Direction Documents** Not later than **2 days** before the Final Hearing **the parties** shall: • Prepare, file and serve the **case management documents** for the Final Hearing as directed by the Court at the PHR • Prepare, file and serve the **court bundle or index of court documents** as directed by the Court at the PHR	All Parties **not later than 2 days before the Final Hearing**
6.3	**The Court's Preparation** Not later than 2 days before the Final Hearing the Court officer shall: • Place any **case management documents** at the front of the court file and at the front of any bundle that is filed by the LA • Deliver the **court file/bundle** to the judge/FPC nominated to conduct the Final Hearing • Ensure that any arrangements for the reception of evidence by video link and telephone conferencing, interpreters, facilities for disabled persons and special measures for vulnerable or intimidated witnesses have been made	Court Officer **not later than 2 days before the Final Hearing**

Action	Party and Timing
6.4 **Orders and Reasons**	Court **at the Final Hearing**

At the conclusion of the Final Hearing the **Court** shall:

- Set out the basis/reasons for the orders made or applications refused in a **judgment** and where appropriate in the form of **recitals** to the order or in the case of an FPC in **form C22**

- Annexe to the order the **agreed or approved documents** setting out the threshold criteria and the care plan for the child

- Where the judgment is not in writing give consideration to whether there should be a **transcript** and if so who will obtain and pay for it

Action	Party and Timing
6.5 **Reserved judgment**	Judge **at the end of submissions**

In a complex case a judge (but not an FPC) may decide to reserve judgment and take time for consideration. Where judgment is reserved the Court will endeavour to fix a date for judgment to be given or handed down within **20 days** (4 weeks) of the conclusion of submissions. Advocates may be invited to make oral or written submissions as to consequential orders and directions at the conclusion of submissions or when the draft judgment is released.

Action	Party and Timing
6.6 **Disclosure**	Court **at the end of the Final Hearing**

At the end of every Final Hearing the **Court** shall consider whether to give directions for **disclosure of documents**, for example:

Action	Party and Timing
• In any case where it is proposed that the child should be placed for adoption and so that subsequent adoption proceedings are not delayed, to the LA adoption panel, specialist adoption agency and/or proposed adopters and their legal advisers for use in subsequent adoption proceedings	
• For any medical or therapeutic purpose	
• For a claim to be made to the CICA	

APPENDIX A/1:
Standard Directions Form

IN THE HIGH COURT OF JUSTICE
FAMILY DIVISION

COUNTY COURT/FPC

Case Number

Application of   Local Authority

Re   Child(ren)

Standard directions by Case Management Judge/Magistrates/Legal Adviser

Date of this order

Upon reading the papers filed by the applicant:

IT IS ORDERED by   **The Honourable**
His/Her Honour
District Judge
Magistrates/Justices Clerk

Allocation Directions

This case is allocated for case management to:

The Honourable
His/Her Honour   and
District Judge
Magistrates/Justices Clerk

Contact Telephone No
(Judge's Clerk/Court Officer/Legal Adviser)

The allocated judge(s) will be responsible for the continuous case management of this case

All future hearings in this case will be conducted by one of the allocated judges and *not* by the urgent applications judge or by any other judge unless on application to one of the allocated judges (if necessary in case of urgency by telephone) the allocated judge releases the case to another judge.
(*Where it is possible to identify the Final Hearing Judge/Magistrates*).

The judge who will be responsible for the PHR and the conduct of the Final Hearing is:

Case Management Conference

There will be a	**The Honourable**
Case Management	**His/Her Honour**
Conference before	**District Judge**
	Magistrates/Justices Clerk

at venue

date

on the

time

at

The parties and their lawyers shall consider each of the matters set out at Steps 1 to 4 of the Protocol and in the CMC Checklist.

The parties shall prepare, file and serve **the Evidence and Case Management Documents** listed below. No documents other than those identified shall thereafter be filed with the Court without the Court's permission, unless in support of a new application.

Local Authority Preparation for the CMC

The LOCAL AUTHORITY shall not later than **2pm 5 days before** the date of the Case Management Conference prepare and file with the Court the following:
(Delete as appropriate)

(a) a Bundle prepared in accordance with the [*Practice Direction (Family Proceedings: Court Bundles)* [2000] 1 FLR 536] [....*or* *specify the form].*
The Local Authority shall at the same time serve on each of the Respondents an Index to the Bundle and on any unrepresented party a copy of the bundle;

(b) an Index of the Documents filed with the Court. The Local Authority shall at the same time serve on each of the Respondents a copy of the Index;

(c) the following case management documents *(delete if not required)*:

- A **case management questionnaire**
- A schedule of the **findings of fact** which the Court is to be invited to make (in particular so as to satisfy the threshold criteria)
- Any update to the **social work chronology**
- The **interim care plan(s)**
- A **skeleton argument** limited to legal questions with accompanying authorities.
- A clear and concise **summary of the background** on one page of A4 paper (only where necessary to supplement the Case Synopsis)
- An **advocates** chronology (only where necessary to supplement the Case Synopsis or the social work chronology)

Respondent's Preparation for the CMC

The RESPONDENTS shall not later than **2pm 2 working days before** the date of the
Case Management Conference prepare and file with the Court and serve on the
Local Authority copies of:

* A statement of evidence in **reply to** the local authorities **initial social work statement**
  (unless already filed).
* A **case management questionnaire**.
* A **position statement** (setting out what is agreed and what is not agreed).

The Advocates Meeting

The parties lawyers and any un-represented party shall attend an **Advocates Meeting**:

at	venue
on the	date
at	time

to discuss those matters set out at Step 4.5 of the Protocol and shall prepare a composite
schedule of issues which shall be filed with the Court:

not later than	time
on the	date

in default of the advocates meeting taking place and in any event, the lawyers for all parties
and any un-represented party shall attend at Court on the day of the Case Management
Conference NOT LATER THAN 1 **hour before** the time fixed for the hearing so that they
can all meet together to discuss the issues and draft the composite **schedule of issues**.

Experts

Any party that proposes to ask the Court's permission to instruct an **expert witness** shall
comply with the **experts code of guidance** and shall set out the required particulars in their
case management questionnaire

Availability and Contact Details

The parties' legal representatives shall bring to the advocates meeting and to the CMC:

* Their professional diaries for the next 12 months.
* Details (so far as can be known) of the names and the availability of anybody who it is
  proposed should conduct any assessment or provide any expert evidence so that a **witness
  availability form** can be prepared and filed at the CMC.

- Details (so far as can be known) of the names and contact details (professional addresses and telephone / fax / DX / e-mail numbers for) so that a **schedule** can be prepared and filed at the CMC with particulars of:
  - the lead social worker
  - the Children's Guardian
  - the solicitors and counsel/advocates for each party
  - any experts and assessors who have been or may be instructed

Disclosure of Documents

Any outstanding disclosure of relevant documents between the parties shall take place:

by   date

Pre-Hearing Review

There will be a PHR before the Final Hearing Judge:

at   venue

on the   date

at   time

with a time   time estimate
estimate of

Final Hearing

The Final Hearing will take place before the Final Hearing Judge

at   venue

on the   date

at   time

with a time   time estimate
estimate of

ADDITIONAL DIRECTIONS (if any)

OBSERVATIONS

                                                                                        Signed

APPENDIX A/2:
Case Management Questionnaire

This questionnaire is completed [by][on behalf of],

In the

[Family Proceedings Court]
[District Registry] [County Court]
[Principal Registry of the Family Division]
[The High Court of Justice]

Note:
Please state
your party
status.

who is the [ ] [Applicant] [Respondent]
[   ] [other]
in these proceedings.

Case Number

Please read the following notes before completing the Case Management Questionnaire.

- **The Local Authority** must file and serve this questionnaire (together with the other case management documents directed at steps 3.4 and 4.1 of the protocol) **not later than 5 days** before the date fixed for the Case Management Conference.

- **All other parties** must file and serve this questionnaire (together with the other case management documents listed at step 4.3 of the protocol) **not later than 2 days** before the date fixed for the Case Management Conference.

- Your answers to the following questions should be given **in summary form only.** However, if you need more space for your answers use a separate sheet of paper. Please put your full name and case number at the top of any additional sheet and mark clearly which question the information refers to. Please ensure that any additional sheets are firmly attached to the questionnaire.

Have you served a copy of the completed questionnaire [and the other documents required by the protocol] on the other [party][parties]?

Yes [ ]   No [ ]

A. Complexity/Urgency

Are the proceedings complex?   Yes [ ]   No [ ]

Are there are any urgent features that the Court should know about?   Yes [ ]   No [ ]

If 'Yes', to either question please explain briefly why the proceedings are complex and or what urgent features the Court should be aware of:

```
┌─────────────────────────────────────────────────────────┐
│                                                         │
│                                                         │
│                                                         │
│                                                         │
│                                                         │
│                                                         │
│                                                         │
│                                                         │
│                                                         │
│                                                         │
└─────────────────────────────────────────────────────────┘
```

B. Urgent/Preliminary Hearings

Do you wish there to be an urgent hearing?   Yes ☐   No ☐

Do you wish there to be a preliminary hearing?   Yes ☐   No ☐

If 'Yes', to either question please explain briefly why such a hearing is required and what question(s) the Court will be asked to answer at that hearing.

```
┌─────────────────────────────────────────────────────────┐
│                                                         │
│                                                         │
│                                                         │
│                                                         │
│                                                         │
│                                                         │
│                                                         │
│                                                         │
│                                                         │
│                                                         │
│                                                         │
│                                                         │
└─────────────────────────────────────────────────────────┘
```

C. Evidence

Part 1 – Witnesses/Reports

Are there any **witness statements** or **clinical reports** upon which you intend to rely?

Yes ☐   No ☐

If 'Yes', please provide the information requested in the box below:

Author	Date of Report:	Nature of Evidence:

Part 2 – Further Assessments/Expert Evidence

Do you propose to ask for a further assessment?   Yes ☐   No ☐

Do you propose to seek permission to use expert evidence?   Yes ☐   No ☐

If you answer 'Yes' to either of the above questions, for each further assessment or expert you propose please give those details required by the Experts Code of Guidance (step 2.3) on a separate sheet and attach it to this questionnaire.

D. Other Evidence including Evidence of Ethnicity, Language, Religion, Culture, Gender and Vulnerability

Is any other evidence needed for example, relating to the ethnicity, language, religion, culture, gender and vulnerability of the child or other significant person?

Yes ☐   No ☐

If 'Yes', please give brief details of the evidence that you propose:

E. Legal and Social Work Timetable

Please give details of the Legal and Social Work timetable that is proposed:

Date Proposed:	Step Proposed:	Party Responsible:

F. Hearing and Reading Time

How long do you think the Case Management Conference will take? [   ] hour(s) [   ] minutes

How long do you think the Pre-Hearing Review will take? [   ] hour(s) [   ] minutes

How long do you think the Final Hearing will take? [   ] day(s) [   ] hour(s)

Give details of the recommended reading list for the Case Management Conference:

G. Proposed Directions

(Parties should agree directions at the Advocates Meeting. A list of proposed directions or orders should be attached to this questionnaire using the standard variable directions forms wherever possible.)

Have you attached a list of the directions (or orders)
you wish the Court to consider at the CMC:

(a) to ensure that the matters set out in the protocol   Yes ☐   No ☐
    are complied with; and

(b) that are required for any other purpose, in particular,   Yes ☐   No ☐
    compliance with the Experts Code of Guidance (Step 2.4)
    and to ensure that disclosure of relevant documents takes place.

H. Other Information

In the space below, set out any other information you consider will help the judge or court to manage this case.

Signed [   ]   date [   ]

[Counsel] [Solicitor] for the
[   ][Applicant] [Respondent] [   ][other]

Please enter your contact name, reference number and full postal address including
(if appropriate) details of DX, fax or e-mail.

Name:	Reference:
Address:	Telephone number:
	Fax number:
	DX number:
	e-mail:

APPENDIX A/3:

Case Management Checklist

Objective

The following checklist is to be used for the First Hearing in the FPC, the Allocation Hearing in the Care Centre, Allocation Directions in the High Court and for the CMC

Representation of the Child

1	Has CAFCASS been notified of any decision to appoint a Guardian? If so, has a Guardian been allocated or is the likely date of allocation known?	☐
2	Are there any other relevant proceedings? If so, was a Guardian appointed and has CAFCASS been informed of the nature/number of the other/previous proceedings and the identity of the Guardian?	☐
3	If a decision has been made to appoint a Guardian but no allocation has yet taken place by CAFCASS: are any directions necessary for the representation of the child including the appointment of a solicitor?	☐
4	Have the parties been notified of the names of the Guardian and of the solicitor appointed in form C47?	☐
5	Should consideration be given to the separate representation of the child?	☐

Parties

6	Have all significant persons involved in the child's care been identified, in particular those persons who are automatically Respondents to the application? Are any directions required to ensure service upon a party?	☐
7	Has consideration been given to notifying a father without parental responsibility and informing other significant adults in the extended family of the proceedings?	☐
8	Should any other person be joined as a party to the proceedings (whether upon application or otherwise)? Are any directions necessary for the service of documents. If so, which documents?	☐

ICO

9   Are the grounds for making an ICO agreed? Have they been recorded on form C22 or in a document approved by the Court?   ☐

10   If the grounds for making an ICO are not agreed has a date been fixed for an urgent hearing of the contested interim application or are the proceedings to be transferred to the Care Centre?   ☐

11   Have all case management directions been given to ensure that the contested interim hearing will be effective?   ☐

Urgency, Transfer and Re-Transfer

12   Are there any features of particular urgency and if so what directions are necessary to provide for that urgency or to minimise delay eg lateral or upwards transfer?   ☐

13   Have any circumstances of complexity, gravity and urgency been considered and has any decision to transfer the proceedings to the Care Centre/High Court been made and notified to the parties?   ☐

14   Have the directions that are set out in the CCP and the FPCP been made upon transfer?   ☐

15   After transfer, have the circumstances of complexity, gravity and urgency that remain been re-considered and is it appropriate to transfer back to the Care Centre or FPC?   ☐

16   In relation to any question of re-transfer, has the availability of the Court been ascertained and have the parties been notified?   ☐

Protocol Documents

17   **LA Documents on Issue of Application.** Are any directions necessary relating to the preparation, filing and service of those LA documents that are required by the protocol within 2 days of the proceedings being issued?   ☐

18   **Case Synopsis.** Are any directions necessary to ensure that the LA or the Child's solicitor prepares, files and serves a case synopsis?   ☐

19   **The Court Bundle/Index.** Are any directions necessary to ensure that a court bundle is prepared and filed or that an index to the Court documents is prepared, filed and served?   ☐

20   Have directions been given to update the court bundle/index, in particular the responsibility for, the format of and arrangements for updating (or the compilation of an application bundle) and whether updates can be provided to the Court/judge by e-mail?   ☐

21	**Local Authority Case Management Documents.** Are any directions necessary to ensure that the LA case management documents are prepared, filed and served?	☐
22	**Other Party's Case Management Documents.** Are any directions necessary to ensure that the case management documents of other parties are prepared, filed and served?	☐
23	**Case Management Questionnaires.** Are any directions necessary to ensure that the parties prepare, file and serve case management questionnaires?	☐
24	**Recommended Reading List.** For any hearing where no case management questionnaire or schedule of issues will be available, are any directions necessary for the parties to provide the Court with a joint reading list?	☐
25	**Witness Non-Availability Form.** Are any directions necessary to ensure that a witness availability form and schedule of contact details are completed/updated?	☐

Preliminary Directions

26	**Statements of Evidence from Each Party.** Have directions been given for the parties other than the LA to prepare, file and serve evidence in reply to the LA's initial social work statement?	☐
27	**Disclosure.** Have directions been given to ensure that all relevant documents are disclosed by the LA within 20 days of the First Hearing?	☐
28	**Allocation.** Have all allocation directions been given?	☐
29	**Standard Directions Form.** Has the SDF been completed and served?	☐

Listing

30	**CMC.** Has a date and time been fixed for the CMC (between days 15 and 60)? Is the date, time and time estimate recorded on the draft SDF?	☐
31	If a CMC is not to be listed have all case management directions been given for the Final Hearing and are they recorded on the draft SDF?	☐
32	**PHR.** Is a PHR necessary? Is the date, time and time estimate recorded on the draft SDF (not later than 2 weeks and no earlier than 8 weeks before the Final Hearing)?	☐
33	If a PHR is not necessary have all case management directions set out in the PHR checklist been considered in giving directions for the Final Hearing?	☐
34	**Final Hearing.** Has a date or hearing window been fixed for the Final Hearing (not later than in the 3 weeks commencing the 37th week after issue) and are the dates recorded on the draft SDF together with the time estimate?	☐

35	**Venue/Technology.** Have directions been given for the venue of each hearing and whether video link, telephone conferencing or electronic communication with the Court can be used? If so, have arrangements been made for the same?	☐

Evidence

36	**Other Proceedings.** Has consideration been given to the relevance of any other/previous proceedings and as to whether the Judgment/Reasons given or evidence filed should be admitted into evidence?	☐
37	**Disclosure.** Has the Guardian read the social work files? If not when will that task be complete? Having read the files has the Guardian confirmed that either they contain no other relevant documents or that an application for specific disclosure is necessary?	☐
38	Are there any applications relating to the disclosure of documents?	☐
39	**The Child's Evidence.** Should evidence be prepared, filed and served concerning the child's wishes and feelings?	☐
40	**The Issues.** What are the issues in the case?	☐
41	Are any directions necessary for the filing of further factual evidence (including clinical evidence of treatment) by any party and if so to which issue(s) is such evidence to be directed?	☐
42	Are any directions necessary for any party to respond to the LA's factual evidence and/or to the LA's proposed threshold criteria and schedule of findings of fact sought?	☐
43	**LA Core Assessment.** Has a core assessment been completed? If not, are any directions necessary for the preparation, service and filing of an assessment?	☐
44	**Additional Assessments and Expert Evidence.** In respect of every question relating to a request for expert evidence, is the request in accordance with the Experts Code of Guidance?	☐
45	What are the issues to which it is proposed expert evidence or further assessment should be directed?	☐
46	Who is to conduct the assessment or undertake the report, what is the expert's discipline, has the expert confirmed availability, what is the timetable for the report, the responsibility for instruction and the likely costs on both an hourly and global basis, what is the proposed responsibility for or apportionment of costs of jointly instructed experts as between the LA and the publicly funded parties (including whether there should be a section 38(6) direction?	☐
47	Are any consequential directions necessary (eg to give permission for examination or interview)?	☐

| 48 | Are any directions necessary to provide the expert with the documents/further documents? | ☐ |

| 49 | Are any directions necessary for the conduct of experts meetings/discussions and the preparation, filing and service of statements of agreement and disagreement? | ☐ |

| 50 | **Ethnicity, Language, Religion and Culture.** Has consideration been given to the ethnicity, language, religion and culture of the child and other significant persons and are any directions necessary to ensure that evidence about the same is available to the Court? | ☐ |

Care Plans and Final Evidence

| 51 | **LA.** Have directions been given for the preparation, filing and service of the final proposals of the LA and in particular its final statements of evidence and care plan? | ☐ |

| 52 | **Other Parties.** Have directions been given for the preparation, filing and service of the parents' and other parties responses to the LA's proposals? | ☐ |

| 53 | **Guardian.** Are any directions necessary for the preparation, filing and service of the Guardian's report? | ☐ |

Other Case Management Steps

| 54 | **Advocates Meetings and Schedules of Issue.** Are any directions necessary to ensure that an advocates meeting takes place and that a composite Schedule of Issues is drafted? | ☐ |

| 55 | **Preliminary/Split Hearing.** Is a finding of fact hearing necessary and if so, what is the discrete issue of fact that is to be determined, by whom and when? | ☐ |

| 56 | **Family Group Conference/ADR.** Has consideration been given to whether a family group conference or alternative dispute resolution can be held and would any directions assist to facilitate the conference resolution? | ☐ |

| 57 | **Twin Track Planning.** Are any directions necessary to ensure that in the appropriate case twin track planning has been considered and where appropriate, directions given in relation to any concurrent freeing for adoption proceedings and for the filing and service of evidence relating to placement options and their feasibility? In particular have dates been fixed for the filing of the parallel plan and in respect of the Adoption/Fostering/Permanent Placement Panel timetable? | ☐ |

| 58 | **Adoption Directions.** Are any directions necessary to ensure that the Adoption Practice Direction is complied with and in particular that any proposed (concurrent) freeing proceedings have been commenced? | ☐ |

59	**Placement.** Are any directions necessary for the filing and service of evidence relating to placement options including extended family placements and their feasibility, information about the timetable for the assessment and planning processes and any proposed referrals to Adoption/Fostering and/or Permanence Panels?	☐

60	**Court's Timetable.** Has a timetable of all legal and social work steps been agreed and is the timetable set out in the Court order or as an approved document annexed to the order?	☐

61	**Monitoring and Compliance.** What directions are necessary to ensure that the Court's timetable and directions are monitored and complied with, in particular have directions been given for the certification of compliance upon ICO renewals and for any further directions or a return to Court in the event of a significant non-compliance?	☐

62	**Change of Circumstance.** What directions are necessary to make provision for the parties to return to court in the event of a significant change of circumstance?	☐

63	**Preparation for Final Hearing.** Is any consideration necessary of the case management directions set out in the PHR checklist in particular:	☐

- Use of interpreters?

- Special Measures for Vulnerable or intimidated witnesses?

- Children's evidence or attendance at court?

- Facilities for persons with a disability?

- Evidence or submissions by video or telephone conference or on paper or by e-mail?

- Video and audio recordings and transcripts?

APPENDIX A/4:
Witness Non-Availability

This questionnaire is completed [by][on behalf of],   In the

who is the [ ] [Applicant] [Respondent]
[   ] [other]
in these proceedings.

[Family Proceedings Court]
[District Registry] [County Court]
[Principal Registry of the Family Division]
[The High Court of Justice]

Case Number

Sheet No.   of

Note: This form may be used for a maximum of six witnesses. If you intend to ask for more than six witnesses to give evidence on your behalf, please continue on a second sheet. You should indicate how many sheets you have used by completing the box above.

Date of Final Hearing (where known)

Location of Final Hearing (where known)

Witness Details:

Witness Number:	Witness Name:	Description:
1.		
2		
3.		
4.		
5.		
6.		

Completion of the Non-Availability Grid:

NOTE:

Mark dates when Experts and other witnesses are <u>NOT</u> available. Codes for use in the grid are as follows: H = Holiday, C = Course, S = Sickness or medical appointment, T = Attendance at another trial/hearing, O = Other

The person signing this form must be fully familiar with all the details of non-availability given on the Grid overleaf. If there are other issues the Court should be aware of concerning witness availability please state these below:

Signed:

Date:

[Counsel] [Solicitor] for the
[   ] [Applicant] [Respondent] [   ]

Date	MONTH					
	Witness Number					
1						
2						
3						
4						
5						
6						
7						
8						
9						
10						
11						
12						
13						
14						
15						
16						
17						
18						
19						
20						
21						
22						
23						
24						
25						
26						
27						
28						
28						
29						
30						
31						

Date	MONTH					
	Witness Number					
1						
2						
3						
4						
5						
6						
7						
8						
9						
10						
11						
12						
13						
14						
15						
16						
17						
18						
19						
20						
21						
22						
23						
24						
25						
26						
27						
28						
28						
29						
30						
31						

Date	MONTH					
	Witness Number					
1						
2						
3						
4						
5						
6						
7						
8						
9						
10						
11						
12						
13						
14						
15						
16						
17						
18						
19						
20						
21						
22						
23						
24						
25						
26						
27						
28						
28						
29						
30						
31						

Date	MONTH					
	Witness Number					
1						
2						
3						
4						
5						
6						
7						
8						
9						
10						
11						
12						
13						
14						
15						
16						
17						
18						
19						
20						
21						
22						
23						
24						
25						
26						
27						
28						
28						
29						
30						
31						

Date	MONTH					
	Witness Number					
1						
2						
3						
4						
5						
6						
7						
8						
9						
10						
11						
12						
13						
14						
15						
16						
17						
18						
19						
20						
21						
22						
23						
24						
25						
26						
27						
28						
28						
29						
30						
31						

Date	MONTH					
	Witness Number					
1						
2						
3						
4						
5						
6						
7						
8						
9						
10						
11						
12						
13						
14						
15						
16						
17						
18						
19						
20						
21						
22						
23						
24						
25						
26						
27						
28						
28						
29						
30						
31						

APPENDIX A/5:

PHR Checklist

Objective

The following checklist is to be used for the Pre-Hearing Review

1	Have the protocol and other practice direction steps been complied with?	☐
2	Have each of the directions given at the CMC and any subsequent hearing been complied with?	☐
3	Have the issues to be determined at the Final Hearing been identified and recorded in the draft PHR order?	☐
4	Which witnesses are to be called, by whom and in relation to what issue(s)?	☐
5	Are any experts required to give oral evidence, if so why and in relation to what issue(s)?	☐
6	What is the extent of the examination in chief and cross-examination of each witness that is proposed?	☐
7	Has a witness template been completed and agreed?	☐
8	What, if any, of the written evidence is agreed or not in issue (and accordingly is to be read by the Court on that basis)?	☐
9	Are interpretation facilities necessary and if so have they been directed and/or arranged (Note the special arrangements to be made for deaf signing)?	☐
10	Are any facilities needed for a party or witness with a disability? If so have arrangements been made?	☐
11	Are any special measures or security measures applied for in relation to vulnerable or intimidated witnesses including, for example, live video link, screens or witness support? If so what are the arrangements, if any, that are directed to be made?	☐
12	Is it intended that the child will attend to see the judge and/or give evidence at the Final Hearing and have the arrangements been agreed and made?	☐
13	Is any evidence is to be taken indirectly by live video link eg for an expert or witness who is overseas or otherwise unable to attend Court. If so have the arrangements been made?	☐

14	Are any video or audio recordings to be used and if so:	☐
	(a) have the relevant excerpts of the recordings been agreed?	
	(b) have agreed transcripts been obtained and?	
	(c) have the arrangements been made to view/listen to the recordings?	
15	Are there questions of law to be determined, and if so when should the submissions be heard and what provision should be made for the consideration of the authorities and skeleton arguments that will be required?	☐
16	Is there a recommended reading list for the Court?	☐
17	What is the timetable for the final hearing including opening and closing submissions and judgment/reasons?	☐
18	What is the estimated length of the Final Hearing?	☐
19	Who is/are the judge/magistrates nominated to conduct the Final Hearing?	☐
20	Where is the venue for the Final Hearing?	☐
21	Does the *Practice Direction (Family Proceedings: Court Bundles)* [2000] 1 FLR 536 apply to the Final Hearing and/or are any other case management documents to be updated, prepared, filed and served by the parties and if so: by whom and when?	☐
22	Are the proceedings ready for Final Hearing and have all steps and directions been complied with so that the PHR can be dispensed with or considered by the Court in the absence of the parties?	☐

APPENDIX B

Standard Documents

Objective

The following documents are identified in the protocol and their contents are prescribed below

1   **Case Synopsis** shall contain such of the following information as is known in summary form for use at the Allocation Hearing and shall normally be limited to 2 sides of A4:

- The identities of the parties and other significant persons

- The applications that are before the Court

- A very brief summary of the precipitating incident(s) and background circumstances

- Any particular issue that requires a direction to be given at the Allocation Hearing (eg relating to a social services core assessment)

- Any intention to apply to transfer the proceedings to the High Court

- The parties interim proposals in relation to placement and contact

- The estimated length of the Allocation Hearing (to include a separate estimate relating to a contested ICO where relevant)

- A recommended reading list and a suggested reading time for the Allocation Hearing

- Advance notice of any other decisions or proceedings that may be relevant, to include: criminal prosecutions, family law proceedings, disciplinary, immigration and mental health adjudications

2   **Social Work Chronology** is a schedule containing a succinct summary of the significant dates and events in the child's life in chronological order. It is a running record ie it is to be updated during the proceedings. The schedule headings are:

- serial number

- date

- event-detail

- witness or document reference (where applicable)

3   **Initial Social Work Statement**. The initial social work statement
      filed by the LA within 2 days of the issue of an application is
      strictly limited to the following evidence:

- The precipitating incident(s) and background circumstances
  relevant to the grounds and reasons for making the application
  including a brief description of any referral and assessment
  processes that have already occurred

- Any facts and matters that are within the social worker's
  personal knowledge

- Any emergency steps and previous court orders that are
  relevant to the application

- Any decisions made by the LA that are relevant to the
  application

- Information relevant to the ethnicity, language, religion,
  culture, gender and vulnerability of the child and other
  significant persons in the form of a 'family profile' together
  with a narrative description and details of the social care
  services that are relevant to the same

- Where the LA is applying for an ICO and/or is proposing to
  remove or seeking to continue the removal of a child under
  emergency protection: the LA's initial proposals for the child
  including placement, contact with parents and other
  significant persons and the social care services that are
  proposed

- The LA's initial proposals for the further assessment of the
  parties during the proceedings including twin track planning

- The social work timetable, tasks and responsibilities so far as
  they are known.

4   **Schedule of Issues**. The composite schedule of issues produced by
      the advocates at the end of the advocates' meetings prior to the
      CMC and the PHR should be agreed so far as is possible and where
      not agreed should set out the differing positions as to the following:

- A summary of the issues in the case (including any diverse
  cultural or religious contexts)

- A summary of issues for determination of the CMC/PHR by
  reference to the questionnaires/checklists

- For the CMC: the timetable of legal and social work steps
  proposed

- The estimated length of hearing of the PHR and the Final
  Hearing

- For the PHR: whether the Final Hearing is ready to be heard
  and if not, what steps need to be taken

- The order which the Court will be invited to make at the
  CMC/PHR

APPENDIX C

Code of Guidance for Expert Witnesses in Family Proceedings

Objective

The objective of this Code of Guidance is to provide the Court with early information to enable it to determine whether it is necessary and/or practicable to ask an expert to assist the Court:

- To identify, narrow and where possible agree the issues between the parties

- To provide an opinion about a question that is not within the skill and experience of the Court

- To encourage the early identification of questions that need to be answered by an expert

- To encourage disclosure of full and frank information between the parties, the Court and any expert instructed

Action	Party and Timing
1 The Duties of Experts	
1.1 **Overriding Duty: An expert in family proceedings has an overriding duty to** the Court that takes precedence over any obligation to the person from whom he has received instructions or by whom he is paid.	
1.2 **Particular Duties:** Among any other duties an expert may have, **an expert shall** have regard to the following duties:	

- To assist the Court in accordance with the overriding duty

- To provide an opinion that is independent of the party or parties instructing the expert

- To confine an opinion to matters material to the issues between the parties and in relation only to questions that are within the expert's expertise (skill and experience). If a question is put which falls outside that expertise the expert must say so

Action	Party and Timing	

- In expressing an opinion take into consideration all of the material facts including any relevant factors arising from diverse cultural or religious contexts at the time the opinion is expressed, indicating the facts, literature and any other material that the expert has relied upon in forming an opinion

- To indicate whether the opinion is provisional (or qualified, as the case may be) and the reason for the qualification, identifying what further information is required to give an opinion without qualification

- Inform those instructing the expert without delay of any change in the opinion and the reason for the change

2	**Preparation for the CMC**	Solicitor instructing the expert
2.1	**Preliminary Enquiries of the Expert**: Not later than 10 days before the CMC the solicitor for the party proposing to instruct the expert (or lead solicitor/solicitor for the child if the instruction proposed is joint) shall approach the expert with the following information:	**10 days before the CMC**

- The nature of the proceedings and the issues likely to require determination by the Court;

- The questions about which the expert is to be asked to give an opinion (including any diverse cultural or religious contexts)

- When the Court is to be asked to give permission for the instruction (if unusually permission has already been given the date and details of that permission)

- Whether permission is asked of the Court for the instruction of another expert in the same or any related field (ie to give an opinion on the same or related questions)

- The volume of reading which the expert will need to undertake

Action	Party and Timing

- Whether or not (in an appropriate case) permission has been applied for or given for the expert to examine the child

- Whether or not (in an appropriate case) it will be necessary for the expert to conduct interviews (and if so with whom)

- The likely timetable of legal and social work steps

- When the expert's opinion is likely to be required

- Whether and if so what date has been fixed by the Court for any hearing at which the expert may be required to give evidence (in particular the Final Hearing).

2.2 **Expert's Response:** Not later than 5 days before the CMC the solicitors intending to instruct the expert shall obtain the following information from the expert:	Solicitor **5 days** instructing **before the** the expert **CMC**

- That the work required is within the expert's expertise

- That the expert is available to do the relevant work within the suggested time scale

- When the expert is available to give evidence, the dates and/or times to avoid, and, where a hearing date has not been fixed, the amount of notice the expert will require to make arrangements to come to Court without undue disruption to their normal clinical routines.

- The cost, including hourly and global rates, and likely hours to be spent, of attending at experts/professionals meetings, attending court and writing the report (to include any examinations and interviews).

Action	Party and Timing
2.3 **Case Management Questionnaire:**	The Party **not later**
Any party who proposes to ask the Court for permission to instruct an expert shall not later than 2 days before the CMC (or any hearing at which the application is to be made) file and serve a case management questionnaire setting out the proposal to instruct the expert in the following detail:	proposing **than 2 days** to instruct **before the** the expert **CMC**

- The name, discipline, qualifications and expertise of the expert (by way of CV where possible)

- The expert's availability to undertake the work

- The relevance of the expert evidence sought to be adduced to the issues in the proceedings and the specific questions upon which it is proposed the expert should give an opinion (including the relevance of any diverse cultural or religious contexts)

- The timetable for the report

- The responsibility for instruction

- Whether or not the expert evidence can properly be obtained by the joint instruction of the expert by two or more of the parties.

- Whether the expert evidence can properly be obtained by only one party (eg on behalf of the child)

- Whether it is necessary for more than one expert in the same discipline to be instructed by more than one party

- Why the expert evidence proposed cannot be given by social services undertaking a core assessment or by the Guardian in accordance with their different statutory duties

- The likely cost of the report on both an hourly and global basis.

- The proposed apportionment of costs of jointly instructed experts as between the Local Authority and the publicly funded parties.

	Action	Party and Timing	

2.4 Draft Order for the CMC:

Any party proposing to instruct an **expert** shall in the draft order submitted at the CMC request the Court to give directions (among any others) as to the following:

Any Party **not later than 2 days before the CMC**

- The party who is to be responsible for drafting the letter of instruction and providing the documents to the expert

- The issues identified by the Court and the questions about which the expert is to give an opinion

- The timetable within which the report is to be prepared, filed and served

- The disclosure of the report to the parties and to any other expert

- The conduct of an experts' discussion

- The preparation of a statement of agreement and disagreement by the experts following an experts discussion

- The attendance of the expert at the Final Hearing unless agreement is reached at or before the PHR about the opinions given by the expert.

3   Letter of Instruction

3.1 The solicitor instructing the expert shall within 5 days of the CMC prepare (agree with the other parties where appropriate) file and serve a letter of instruction to the expert which shall:

Solicitor instructing the expert **within 5 days of the CMC**

- Set out the context in which the expert's opinion is sought (including any diverse ethnic, cultural, religious or linguistic contexts)

- Define carefully the specific questions the expert is required to answer ensuring

  - **that they are within the ambit of the expert's area of expertise and**

  - **that they do not contain unnecessary or irrelevant detail**

Action	Party and Timing

- **that the questions addressed to the expert are kept to a manageable number and are clear, focused and direct**

- **that the questions reflect what the expert has been requested to do by the Court**

- List the documentation provided or provide for the expert an indexed and paginated bundle which shall include:

  - **a copy of the order (or those parts of the order) which gives permission for the instruction of the expert immediately the order becomes available**

  - **an agreed list of essential reading**

  - **all new documentation when it is filed and regular updates to the list of documents provided or to the index to the paginated bundle**

  - **a copy of this code of guidance and of the protocol**

- Identify the relevant lay and professional people concerned with the proceedings (eg the treating clinicians) and inform the expert of his/her right to talk to the other professionals provided an accurate record is made of the discussion

- Identify any other expert instructed in the proceedings and advise the expert of his/her right to talk to the other experts provided an accurate record is made of the discussion

Action	Party and Timing
• Define the contractual basis upon which the expert is retained and in particular the funding mechanism including how much the expert will be paid (an hourly rate and overall estimate should already have been obtained) when the expert will be paid, and what limitation there might be on the amount the expert can charge for the work which he/she will have to do. There should also be a brief explanation of the 'detailed assessment process' in cases proceeding in the Care Centre or the High Court which are not subject to a high cost case contract	
• In default of agreement the format of the letter of instruction shall be determined by the Court, which may determine the issue upon written application with representations from each party.	

Action	Party and Timing
4 The Expert's Report **Content of the Report:**	The Expert **in accordance with the Court's timetable**
4.1 The expert's report shall be addressed to the Court and shall:	
• Give details of the expert's qualifications and experience	
• Contain a statement setting out the substance of all material instructions (whether written or oral) summarising the facts stated and instructions given to the expert which are material to the conclusions and opinions expressed in the report	
• Give details of any literature or other research material upon which the expert has relied in giving an opinion	
• State who carried out any test, examination or interview which the expert has used for the report and whether or not the test, examination or interview has been carried out under the expert's supervision.	
• Give details of the qualifications of any person who carried out the test, examination or interview	

Action	Party and Timing

• Where there is a range of opinion on the question to be answered by the expert:
 	
    • summarise the range of opinion and
 	
    • give reasons for the opinion expressed
 	
• Contain a summary of the expert's conclusions and opinions
 	
• Contain a statement that the expert understands his duty to the Court and has complied with that duty
 	
• Where appropriate be verified by a statement of truth.	

4.2	**Supplementary Questions:** Any party wishing to ask supplementary questions of an expert for the purpose of clarifying the expert's report must put those questions in writing to the parties not later than 5 days after receipt of the report. Only those questions that are agreed by the parties or in default of agreement approved by the Court may be put to the expert The Court may determine the issue upon written application with representations from each party.	Any party **within 5 days of the receipt of the report**
5	**Experts Discussion (Meeting)**	The Court **at the CMC**
5.1	**Purpose:** The Court will give directions for the experts to meet or communicate: • To identify and narrow the issues in the case. • To reach agreement on the expert questions • To identify the reasons for disagreement on any expert question and to identify what if any action needs to be taken to resolve any outstanding disagreement/question • To obtain elucidation or amplification of relevant evidence in order to assist the Court to determine the issues	

Action	Party and Timing	
• To limit, wherever possible, the need for experts to attend Court to give oral evidence.		
5.2 **The Arrangements for a Discussion/Meeting: In accordance with the directions given by** the Court **at the CMC,** the solicitor for the child or such other professional who is given the responsibility by the Court shall make arrangements for there to be a discussion between the experts within 10 days of the filing of the experts reports. The following matters should be considered: • Where permission has been given for the instruction of experts from different disciplines a global discussion may be held relating to those questions that concern all or most of them. • Separate discussions may have to be held among experts from the same or related disciplines but care should be taken to ensure that the discussions complement each other so that related questions are discussed by all relevant experts • 7 days prior to a discussion or meeting the solicitor for the child or other nominated professional should formulate an agenda to include a list of the questions for consideration. This may usefully take the form of a list of questions to be circulated among the other parties in advance. The agenda should comprise all questions that each party wishes the experts to consider. The agenda and list of questions should be sent to each of the experts not later than 2 days before the discussion	Child's Solicitor	**within 10 days of the filing of the experts' reports**

Action	Party and Timing
• The discussion should usually be chaired by the child's solicitor or in exceptional cases where the parties have applied to the Court at the CMC, by an independent professional identified by the parties or the Court. In complex medical cases it may be necessary for the discussion to be jointly chaired by an expert. A minute must be taken of the questions answered by the experts, and a Statement of Agreement and Disagreement must be prepared which should be agreed and signed by each of the experts who participated in the discussion. The statement should be served and filed not later than 5 days after the discussion has taken place	
• Consideration should be given in each case to whether some or all of the experts participate by telephone conference or video link to ensure that minimum disruption is caused to clinical schedules.	
5.3 Positions of the Parties:	Any Party **at the PHR**
Where any party refuses to be bound by an agreement that has been reached at an experts' discussion that party must inform the Court at or before the PHR of the reasons for refusing to accept the agreement.	
5.4 Professionals Meetings:	
In proceedings where the Court gives a direction that a professionals meeting shall take place between the Local Authority and any relevant named professionals for the purpose of providing assistance to the Local Authority in the formulation of plans and proposals for the child, the meeting shall be arranged, chaired and minuted in accordance with directions given by the Court.	
6 Arranging for the Expert to attend Court	Every Party **by the PHR**
6.1 Preparation:	responsible for the
The party who is responsible for the instruction of an expert witness shall ensure:	instruction of an expert

Action	Party and Timing

- That a date and time is fixed for the Court to hear the expert's evidence that is if possible convenient to the expert and that the fixture is made substantially in advance of the Final Hearing and no later than at the PHR (ie no later than 2 weeks before the Final Hearing)

- That if the expert's oral evidence is not required the expert is notified as soon as possible

- That the witness template accurately indicates how long the expert is likely to be giving evidence, in order to avoid the inconvenience of the expert being delayed at Court.

6.2   **All parties shall ensure:**   All Parties   **at the PHR**

- That where expert witnesses are to be called the advocates attending the PHR have identified at the advocates meeting the issues which the experts are to address

- That wherever possible a logical sequence to the evidence is arranged with experts of the same discipline giving evidence on the same day(s)

- That at the PHR the Court is informed of any circumstance where all experts agree but a party nevertheless does not accept the agreed opinion so that directions can be given for the proper consideration of the experts' evidence and the parties reasons for not accepting the same

- That in the exceptional case the Court is informed of the need for a witness summons.

Action	Party and Timing	
7 **Post Hearing Action**	Solicitor instructing the expert	**within 10 days of the Final Hearing**
7.1 Within 10 days of the Final Hearing the solicitor instructing the expert should provide feedback to the expert by way of a letter informing the expert of the outcome of the case, and the use made by the Court of the expert's opinion. Where the Court directs that a copy of the transcript can be sent to the expert, the solicitor instructing the expert should obtain the transcript within 10 days of the Final Hearing.		

APPENDIX D

Note—*President's Direction of 10 March 2000 (Family Proceedings: Court Bundles)*, which is contained in Appendix D, is not reproduced here as it can be found in Part IV of this work in its chronological position.

APPENDIX E/1

The Care Centre Plan

Objective

To implement the protocol (without modification) on a local basis and to ensure that in each Care Centre judicial and administrative resources are deployed in order to achieve the highest practical level of continuity of judicial case management and the earliest possible resolution of cases

1 **Responsibility for the Preparation and Operation of the CCP:** The Designated Family Judge (DFJ) in each Care Centre shall be responsible for the preparation and operation of the CCP

2 **Consultees:** When preparing the CCP the DFJ shall consult fully with each of the Circuit and District Judges nominated to do Public Law work at the Care Centre as well as with:

- The Court Service
- All relevant Family Proceedings Courts (FPCs)
- CAFCASS
- All relevant Local Authorities
- Other local professional bodies

3 **Contents of the CCP:** The CCP shall provide for the following:

(a)   The arrangements for transfer and retransfer of cases between the FPCs and the Care Centre and the job title and contact particulars of the person responsible for administering transfers at each court

(b)   How and when cases will be allocated to one and not more than two case management judges (one of whom may be and where possible should be the judge who will conduct the Final Hearing) to case manage the proceedings in accordance with the protocol and the CCP

(c)   Where two judges are allocated, for the division of work between them

(d)   Where the case management judge or judges are not able to be the Final Hearing judge, how and when the Final Hearing judge for the case is to be identified

(e)   Wherever possible, for the release of the allocated judges from other business to hear applications and the arrangements for the case to follow the allocated judge or to be heard by telephone conferencing or video link.

(f)   Where, exceptionally, no allocated judge is available to hear an application, for the referral of the proceedings to one of the allocated judges or the DFJ before it is listed before another judge

(g)   The identity of the DFJ, the judges to whom cases may be allocated for case management and the other Nominated Circuit Judges and Nominated District Judges at the Care Centre (All judges of the Family Division of the High Court are available to act as case management judges)

(h)   The local agreement with each MCC as to the directions to be given by FPCs on the transfer of cases to the Care Centre

(i)   The local arrangements for joint directions in cases where there are concurrent relevant criminal proceedings

(j)   The arrangements in the Care Centre for the allocation of the judiciary to conduct Public Law Children Act cases

(k)   The arrangements for the monitoring by the local Family Court Business Committee of the implementation of the protocol and the CCP

(l)   The arrangements for active liaison between the Care Centre and the FPCs

4   **Authorisation of the Care Centre Plan:** Each CCP shall be subject to the final approval of the Family Division Liaison Judge (FDLJ) of the relevant Circuit before implementation.

5   **Timetable for Preparation and Lodging of the CCP:** The first CCP for each Care Centre shall be submitted to the FDLJ by the DFJ by the 1st October 2003. The CCP as approved by the FDLJ shall be lodged at the office of the President of the Family Division by the 31st October 2003.

6   **Review and Amendment of the CCP:** Not later than 1st October 2004 the first CCP shall be reviewed in the same way as it was prepared. Thereafter the CCP shall be reviewed in the same way every 2 years unless the DFJ determines that it is necessary to do so earlier or the President or the FDLJ so direct. Revised or updated plans shall be lodged at the President's office within 10 days of their approval by the FDLJ.

APPENDIX E/2

The Family Proceedings Court Plan

Objective

To implement the protocol (without modification) on a local basis and to ensure that in each Family Proceedings Court (FPC) and administrative centre resources are deployed in order to achieve the highest practical level of continuity of case management and the earliest possible resolution of cases

1   **Responsibility for the Preparation and Operation of the FPCP:** The Justices' Chief Executive (JCE) for each Magistrates Courts Committee (MCC) area shall be responsible for arranging for the preparation and administrative operation of the Family Proceedings Court Plan (FPCP).

2   **Consultees:** When preparing the FPCP the JCE should consult fully with each of the Chairs of the Family Panels, the District Judges (Magistrates Courts) nominated to do Public Law cases in the MCC area and the Justices Clerk(s) as well as with:

- The Court Service

- CAFCASS

- All relevant Local Authorities

- Other local professional bodies.

3   **Contents of the FPCP:** The FPCP shall provide for the following:

(a)   The arrangements for transfer and retransfer of cases between the FPCs and between FPCs and the Care Centre and the job title and contact particulars of the court officers responsible for administering transfers at each court

(b)   The local arrangements with the Care Centre as to the directions to be given by FPCs on the transfer of cases to the Care Centre

(c)   The best practical arrangements to maximise effective and continuous case management. Where practicable within existing resources, this could include allocation to no more than 2 legal advisers and to no more than 6 identified magistrates (or 2 DJs(MC)); or to a team of specialist family legal advisers. If possible, however, the objective of continuous case management by allocation of each case to a single legal adviser and to a single bench for case management and Final Hearing should be pursued.

(d)   Arrangements for active liaison between the FPCs and the Care Centre.

4   **Authorisation of the FPC Plan:** The FPCP for each MCC shall be subject to the final approval of the JCE after consultation with the relevant Designated Family Judge(s) (DFJ) and the Family Division Liaison Judge (FDLJ) of the relevant Circuit before implementation.

5   **Timetable for Preparation and Lodging of the FPCP:** The first FPCP for each MCC area should be returned to the FDLJ by the JCE by the 1st October 2003. The FPCP should be lodged at the office of the President of the Family Division by the 31st October 2003.

6   **Review and Amendment of the FPCP:** Not later than the 1st April 2004 the first FPCP shall be reviewed in the same way as it was prepared. Thereafter the FPCP shall be reviewed in the same way every year unless the JCE determines that it is necessary to do so earlier (in consultation with the FDLJ). Revised or updated plans shall be lodged at the President's office within 28 days of their submission to the FDLJ.

APPENDIX F

Social Services Assessment and Care Planning Aide-Memoire

Days

The reference in this appendix to "DAYS" is independent of the "DAYS" referred to in The 6 Steps

Recommended Guidance	Recommended timetable
1 **Referral** A referral to a Council with Social Services Responsibilities (CSSR) in England and a Local Authority in Wales (ie a request for services including child protection) triggers the following Government guidance:	**On DAY 1**

	Recommended Guidance	Recommended timetable
2	**Initial Decision** Within 1 working day of a referral social services should make a decision about what response is required including a decision to take no action or to undertake an initial assessment. The parents or carers (the family), where appropriate, the child and (unless inappropriate) the referrer should be informed of the initial decision and its reasons by social services	On DAY 2
3	**Initial Assessment** An initial assessment (if undertaken) should be completed by social services within a maximum of 7 working days of the date of the referral (ie 6 working days from the date of the decision about how to respond to a referral)	By DAY 7
4	As part of an initial assessment social services should: • Obtain and collate information and reports from other agencies • Interview family members and the child • In any event, see the child	
5	At the conclusion of an initial assessment social services will make a decision about whether the child is a child in need and about further action including whether to undertake a core assessment. It will inform the family, the child and other relevant agencies of the decision and its reasons. Social services will record the response of each person and agency consulted	
6	**Initial Assessment Record** Social services will make and keep a record of the initial assessment and decision making process. The Department of Health (DH) and Welsh Assembly Government (WAG) publish an 'Initial Assessment Record' for this purpose.	
7	**Child in Need Plan** Where social services decide that the child is a child in need they will make a plan which sets out the services to be provided to meet the child's needs.	

	Recommended Guidance	Recommended timetable
8	**Strategy Discussion/Record** Where social services has evidence that the child is suspected to be suffering or is likely to suffer significant harm it should ensure that an inter agency strategy discussion takes place to decide whether to initiate an enquiry under section 47 of the Children Act. This should also result in the child in need plan being updated. A record of the strategy discussion will be made.	
9	**Achieving Best Evidence in Criminal Proceedings** Where a child is the victim of or witness to a suspected crime the strategy discussion shall include a discussion about how any interviews are to be conducted with the child. These may be as part of a police investigation and /or a section 47 enquiry initiated by social services, These interviews should be undertaken in accordance with Government guidance 'Achieving Best Evidence in Criminal Proceedings'.	
10	**Complex Child Abuse Investigations** Where a complex child abuse investigation has been initiated by social services or the police there will be inter agency strategy discussions to make recommendations relating to the planning, co-ordination and management of the investigation and assessment processes in accordance with the guidance given in 'Working Together', 'Complex Child Abuse Investigations: Inter Agency Issues' (England only - to be published in Wales, Summer 2003)	

	Recommended Guidance	**Recommended timetable**
11	**Section 47 Enquiries** If during a strategy discussion it is decided that there is reasonable cause to suspect that the child is suffering or is likely to suffer significant harm, section 47 enquiries will be initiated by social services. This means that a core assessment will be commenced under section 47 of the Children Act 1989. It should be completed within 35 working days of the completion of the initial assessment or the strategy discussion at which it was decided to initiate section 47 enquiries.	**By DAY 42 or within 35 days of the last strategy discussion**
12	**Core Assessment** Where social services decides to undertake a core assessment it should be completed within 35 working days of the initial assessment or the date of the subsequent strategy discussion. A timetable for completion of specialist assessments should be agreed with social services	**By DAY 42 or within 35 days of the last strategy discussion**
13	At the conclusion of a core assessment social services should consult with the family, the child and all relevant agencies before making decisions about the plan for the child. Social Services will record the response of each person and agency consulted.	
14	**Core Assessment Record** Social services will make and keep a record of the core assessment and decision making process. The DH and WAG publish a 'Core Assessment Record' for this purpose.	

Recommended Guidance	Recommended timetable

15	**Child Protection Conferences** Where social services undertakes section 47 enquiries and it is concluded that a child is at continuing risk of suffering or is likely to suffer significant harm, social services will consider whether to convene a child protection conference. A child protection conference determines whether the child is at continuing risk of significant harm and therefore requires a child protection plan to be put in place when determining whether to place the child's name on the child protection register. It agrees an outline child protection plan. An initial child protection conference should take place within 15 working days of the last strategy discussion (ie by day 22) in accordance with the Government guidance given in 'Working Together to Safeguard Children: a guide to inter-agency working to safeguard and promote the welfare of children'	**By DAY 22 or within 15 days of the end of the last strategy discussion**
16	**Decision to Apply for a Care Order** At the conclusion of the core assessment which may have been undertaken under section 47 of the Children Act and where no earlier decision has been made social services should decide whether to apply for a statutory order and should be able to identify by reference to the conclusions in the core assessment	

- The needs of the child (including for protection),

- The services that will be provided,

- The role of other professionals and agencies,

- Whether additional specialist assessments are to be undertaken,

- The timetable and

- The responsibilities of those involved.

17	**Plans** At the conclusion of a core assessment social services will prepare one or more of the following plans:

- A children in need plan

Recommended Guidance	Recommended timetable
• A child protection plan for a child whose name is on the child protection register • A care plan (where the child is a looked after child) The DH and WAG publish formats and/or guidance for each of these plans.	
18 **Interim Care Plans** Where social services decide to make an application to the Court it will be necessary to satisfy the Court that an order would be better for the child than making no order at all. An interim care plan should be prepared, filed and served so as to be available to the Court for the CMC in accordance with steps 3.4 and 4.1 of the protocol.	
19 In cases where no core assessment has been undertaken (eg because the interim care order had to be taken quickly before one could be begun/completed) it should be begun/completed as soon as possible. The interim care plan should be developed from the initial assessment information	

20 **Care Plans** Care Plans should be written so as to comply with the Government guidance given in **LAC(99) 29** in England and *Care Plans and Care Proceedings under the CA 1989* **NAFWC 1/2000** in Wales. While interim care plans will necessarily be in outline and contain less comprehensive information, the plan should include details of the following:
 	
• The aim of the plan and a summary of the social work timetable
 	
• A summary of the child's needs and how these are to be met including
 	
  • placement
 	
  • contact with family and other significant persons
 	
  • education, healthcare and social care services	

Recommended Guidance	Recommended timetable
• the role of parents and other significant persons • the views of others • Implementation and management of the plan	

21	**Emergency Protection** Where at any time there is reasonable cause to believe that a child is suffering or is likely to suffer significant harm, an application for a child assessment order or an emergency protection order may be made (among others) by social services. The child may be removed or remain in a safe place under police powers of protection. In each case agency and/or court records of the application and reasons will exist.	
22	**Adoption** Government guidance is given on the assessment and decision making process relating to adoption in England in **LAC (2001) 33** which from the 1st April 2003 incorporates the 'National Adoption Standards for England'. The processes and timescales of assessment and decision making for a child for whom adoption is identified as an option are set out in detail in the Standards.	

APPENDIX G

Section 37 Request

Objective	Target time: by DAY 40

To provide a recommended procedure within the existing rules for the timely determination of section 37 requests by the Court

Days

The reference in this appendix to **"DAYS"** is independent of the **"DAYS"** referred to in The 6 Steps

Action	Party and Timing
1 **The Test** Where, in any family proceedings in which a question arises with respect to the welfare of any child, it appears to the Court that it may be appropriate for a care or supervision order to be made with respect to the child, the **Court** may direct the appropriate local authority (LA) to undertake an investigation of the child's circumstances.	Court **on DAY 1**
2 **The Court's Request** On the same day the **Court** shall: • Identify the LA that is to prepare the s 37 report • Fix the date for the next hearing • Specify the date for the s 37 report to be filed by the LA • Direct the court officer to give notice of the order and the form C40 to the LA court liaison manager/lawyer (as set out in the CCP) by fax on the day the order is made • Direct each party to serve upon the LA all further documents filed with the Court.	Court **on DAY 1**
3 Where a s 37 report is required in less than 8 weeks, the **Court** should make direct enquiries of the Court liaison manager/lawyer of the LA to agree the period within which a report can be written.	Court **on DAY 1**
4 Within 24 hours of the order being made (on **DAY 2**) the **court officer** shall serve on the LA a sealed copy of the order and such other documents as the Court has directed.	Court **on DAY 1** Officer
5 **LA Responsibility** Within 24 hours of the receipt of the sealed order (on **DAY 3**) the Court liaison manager/lawyer of the **LA** shall ensure that the request is allocated to a social services team manager who shall:	LA **on DAY 3**

Action	Party and Timing
• Be responsible for the preparation of the report and the allocation of a social worker/team to carry out any appropriate assessment	
• Ensure that the request is treated and recorded as a formal referral by social services in respect of each child named in the order	
• Notify the Court and the lawyers acting for all parties of his/her identity and contact details and the identity of the team that has been allocated	
• Follow Government guidance in relation to referral and assessment processes (see appendix F).	
6 Any **assessment** including a core assessment that is undertaken by social services should be completed within 35 days of the allocation above ie within 36 days of the service of the sealed court order.	Social Services **by DAY 38**
7 At the conclusion of the social services enquiries **social services** shall: • Consult with the family, the child and all relevant agencies before making decisions about a plan for the child. The LA will record the response of each person and agency consulted • Decide whether to apply to the Court for a statutory order • File the section 37 report with the Court and serve it upon the parties on or before the date specified in the Court's order.	Social Services **between DAYS 38 and 40**
8 Where social services decide not to apply for a care or supervision order they should as part of their report set out the decisions they have made and the reasons for those decisions and any plan they have made for the child (including the services to be provided) in accordance with Government guidance (see appendix F).	

PRACTICE DIRECTION

Practice Direction (Care Cases: Judicial Continuity and Judicial Case Management)

1.1 This Practice Direction, which includes the annexed Principles and the annexed Protocol, is issued by the President of the Family Division with the concurrence of the Lord Chancellor. It is intended to implement the recommendations of the Final Report, published in May 2003, of the Lord Chancellor's Advisory Committee on Judicial Case Management in Public Law Children Act Cases chaired by Munby and Coleridge JJ.

1.2 The Practice Direction, Principles and Protocol apply to all Courts, including Family Proceedings Courts, hearing applications issued by local authorities under Part IV (Care and Supervision) of the Children Act 1989 ("care cases") where

 (a) the application is issued on or after 1 November 2003; or

 (b) the proceedings are transferred on or after 1 November 2003 from the Family Proceedings Court to a Care Centre, or from a County Court to a Care Centre or from a Care Centre to the High Court.

1.3 *Practice Direction (Family Proceedings: Court Bundles)* [2000] 1 WLR 737, [2000] 1 FLR 536, remains in force and is to be complied with in all cases to which it applies, subject only to the Protocol and to any directions which may be given, in any particular care case by the case management judge.

1.4 Paragraph 2 of the *President's Direction (Judicial Continuity)* [2002] 2 FLR 367 shall cease to have effect in any case to which this Practice Direction applies.

2 **Purpose of the Practice Direction, Principles and Protocol**

2.1 The purpose of the Practice Direction, Principles and Protocol is to ensure consistency in the application of best practice by all Courts dealing with care cases and, in particular, to ensure:

 (a) that care cases are dealt with in accordance with the overriding objective;

 (b) that there are no unacceptable delays in the hearing and determination of care cases; and

 (c) that save in exceptional or unforeseen circumstances every care case is finally determined within 40 weeks of the application being issued.

2.2 The Principles are the principles which govern the application of the Practice Direction and Protocol by the Courts and the parties.

3 **The Overriding Objective**

3.1 The overriding objective is to enable the Court to deal with every care case

 (a) justly, expeditiously, fairly and with the minimum of delay;

(b)   in ways which ensure, so far as is practicable, that

    (i)   the parties are on an equal footing;
    (ii) the welfare of the children involved is safeguarded; and
    (iii) distress to all parties is minimised;

(c)   so far as is practicable, in ways which are proportionate

    (i)   to the gravity and complexity of the issues; and
    (ii) to the nature and extent of the intervention proposed in the private family life of the children and adults involved.

3.2   The Court should seek to give effect to the overriding objective when it exercises any power given to it by the Family Proceedings Courts (Children Act 1989) Rules 1991 or the Family Proceedings Rules 1991 (as the case may be) or interprets any rule.

3.3   The parties are required to help the Court to further the overriding objective.

3.4   The Court will further the overriding objective by actively managing cases as required by sections 11 and 32 of the Children Act 1989 and in accordance with the Practice Direction, Principles and Protocol.

4   Avoiding Delay

4.1   Section 1(2) of the Children Act 1989 requires the Court to "have regard to the general principle that any delay in determining any question is likely to prejudice the welfare of the child".

4.2   Decisions of the European Court of Human Rights emphasise the need under article 6 of the European Convention for the Protection of Human Rights and Fundamental Freedoms for "exceptional diligence" in this context: *Johansen v Norway* (1996) 23 EHRR 33, para [88].

4.3   One of the most effective means by which unnecessary delay can be avoided in care cases is by active case management by a specialist judiciary.

5   Judicial Case Management
5.1   The key principles underlying the Practice Direction, Principles and Protocol are

(a)   **judicial continuity**: each care case will be allocated to one or not more than two case management judges, who will be responsible for every stage in the proceedings down to the final hearing and one of whom may be, and where possible should be, the judge who will conduct the final hearing;

(b)   **active case management**: each care case will be actively case managed by the case management judge(s) with a view at all times to furthering the overriding objective;

(c)   **consistency by standardisation** of steps: each care case will so far as possible be managed in a consistent way

    (i)   in accordance with the standardised procedures laid down in the Protocol; and

(ii) using, wherever possible, standardised forms of order and other standardised documents;

(d) **the case management conference**: in each care case there will be a case management conference to enable the case management judge to actively case manage the case and, at the earliest practicable opportunity, to

    (i) identify the relevant issues; and

    (ii) fix the timetable for all further directions and other hearings (including the date of the final hearing).

6   Implementing the Protocol

6.1   The Protocol is based on, and is intended to promote the adoption in all Courts and in all care cases of, the best practice currently adopted by Courts dealing with care cases.

6.2   The Protocol will be implemented:

(a) in each Care Centre by reference to the Care Centre Plan which will be drafted locally (see appendix E/1 to the Protocol); and

(b) in each Family Proceedings Court by reference to the FPC Plan which will be drafted locally (see appendix E/2 to the Protocol).

6.3   The target times specified in the Protocol for the taking of each step should be adhered to wherever possible and treated as the maximum permissible time for the taking of that step. Save in exceptional or unforeseen circumstances every care case should be finally determined within 40 weeks of the application being issued. Simpler cases can often be finally determined within a shorter time.

6.4   Unless the case management judge is satisfied that some other direction is necessary in order to give effect to the overriding objective, the case management judge should, and, unless the case management judge has otherwise ordered, the parties and any expert who may be instructed in the case must (as the case may be):

(a) use or require the parties to use the forms and standard documents referred to in Appendix A to the Protocol;

(b) prepare or require the parties to prepare the documents referred to in Appendix B to the Protocol in accordance with that Appendix;

(c) comply or require the parties and every expert to comply with the Code of Guidance for Expert Witnesses in Family Proceedings contained in Appendix C to the Protocol; and

(d) make every order and direction in the form of any relevant form which may from time to time be approved by the President of the Family Division for this purpose.

6.5   Appendix D to the Protocol contains the text of the President's *Practice Direction (Family Proceedings: Court Bundles)* [2000] 1 WLR 737, [2000] 1 FLR 536.

6.6	Appendix F to the Protocol contains the Social Services Assessment and Care Planning Aide-Memoire, which is a summary of existing guidance relating to assessment and care planning.

6.7	Appendix G to the Protocol is a summary of best practice guidance relating to requests made under section 37 of the Children Act 1989.

6.8	Cases in which there are concurrent care proceedings and criminal proceedings are to be dealt with in accordance with the Care Centre Plan.

7	**Monitoring and Compliance**
7.1	It is the responsibility of the Designated Family Judge in conjunction with the Court Service and in consultation with the Family Division Liaison Judge

> (a) to monitor the extent to which care cases in the Courts for which he is responsible are being conducted in compliance with the protocol and with directions previously given by the Court;

> (b) to arrange for the collection and collation of such statistical and other information and in such form as the Family Division Liaison Judge and the President of the Family Division may from time to time direct.

ANNEX TO THE PRACTICE DIRECTION

Principles of Application

The principles which govern the application of the Practice Direction and Protocol by the Courts and the parties

1	The **Aim** of the Practice Direction and Protocol is to reduce delay and improve the quality of justice for children and families by the following means:

- Proper Court control of proceedings
- Identifying and promoting best practice
- The consistent application of best practice by all Courts
- Providing predictable standards which the Courts will treat as the normal and reasonable approach to the conduct of proceedings by parties

2	In order to achieve the **Aim** the Practice Direction gives effect to:

- A **protocol** which sets out predictable standards as specific steps to be taken in all care proceedings by reference to identified best practice

- An **overriding objective** to provide consistency of case management decisions

- **Court plans** to maximise the use of judicial and administrative resources

- Best practice **guidance**

3   **Court Control:** Proper Court control of care proceedings requires forward planning so that:

- A specialist judiciary is identified and trained

- Arrangements are made for continuous case management in the High Court, and in each Care Centre and Family Proceedings Court

- The arrangements for continuous case management are supervised by the specialist judiciary in conjunction with dedicated court officers, in particular

  - the matching and allocation of judicial and administrative resources to cases; and

  - the allocation and listing of cases,

- There is continuous and active case management of each case by allocated case management judges/benches

- There is continuous monitoring of the progress of all proceedings against target times to help minimise delay

4   **Continuity of Case Management:** The continuity of case management is to be achieved:

- In the Care Centre and the High Court by a **care centre plan** (CCP); and

- In the Family Proceedings Courts, by a **family proceedings courts plan** (FPCP)

- By the **identification of the specialist judiciary** and the **dedicated court officers** in the plans

Guidelines for the preparation and implementation of the plans are set out at appendix E to the protocol.

5   **Active Case Management:** Active case management is to be achieved by giving directions to ensure that the determination of proceedings occurs quickly, efficiently and with the minimum of delay and risk to the child (and where appropriate other persons) by:

- Identifying the appropriate Court to conduct the proceedings and transferring the proceedings as early as possible to that Court

- Identifying all facts and matters that are in issue at the earliest stage and then at each case management step in the proceedings

- Deciding which issues need full investigation and hearing and which do not

- Considering whether the likely benefits of taking a particular social work or legal step justify the delay which will result and the cost of taking it

- Encouraging the parties to use an alternative dispute resolution procedure such as a family group conference and facilitating the use of such a procedure

- Helping the parties to reach agreement in relation to the whole or part of a case, quickly, fairly and with the minimum of hostility

- Encouraging the parties to co-operate with each other in the conduct of the proceedings

- Identifying the timetable for all legal and social work steps

- Fixing the dates for all appointments and hearings

- Standardising, simplifying and regulating:

  - the use of case management documentation and forms

  - the court's orders and directions
- Controlling:

  - the use and cost of experts

  - the nature and extent of the documents which are to be disclosed to the parties and presented to the Court

  - whether and if so in what manner the documents disclosed are to be presented to the Court

- Monitoring the Court's timetable and directions against target times for the completion of each protocol step to prevent delay and non-compliance

6	**Standard Directions, Forms and Documents:** In order to simplify and provide consistency in the exchange of information: such standard variable directions, forms (appendix A) and standard documents (appendix B) as may be approved from time to time by the President are to be used unless otherwise directed by the Court.
7	**Controlling the Use and Cost of Experts:** Expert evidence should be proportionate to the issues in question and should relate to questions that are outside the skill and experience of the Court. To assist the Court in its control of the use and cost of experts a Code of Guidance is incorporated as appendix C to the protocol. The Code of Guidance is to be followed by the parties when a party proposes that the court gives permission for the use of an expert. The Code of Guidance should form part of every letter of instruction so that experts can adopt best practice guidance in the formulation of their reports and advices to the Court.
8	**Disclosure:** Disclosure of relevant documents should be encouraged at the earliest opportunity. Where disclosure is in issue the Court's control of the extent of disclosure will have regard to whether the disclosure proposed is proportionate to the issues in question and the continuing duty of each party to give *full* and frank disclosure of information to each other and the Court.

9   **Inter-Disciplinary Good Practice:** The Court's process and its reliance
        upon best practice should acknowledge and encourage inter-disciplinary
        best practice and in particular pre-application investigation, assessment,
        consultation and planning by statutory agencies (including local
        authorities) and other potential parties (an aide-memoire of local authority
        guidance is annexed to the protocol at appendix F).

10   **Target Time:** The target times specified in the protocol for the taking of
        each step should be adhered to wherever possible and treated as the
        maximum permissible time for the taking of that step. Where target times
        are expressed in days, the days are 'court business days' in accordance
        with the Rules. Save in exceptional or unforeseen circumstances every
        care case should be finally determined within 40 weeks of the application
        being issued. Simpler cases can often be finally determined within a
        shorter time. Target times should only be departed from at the direction of
        the Court and for good reason in accordance with the overriding
        objective.

11   **Monitoring and Compliance:** To facilitate directions being given to deal
        with a change of circumstances or to remedy a material non-compliance
        at the earliest opportunity the Court should consider requiring regular
        certification of compliance with the Court's timetable and directions by
        the parties, for example on interim care order renewal certificates. In
        addition the Court might consider other mechanisms to monitor the
        progress of a case without the need for the parties or their representatives
        to attend Court.

12   **Technology:** Where the facilities are available to the Court and the
        parties, the Court should consider making *full* use of technology
        including electronic information exchange and video or telephone
        conferencing.

LORD CHANCELLOR'S ADVISORY COMMITTEE ON JUDICIAL CASE MANAGEMENT IN PUBLIC LAW CHILDREN ACT CASES

Final Report

May 2003

1. Introduction

1.1. This is the final report of the Lord Chancellor's Advisory Committee on Judicial
Case Management in Public Law Children Act Cases ('the committee'). It has been
chaired by the Hon. Mr Justice Munby and The Hon. Mr Justice Coleridge. A list of
the Committee members and other consultees is given in the Annex.

1.2. The committee was established in May 2002 by the Lord Chancellor at the
instigation of the President of the Family Division. Its purpose was to consider the
whole question of case management in Public Law Children Act cases (PLCACs). Its
specific terms of reference were:

> 'to consider and approve a draft protocol based on the models of best practice
> collated from Care Centres and Family Proceedings Courts and agree on target
> time-scales for each stage of the Public Law Children Act process'

1.3. The committee had four plenary sessions (beginning in November 2002) but sub-groups representing particular interests met on a number of other occasions as did the core judicial group concerned with detailed drafting.

1.4. As can be seen from the list of represented organisations and consultees, this large committee drew on the experience and expertise of all those agencies which participate at any stage in PLCACs which, by their nature, often involve many parties and are complex. At all times the intention has been to achieve complete consensus amongst participants to ensure the maximum level of voluntary and whole-hearted co-operation after implementation.

1.5. We are very happy to record the overwhelming and enthusiastic support which this project and the resulting Protocol has attracted from all participants. This degree of support undoubtedly reflects the dedication of each individual organisation to doing the best for the children involved in the process and the desire to make improvements whenever possible and within the constraints created by lack of public resources (for which, of course, there is predictably an incessant demand) in a number of related areas.

2. Background

2.1. Section 1(2) of the Children Act 1989 requires the Court to 'have regard to the general principle that any delay in determining any question is likely to prejudice the welfare of the child'.

2.2. Decisions of the European Court of Human Rights emphasise the need under article 6 of the European Convention for the Protection of Human Rights and Fundamental Freedoms for 'exceptional diligence' in this context: see *Johansen v Norway* (1996) 23 EHRR 33, para [88]

2.3. The problem of delay in care cases has long been recognised and specifically considered on previous occasions including:

(*a*)   by Dame Margaret Booth in her report in July 1996 'Avoiding Delay in Children Act Cases';

(*b*)   by the Lord Chancellor's Department in its March 2002 'Scoping Study on the Causes of Delay'.

2.4. The Lord Chancellor's Department has been pursuing a programme of work to reduce delay in these cases since the publication of the Scoping Study. That study identified case management as an area which, if improved, could have a substantial impact on delay. And all members of the Committee are agreed that one of the surest means by which unnecessary delay can be avoided in PLCACs is by the proper management and control of cases by a specialist judiciary.

2.5. Many Care Centres around the country and the Family Division of the High Court in London have, over the last few years, established protocols/best practice guides/ practice directions for improving case management. They have emerged partly as a result of a need to tackle serious issues of localised delay and partly as a result of the national civil case management protocols (following the introduction of the CPR reforms). Similarly, the successful introduction of the new Family Proceedings Rules governing the procedure for ancillary relief cases has demonstrated how court-led case management can alleviate delay and make significant savings in both court time and cost per case.

2.6. The protocol (agreed by the Advisory Committee at its final meeting on 6 March 2003) represents a collation of the best practice from around the country and is the

first National statement of common practice and solutions. The annexes have, in addition, been drafted partly by those with specialised experience in particular areas.

2.7. It is proposed that the protocol will be introduced by attachment to a President's Practice Direction in May or June 2003 with a view to National implementation on 1 November 2003. The period between May/June and November has been provided to enable familiarisation and training to be achieved amongst all potential users.

3. Format and content

3.1. The format of the protocol is designed to be as simple and user friendly as possible recognising the fact that it will be used by staff in all agencies (legal and non legal) and at all levels of the process. It is the culmination of a process of reduction to six essential steps covering all the stages of a case, from issue of the application to conclusion of the final hearing.

3.2. The time periods for each stage are expressed as 'target times' to reflect the fact that some degree of limited flexibility is necessary and desirable and also that resource limitations in certain areas, at present, do not admit of the imposition of a more stringently enforceable timetable. However, it is hoped and expected that every reasonable effort will be made not to exceed them and wherever possible to improve upon them.

4. Paramount objective

4.1. **The paramount objective** of the protocol has been to **improve the outcomes for children by reducing unnecessary delay** in PLCACs and, to this end, to achieve the completion of all cases within an overall timetable of **not more than 40 weeks** (save in exceptional or unforeseen circumstances).

4.2. The following **key elements** have been identified to the achievement of that paramount objective:

4.2.1. The highest practical level of judicial continuity and case management by one or not more than two judges per case. The precise achievement of this key element will be by:
- **Care Centre Plans** drafted by individual Designated Family Judges in consultation with all local judiciary and local agencies. These plans will be finally approved by Family Division Liaison Judges and then lodged with the President. The plans will be periodically reviewed to ensure they remain current.
- **Family Proceedings Court Plans** similarly drafted by the Justices Chief Executive in consultation with Family Panels, Justices Clerks and other local agencies and also lodged with the President.
- **Improved listing arrangements**

4.2.2. **Consistency** of all aspects of case management at all levels of court together with identification of cases requiring 'transfer up' at the earliest opportunity.

4.2.3. **Time-tabling to final hearing** at the earliest practical stage and the reduction of intermediate hearings to no more than four (First Hearing, Allocation Hearing, Case Management Conference and Pre Hearing Review) save in exceptional or unforeseen circumstances.

4.2.4. A more rigorous control of the use of experts.

4.2.5. A more rigorous **control of the content and quantity of Court documentation** including standardisation where possible.

4.3. The Protocol has been produced to assist all participants in the process (including judges, lawyers, guardians, social workers and other experts) by providing them with a common, timed framework for the case management of every case at every stage and every level. To this end, it sets out the 'Six Steps' that every PLCAC should go through and includes guidance on and documentation for the conduct of each of the steps. As is apparent the protocol does not radically change the procedure (no rule changes are required), rather it seeks to distil and streamline the process to its essentials and change the culture within which the proceedings takes place.

4.4. Although the paramount objective of the protocol has been to improve outcomes for children by reducing delay, the Committee believes also that it has a very real potential for reducing the cost (per case) to the public purse. Certain figures were shown to us during the period when the Committee was deliberating. These figures suggested that there might be (on a worst case basis) a small increase in overall cost. However, on a best case basis the savings were evidently very considerable. Our experience of the High Court London Practice Direction is that it is already delivering higher settlement rates (and at an earlier stage in the process) and shorter final hearings. If this is replicated nationwide, savings of both time and money will follow. For our part we are unable to envisage a situation where better managed cases could cost more than the present less formalised, drawn out procedures. Similarly, our experience in the parallel ancillary relief field is entirely supportive of the assertion that savings of time and money result from a properly managed and disciplined system of case handling.

4.5. Apart from direct cost savings, there is also potential for indirect savings where cases take less time and children are eg. retained for less time within the care system.

5. Major obstacles to success

5.1. PLCACs are complex and involve many agencies, all of them publicly funded in one way or another. The Committee was able to resolve many current concerns and other issues that arose during its deliberations from different quarters on its way to achieving consensus. However, there remains an overarching concern that better outcomes for children and further reductions in delay require further work and investment to complement and reinforce the efficacy of the Protocol.

5.2. The Protocol is an essential step forward, but the Committee would like to record the following major obstacles to real success in this area:

     5.2.1. **Social services departments** continue to be seriously understaffed, suffering both recruitment and retention of staff problems. This critically limits their ability to speed up the pre-application stages in the care process. It also has the effect that, were they to focus more of their precious human resources on the actual litigation stage, their other roles in care, prevention and education would be likely to be compromised

     5.2.2. **CAFCASS** has a shortage of guardians which, in parts of the country, remains significant. Effective case management within the Courts and CAFCASS will alleviate some of the pressure. Increased funding for the next financial year is obviously welcome and helpful. However, until guardians can be promptly allocated at the start of each case throughout England and Wales neither the children nor the Courts will be receiving the essential and proper service.

     5.2.3. **Publicly funded remuneration** for the legal profession must reflect the fact that PLCACs require the full input and co-operation of experienced, specialist practitioners. Without such practitioners the protocol will not work to its best advantage. Underpayment of the practitioners who do

this work will inevitably lead to a shortage of such specialist lawyers (and accordingly in the future to a shortage of specialist judges, both part and full time) as the brightest and best turn to better remunerated fields of practice. Remuneration must also be structured to reflect the fact that the Protocol requires advocates to do considerably more work at the early stages of a case to ensure the early identification and narrowing of issues.

5.2.4. The need for significantly more **family sitting days** in some areas

5.2.5. A **shortage of experts** in a number of fields prevents the swift hearing of cases in some areas. The Protocol should help but the problem persists.

5.2.6. **Local listing practices** in some places call for a radical change of culture. Specialist judges are at the heart of the Protocol's success but even those judges cannot case manage effectively if the listing arrangements do not accommodate the need for continuity and also allow for a sensible amount of reading time prior to hearings. In less busy courts and rural areas this is sometimes hard to achieve and requires special attention. The proper exploitation, at the case management stage, of the available expertise of many District Judges is also sometimes overlooked. Finally, proper training and support from all departments of the Lord Chancellor's Department and the Court Service is essential.

6. The introduction of the protocol should lead to better use of available resources and so reduction of unnecessary delay. However, it must be remembered and emphasised that PLCACs, by their very nature, sometimes call for flexibility and delay. The target in every case is to get the best possible outcome for the child concerned. There will always remain cases where there is a need for adapting or prolonging the procedure to fit changing circumstances or allow for constructive delay. The right answer cannot be sacrificed on the altar of speed and efficiency.

7. Conclusion

7.1. The work of the Committee has been facilitated by an exceptional level of commitment to the cause of improving the use of available resources, reducing delay and an overwhelming consensus on the need for better and more effective continuous case management by specialist judges. The Committee is confident that this consensus and commitment will be transmitted through the organisations represented on the Committee, through the Court system and through Government and that this will result in real reductions in delay and corresponding cost savings.

7.2. We have from time to time expressed anxiety at the suggestion that the Protocol might be introduced initially on a pilot basis. We repeat that we believe that to be an unnecessary and retrograde step. We strongly recommend that the Protocol be implemented nationally in accordance with the timetable set out in para 2.7 of this report. At the same time on-going careful but simple monitoring by the Care Centres and FPCs to measure the effect of the Protocol should be put in place (as is already happening in the High Court in London).

7.3. We would like to express our most sincere gratitude to all the members of the Committee for the enormous amounts of both time and effort they have invested in this project. Many of them are from the private sector and gave much precious time without reward. In this regard Ernest Ryder QC calls for special mention. He has been the 'drafter-in-chief' without whose encyclopaedic knowledge and dedication to the cause this Protocol would not have finally emerged. His Honour Judge Cryan's input

on the Care Centre and FPC Plans and other ancillary documents has also been
particularly demanding of time and sensitivity.

Hon Mr Justice Munby

Hon Mr Justice Coleridge

****

INDEX

References are to paragraph numbers.